POLYCENTRISM

POLYCENTRISM

The New Factor in International Communism

Edited by WALTER LAQUEUR

and LEOPOLD LABEDZ

FREDERICK A. PRAEGER

Publisher • New York

BOOKS THAT MATTER

Published in the United States of America in 1962
by Frederick A. Praeger, Inc., Publisher
64 University Place, New York 3, N.Y.

Most of the material in this book was
First published in Great Britain in 1962
as a special issue of *Survey*

Library of Congress Catalog Card Number: 62-18268

POLYCENTRISM is published in two editions:
> A Praeger Paperback PPS-99
> A clothbound edition

This book is Number 116 in the series of
Praeger Publications in Russian History and World Communism

Printed in the United States of America

Publisher's Note

POLYCENTRISM is based on a special issue of *Survey*, A Journal of Soviet and East European Studies, which provides both expertise for the specialist, and stimulating material for the general student of contemporary affairs.

Survey covers the social and cultural trends in the Soviet bloc extensively and systematically. It has published articles on recent developments in Soviet historiography and economic thought, on Soviet psychological studies and philosophical publications, on the state of the social sciences, on educational reform, on painting, music, and even astronomy. *Survey* draws attention to all the symptoms of intellectual ferment in the Soviet bloc, and was the first Western journal to publish comprehensive articles on such young heretics as Kolakowski and Yevtushenko, long before their names became familiar to the Western reading public. It was also the first English-language magazine that printed an essay (and later a short story) by the anonymous Soviet author who writes under the pen name of Abram Tertz. Recent special issues have dealt with present-day Poland, Hungary, and Bulgaria; *Soviet Literature Yesterday and Today* presented a broad panorama of the Soviet literary scene.

Survey is edited in London by Walter Laqueur and Leopold Labedz. Since its first appearance in January, 1956, it has established itself as the leading magazine in its field and is read in more than sixty countries. Its articles have been quoted in *The Times* of London, *The New York Times*, the *New York Herald Tribune*, *The Washington Post*, *The Guardian*—and in the Soviet press.

CONTENTS

POLYCENTRISM

THE SCHISM

Walter Laqueur

WHAT happens when believers cannot agree about the essentials of their creed, its interpretation and application? The last two thousand years have provided abundant material and food for thought about the natural history of heresy and schism. We know, for instance, that usually there is no clear and sudden break; the final division of the Christian church into Eastern Orthodox and Western Catholic came only after disputes which were prolonged over two centuries. Rome wavered between declarations that no one see had jurisdiction over any other but all were equal before God, and a more adamant stand renewing the Petrine claim of world jurisdiction. Constantinople (the ' second Rome ') accepted the authority of the Ecumenical Councils, seven in number, but for the most part refused to recognise *ex cathedra* pronouncements by the pope. The sees of Alexandria and Antioch tried for centuries to play Rome off against Byzantium, and vice versa; when the great split came they remained with the East, presumably because Constantinople was more liberal than the Catholic church of the West, recognising autocephalous churches in its camp. From time to time believers excommunicated each other as companions of the devil and his brood, or as wild boars determined on overthrowing truth.[1] But the separation was by no means complete and relations ranged from open warfare (the fourth crusade) to full reconciliation (Michael VIII and the Council of Lyon); however bitter and deep-reaching the split, there were outside enemies threatening all Christendom, and to counter this menace unity of action was from time to time restored.

All this sounds very familiar and it is not surprising that the eruption of the Sino-Soviet conflict should awaken a new interest in the history of schism, not only within the Christian church. Nevertheless it is more than doubtful whether such a study provides anything but erudite footnotes. Not only is every historical situation unique, and parallels therefore of doubtful validity; in some respects the differences between conflicts within religious and within totalitarian secular movements are very striking indeed. The debate on revolutionary war and peaceful co-existence is of greater immediate consequence than the quarrel about the *filioque* clause.

*　　*　　*

Polycentrism, a term coined by Palmiro Togliatti six years ago, has become one of the most important realities in world affairs, though the lexicographers have not yet taken note.[2] After Stalin's death important

---

[1] Cf. A. A. Vasiliev, *History of the Byzantine Empire* (1928); Steven Runciman, *Byzantine Civilization* (1933).

[2] The *Malaya Sovetskaya Entsiklopedia* has an entry on *Politsentrism* referring to ' the theory about the origin of the present human races from the different kinds of

changes had to be made both inside the Soviet Union and within the bloc: de-Stalinisation greatly promoted the spread of polycentrism, the growth of independence among states and parties within the camp, and the emergence of one real and several potential rival centres. The doctrine of the unshakeable unity of the camp had been based on the dogma of infallibility of the Soviet leadership; the destruction of one could not but decisively affect the other. Nevertheless there is good reason to believe that the centrifugal trends would in any case have prevailed in the bloc even if Khrushchev had never debunked Stalin and his system; it might have taken longer but might in the end have caused even more violent dissension. Stalinism after all could not prevent Tito's defection and the gradual Chinese estrangement. Under Stalin Peking was for a number of reasons more willing to follow the Soviet lead, but as China grew stronger it was bound to press for more and more influence in the camp; Peking undoubtedly intended to graduate from the status of a junior partner to equality with Russia, and ultimately to senior partnership because of its bigger population and as a reward for its greater doctrinal purity. Relations within the ' socialist world system ' had to be modified after 1953, but while the Soviet state had the means of physical control to keep internal de-Stalinisation in bounds, there were no such means to check the transformation of the camp. There were no other means but common ideological belief, friendly persuasion (backed admittedly by military, economic, and political assistance or their withdrawal) to bring about the desirable measure of co-operation and cohesion between the countries of the bloc. But this was not sufficient to prevent conflicts and crises. I have pointed out elsewhere that Khrushchev can hardly be blamed for bringing out into the open a crisis that was not of his own, but of Stalin's making; the communist system had ceased to be united long before, and the Russians merely decided to make an end to what appeared to them a harmful, perhaps intolerable pretence of agreement where no real agreement existed.[3]

The communist polycentrism debate goes back to the now famous Togliatti interview with *Nuovi Argomenti* in the summer of 1956 which provoked a reply in the French communist press.[4] It was decided at the time, however, not to continue these polemics and the second act opened five years later with yet another Togliatti speech—his report on the 22nd CPSU congress,[5] in which he declared, *expressis verbis*, that the spread of communism to distant countries, and the great objective differences in the methods and conditions of work made polycentrism absolutely

---

Neanderthals, which developed in a parallel way in the direction of the present species of man '. On second thoughts this definition—Neanderthals and all—is not entirely unconnected with the present-day predicament. See below on cultural heritage and national peculiarities as one of the factors in the spread of polycentrism.

[3] 'The end of the monolith', *Foreign Affairs*, April 1961. Writing about this ' fiction of unity', Richard Lowenthal has pointed out that it remains to be seen whether the Russians will in future be willing to maintain it without a minimum of submission to majority rule (*Problems of Communism*, January–February 1962).

[4] Roger Garaudy in *Cahiers du Communisme*, January 1957.

[5] *Unità*, 11 November 1961.

necessary. Against this the French communist leaders rallied and stressed the necessity for unity in the world movement and the danger of the emergence of factions.[6] Togliatti's reply revealed that it had been suggested back in 1956 at an assembly of leaders of the old Comintern parties to establish regional communist centres, but that this proposal had not come from his party, and that the attempts to follow up the suggestion had not been successful.[7]

With this the open polycentrism debate has come to a halt for the time being, though the East Germans, Poles, and Chinese have put some rather vague declarations on record; but it can be taken for granted that there must have been internal discussion on the subject. Recent official statements at any rate are not very illuminating; sometimes they recall nothing so much as the disputations between Greek and Latin monks in the Middle Ages. The Hungarian ideologist Szanto has emphasised that while the Soviet Communist party is no longer a leading party in the administrative sense, it still is a leading group, and the attitude to it is the test of internationalism. This may be very close to the actual state of affairs, but the ambiguities hidden in this situation clearly make it not very easy to restore the unity of the camp. Nor have Soviet declarations been very helpful. *Pravda* (22 February 1962) has stressed the international significance of the 22nd congress and it has quoted many foreign communist leaders to the effect that the Soviet Union is still the centre of the socialist camp; Soviet spokesmen have admitted at the same time that the declarations of one party are not binding on the parties of other countries.[8] Such equivocations admittedly reflect more than individual inconsistencies; they are inherent in a complex situation.

*   *   *

Consciousness—or at any rate official acknowledgment—frequently lags behind political realities. With very few exceptions the leaders of what used to be the Soviet camp have so far refused to take cognisance of that new fact of political life—polycentrism. It is freely admitted that the bloc no longer has one centre, but the obvious inference—that it now has several centres—is not drawn. The emergence of two major and several minor such centres is an irreversible fact; certain trends may in effect lead the communist countries *beyond* polycentrism. For polycentrism, after all, implies a measure of common ground and the existence of a world system of communist states; but what if, at a certain point, the divisive factors should cause a break up of the system and lead beyond it?

It has been maintained that this is bound to happen in the end, and it is also urged, on the other side, that the present conflicts may be nothing

---

6 Waldeck Rochet in *Humanité*, 27 November; Maurice Thorez, *ibid.*, 30 November 1961.
7 *Unità*, 2 December 1961. According to press reports the Indonesian communist leader Aidit has since come out with a proposal to establish a quasi-independent South-East Asian regional communist centre.
8 V. Rudin in *World Marxist Review*, February 1962.

more than the birth-pangs of a new international order. Every social order, the argument runs, has its own forms of conflicts; feudal rivalries were concerned with territory, prestige, and status within the hierarchical structure of society; in the bourgeois age nations fought over spheres of interest, and to some extent over ethnic claims. Communism has now produced its own 'world system' with eleven countries and eighty-three parties. Will it transpire that they are incapable of coexisting with one another, or will they be able to resolve their conflicts within whatever framework they develop for that purpose? Divergent interest, hostility, and open conflicts do not necessarily lead to the break-up of the system; is it not at least a possibility that the communist states and parties will develop their own forum to deal with such emergencies?

Speculations of this kind must be based on an analysis of the causes of polycentrism. Five years ago Professor Wiles asked in these pages whether communism could go on being 'papal' or whether it would by necessity become 'conciliar'. 'Or would a compromise like the original Comintern do—conciliar in that it is genuinely multi-national, papal in that its majority decision is final and binding?'[9] This question has been answered, for the compromise has not really worked, and the majority decisions have not been accepted as final and binding. In 1957, when Peter Wiles wrote, Poland was the great protagonist of polycentrism. ('If Hungary is a wound, Poland is an infection . . . The admitted poly-centricity of ideology casts doubt on all ideology . . . But things are worse than that: for one of the centres has in effect abandoned ideology'.) In 1962 Poland is no longer an infection, at best a local irritation in the Soviet bloc, and yet polycentrism is more rampant than ever before. In the present phase it is not the 'liberals' but their antagonists, the neo-Stalinists, who have made the conflict more acute. What then are the prime causes of the spread of polycentrism?

The most common explanation refers to the different stages of Russian and Chinese economic, social, and political development, the fact that China has only recently entered its 'Stalinist' phase while the Soviet Union seems on the way out of it. This economic and social disparity has of course weighty political repercussions on China's domestic and international policy, but it cannot serve as a full and satisfactory explanation for a more complex phenomenon. Following this explanation to its logical end, it would mean that once China emerges from the Stalinist phase as a result of economic development—say, in twenty, thirty, or fifty years' time—the 'objective basis' for conflict will disappear and harmony prevail. Conversely, it means that if Russia and China were at present more or less on the same level of economic and social development, peace and unanimity would already reign. Unfortunately, historical experience shows that big powers have clashed whether or not they had reached the same level of economic and social development. Only the assumption that the current conflicts between Russia and China are

[9] *Survey*, May 1957.

exclusively ideological in character would justify the belief that the conflict will 'wither away'. But this makes no allowances at all for the automatism of totalitarian rule, or for big power rivalries and clashes. Totalitarian states have a tendency to expand, they have a messianic mission, and a monopoly of the means of grace; they find it, as a rule, more difficult to coexist with each other than do old-fashioned big powers, which, with all their rivalries, practise a certain amount of toleration. Their dynamism is greater and their ideological motivation prevents them from seeking compromises that would have been possible in bygone ages. Spain and Portugal could divide the world between themselves along a certain meridian; Russia and China cannot do so—unless, of course, the gradual end of Stalinism were also to mark the end of totalitarian rule and the far-reaching transformation of the whole communist world. Such a development, while highly desirable, can at present be no more than a pious wish. The backwardness-of-China thesis also disregards the existence of a great many factors apart from the Sino-Soviet conflict that are conducive to the spread of polycentrism, such as the emergence of independent and quasi-independent communist centres in Africa, South-East Asia, and Latin America, the quarrels among European communists (such as the French and the Italian communist parties). It omits from view, in particular, the fact that the very success of communism in the under-developed countries seems to be its undoing. It has been adulterated and produces a strange harvest: Under a veneer of Marxist-Leninist ideology, of anti-imperialist slogans, state control of the economy and one-party rule, influences are at work which have very little to do with Marxism or even Leninism. Communism is Africanised and Asianised even faster and more thoroughly than Christianity, because it is a secular movement and therefore in greater need of adaptation. The outcome is a mixture of communist elements and components alien to it. This, from the point of view of communist unity, is highly regrettable, but the irony of it is that any progress by world communism can now be achieved only by strengthening the centrifugal trends and thus weakening the movement from within.

If Chinese (and Albanian) economic and social backwardness are at best only part of the explanation for a very complex phenomenon, what are the other factors that cause, or accentuate polycentrism? Reference has been made to the dynamics of totalitarian rule; the great importance of differences in national make-up, cultural heritage, and general outlook in the different parts of the world must also be mentioned. These imponderabilia have been consistently under-rated in communist history, sometimes with near-fatal consequences. (The importance of the national factor in the rise of fascism!) In theory it was recognised that different conditions prevailed in different countries, in practice the measure of national autonomy granted was the smallest possible; each attempt to work out a 'national road' to communism was branded as a deviation from proletarian internationalism. But these national peculiarities were not pretexts invented by faint-hearted comrades; they were stubborn facts, in East Europe and elsewhere, and with the spread of communism to the Far and Middle East, to Africa and Latin America, the attempts to find common solutions to different problems became more and more unrealistic. Some efforts were made to accommodate the old doctrine to the new realities; the invitation to the 22nd CPSU congress of various radical nationalist African parties could serve as an illustration. But the case of Guinea at once shows the limits of such attempts at integration by friendly persuasion, when no discipline is demanded and none shown.

Cultural heritage and national peculiarities, then, are of great importance in this context and one can, with reservations, agree with George Lichtheim's observation that the further spread of polycentrism is likely to occur along the cultural frontiers embedded within the communist orbit.[10] On purely cultural grounds a split between 'Eastern' and 'Western' communism would appear extremely likely, but the overall picture is distorted by the intrusion of other factors. A number of Asian communist parties (and some of the most important among them) have been deeply antagonised by Chinese pretensions to leadership over a communist Asian co-prosperity sphere. They are rightly afraid of Chinese political ambitions and will gravitate to any countervailing centre, however close their cultural (or ethnic) affinity with Peking. Some African and Latin American communist parties, on the other hand, may incline towards Peking for political reasons, notwithstanding an almost total absence of cultural ties or other common interests with the Chinese. Which brings one back to the problem of Sino-Soviet relations, a topic analysed at length in a number of recent studies. Of late hardly any international communist gathering has passed without a show of open conflict and dissension between Moscow and Peking (the meeting of the World Peace Council in Stockholm, the Afro-Asian writers conference in Cairo, the Afro-Asian solidarity meeting in Gaza, etc.); this uneasy co-existence, based not on toleration ('agreement to disagree') but rather on the inability to overthrow the rival, will presumably continue for a long time, attempts to iron out existing difficulties alternating with fierce political warfare. It is very likely that a sizeable fraction of Soviet and East European communists feels extremely unhappy about the split with Peking and may be willing to undertake new attempts to achieve a fresh rapprochement if not total reconciliation. Lasting reconciliation, however, seems impossible in the foreseeable future, not so much because of divergent views on war and peace, on the organisation of agriculture or the place in history of the late Josef Stalin, but because both Russia and China are big powers, and the voluntary abdication by a big power of its position, a renunciation of its interests for any length of time, can be ruled out. But 'interests' in our time and age does not simply mean territory and spheres of interest, it stands for control over party organisation—at home, in other parts, and ultimately over the whole bloc. The

10 *New Leader*, 19 March 1962.

dilemma of the Chinese communists is similar in character. They are deeply committed to the image of total unanimity, as Benjamin Schwartz has recently pointed out.[11] They strongly desire bloc solidarity, and yet are equally committed to the supremacy of their own political and ideological authority within China as well as to their right to pursue their own national interests. ' These sundry commitments can only be reconciled by what Chou En-lai refers to as " unanimity through consultation ".' Both China and Russia have made concessions, revealed in a great number of official communiqués in recent years, which try to make up in length for lack of precision and absence of agreement. There has been no unanimity as to how these resolutions should be interpreted. Like the heroes in the old farm ballad:

> *We arg'ed the thing at breakfast,*
> *we arg'ed the thing at tea,*
> *And the more we arg'ed the question*
> *the more we didn't agree.*

* * *

The present volume deals with both the cohesive and the centrifugal tendencies in world communism today; in this extremely fluid situation most contributors have rightly refrained from going on record with predictions. In the near future almost anything may happen—from a new rapprochement between Moscow and Peking to a ' final break ' (assuming that both ' final ' and ' break ' have been defined in a satisfactory way). In a longer perspective a number of trends which can already be discerned now will almost certainly make their impact. One is the emergence of factions in communism both nationally and internationally. If factions are recognised on the international level, how can their emergence within one party be prevented? How, in the long run, can ' iron discipline ' be kept *within* a national party if there is none in the international movement? This process, if unchecked, could have incalculable consequences —the communist parties would gradually come to resemble other parties. It would be the end of communism as we have known it.

Another probable development is the emergence of communist centres outside Moscow and Peking. The Sino-Soviet conflict has overshadowed all other divisions and rivalries in the bloc, but once the principle of *una sancta* is abandoned, there is no limit, in theory at any rate, to the number of possible autocephalous churches. In practice their number may be restricted; but the emergence of a Latin American, an African, and a West European communist centre is highly probable. Once such a division has become an established fact, development along diverging and probably conflicting lines is accelerated; whether West European communists, for instance, will still find much in common with the Chinese after a while is an open question. The differences may be even more marked in the newly independent countries of Asia and Africa, and perhaps also in Latin America; Russians may scoff at ' African socialism ',

[11] *Ibid.*

but this lack of sympathy is mutual; there is not much room for orthodox Leninism, not even for Maoism in the blueprints of the national revolutionaries of Africa, South East Asia, and, *pace* Dr Castro, Latin America.

These then are the long range probabilities. In the immediate future there exist, broadly speaking, three: A reconciliation between Moscow and Peking, though perhaps not impossible, would in all probability be of short duration, given the constant factors that make for friction inside the communist bloc. A radical break between the two centres and the consequent establishment of two camps is equally unlikely, for the unifying forces—the common traditions and ideology, the existence of an outside threat—are still too strong. Most likely, then, is a prolonged period of competitive coexistence and peaceful conflict, a series of lateral or ecumenical councils trying to reach a modus vivendi if it should prove impossible to resolve the existing conflicts. This may take (as Benjamin Schwartz has put it) either the form of an open agreement to disagree on certain issues in the interest of solidarity on overriding common interests, or an affirmation of solidarity in terms of common interests without a resolution of issues and without any agreement to disagree. In either case this would only mean the perpetuation of an anomalous situation; such an arrangement may be workable among saturated, conservative nations, but not among dynamic powers with a strong sense of mission to bring about the redemption of this whole sinful world.

The schism opens entirely new perspectives; polycentrism is no longer a possibility, but an established fact. The question is not whether the various communist parties and states will follow independent lines that may conflict with one another, but rather how fast and how far this development will proceed. It may be retarded by a faction in Moscow that demands yet another attempt to reach agreement with the Chinese, or by a group in Peking that believes an understanding with the Russians to be of paramount importance. But the logic of events, the very dynamic of communist parties and states, propel them in different directions.

It remains to be seen how the various factions in world communism will crystallise; like big planets, the major parties and states will probably constitute autonomous systems with their own satellites revolving round them. And it remains to be seen, above all, whether the ' socialist world system ' will be able to contain these new developments or whether polycentrism, bursting through the old framework, will sweep it aside; whether a common ideological heritage will for much longer prove more powerful than the many divisive factors which, with each year, are becoming more and more important.

COMMUNIST INTERNATIONAL RELATIONS

Melvin Croan

Now that the building of socialism is no longer confined to one country and a world socialist system has been formed, new theoretical problems of the struggle for the victory of socialism and communism have arisen.
—N. S. Khrushchev, *Report to the 21st (Extraordinary) Congress of the CPSU, January* 1959.

Here there arises an important question of principle: How to interpret internationalism?
—V. I. Lenin, ' *On the Question of Nationalities or " Autonomizing",'* 30 *December* 1922.

IT is a cardinal tenet of the Leninist school of Marxism that without a revolutionary theory, there can be no revolutionary practice. Adherents of the Marxist-Leninist persuasion never tire of proclaiming that theory is the key to action. Apart from the theory which articulates and interprets it, reality is devoid of meaning. Even more crucially, theory should provide a reliable guide to conscious exertions purposively undertaken in order to achieve doctrinally desirable ends. Thus conceived, Marxist-Leninist theory is meant to be more than either normative prescription or existential description, not to mention mere rationalisation. From the point of view of the committed communist, theory and practice must be indissolubly linked in a dynamic reciprocal relationship. Actual practice should constantly enrich theory but the decisive test of theory at any given point in time is to be found in practice. As A. Rumyantsev, the editor-in-chief of *Problems of Peace and Socialism* (*World Marxist Review*), recently expressed it, interestingly enough in an authoritative editorial on the present distress within the international communist movement, ' the supreme criterion of any theory is practical experience '.[1]

' Practical experience ' does suggest that in some crucial respects Marxist-Leninist theories of international politics may well have served Soviet policy-makers better than any comparable frame of reference available to their Western counterparts.[2] For all its pedantry and polemicism, Lenin's analysis of ' imperialism ' does instruct its disciples in an elementary appreciation of the reality of international conflict and has directed their attention to some of the basic springs of change in world affairs.[3] How striking, by contrast, the failure of the same general body

---

[1] A. Rumyantsev, ' Our Common Ideological Weapon ', *World Marxist Review*, January 1962, p. 4.

[2] Cf. Robert C. Tucker, ' Russia, the West and World Order ', *World Politics*, October 1959, and Z. K. Brzezinski, ' Communist Ideology and International Affairs ', *Journal of Conflict Resolution*, September 1960.

[3] It may be argued that with the attainment of independence by the former colonial peoples, the Marxist-Leninist sensitivity to backward (' colonial ') areas has already spent itself. On the other hand, the Leninist view of international politics as a process of change, conflict, and ' uneven development ' still constitutes an operative if highly generalised and questionably deduced insight.

of theory—or at least of its latter-day Soviet exponents—to penetrate the political dynamics of international communism. Comrade Rumyantsev notwithstanding, contemporary Soviet theory can no longer control and really does not even comprehend the sources of conflict and the dynamics of change within the international communist system itself.

If, as N. S. Khrushchev confidently reported to the twentieth congress of the CPSU in 1956, ' the chief feature of our epoch is the emergence of socialism from the confines of one country and its transformation into a world system ',[4] the character of that transformation has remained elusive and its consequences increasingly unmanageable. Although there has been no lack of Soviet theorising since 1956, events since the twenty-second congress have made it unmistakably clear that the quest for an operative theory of communist international relations has proved abortive. If anything, the inadequacies of theory now threaten further to compound the frustrations of practice.

THE problem posed by the existence of communist movements, if not yet communist states, beyond ' the confines of one country ' has, of course, a rather lengthy pre-history. Before World War II the issue was typically formulated as a question of the relation between the ' national power interests ' of the Soviet state and the claims of ' world revolution '. Although outside observers espied competition and potential conflict between these two hinges of Soviet commitment, no communist and certainly no Soviet communist dared accept the validity of such an analysis. In fact, terrible simplifier that he was, Stalin had effectively ' solved ' the theoretical dilemma. What other purpose had his demonstration that whatever best served the Soviet power *eo ipso* benefited the cause of world revolution? A syllogism, perhaps; but woe unto them who questioned the logic!

Stalin's reduction of the Comintern to an obedient instrument of Soviet foreign policy is a familiar enough story in the West. The story is now being acknowledged in some detail inside the communist world.[5] Yet at a time when the Soviet leadership is ever more insistently invoking Leninism as a source of inspiration and justification, it may be safely assumed that Lenin's responsibility for the fate of international communism at Stalin's hands will go unmentioned. All the same, Stalin's success in mastering the machinery of the international movement and directing it towards his own ends was in fact enormously facilitated by Lenin's own achievements in the international movement. The 21 conditions of admission to the Comintern (1920) mark a conscious and, as it turned out, a successful projection on to the international plane of Lenin's precepts of democratic centralism. The very same elitist organisational

4 *Pravda*, 15 February 1956.
5 Cf. ' Kierunek odnowy i marszu do kommunizmu ', *Nowe Drogi* (Warsaw), December 1961, and Tadeusz Daniszewski, ' Kult jednostki i miedzynarodowy ruch robotniczy ', *Polityka*, 2 December 1961. For a Soviet evaluation of the consequences of Stalinism in the international sphere, see Yu. Andropov, ' XXII. s'ezd i razvitie mirovoy sotsialisticheskoy sistemy ', *Pravda*, 2 December 1961.

norms which Lenin had earlier applied to one segment of Russian Marxism were, in effect, also internationalised by him. The stipulations of 1920 anticipated the subordination of international communism to the Soviet party and their joint subjection to the caprices and excesses of the Stalinist dictatorship. Moreover, as the late Franz Borkenau once suggested, the Leninist belief in the ineluctable efficacy of a set of ' proper ' organisational norms in combination with the ' correct' tactical manoeuvres also rationalised the practice of the international purge whenever a ' national section ' of the Comintern suffered a substantial political setback.[6]

The unconditional subordination of the international communist movement to Moscow was, then, an incontestable reality long before World War II. The expansion of Soviet power into East Europe and the installation of ' people's democratic ' regimes there after 1945 in no way altered either the Stalinist practice or the Leninist theory of the international communist movement. Stalin's campaign against Titoism throttled a hesitant and tentative emergence of what Professor Brzezinski has termed ' domesticism ', i.e. the tendency of some newly invested communist leaders to make domestic adjustments the better to counter local pressures and solve particular problems, while at the same time accepting ultimate Soviet leadership.[7] It is even open to question whether divergent domestic practices in the countries of East Europe before 1948 are to be understood as the incipient strivings of the local communist leaders for a measure of autonomy—however small—or as testimony to Stalin's reluctance at the time, for foreign policy reasons of his own, to clamp tight the full force of his totalitarian panoply over the entire area.[8] Even after 1948–49, the internal politics of the states subject to Soviet power could not be totally ' coordinated ' down to the very last detail. The fact that the party purges inaugurated in the wake of the campaign against Titoism were more brutal and bloody in Hungary and less so in Poland was to assume enormous importance at a later date when the time came to rehabilitate the disgraced and fallen leaders.

However pertinent such internal distinctions for subsequent developments, they did not count for very much in the immediate context of Stalinist control of the entire satellite bloc. After the Tito affair Soviet dominance over the communist inter-state system was effectively guaranteed by the extension to the East European satellites—China was another matter again—of the same network of totalitarian controls through which Stalin presided over the Soviet Union. While this kind of international arrangement did secure Soviet power, as exercised in the last analysis by Stalin personally, its radical political simplicity did not necessarily produce the intended social and economic consequences. The decision of the post-Stalinist rulers to loosen the Soviet grip on the satellites soon

---

6 Franz Borkenau, *World Communism* (New York, 1939), passim.

7 Z. Brzezinski, ' The Challenge of Change in the Soviet Bloc ', *Foreign Affairs*, April 1961. Cf. his *Soviet Bloc* (Harvard, 1960).

8 See Paul Kecskemeti, ' Diversity and Uniformity in Communist Bloc Politics ', *World Politics*, January 1961. The two interpretations are not, of course, mutually exclusive.

after the old dictator's death reflected their conscious recognition of the socio-economic costs of Stalinism abroad no less than at home.

THE momentous events of 1956 in Poland and Hungary should not, however, be understood as the simple consequence of this relaxation. As Richard Lowenthal has pointed out, any adequate explanation must take account of the convergence of relaxation and a 'triple crisis of authority', involving the disclosure and disavowal of Stalin's crimes, the prior involvement of many satellite bosses in the 'anti-Titoist' phase of these crimes, and the uncertainty of the succession crisis in the Soviet Union itself.[9]

Paradoxically, the events of 1956 at once made a new definition of communist international relations most urgent and the implementation of any novel principles most difficult. In fact the restoration of a semblance of international communist harmony as well as of internal order in the East European states was achieved through the struggle against revisionism, which posed a common menace to the survival of communist dictatorships everywhere. That achievement, however, was purchased at the price of the renewed exclusion of Tito from international communist affairs and, even more significantly, the introduction of Maoist influence into Eastern Europe.

The unprecedented participation of the Chinese in the affairs of the entire bloc proved to be the harbinger of a much more serious challenge to the coordination of the 'socialist system' and indeed to its very unity as a system.[10] It would be wrong to assume that the Chinese at that time aspired to an institutional realisation of the formula of joint Sino-Soviet leadership of the camp, pronounced, probably inadvertently, by Molotov in 1955.[11] In fact in 1957 the Chinese proved most zealous in their lobbying for an unequivocal statement by the ruling communist parties upholding the unqualified leadership of the Soviet Union over the entire camp. Yet the more anxious the Chinese were to preserve a unified international movement led from a single centre, the more concerned they became that the doctrines expounded and the policies pursued by the centre should be, in their own view, the 'correct' ones, and the more ominous, for that reason, the growing divergence between Chinese and Soviet interpretations of such abstract and yet intensely practical questions as 'the definition of the present epoch', 'the meaning of peaceful coexistence', 'the character of national liberation movements', 'roads to socialism', 'the timing and methods of arrival at communism', and the like. As early as

9 Richard Lowenthal, 'Schism Among the Faithful', *Problems of Communism*, January–February 1962.

10 For a cogent discussion of the distinctive attributes of the communist international system up to 1960, see George Modelski, *The Communist International System* (Princeton, 1960).

11 His 1955 formulation (in a speech to the Supreme Soviet) of 'the socialist camp headed by the Soviet Union, or more properly speaking, by the Soviet Union and the People's Republic of China', has made him fair game for the speculations of the Kremlinologists as well as the recriminations of the Khrushchevites.

1958 it had become quite clear that the Chinese were intent on 'genera-lising' their own views on the international situation and even their own domestic policies and programmes. This was precisely the behaviour which the Soviet leadership had found so reprehensible two years earlier in the case of Tito; pretensions to which the Chinese up to that point had been immune.[12]

The manner in which the Sino-Soviet dialogue became embittered during 1960 is a matter of general public knowledge in the West. Suffice it to record that the verbose Statement of the 81 Communist parties, adopted after a protracted and impassioned debate in November 1960, failed to resolve the outstanding issues. On the contrary, the Chinese continued and even intensified their moral and material support of the staunchly Stalinist Albanian regime of Enver Hoxha, and may well have deliberately provoked the Soviet First Secretary by encouraging anti-Khrushchev elements elsewhere, not excluding the Soviet Union. The open Soviet attack on Albania at the 22nd CPSU congress and the subse-quent rupture of diplomatic relations, together with the persistence of an undisguised Chinese commitment to Hoxha and further exacerbation of mutual recrimination between the Chinese and Soviet leaders, are only the most recent chapters in the uncompleted story of communist inter-state competition and conflict. The 'moral and political unity' of inter-national communism has been unmistakably shaken, perhaps irreparably shattered. In the absence of a single centre of uncontested leadership, the Leninist norms of democratic centralism have lost all relevance as a guide to communist international relations.

S UCH, briefly, are the broad outlines of major political developments within the communist camp, as they appear to an outside observer. The pace of recent events has clearly outdistanced the theory that ought to have governed them. The direction of these events posits a supreme challenge to theory itself. How, indeed, to interpret 'proletarian' or 'socialist internationalism'? Where to find an operative Soviet theory of communist international relations?

There is, of course, no dearth of formalised verbal statements about the relations that *should* obtain among communist states and the prin-ciples upon which these relations ought to be based. Both the Statement of the 81 parties (December 1960) and the new Soviet Party Programme

---

12 See 'For Further Consolidation of the Forces of Socialism on the Basis of Marxist-Leninist Principles', *Pravda*, 23 November 1956, the Soviet reply to Tito's speech at Pula on the Hungarian uprising. Cf. the following charge against Tito: 'Is it correct to disparage the socialist system of other countries, to extol one's own experi-ence, publicising it as universal and best? One cannot but see that the idea is appearing more and more often in the Yugoslav press that the Yugoslav "road to socialism" is the most correct or even the only possible road for almost all countries of the world . . .' with the laudatory observation that 'the wisdom of the Communist party of China is also seen in the fact that it does not counterpose the experience of building socialism in its country to the experience of other countries but skilfully uses the experience of all the socialist countries for the successful solution of problems in building a new society in China'.

(October 1961) meticulously delineate the ideals of 'complete equality, mutual respect for independence and sovereignty, and fraternal mutual assistance and cooperation.'[13] Both pronouncements, and the numerous official Soviet commentaries on them, also stress the need for international communist unity and express the certainty that the desired unity is embedded in the solid foundations of common ideological convictions and shared economic and political interests.

These are the basic norms and fundamental assumptions of what can be called 'Khrushchev's vision' of international communism. Yet the ascription of this vision to Khrushchev personally requires modification in at least two vital respects. First, so personalised a designation is quite misleading from the point of view of doctrinal genealogy. Second, the relationship postulated between the harmonious unity of the entire system and the absolute equality of its individual members ignores the most recent Soviet gloss on the doctrine of equality, which gives a substantially different 'vision' but one which, nonetheless, cannot be detached from the name of N. S. Khrushchev.

In the first place, Khrushchev's norms, if not his assumptions, antedate his accession to the Soviet leadership. The very same norms were in fact proclaimed in Stalin's time. Although Stalin's monopoly of personal power in the Soviet orbit was characterised by egregious violations of these and all other norms, it was not at all the case that Stalinist theory simply neglected the problem of relations among communist states. Still less will it suffice to suppose that the theoretical issue of international communist relations was exhausted by that masterpiece of understatement, in which Malenkov dismissed Stalinist relations with the satellites as ' an example of entirely new relations among states, relations never yet encountered in history'.[14] However embryonic and ultimately irrelevant the elaboration of a theory of communist international relations under Stalin, there was at least the formal acknowledgment of the principles of equality, independence, non-interference in domestic affairs, close economic co-operation, and mutual assistance. As Gomulka observed in his remarkable address to the historic eighth plenum of the Central Committee of the Polish Communist party in October 1956:

> Stalin as the leader of the party and of the Soviet Union formally recognised that all the principles enumerated above should characterise the relations between the countries of the socialist camp. Not only did he recognise them, but he himself proclaimed them. In fact, however, these principles could not fit within the framework of what makes up the cult of personality.[15]

[13] *Programme of the Communist Party of the Soviet Union* (Moscow, 1961), p. 22. Cf. 'Statement of the Meeting of Representatives of the Communist and Workers Parties', Supplement to *New Times*, No. 50, 1960, p. 6.
[14] Report of the Central Committee to the 19th CPSU congress (by Malenkov), *Pravda*, 6 October 1952.
[15] *Trybuna Ludu*, 21 October 1956, in Paul Zinner, ed., *National Communism and Popular Revolt in Eastern Europe* (Columbia University Press, 1956), pp. 227–228.

In yet another respect Khrushchev's initial theory of communist international relations owes an unacknowledged debt to its Stalinist antecedents. Both before 1953 and afterwards—recurrently until at least 1959—Soviet theory postulated an explicit analogy between the Soviet treatment of the problem of nationalities inside the USSR and the future prospects for the communist inter-state system [16]; as a state which was both multinational and monolithic, the Soviet Union held a special place in the international communist system. [17] In addition to such practical topical conclusions, however, the analogy between the Soviet nationalities problem and the international communist system may well have proved conducive to utopian thinking, as reflected in Khrushchev's grandiloquent use of the analogy on more than one occasion. Consider, for example, his remarks at Leipzig on 7 March 1959:

> The old concept of frontiers as such will be gradually obliterated. With communism winning on a world-wide scale, the state frontiers will disappear as Marxism-Leninism teaches us. And then, in all probability, there will remain, for the time being, only the ethnographic boundaries. And even they will be purely of a conventional nature. Such frontiers, if one can call them that, will have, naturally, neither frontier guards, nor customs officials, nor any incidents. They will simply demarcate the historically created pattern of the distribution of one or another people or nationality on a particular territory. That this will be so, *is demonstrated by the process going on in the Soviet Union, which is a country of many nations.* (Italics added.—M. C.)

Short of this splendidly utopian image of a future world communist society, could not one conclude by reasoning in terms of the analogy that once certain Stalinist excesses were corrected in communist international relations, as they were to be corrected in internal nationality affairs, the international system would run smoothly? Such indeed seems to have been the inspiration behind Soviet policy towards China in 1954, Khrushchev's 'new course' for East Europe through 1956, and, more especially, his efforts to restore state and party relations with Yugoslavia. Unfortunately, the analogy from which these international policies may have been derived was never a wholly sound one. As Mukhitdinov reminded the delegates to the 21st CPSU congress, the 'main thing' guaranteeing the success of Soviet nationality policy is 'the leading and directing role of the Communist Party'. [18] And that is precisely the rub. Who, in fact, leads the socialist system? How are common decisions to

---

[16] Cf. Beria's speech to the 19th CPSU congress with those sections of Khrushchev's public report to the 20th which deal with the nationalities problem, Soviet patriotism, and the international communist system.

[17] To cite one example: 'Soviet Communists consider it their sacred duty to set an example of the practice and principles of socialist internationalism as befits representatives of a multinational socialist country in which the nationality question has been solved consistently on the basis of Marxist-Leninist theory', Editorial, *Pravda*, 16 July 1955.

[18] *Pravda*, 31 January 1959.

be reached? What kind of decisions should be binding on all the 'equal members' of the system?

THAT this kind of question never arose during Stalin's lifetime is testimony to the practical significance of Stalin's personal role in the entire system. Whether the emergence of such issues could have been permanently deferred is itself a moot question in view of the Tito case and, more particularly, the patent impossibility of imposing the Stalinist pattern of Soviet totalitarian control on China. In any case, as long as Stalin was alive, Soviet theory could postulate the absolute equality of all members of the socialist camp, much as Hobbes' *Leviathan* stipulated the principles of extreme individualism and radical equality. Once the 'sovereign' died, however, and once both the international and internal excesses of his rule were acknowledged, the need to discover an institutional substitute for the defunct personal monopoly of international power became an extremely urgent one. Regrettably for the Soviet party, the very sequence of first quietly correcting and then publicly denouncing the Stalinist legacy undermined its international moral authority at precisely the time when, because of the increasingly obvious limitations of its operative power within the socialist camp, it needed to be maximised.

It should be observed that Khrushchev, as befits a hardened Bolshevik, has been especially sensitive to the problem of leadership. To be sure, during the uncertain days of 1956, a Togliatti could advance, although not without challenge even then, the notion of 'polycentrism'. The very next year, however, produced, in the Moscow Declaration of November 1957, an unequivocal affirmation of the 'leading role' of the Communist Party of the Soviet Union. While it lasted, the assertion of Soviet predominance was reasoned in terms which variously stressed the historical precedence of the Russian Revolution, the primacy of Soviet power, and the pre-eminence of Soviet achievements in the construction of Socialism. As Khrushchev formulated it in his report to the 21st congress:

> As regards the Soviet Union, its role, as is known, consists not in controlling other countries, but in having been the first to blaze the trail to socialism for mankind, in being the most powerful country in the international socialist system and the first to have entered into the period of extensive building of communism.[19]

Thus elaborated, the assertion of Soviet leadership implied a special Soviet right to pass judgment on internal practices and developments in other communist countries, and reserved for the CPSU the 'last word' on matters of doctrinal interpretation and international strategy. Yet disputes on these very matters of doctrine and strategy since 1958, as well as the further development of internal diversity (between the Soviet Union and China, Poland and Albania, to mention only the most striking examples), prompted the subsequent Soviet admission that it had in fact

19 *Pravda*, 28 January 1959.

become 'impossible to lead all the socialist countries and communist parties from any single centre'.[20]

Where does the renunciation of the leading Soviet role in the communist international system leave the norm of absolute equality of all socialist states and communist parties? If Poland is to pursue its own special course in agriculture—with or without explicit Soviet endorsement—on what basis to contest Albania's perpetuation of Stalinist practices, or, for that matter, China's distinctive views on world affairs? When the Albanians openly raised this question in their own case, Soviet spokesmen replied that certain Soviet decisions (e.g. those of the 20th congress), as ratified by representative international communist meetings (e.g. the meeting of the 81 parties) must be considered binding on all socialist states and communist parties.[21]

Unfortunately, rudimentary parliamentarism in international communist relations has also generated its own special dilemmas, not the least of which is the basic incompatibility of the compromise which parliamentarism requires to be effective with the ideological pretensions of international communism in general and the monolithic practices of individual communist parties in particular. Ideology, by its nature, vitiates the parliamentary solution. Where there can be only one 'correct' policy, only one 'right' answer, pragmatic compromise between divergent points of view is clearly impossible. Thus, common adherence to Marxism-Leninism, which Soviet theory regards as the basic cohesive factor in communist international relations, has, in the absence of a single centre of authoritative interpretation, proved to be a disruptive one.

The renunciation of the Soviet 'leading role' and the impracticability of a parliamentary substitute have belatedly required a reassessment of the norm of absolute equality. [In effect, it is now asserted that the Soviet party must be 'more equal' than other parties on certain basic matters, especially on the question of war and peace.[22] Yet if the Soviet theory of international communist unity based upon the assumptions of common ideological conviction and shared interests and mutual assistance were really viable, the entire complex of knotty problems relating to international leadership, decision-making, and obligation would never have arisen in this form at all.] The assumptions themselves suggest almost a communist version of the old liberal notion of automatic harmony in international relations. The communist version has proved no more

20 Khrushchev's speech of 6 January 1961, in *World Marxist Review*, No. 1, 1961. Cf. the statement of the meeting of the 81 parties.
21 Cf. Hoxha's speech of 8 November 1961 on the 20th anniversary of the founding of the Albanian Communist party, with, e.g., 'Na opasnom puti' (On a dangerous path), *Pravda*, 14 December 1961, on the occasion of the rupture of diplomatic relations.
22 For a recent statement on the requirement for unanimity on the question of war and peace (in its Soviet interpretation), see Mieczyslaw Rakowski, 'Tresci i formy jednosci', *Nowe Drogi*, January 1962. As far as some of the other matters are concerned, consider the following Soviet assertion: 'Our party did not boldly and openly condemn the cult of the individual in order to stand by indifferently while dogmatists and nationalists attempt in the name of this cult to weaken the communist movement and to erase everything Marxism-Leninism has gained in recent years' Yu. Andropov, *Pravda*, 2 December 1961.

tenable than its liberal predecessor. Its breakdown has resulted in a modification of the norm of complete equality of all socialist states which, in turn, further undermines the basic assumptions underlying the Soviet theory of communist international relations.

THE current confusion in communist international politics and the unmistakable miscarriage of its theory have prompted many Western observers to predict—perhaps prematurely—additional dramatic convulsions in international communism, and even the inevitable transformation of the Soviet dictatorship itself as yet a further consequence of these international mutations. Following the death of Stalin, it was something of an intellectual fashion to argue the demise of Soviet totalitarianism exclusively in terms of the growing irrelevance of Marxist-Leninist ideology to the aspirations of a maturing society inside the Soviet Union. Now the inadequacies of ideology have been demonstrated in the arena of communist international relations as well. Not only has Marxism-Leninism failed to produce a viable theory of communist international relations but, even more significantly, the ideological coloration of these relations has itself militated against any pragmatic solution to the conflicts that have arisen between communist states. Thus there now exists an additional basis on which to argue the case for the end of ideology.

Such an argument, however, comes most easily to the outside observer who does not himself subscribe to the tenets of Marxism-Leninism. To suggest that the Soviet leaders should appreciate the complicating role played by ideology in communist international relations (and elsewhere) presupposes that they have already liberated themselves from their own ideological commitment to a far greater degree than is yet the case. The vitality of the Soviet commitment to the official ideology has disappointed its critics so often in the past that some caution in proclaiming its demise is called for. Assuming the persistence of ideology as a basic component in communist international relations, the *immediate* prospects for international communism need not necessarily be exhausted by the alternatives of ' polycentrism ' or a clean break between Moscow and Peking. The perpetuation of the present situation, of a measure of outward unity in the face of the competition between the socialist camp and the Western alliance—still the basic factor in world affairs—punctuated by occasional eruptions of violent altercations, cannot be entirely dismissed.

Yet even such an outcome—a pragmatic solution dictated by the overall logic of international politics—seems at best to be only a transitional arrangement. The preservation of this kind of international communist unity by its very nature will permit some degree of polycentrism. Ironically, the spectre of nationalism, which Soviet theory quite correctly perceives as both a cause and a consequence of the isolation of individual states from the communist international system,[23] is no less a reality in the context of a superficial unity based upon even a limited polycentrism. To the extent to which the entire socialist international system is suffused with repressed nationalism, the individual ruling parties will, in the absence of a single international centre, be increasingly subject to its infection.

However these developments may turn out, the period between the 20th and 22nd CPSU congresses will certainly be remembered as a time of an involuntary and ultimately abortive search on the part of the Soviet leadership for an operative theory of communist international relations. The theories enunciated in those five years have ranged from grandiose schemes depicting a conflict-less communist utopia embracing the entire globe, through a series of *ad hoc* rationalisations of concessions wrenched from the Soviet party in the course of a continuing and conflict-laden political process, to a belated effort to preserve intact special Soviet prerogatives. None of these efforts has accomplished the desired result in either theory or practice. The doctrinal tenet, enshrined in the new CPSU programme, that communist international relations are not afflicted by 'uneven development' and are therefore characterised by co-operation rather than by conflict, was dramatically challenged by the public display of Sino-Soviet hostility in the course of the proceedings of the very congress which adopted the programme. The assumption of an absolute identity between the interests of Soviet power and those of international communism, at the core of all recent theory, can now be regarded as finally disproved.

---

[23] The new CPSU programme asserts, *inter alia*, that 'nationalism is the chief political and ideological weapon used by international reaction and the remnants of the domestic reactionary forces against the unity of the socialist countries'.

POST-CONGRESS ROUNDUP

C. H. F.

A S the 22nd Soviet Party congress progressed, it became evident that it would promote even more far-reaching repercussions in the world communist movement than had the original denunciation of Stalin in Khrushchev's secret speech at the 20th congress. Now, in contrast to 1956, not only was the renewed denunciation of Stalin made in public and carried to the extreme of the removal of his body from the Mausoleum in Red Square, but a number of former Soviet leaders, previously revered as 'true disciples of V. I. Lenin', were indicted on what amounted to a charge of large-scale political gangsterism.

The latter issue was bound to lead to questions in the minds of many foreign delegates about the nature of the Soviet political system as a whole and the probity of the present Soviet leadership. Finally, and most importantly, the Soviet attack on the Albanian leadership and the explicit criticism of this by the leader of the Chinese delegation revealed the continuing gravity of Sino-Soviet differences and the illusory and temporary nature of the 1960 compromise. It faced delegates with the possibility of an eventual direct split in the international communist movement.

Initial reactions ranged from open disapproval of the removal of Stalin's body to direct and open criticism of the Chinese position advanced by many European communist leaders with their vested interest in the Soviet interpretation of peaceful coexistence.

The Italian communist leader, Longo, in a speech reported by *Unita* on 23 December, criticised views that the advanced ' socialist' countries should retard their future progress so as to put all their material advantages at the disposal of the more backward ones on the grounds that if this were to be accepted :

> You cannot approve of the Soviet Union's economic challenge to the United States; you do not agree on the tactical and strategic plans for peaceful coexistence, economic aid given by the Soviet Union to ex-colonial countries, nor even on the programme for the move from socialism to communism and the measures to make institutions more democratic. The Chinese comrades do not hide their disagreement ... We, on the contrary, think that Soviet policy is the most useful for progress in the whole socialist field.

The façade of the monolithic unity of the international communist movement was effectively exploded at the congress itself, when, faced with the Soviet-Albanian-Chinese dispute, only a bare majority of foreign delegations were prepared immediately to support the Soviet position. The effect of geographical areas of influence was plainly to be seen.

Within the bloc the Soviet leadership was supported by all the East European delegations and the Mongolian delegation, but not by the North Korean and the North Vietnamese.

Outside the bloc similar divisions were apparent. Of the Asian parties only the delegations from Ceylon and the island of Reunion supported the Soviet Union. This contrasted with the total support given by the delegations from Middle East parties and the almost total support of those from Latin America. Of the latter only the delegations from Guatemala, Paraguay, and the Dominican Republic failed to denounce the Albanian leadership.

For the rest, the African parties were more or less evenly split, with support for the Soviet leaders coming from the Tunisian and Sudanese, but not from the Moroccan, Algerian, and South African delegations. Support was also to come from the United States delegation though not from those from Canada, New Zealand, Australia, and the Caribbean parties of Guadeloupe and Martinique.

Perhaps the most surprising feature at the time was the limited support given by the West European parties, of which only the French, Italian, Spanish, Austrian, Greek, Portuguese, Finnish and San Marino delegations directly associated themselves with the Soviet attack on Albania. However, as subsequent events were to show, the majority of these abstentions were motivated primarily by the fear of further exacerbating the dispute, coupled without doubt in some cases with pique at the complete lack of prior consultation over these issues. In some instances, too, the need to overcome pressure from vigorous pro-Chinese elements in their parties before coming out openly on the Soviet-Albanian-Chinese dispute also played a part.

WITH the exception of Poland, where it is officially contended that the effects of the personality cult have already been eradicated, the problem facing the various leaderships within the bloc has been how to de-Stalinise further without threatening the stability of the regimes. In practical terms this has involved coping with one or all of the following three tasks:

(i) a re-organisation of the existing leadership in order to remove Stalinist elements;

(ii) a reappraisal of recent Party history, in order to account for Stalinist practices in the past and to explain away any remaining vestiges of the cult of personality adhering to the present leaders; and

(iii) the elimination of the remaining physical signs of the Stalin cult by removing statues, renaming towns called after Stalin, etc.

At the same time the 22nd congress has given rise in intellectual circles to a ferment reminiscent of 1956; literary and scholarly publications are again producing articles openly critical of various aspects of communist development and calling for greater internal liberalisation. In the present circumstances, however, it appears unlikely that this will lead to a repetition of the popular unrest of 1956 in view of the object lessons learnt then by the Poles and Hungarians and of the relaxation since then of the harsher aspects of life in these countries. However, this possibility cannot be ruled out entirely. It was plainly in Khrushchev's mind when in his opening speech at the congress he gave the warning that the imperialist-inspired ' counter-revolutionary rising in Hungary and the intrigues of enemies in Poland and the German Democratic Republic ' might well have their counterparts in the future, with attempts by the remnants of internal reaction to ' rend this or that country from the socialist system, in their striving to restore the bourgeois order '.

The Asian bloc countries: Here the Soviet-Albanian-Chinese dispute has been the main issue bequeathed by the congress. In further defining their attitudes both the Mongolian and North Vietnamese parties have reaffirmed their different position, although Ho Chi Minh's apparent determination to continue to play the honest broker between the two major Communist Powers has been accompanied by considerable North Vietnamese deference to the Albanians. This was particularly evident in the month following the congress when the North Vietnamese party sent a message of congratulations on the 20th anniversary of the Albanian party and simultaneously published an article under the title of ' Brilliant and Victorious Twenty Years of the Albanian Workers' Party ' in its daily organ *Nhan Dan*.

In contrast, the North Korean party, while conceding the Stalin issue as an internal affair of the CPSU and emphasising its unity with ' the great CPSU ' as well as its ' militant friendship ' with the Chinese Communist party, has tended to substitute direct alignment with the Chinese for the formally neutral line it had adopted at the congress. North Korea, for example, was the only bloc country except Albania to express public approval of the Chinese stand in the latest border dispute with India. It has also been reported that at the recent meeting of the World Peace Council, North Korea was the only bloc country to give its support to the Chinese and Albanians.

Yugoslavia: While in the communist bloc itself the airing of the Soviet-Albanian-Chinese dispute has thus served to emphasise different basic loyalties, it has also had a material, if incidental, effect on the position of the one European non-bloc communist country of Yugoslavia. The marked deterioration in the relations of the Soviet Union and its East European supporters with the arch-denunciators of ' Yugoslav revisionism ' and ' the Tito clique ', the Chinese and Albanians, has naturally led to an increase in cordiality in state relations between Yugoslavia and the Soviet Union and its bloc allies. This has been exemplified by the increase in exchanges between Yugoslavia and these countries on the government, cultural, trade, and trade union levels, which in the period from the opening of the congress to 30 January 1962, were to total no fewer than seventy. It was also shown in December 1961, by the despatch by Khrushchev and Brezhnev of messages of congratulation to Tito on Yugoslavia's National Day, a practice suspended the previous year after ' Yugoslav revisionism ' had been denounced by the meeting of the 81 Communist parties in Moscow.

On 30 January 1962, further testimony to this increase in cordiality was demonstrated by Khrushchev's telegram of sympathy and offer of assistance to Tito in connection with a recent earthquake, and, more important, by a message which, Yugoslav official sources stated on 3 February, concerned the Soviet Government's statement on the German problem.

OUTSIDE the bloc developments in the Asian parties, most of which have pro-Soviet and pro-Chinese factions, have stressed their divided loyalties. The Indonesian party, the largest non-bloc party in the world, has demonstrably come out on the Chinese side. Aidit made this clear on 27 November when in a speech at Jakarta he remarked that he was not convinced that criticism of a Communist party at the congress by another Communist party was a sure way of settling differences of opinion. He urged party members to study the statements of both the Soviet and Albanian leaderships.

At a central committee plenum at the end of December this pro-Chinese line was reaffirmed; Aidit, while conceding that the Stalin issue was essentially an internal Soviet affair, claimed that foreign parties were also entitled to have a say in the matter because of Stalin's international standing. He proceeded to pay an almost provocative tribute to Stalin who, he said, continued Lenin's effort to build socialism in the Soviet Union and took an active part in defeating fascism. Aidit further emphasised that Indonesian communists would continue to consider Stalin's speeches and writings, for instance those devoted to the revolution in Eastern countries, as a reliable ideological guide. These passages were pointedly omitted by *Pravda* in its summary of his speech in its issue of 6 January 1962.

It was further reported in February that Aidit had canvassed the leaders of all the Asian Communist parties for support for the establishment of a purely Asian Communist international secretariat to co-ordinate policies. On 6 March, Aidit, in an interview with the party daily *Harian Rajkat*, echoed Chinese views on international issues by describing President Kennedy's government as ' more aggressive and more undemocratic than Eisenhower's ', and by attacking Yugoslavia.

In India the impact of the 22nd congress has been decisive in re-emphasising the differences between the generally pro-Soviet leadership and pro-Chinese factions in the party. Previously there had been vigorous attempts to paper over the cracks with an eye to the February elections. Indeed the only common ground in Indian communist reactions to the congress has been the general distaste for the removal of Stalin's body from the Mausoleum, which led to the Indian party sending a telegram to Khrushchev deploring this. The vehemence of this distaste was demonstrated in an open letter sent by three members of the Rajkot district council to Khrushchev urging him ' to reconsider the propriety of the decision to remove the embalmed body of Joseph Stalin from the Mausoleum in Red Square ', and questioning whether ' the removal of his rivals one by one from power was not aimed at concentration of powers to himself' (*Statesman* (Delhi), 6 November 1961).

Outside this one issue, the gravity of differences within the Indian CP has been emphasised by the caution manifested by the pro-Soviet leadership in consistently advocating the postponement of any discussion of the Soviet-Albanian-Chinese dispute until the meeting of the National Council after the elections; this, despite a number of open provocations such as the publication in November of an article ' Albania, the Model of Socialist Construction ' in the Hindi weekly of the pro-Chinese Uttar Pradesh faction.

This attitude has contrasted strongly with the leadership's denunciation of Chinese territorial encroachments and its pledge of full support to the Indian Government for any measures designed to curb them. But here the leadership probably considered it was on much safer ground, as its failure to do this would have marred the party's electoral chances. A majority of the party branches is pro-Soviet in orientation, but the party organisations in Andhra, Kerala, Madras, and West Bengal have urged a more militant policy on Chinese lines.

The third major Asian party, that of Japan, has maintained a neutral attitude to the dispute, a necessary consequence of the leadership's general agreement with Soviet policies on the one hand and the considerable influence of the Chinese on the other, the latter due to reasons of geography and also to the major contributions made by the Chinese to the Japanese party's finances.

Of the other Asian parties, support for the Albanian leadership has come since the congress from the Thai, Burmese, and Malayan parties. These are all illegal organisations, the latter two being engaged in open armed struggle. Their natural sympathies thus lie with the Chinese, both from practical considerations of effective military assistance and also on ideological grounds, as for them gradualist policies and emphasis on the possibility of a peaceful transition to socialism can be of little appeal.

Latin America: Here the main developments stemming from the congress have been the expulsion of two communists from the Brazilian party on charges of Stalinism and the abandonment by the Guatemalan and Paraguayan parties of their neutral attitude towards the dispute at the congress, in favour of direct association with the Soviet position.

The declaration of the Paraguayan party (published in the Uruguay communist paper *El Popular* on 28 December 1961) was particularly notable for its outspoken criticism of the Chinese. In touching on the 1960 meeting of 81 Communist parties, this declared:

> The delegation of the Chinese Communist party promised solemnly to carry out the agreement expressed in the Declaration of the 81 Communist parties and to defend the unity of the Communist movement against any act which might harm the future. We took part in the general joy aroused by the Chinese Communist party's promise. For this very reason we have been grieved that the Chinese comrades allowed the Albanian leaders to attack the USSR . . . to

boast openly of the Chinese People's Republic's support in its struggle against the USSR without rectifying this extremely grave and bold assertion.

The declaration then expressed the hope that

the comrades of the Chinese Communist party . . . observing the prejudicial result which their position in relation to the schismatic activities of Hoxha's group has produced, will correct this erroneous position in accordance with the 1960 agreements.

In other parts of the non-communist world a number of parties whose delegations had failed to mention the Albanian issue at the 22nd congress have also clarified their positions. Among those which have associated themselves with the Soviet position have been the Canadian, Martinique, Moroccan and, surprisingly in view of their past close associations with the Chinese, the Algerian parties. In contrast, the Australian party appears to have adopted a pro-Chinese line, with the exception of the Sydney organisation which in February demonstrated its pro-Soviet sympathies on the Albanian issue.

IN Western Europe most of the parties which had originally abstained on the crucial Albanian issue, have rallied since the congress to the Soviet position. These have included the parties in Belgium, Denmark, Great Britain, Luxemburg, the Netherlands, Norway, and Sweden. While, in the majority of these, this clarification of their position has in all probability been largely a formality, in at least two instances, those of the Swedish and Belgian parties, there have been indications that this was only achieved after overcoming opposition from pro-Chinese elements.

In Sweden the procession of events which suggested this began in mid-October when, with the Party chairman, Hagberg, away at the congress, the party's daily *Ny Dag* began to publish more items than usual from Chinese and Albanian as opposed to Soviet news sources. Significantly, this ceased after Hagberg had paid a short return visit to Stockholm, in the course of which, in an interview with *Ny Dag* on 27 October, he came out against the Albanian leadership. However, in his subsequent speech at the congress (*Pravda*, 30 October) he pointedly avoided the Albanian issue; he did not come out with criticism of the Chinese patronage of the Albanian leaders until some four weeks later.

In Belgium, the reverse process apparently operated, with the Belgian party president, Burnelle, appearing to play the pro-Chinese role. This is the most obvious interpretation of his gesture, after ignoring the Albanian issue at the congress, in sending a message of congratulations to the Albanian leaders on the occasion of the 20th anniversary of the Albanian party on 7 November. The gesture was to be swiftly disavowed by the Belgian central committee, when, in the course of its meeting on 11–12 November, it passed a resolution approving the criticism of the Albanian leadership at the congress as being ' in line with the successful

efforts in recent years to eliminate dogmatism from the communist movement' and urging that 'the party must fight against all sectarian and
adventurist attitudes'.

Outside this question of basic loyalties in the dispute, the political
issues raised by the 22nd congress have created the greatest furore in
the Italian communist party which, as well as being the largest of the
non-bloc European parties, is also the one most given to uninhibited
debate.

Here, the congress' re-denunciation of Stalin and its association of the
'anti-party group' with his excesses has not been blindly accepted, but
has been widely held to reflect on the Soviet political system itself. Thus,
a young communist, Minuti, writing in November in the communist youth
organ *Nuova Generazione*, said there were facts to suggest that 'the
denunciation of Stalinism is, in part at any rate, only an instrument in
the struggle for power'. He went on to complain that, as in Stalin's time,
'the point of view of the anti-party group was not discussed and it was
even denied that they had one'.

While *Nuova Generazione* was subsequently attacked for airing
erroneous views, a broadly similar line was followed by leading Italian
communists at meetings of the central committee in attempts to analyse
the factors motivating the excesses of the Stalin period and the continuing
limitations placed on socialist democracy in the Soviet Union. Secchia,
a senator and a member of the party's old guard, declared:

> One has the impression that some errors have persisted and
> reappeared. Let us remember [that the Russians] did not come to
> executions without a long process which started neither in 1937 nor
> in 1934, but much earlier when minorities were deprived of the right
> of expressing their views and then were isolated and kept under
> suspicion, and eventually expelled and imprisoned. That is why we
> should not be satisfied by the mere fact that today there are no more
> opponents of the regime in prisons. This in itself is not sufficient
> (*Unità*, 12 November 1961).

At the same meeting Terracini, another communist Senator and a
member of the party directorate, raised the question whether further
denunciations might not engulf Khrushchev himself, and other speakers
cited Lenin's tolerance of a genuine vote before the adoption of decisions
in order to advocate that in future minority views should get a hearing at
congresses. On this point Velio Spano, a member of the party directorate,
stated that if the 22nd congress had discussed Molotov's theses it might
have been easier to defeat and overcome them. Nor was this criticism of
Soviet institutions confined to the political system. Antonello Trom-
badori, a member of the central committee, in calling for discussion on
how democracy and liberty could be incorporated in institutions in a
socialist society, referred to Soviet cultural institutions as showing how
the false concept of the purely didactic function of art gave rise to institutions prejudicing the liberty of research and creation.

In addition, the Italian communist party raised the question of the principles which should govern relations between parties in the international communist movement now that 'the 22nd congress has made an end of fictitious unity'. On the grounds that 'the system of bilateral contacts, of internal polemics, of summit meetings and of conferences' (as laid down in the Statement of the 81 communist parties) was not enough to take into account 'the different kinds of situation and positions existing, for example, between Russia and China, Italy and France, and Yugoslavia and Cuba', the concept of polycentrism, originally advanced by Togliatti in 1956, was again revived.

As at first re-expounded in November 1961, this concept implied the establishment of a multiplicity of regional centres of direction for the international communist movement, and as such was supported by the Swiss party, while being rejected by Thorez and the French party on the grounds that it covered 'the tendency to fractionalism'.

Polycentrism in this interpretation was also attacked by a number of other party leaders in both Western and Eastern Europe. The Czech Party secretary, Vladimir Koucky, for example, rejected it because it reflected a lack of confidence in the correctness of the policy of the Soviet Union, would let loose the forces of nationalism in the communist movement, and would prevent the European parties from having any say about Asian problems (*Rude Pravo*, 24 November 1961).

Later, a meeting of the Italian central committee (21–23 December) passed a resolution which stated that this interpretation was incorrect. The party's term 'polycentrism' was simply meant to rule out any concept of a single centre and guide-party and to affirm autonomy in the responsibility of every party towards the proletariat, the people of its country and the international workers movement (*Unità*, 24 December 1961).

A greater measure of autonomy for individual parties may indeed be an eventual by-product if the present impetus towards bi-polarity continues in the communist movement. It is to be noted that the *World Marxist Review* (in its non-English editions *Problems of Peace and Socialism*) has long since ceased to provide a generally-accepted line for the international communist movement. Chinese association with this journal was terminated at the end of 1960 and it demonstrated beyond all doubt that it now speaks only for the Soviet and associated parties by publishing in its December 1961 issue a leading article in which the Albanian leadership was denounced and the Soviet decision to raise this issue at the congress justified.

COEXISTENCE WITHIN
THE BLOC

Boris Levitski

IMMEDIATELY after Stalin's death, together with other momentous problems of internal policy, that of reorganising relationships between the CPSU and other communist parties became a matter of urgency. There were various reasons why the Soviet leaders were at that time not in a position to elaborate a concrete plan for the solution of these problems. The internal struggle for power and a crisis in the party leadership were not the all-important reasons. To be able to achieve a satisfactory solution of the relationships between the various communist parties within the Eastern bloc, it was necessary in the first place for relationships between the Soviet Union and the People's Democracies to be reorganised and for the worst elements of the Stalin era to be removed. At the 20th CPSU congress Mikoyan listed the following ' courageous ' steps taken by Moscow: ' The surrender of our military bases in China and Finland, and the dissolution of the " mixed companies " in the people's democracies '. He also included the efforts to mitigate the Soviet-Yugoslav dispute. All this was in line with the restoration of ' Leninist principles '. It appeared that the Soviet leaders regarded the restoration of normal relations between Moscow and Belgrade as the appropriate key to the reshaping of the organisational forms of world communism.[1]

It would, however, be wrong to suppose that the 20th congress provided a platform for all these aspirations: it merely supplied an impulse. The immediate initiative for the reorganisation of world communism came from outside the USSR. The rapid emancipation of the Chinese Communist party and events inside the Polish Communist party and in Hungary were the main sources of the movement inside the Eastern bloc. Various processes inside the Italian Communist party formed the point of origin outside the Eastern bloc. At the eighth congress of the Chinese Communist party in September 1956, Mikoyan stated for the first time that the Soviet Union recognised the ' Chinese road to socialism '. Many observers also believe that the report made after his return by E. Ochab, the leader of the Polish delegation in Peking, had some influence on the October events in Warsaw.

The second half of 1956 was dominated almost entirely by a great discussion within the communist movement, in which the dramatic climaxes were provided by Gomulka in Poland and the Hungarian revolt of October–November 1956. Whereas the Soviet theorists were concerned primarily with the consequences of the personality cult, Palmiro

---

[1] In July 1955 a plenary meeting of the CPSU central committee approved all the measures taken by the Soviet leaders to normalise relations with Yugoslavia and also announced the return to ' Leninist principles ' in relations between the CPSU and other communist parties. See the leading article in *Kommunist*, 1955, No. 11.

Togliatti and, later, Gomulka, raised the problem of the sociological roots of Stalinism. Whilst reference was made in the official terminology to 'Stalin's errors', the American communist paper *Daily Worker* and a large section of the Polish press called the same thing 'Stalin's crimes'. Whereas all the communist parties welcomed in principle the intention of the CPSU to eradicate the consequences of the 'personality cult' in the Soviet system, the French Communist party declared that the fight against the personality cult was not its business, since it was not threatened by this danger. At that time the Yugoslav problem was also one of the bones of contention in the international communist world. Some parties pressed for an improvement in relations with Yugoslavia, others issued urgent warnings of the dangers lurking in any imitation of the Yugoslav line.

The thesis which Togliatti propounded in 1956 on the need for polycentrism in the communist movement, and the even stronger development of the independence of the communist parties, represented a potentially important contribution to the problem of the new relationships between communist parties. The question became even more embarrassing when the Polish communists made public the relations which had existed between the Soviet Union and Poland during the Stalin era. These revelations were contained in the speech which Gomulka made at the eighth plenary session of the Polish Central Committee in October 1956. His account of the situation was supplemented by various other speeches.[2]

The end of the year 1956 was marked by further dramatic events. After the Hungarian rising and its suppression by the Soviet army, Tito made an important political speech on 11 November in which, in addition to criticising Soviet intervention in Hungary, he also raised the question of a more effective de-stalinisation of the communist world movement. In December 1956 there took place the eighth congress of the Italian Communist party, at which Togliatti denounced the 'errors' committed during the Stalin period not only in the Soviet Union but also in the people's democracies, and in doing so made his own views on the organisation of the communist world movement clear:

> The communist movement must be homogeneous on the international as well as the national level. This unity may be understood in two ways: as the result of pressure from without, of the mechanical endorsement of or slavish adherence to all directives. This kind of unity we reject. But there can also be a unity which is based on the differences and originality of individual experience, on mutual criticism and the enhanced autonomy of the various parties: we feel the need for a unity of this second type.

At the Italian congress guiding principles were worked out for an 'Italian way to socialism'. On 29 December the Chinese party organ *People's Daily* made its contribution to the discussion in an important article entitled 'More on the historical experience of the dictatorship of

---

2 *Nowe Drogi*, 1956, Nos. 10, 11/12.

the proletariat ', one of the most significant political documents of the period.[3]

WHAT part did the CPSU play in these dramatic events? It is quite clear that almost up to the end of 1957 the Soviet communists were entirely on the defensive. When criticism of the Soviet Union was nearing its climax in the second half of 1956, the Government of the USSR published a statement on ' The foundations of the development and further consolidation of friendship and cooperation between the Soviet Union and other socialist states '.[4]

This included the following declaration :

> In the process of constructing a new system and effecting profound revolutionary changes in social relationships, there have arisen many difficulties, unsolved problems and outright errors. The latter have included infringements of the mutual relationships between socialist countries and mistakes which have weakened the principle of equality of rights in the mutual association of the socialist countries.

This statement referred primarily to the economic and military problems of the Eastern bloc and was made under the pressure of the events which were under way in Hungary. After its military intervention in that country, Moscow endeavoured to restore normal relations with Poland as rapidly as possible. Between 15 and 18 November 1956 negotiations between Party and Government delegations of the Soviet Union and Poland took place in Moscow, which led to a number of important concessions to Poland. *Pravda* (23 November 1956) published an editorial article ' On the further amalgamation of the forces of socialism on the basis of Marxist-Leninist principles '. This was in fact an official comment by the Communist party and Government of the USSR on the events in Hungary and at the same time a sharp criticism of Tito's speech.[5] There followed further feverish efforts to improve relations with the people's democracies. Between 26 November and 3 December 1956, discussions took place with a Party and Government delegation from Rumania; between 3 and 8 January 1957 with the German Democratic Republic (DDR); and on 10 January 1957 a meeting was held in Moscow of Party and Government delegations from China, Hungary, and the Soviet Union. In a brief communiqué issued after these discussions it was stated that relations between the parties ' will be strengthened and systematic contacts and fraternal associations will be developed on the basis of the great Marxist doctrine and the principles of proletarian internationalism ' (*Pravda*, 12 January 1957). Soviet-Chinese discussions took place

---

[3] Also published in *Pravda*, 3 January 1957.

[4] *Pravda*, 31 October 1956.

[5] It is of some topical interest to recall that in this document the Soviet leaders protested vehemently against the use of ' coarse and insulting language ' in Tito's references to the Albanian comrades. ' Why may comrade Hodja not have his own opinion? Why should he not enjoy the right to criticise which is claimed by the Yugoslav comrades?'

between 7 and 11 January and 17 and 19 January 1957. A joint communiqué stated: 'A high international duty for the Soviet Union and China is the strengthening and consolidating of the unity of the socialist countries' (*Pravda*, 19 January 1957).

The situation which had arisen in 1957 in the relations between the Soviet Union and the other communist parties may be described as follows: On the one hand, there was a spontaneous and irresistible process of emancipation of the communist parties which the Soviet Union was being forced to take into account. On the other hand, events in Hungary and the obvious failure, at the end of 1956, to incorporate Yugoslavia in the Eastern bloc, showed that a second important complex of problems existed in connection with the maintenance of the unity of the communist movement. Whereas the aspirations to independence of the communist parties had forced Moscow on to the defensive, the recognition by the majority of the communist leaders of the threat of schism involved in the cases of Hungary and Yugoslavia made it possible for Moscow to move over to the offensive. The situation was therefore ripe for the most important event in the field of co-operation between the Soviet Union and the other communist parties—the discussions that took place in Moscow in November 1957.

ON the eve of the Moscow discussions, the 40th anniversary of the October Revolution was celebrated on a lavish scale in the Soviet Union. The Soviet leaders skilfully exploited the event in the interest of their offensive in the international field. During the anniversary session of both houses of the Supreme Soviet on 6 November 1959, Khrushchev made a speech in which numerous passages were devoted to relations between the CPSU and other communist parties and between the USSR and other communist countries. He reminded his audience that Lenin had said that ' all nations and countries will achieve socialism but they will not all attain the goal in the same way '. He did not, however, stress the different ways to socialism. On the contrary, he declared that ' the most important common factors underlying the struggle for socialism must be placed in the foreground '. He listed the constituents of the common cause and then uttered a warning against ' too many roads to socialism '. The ' enemies of socialism ' proposed to proceed to socialism individually, singly and separately, by different paths. If such a method were adopted there would in the end be so many roads that men would lose their way, as in a wood, and would fail to achieve their great goal. The most sacred duty of international communism was the consolidation of the unity of the socialist countries—this was the tenor of Khrushchev's speech and it later became the main theme of the November discussions in Moscow.[6]

A few days after the anniversary session two important international communist events took place in Moscow: from 14 to 16 November the

[6] Full text in *Pravda*, 7 November 1957.

deliberations of the delegations from the communist countries and from 16 to 19 November the conference of representatives of 64 communist parties from all over the word. This subdivision reveals with what finesse the organising body—the communist party of the Soviet Union—had arranged the discussions: it is clear that the Soviet communists attached a great deal more importance to everything that was to take place in the communist camp than to forthcoming events in world communism. The first conference closed with a communiqué entirely in accordance with the Soviet line. As far as the bases of the relations between the countries and communist parties of the ' socialist world system ' were concerned, they were formulated thus:

> Complete equality of rights; respect for territorial integrity and political independence and sovereignty; non-interference in internal affairs . . . [But] the nature of the relationships between the socialist countries is not thereby exhausted. Mutual fraternal assistance is an absolutely essential element in these relationships. . . . All problems of the relations between the socialist countries can be solved to the fullest extent by friendly discussion on the basis of strict adherence to the principles of socialist internationalism.

The first Moscow discussion outlined the organising principle of world communism as follows:

> Following their exchange of views, the participants in the discussion have come to the conclusion that in the present circumstances it would be expedient, in addition to the meetings of leading officials and in addition to an exchange of information on a bilateral basis, to arrange more far-reaching conferences of the communist and labour parties in order to discuss topical international problems, to exchange experiences, to get to know one another's views and attitudes and to co-ordinate the common struggle for common aims, for peace, democracy, and socialism.[7]

This was not a detailed recognition of polycentrism but *de facto* a great step in that direction.

The conference of representatives of 64 parties was politically unimportant, at any rate in the present context; it ended with the signing of a ' Peace Appeal '. The representatives of Yugoslavia were among the signatories. The Yugoslavs had refused to take part in the first conference; hence the attacks on the Yugoslav communists which have been going on ever since. In the first discussion of the ruling communist parties the struggle against ' revisionism ' was described as their most pressing task. Imre Nagy and Milovan Djilas were skilfully woven into the argument but no reference was made to Tito or Kardelj.

IN 1958, however, events piled up rapidly: the differences between the Soviet Union and China on the one hand and the communists of Yugoslavia on the other entered a phase of acute crisis. There is no need to recapitulate these familiar events here; but they explain the

[7] *Ibid.*, 22 November 1957.

purpose of Moscow's constantly increasing inflammatory campaign against Yugoslavia, which was intended to cement the unity of the communist world movement by exaggerating the dangers of the dispute with Yugoslavia. Against this background further offensive measures were taken by the Soviet communists. Between 20 and 23 May 1958 there took place in Moscow a conference of representatives of the communist parties of the member-states of the Council for Mutual Economic Aid (Comecon). The Soviet press attached a great political importance to this conference, which marked a further step towards the establishment of certain guiding-principles within the framework of an ultimate 'integration'. At that time it was not yet known that the Soviet leaders were already working on the seven-year plan. It is quite clear that the task of the Comecon conference was to enforce within the area measures which would suit this plan.

On 12 November 1958 the Central Committee of the CPSU decided to convene the extraordinary 21st congress of the CPSU on 27 January 1959 to discuss the draft of Khrushchev's proposed plan for 1959–1965, published in *Pravda* (14 November 1958). This contained a new and more concrete conception not only of Soviet internal policy but of communist strategy in general, and this was fully endorsed by the congress itself.

On 22 November 1958 *Pravda* published an article by O. Kuusinen on 'A Charter of Unity for the International Communist Movement', prompted by the first anniversary of the signing of the Moscow declaration. It did not merely draw a balance of what had taken place in the interim in the communist world movement, but also prepared the 'fraternal parties' for the new and more rigid standpoint of Moscow on the fundamental questions of world communism.

> In recent years, in particular since the conference of the representatives of the communist and labour parties in Moscow, the CPSU has by its creative efforts greatly enriched the theory and practice of communist society and its development. The further study of the practical and theoretical problems connected with the development of the socialist world system is of tremendous importance.

During the 21st party congress, Khrushchev formulated Moscow's new attitude to the other communist parties as follows: 'All communist parties are independent and their work proceeds from the concrete circumstances of the country in which they are situated'. He spurned the accusation that the other communist parties are dependent on Moscow. It is true that he did not deny the leading role of the CPSU, but he considered that this was acknowledged quite spontaneously by the other communist parties. He thanked them for this but assured them that 'in fact the CPSU does not lead the other parties and the Soviet Union does not lead other countries: in the communist movement there are no "superior" or "inferior" parties. We have always followed the great teaching of Marx, Engels and Lenin . . . our party considers itself, figuratively speaking, as one of the vanguards of the communist world movement, the first to climb the heights of communism and on the way to these heights no avalanches and no falling stones will impede us'.

Once again Khrushchev touched on the question of the different roads to socialism, referring to the Chinese example: 'We are in all things in complete accord with the fraternal Chinese Communist party although their methods are in many respects different from ours. . . . The question of the methods and practice of the development of socialism is the internal affair of each individual country'. He also suggested that the methods employed by the communists in Yugoslavia did not provide a reason for differences; the differences were caused by the fact that the Yugoslav leaders wanted to set up their own form of socialism and that they were pursuing a policy of their own outside the bloc.

As a result of all the changes that have taken place in the Soviet Union these purely organisational matters have in fact become of secondary importance. The foreground is now occupied by the new and rigid Soviet conception of the prospects of the communist world movement, of the significance of the 'socialist world system', and in particular of the role of the contest between the Soviet Union and the United States for the future of communism.

SOVIET teaching on the role and structure of the 'socialist world system' forms the main item in Soviet communist theory on the further evolution of human history and the tasks and prospects of world communism. The general principles which determine the relations between the countries in the communist world system were—as we have already said—outlined for the first time in the statement issued after the November 1957 conference. But they are of an essentially formal nature. It is the thesis on the role of the Soviet Union within this bloc and the thesis on the varying stages of socialist development which are of decisive importance.

Even before the 21st CPSU congress Soviet theorists were engaged in discussion on the transition to communism. Nearly all the writers agreed that 'historical experience shows that during the process of the development of socialism, states which were formerly backward, by relying on the help of the progressive socialist nations, rapidly make up for lost time, improve their commerce and culture, and develop as equals alongside the progressive states'.[8] In spite of this optimistic thesis a debate ensued on the basic question: Will the countries of the 'socialist world system' enter the communist phase together or at different times? When the Chinese communists introduced the people's communes in the summer of 1958 and spoke in numerous articles of the possibility of shortening the socialist phase and of an immediate transition to communism, the discussion became quite vehement, and in the course of it the Soviet and Chinese views became clear.

[8] I. A. Dunaeva, *Sotrudnichestvo sotsialisticheskikh natsii v stroitelstve kommunizma* (Moscow, 1960), p. 250.

The Bucharest conference of delegates from 12 communist parties in communist and 39 in other countries in June 1960 was dominated by the struggle for recognition of the Soviet point of view. It was a preparation for the November–December conference of representatives of 81 communist parties all over the world. The Soviet conception of the ' socialist world system ' was laid down in the statement issued after this conference:

> The Soviet Union is realising successfully the comprehensive development of communist society; the other countries in the socialist camp are successfully laying the foundations of socialism: some of them have already entered the period of the construction of the fully-developed socialist society. (*Pravda*, 7 December 1960.)

From what was said about other communist countries, including China, it may be inferred that they were assigned to the lowest category.

THE conception of the pyramidal structure of the ' socialist world system ' is of decisive importance for the whole Soviet attitude to the communist world movement. It established for the first time the reasons why the leading role falls in all circumstances to the CPSU. Gone now are the old arguments about ' the first country to make the socialist revolution ', and the country that accumulated tremendous experience in the development of socialism being naturally entitled to first place. The new thesis is that the Soviet Union is the only country in the world to have already entered the stage of communist development. The claim to priority arises not from any moral grounds but from the phase of social development which the Soviet Union has now attained.

Many Soviet sources refer to the importance of the contest between the socialist and the capitalist system. This leads inevitably to the second thesis, that the development of communism in the Soviet Union and the race between the Soviet Union and the United States is becoming the most fateful issue for the ' socialist world system '.

As to the significance of this thesis for the integration of the socialist world system, the Soviet communists maintain that only two states are in a position to develop a complex economy: the Soviet Union and the Chinese People's Republic. The people's democracies which belong to Comecon are therefore regarded as a single area for a complex economic policy. Although Comecon has been in existence for 13 years, a genuinely integrated economy is still only in its infancy. Considerable successes have been achieved only where the Soviet Union was itself specially interested (specialisation in the mechanical engineering industry, for example).[9]

Many Western observers have underestimated the importance of the pyramid theory or even completely ignored it. But it is precisely in connection with such problems as the ' united ' or ' separate ' transition

9 Cf. W. Kunz, ' Die Ausgleichung des ökonomischen Entwicklungsniveaus der sozialistischen Länder ' in *Wirtschaftswissenschaft* (East Berlin), February 1962.

to communism, the 'exclusive development of communism in the Soviet Union' or integration within the bloc in accordance with the 'authentic spirit of proletarian internationalism' that we come close to the roots of the latest struggle within world communism.

At the plenary session of the central committee of the Italian Communist party (20 to 24 December 1961) it was Luigi Longo who provided the most detailed information on this subject. His observations are particularly noteworthy because he was speaking directly after returning from Moscow and after intimate discussions with Polish communist leaders.

> The quarrel between the Soviet and the Chinese Communist parties refers to a much more important question than that of peaceful coexistence, possibilities of avoiding atomic war or the dispute over the cult of Stalin's personality. The real issue is a difference between their views on the true way to socialism and communism. The Chinese believe that the development of communism in the various countries of the socialist bloc should be indivisible. The countries that are more advanced economically should therefore take more interest in the troubles and sufferings of the more backward socialist countries and place all their material resources at their disposal. Those who hold this view cannot accept the competition between the Soviet Union and the United States and the capitalist countries. Nor can they accept peaceful coexistence or Soviet aid to under-developed countries. This help should be given to the economically backward countries in the socialist camp. The Chinese comrades do not hide their misgivings but we Italian communists believe that the Soviet policy of competition with the United States is more useful for the development of world communism than a concern for the equal economic development of all the countries in the socialist camp. The effect of Soviet policy is to accelerate the development of conflicts within the capitalist camp and to draw the colonial peoples into the socialist camp. (*L'Unità*, 23 December, 1961.)

IT is possible by studying Soviet sources to describe Moscow's current conception of the organisational forms of communism. It is, as we have seen, the result of a transformation of Soviet communist theory as a whole. At the centre of the conception is the fateful thesis laid down by Stalin on the 'construction of socialism in one country', which Khrushchev and his followers, adapting it to the problems of developing a modern industrial society, have turned into the 'construction of communism in one country'. The new theory was finally hammered out about the time of the 21st party congress and it had important consequences for the international communist movement and especially for the countries of the Eastern bloc. Economic competition with the capitalist world was described as the 'main field' of activity for the communist parties,[10] and the race between the Soviet Union and the United States as a factor which would decide the future history of mankind.

All this has certain obvious implications for the organisational forms and the whole strategy of international communism. To a certain extent polycentrism is even advantageous from Moscow's point of view. Since the CPSU is concerned with the development of communism, that is, with the solution of problems qualitatively different from those of other ' socialist ' countries, the thesis of the ' different roads to socialism ' is automatically justified. As a matter of course, this policy must include greater autonomy for the individual communist parties. Moscow's ' pyramid theory ' does not imply a denial of this autonomy, but it does involve recognition of the Soviet Union, not as a headquarters issuing orders, but as a society which from the standpoint of Marxism-Leninism has attained the relatively highest stage of development. The Sino-Soviet conflict can be understood only in the light of these events. The fact is that the Soviet communists are not in a position to meet the Chinese communists' most important demand and to make their material resources available to backward socialist countries. If they were to accept the Chinese proposal which Luigi Longo reformulated so exactly, the Soviet leaders would have to tell their own people that for another ten or twenty years the greatest sacrifices would be required of them on behalf of their ' socialist brethren '.

The Moscow conception of polycentrism is Janus-faced. On the one hand, the autonomy of the other communist parties is in theory accepted by the CPSU. There are no public institutional channels to transmit orders from the Kremlin. The following information about the present position comes from a Soviet source:

> There is at the moment no headquarters issuing orders to the international communist movement or co-ordinating the activities of the communist parties and making possible the mutual interchange of experiences. A central office of that kind did exist between 1947 and 1956 in the shape of the Information Bureau of Communist Parties.[11]

The same source states that at the present time periodical discussions between representatives of communist parties on a regional and international level are the most important form of mutual contact between the parties. The international conferences of representatives of the communist parties are of particular importance in the field of cooperation between them.

---

10 There is an extensive Soviet literature—polemical as well as programmatical—on this. See, for example, the article by Starushenko in *Kommunist*, 1962, No. 2, and Khrushchev's speech at the 22nd congress.
11 G. F. Sazepilin, *The powerful transforming force of our epoch* (Kiev, 1961), pp. 7–8 (in Ukrainian).

On the other hand, Moscow's attitude to polycentrism is naturally enough concerned with the limits of the communist parties' autonomy. From two concrete examples from the recent history of the communist movement—Yugoslavia and Albania—the communists know that 'autonomous development' may reach a point where the unity of the communist movement is endangered. The Polish party organ *Nowe Drogi* (January 1962) deals with this problem in some detail. The attitude of the Polish communists resembles that of the Soviet communists: if a particular communist party pursues a policy damaging to the 'interests of socialism', then it is the duty of the other parties to protest, even if it may allegedly only be a matter of the 'internal affairs' of the party in question; they should certainly demand an explanation and if necessary disavow the offending party.

We are witnessing today a desperate and uncompromising struggle on the part of Moscow to lay down the ultimate limits to which the autonomy of the individual communist parties must be subject. Just as in 1957 the propaganda campaign against Yugoslavia and against 'revisionism' was used by the Soviet communists as an excuse to channel the dramatic wave of emancipation of the communist parties into the question of unity, so at the present time the Albanian dispute is being used in a similar way. Hodja is providing an excuse for Moscow's effort to curb the communist movement in the present phase. But the situation today is far more difficult than in 1957, when the most powerful communist party after the CPSU—the Chinese Communist party—recognised the dangers of schism inherent in 'revisionism' and became Moscow's chief ally. The insistence by the Chinese that their economic development is no less important for the future of world communism than the Soviet development prevents their being Moscow's allies in the manipulations which it is at present carrying on inside world communism. This is the fundamental reason for the present crisis in the mutual relationships of the communist parties.

RUSSIA AND CHINA

Geoffrey Hudson

IN the history of China's international relations over the last two decades two events have been of outstanding importance. One was the treaty of military alliance with the Soviet Union concluded at the beginning of 1950 after the communists' victory in the civil war and the founding of the Chinese People's Republic. The other, nearly five years earlier in time, was the formal recognition of China as a Great Power by the assignment of a constitutional status as one of the five permanent members of the Security Council of the United Nations in 1945. This status belongs to China as such, irrespective of whether the seat is held by a delegate from Peking or from Taipeh.

The elevation of China to the select category of the Great Powers was primarily due to President Roosevelt and reflected the American official view at that time that China in the post-war period would emerge as the most important nation in Asia, apart from the Soviet Union, but would remain a friend and *protégé* of the United States. Roosevelt had previously been ready to include China in an even more select group of four, since France had been ruled out after her collapse in 1940; in one of his schemes for ordering the world after the war, he designated the United States, Britain, the Soviet Union and China as the 'Four Policemen' who would keep the peace of the world. The contemporary strength of China, however, was hardly sufficient to justify her advancement to the highest rank among the nations, and Churchill regarded Roosevelt's predilection for China as sentimental nonsense; nor did Stalin show any enthusiasm for admitting Chiang Kai-shek to equality with the Big Three of Teheran, Yalta, and Potsdam; the wording of the Yalta secret agreement on Manchuria, which laid down that the promised Soviet gains at the expense of Chinese sovereignty were to be 'unquestionably fulfilled' whether China consented to them or not, showed clearly enough the real Soviet estimate of Chinese importance at that time. Both Britain and the Soviet Union, however, were willing to yield to American insistence in the matter of permanent membership of the Security Council. China thus replaced Japan (which had been a permanent member of the Council of the League of Nations) as the sole indigenous Asian state recognised as belonging to the Great Power group.

The consequences of this status, if taken seriously—and the Chinese do take it seriously—are very far-reaching. If China is the equal of the other four nations in the Great Power class, she cannot accept any restrictions which are not equally applicable to them; in particular, she cannot agree to renounce nuclear weapons as long as the other four have them. Further, since all nations other than the Big Five are in an inferior status, China cannot agree that any of them should be associated with her on terms of equality in Great Power conferences, still less that any should be substituted for China as representative of Asia in such a conference.

The importance which the Chinese attach to the question of their international status can only be fully understood in relation to the vicissitudes of their past history—the background of imperial greatness, economic and cultural self-sufficiency, and ethnocentric pride, and the subsequent period of coercion and humiliation at the hands of the Western powers. To build a great new China worthy to be compared with the old empire became the aspiration of the patriotic intelligentsia; resentment against the nations of the West was combined with the desire to learn from them the secrets of their strength and to obtain their assistance. The pupose was to restore China's national strength and position in the world, but this could not be done through a return to the old isolation and self-sufficiency; China now needed to acquire a new ideology from the West to go with technological modernisation (for which the indigenous Confucian tradition was inadequate), to get financial and technical aid for her retarded industrialisation, and to obtain the support of an alliance or quasi-alliance with a foreign Great Power for her security and her standing in world affairs.

For a new ideology the choice was between liberal democracy as represented by America and totalitarian collectivism as represented by Soviet Russia, and both the source of economic aid and the political-military alliance would depend on the ideological choice. If China were to follow the democratic path, economic aid would come from America and a measure of American protection, even if not a full military alliance; if China were to choose communism, she would have to look to Russia, not only for her ideology, but also for economic and strategic support. The victory of the communists in the Chinese civil war thus meant a complete switching of Chinese policy from a pro-American to a pro-Russian alignment. It may be noted in passing that the communist victory meant a much closer ideological conformity initially to the Russian pattern than the Kuomintang regime had previously shown to the American model; although the Kuomintang political doctrine retained the ideal of a multi-party democracy which had been professed by the republican revolutionaries of 1911, the introduction of the idea of a period of 'tutelage' under a single party dictatorship had rendered the actual practice of Kuomintang rule widely divergent from American principles, so that the American government after the end of the Pacific war felt that it could not with a good conscience support such a regime unless it were reformed, and the resulting half-hearted and ambiguous policy towards it was a major factor in bringing about its downfall. Moscow did not need to have any such qualms about supporting the Chinese communist regime once it had been established, for the latter was ready to conform its institutions fully to the Russian model, or rather to the scheme for communist-controlled 'coalition' government which had been laid down for the 'people's democracies' of Eastern Europe. At the outset it appeared that China was going to have a more harmonious and intimate political relation with Russia than she had ever had with America, even during the common struggle against Japan. Since 1949, nevertheless, the manifest strains and conflicts in Soviet-Chinese relations have shown that a common adherence to Marxist-Leninist ideology has not been enough to ensure a smooth adjustment of interests and co-ordination of policies between the two countries.

IT should be emphasised in the first place that it goes very much against the grain for the Chinese to draw their ideology from a foreign country at all. They had formerly lived by a political and cultural system which they had evolved for themselves; they had been accustomed to regard themselves as originators, and not borrowers of civilisation. Buddhism, which had been introduced into China from India, had for several centuries been marginal rather than central in the Chinese tradition, and the Confucian scholar-gentry of the eighteenth century regarded all outside 'barbarian' peoples with disdain. 'Learning from the West' was the response to the bitter experience of the era which began with the Nanking Treaty of 1842 and the loss of self-esteem and self-confidence which resulted from it. But in the long run acceptance both of a foreign doctrine and of a foreign authority to interpret it were incompatible with the spirit of the intense nationalism which sought to restore the past greatness and creativeness of China's civilisation.

It was only to be expected that, whatever foreign ideology or institutional forms the Chinese might adopt, they would sooner or later strike out a path of their own in transforming what they had received into something different from its original. On the other hand, the notion so widespread in the West in 1949, that the Chinese communists were not real communists but 'agrarian reformers', and that their victory would make little difference in practice to China's international alignments, was doomed to disappointment. The 'russification' of China was to be a temporary phenomenon, but it was real enough while it lasted. Among the converts to Marxism-Leninism there was a genuine emotional enthusiasm for the land of its birth; there was eagerness to profit from the Soviet experience—the key that was to unlock all doors; the party leadership did all it could to promote the cult of all things Russian in order to wipe out the prestige and influence of America which were strong particularly among the intellectuals. As late as the end of 1958, when the Indian demographer Dr S. Chandrasekhar visited China, he was deeply impressed with the extent of the Russian presence in China, and wrote in his book *Communist China To-day*:

> From menus to theatre notices, from directions at stations and airports to travel information we find only two languages—Chinese and Russian. . . . Soviet books have taken the place of American books in college and university libraries. In every factory I visited I was told the same story of the 'selfless help' of the Soviet Union in giving technical assistance and machinery. . . . Russian literature, Russian ballet, Russian teachings have invaded China from Mukden

to Canton. China is fast becoming an image of Russia. It is no wonder that the Chinese have erected massive structures in honour of Sino-Soviet co-operation and friendship, and these buildings usually house permanent exhibitions of the technological achievements of the Soviet Union—which are extremely impressive.

Yet, even before Dr Chandrasekhar made his observations, there had already been rifts in Soviet-Chinese political relations which foreshadowed the disputes of the more recent period. The first serious clash was over Khrushchev's attack on Stalin in his speech at the secret session of the 20th congress of the CPSU in February 1956. It is not known how far Mao Tse-tung had been informed of an intention to demote Stalin from the eminence hitherto accorded to him in the faith of all good communists, but the laudatory reference to Stalin in his fraternal message of greeting to the congress showed that he had either not been consulted or had disapproved of the proposed action. The demotion of Stalin was in fact very embarrassing for the Chinese communists; they had taken great trouble to build up in China a glorious image of the 'party of Lenin and Stalin', and now they had to explain that they had been all wrong about it. Moreover, the attack on the 'cult of personality' could not but reflect indirectly on the cult of Mao in China, which was, and is, comparable to that of Stalin in its adulation, though its consequences have not up to now been so dire for lives of party members. Khrushchev might regard the demotion of Stalin as a matter of Soviet internal politics to be decided according to the tactical needs of his own struggle for power, but the consequences of such a move for the communist cause all over the world clearly made it the business of the whole international communist movement and not of the CPSU alone.

The European Communist parties which had always been accustomed to take their line from Moscow conformed to the wishes of the CPSU leadership, though not without serious misgivings, and the objections of Peking were not enough to deflect the course of events at the 20th congress. But the outcome raised for the Chinese communists a question which has since then assumed a vital importance in their political thinking. Could a congress of the CPSU alone determine policy for the whole international communist movement, or should there be a new world-wide organisation to replace the defunct Comintern? If decisions of a Soviet Party congress are to be valid and binding for all Communist parties of the world, this would mean a permanent Soviet domination not only over parties which are struggling to attain power in their respective countries, but also over those which already possess the governments of sovereign states. The Chinese have come more and more to take the view that only representative conferences of all the parties, and particularly of all those which hold state power, can take full authoritative decisions on fundamental questions of Marxist-Leninist doctrine and political strategy. The Russians, while continuing to claim general authority for the decisions of their own Party congresses, have since 1956 yielded to pressures in favour of 'oecumenical councils' to the extent of summoning two world conferences of Communist parties; the first, at the end of 1957, conveniently coincided with the celebrations of the fortieth anniversary of the October Revolution, and the second, held three years later, was assembled specifically for the purpose of ironing out the differences which had arisen between Russia and China. Although the prestige and influence of the CPSU have been sufficient on both occasions to obtain conference resolutions more or less to its advantage, the declarations issuing from these conferences have differed considerably in tone and emphasis from the pronouncements of Soviet Party congresses under Khrushchev's leadership. Khrushchev would undoubtedly like to be able to lay down the law for the world communist movement as Stalin did during his later years; reaching agreed decisions in world conferences of Communist parties is a difficult process having more in common with international diplomacy than with the management of a congress of the CPSU by the boss of its organisational apparatus.

BETWEEN the Soviet twentieth congress and the international gathering in Moscow in the autumn of 1957 there took place the upheavals in Poland and Hungary and the East European tour of Chou En-lai, which had the special purpose of mediating between Moscow and Warsaw. This was the first historical Chinese political intervention in the affairs of Europe, and as such was a highly significant event; it reflected the dismay and embarrassment of the Soviet leadership in a crisis which shook to its foundations the structure erected by Stalin in Eastern Europe at the end of the Second World War. The Chinese took the opportunity to advance their own conception of how the communist bloc should operate internationally, but this conception was far from being simply one of reducing the authority of the Soviet Union; indeed, it came as rather a surprise to the Poles, who had believed that the Chinese stood for the complete equality and independence of all Communist parties. What Chou urged, certainly on instructions from Mao Tse-tung, was that parties should follow their own ' roads to socialism ' in their domestic policies, but that internationally there should be solidarity of the ' socialist camp ' under the leadership of the Soviet Union. At Moscow, at the November conference of 1957, it was the Chinese who most strongly pressed recognition of this leadership of the Soviet Union on the Poles, who were extremely reluctant to endorse it.

At first sight it may seem strange that the Chinese communists should have taken this line in 1957, when they had already themselves shown recalcitrance towards Soviet leadership. There can be no doubt, however, that military considerations were at this time foremost in Chinese thinking about Europe. The bloc of communist states was regarded in Peking primarily as a military alliance against the West; the Soviet alliance had been of decisive importance for China during the Korean war and continued to compensate for Chinese weakness in confrontation with American power in the Far East. But what if Soviet power were to be seriously reduced in Europe by the break-up of Stalin's system of satellite states? Yugoslavia had already adopted a policy of neutrality between the power blocs, and Hungary had tried to do the same. The Polish insistence on the total independence of Communist parties seemed to the Chinese to be too careless of the threat of American imperialism and to be incompatible with the maintenance of a tight system of military alliances. If the bloc was to be effectively organised strategically, the Soviet Union must be given the leading role, since Soviet military strength so far exceeded that of all other members of the bloc. But this acknowledgment of Soviet primacy was intended to be executive only; it did not imply that Moscow had the right to determine ideology or to act contrary to basic world-revolutionary aims. Russia was to lead, but to lead in a given direction, against the Western world, and to a lesser extent against all non-communist states; non-Soviet communists were to follow where Russia led, but on the understanding that Russia would always put their interest first and never make deals with imperialism at their expense or give preference to countries outside the pale of the Marxist-Leninist faith. The assertion of Soviet leadership was to be contained in a document which would set the goals of policy in accordance with the will of all the parties of the bloc, thus setting up an authority higher than that of the Kremlin as the norm by which all actions were ultimately to be judged.

Peking appears to have been well satisfied with the results of the 1957 conference, but only a few months later the Soviet Government, certainly without consultation with Peking, took a step in its foreign policy which was most injurious to the interests of China. In response to the American landings in the Lebanon in the summer of 1958, Khrushchev demanded a summit conference on the situation in the Middle East, to include India as representative of Asia alongside the three Western Great Powers and the Soviet Union. This meant in effect the substitution of India for China as a member of the Big Five. Khrushchev should have known what a provocation to Peking such a move must be. It can be argued that since the United States would in any case have refused to sit down with communist China at a summit conference, and since Mr Nehru could be counted on to support Soviet opposition to the 'Eisenhower Doctrine' for the Middle East, Khrushchev was merely acting with a view to an immediate tactical advantage in proposing a conference with India instead of China. But there were, and have since been many more, signs that Soviet policy was set on wooing India to an extent which disregarded the special position of communist China as both the principal communist state of Asia and one of the five formally recognised Great Powers of the world.

Up to a point it was clearly in the interest of the communist bloc as a whole that favourably inclined neutral countries such as India, Indonesia, or Egypt should be drawn by diplomatic manoeuvres, flattery, and economic assistance away from the West and closer to the communist camp. But it was not compatible with communist bloc solidarity to give such countries preference over a communist state where rivalries of

interest or status were involved. That the Soviet Union was inclined to
do just this in its endeavours to increase its influence in India was shown
very definitely at the time of Khrushchev's tour of India and Indonesia
at the beginning of 1960. Both these states under ' bourgeois nationalist '
governments were in conflict with China, the one over frontier disputes
and the other over the rights of Chinese residents engaged in local trade,
but in spite of these tensions with his principal partner in the communist
camp, Khrushchev did not, as far as can be ascertained, do anything
whatever to plead China's case and use his good offices for a settlement;
his public speeches and remarks were devoted to flamboyant boasting
about the achievements of the Soviet Union without any reference to
Mao's China. Such behaviour can hardly be explained solely by the
desire to align India and Indonesia against the West; it indicates also a
will to extend an exclusive Soviet sphere of influence into regions
adjacent to China and to reduce China's relative stature by patronage
of rival power centres in Asia.

IF, however, Soviet diplomacy towards India and Indonesia showed a
disregard of China's interest and susceptibilities, the approaches to the
United States during the year 1959 were a far more serious matter. This
was a matter, not of any mere excess in courting ex-colonial neutrals, but
of an apparent purpose of concluding with the imperialist enemy a bargain in which there was no guarantee that China's most vital concerns
would be taken seriously into account. There is no reason to believe that
the Soviet leadership at any time engaged in the kind of consultation with
Peking which the American government normally maintains with its
principal NATO allies when important negotiations with Russia are in
train. Krushchev's way appears to have been to reserve to the Soviet
Union an unfettered right of developing foreign policy with a minimum
of consultation with other governments of the communist bloc. It should
be no cause for wonder if the Chinese communists began to feel that they
were expendable. The propaganda campaign in the Chinese press which
brought the Sino-Soviet conflict for the first time into the open was
launched shortly before the summit meeting in Paris at which Khrushchev
had hoped to get his way over Berlin; Peking was desperately anxious to
prevent a Soviet-American agreement from which China would be left
out. The cancellation of the summit was not due to Chinese pressure any
more than it was to its pretext, the U.2 incident, but to Khrushchev's
realisation from American policy statements that he was after all unlikely to get his way over Berlin, Camp David spirit notwithstanding;
on the other hand, the derisive criticism directed from Peking at the
appeasement of imperialism made it more dangerous than it would
otherwise have been for Khrushchev to engage in a top-level conference
at which his demands might be rejected.

Although the controversies of 1960 were patched up at the conference
of fraternal parties in Moscow at the end of the year, there was no real
restoration of Chinese confidence in the loyalty of the Soviet Union to its

Asian partner, and with the twenty-second congress of the CPSU the conflict broke out afresh, this time with Albania as the bone of contention. Khrushchev's vendetta against Hoxha has not been due to the latter's venial sin in promoting a personality cult in Albania, but to his mortal sin in having been the only European communist leader to give open support to China against Russia, and this in turn was due to China's implacable hostility towards Albania's enemy, Yugoslavia, in contrast to Moscow's long-suffering forgiveness for the heretic Tito. China's policy in this matter is not determined by any national interest, for China and Yugoslavia as nations do not in any way impinge on each other, but by Chinese communist detestation of Yugoslavia as the symbol of the undermining of Marxism-Leninism and of the revisionism towards which the Soviet Union itself is considered to be moving. Fundamentally, the Chinese case against the Soviet Union is that instead of drawing a sharp line of division between communist and non-communist states and conducting political relations with the latter only in full concert with its ideological partners, the Soviet Union carries on a solitary and selfish foreign policy seeking its own advantage wherever opportunity offers, whether in heretic Yugoslavia, bourgeois nationalist India or imperialist America.

How long can the communist bloc survive the strains imposed by such a situation? The question is somewhat different for China and for the East European associates of the Soviet Union. The latter are relatively small nations which, however strong their patriotic sentiments, cannot aspire to play Great Power roles and from past experience are deeply conscious of their weakness in a world of *Realpolitik*. Rumania and Hungary can be directly coerced by Russia; Poland and Czechoslovakia are bound to Russia by their fear of German *revanche*. But China, whatever her current weakness, thinks of herself as a Great Power, and struggles to match her strength to her pretensions; with a vast territory, immense natural resources, and a population well over three times that of the Soviet Union, China will not toe a line marked out by Moscow. The Chinese have not rebelled against Western tutelage and repudiated past submissions to Britain, Japan, or America in order now to be coerced and humiliated by Russia. They continue to seek a co-ordination of policies by collective decisions of the communist bloc, but the wilfulness and arrogance of Khrushchev leaves them little room for manoeuvre between absolute submission to Moscow and a recalcitrance which entails much hardship and frustration for a country in the midst of a prodigious effort of economic development and deeply in need of outside aid.

At present the Russians appear to be relying on economic pressures to break the Chinese will to resist. According to recent reports they have not only refused to grant China any new credits, but have demanded repayment of all debts incurred by China in fighting the Korean war, while Russian technicians withdrawn from China have in some cases left projects half finished and have taken away construction blue-prints with them. The signing of the Sino-Soviet trade agreement for the current year does not seem to change the picture very much, particularly in view of the fact that Patolichev's mission to Peking coincided with Gromyko's visit to Belgrade. Chou En-lai's speech at the opening of the People's Congress on 27 March suggests that, because of their present economic difficulties, the Chinese are not in a position to advertise their differences with the Russians, and may even have to subdue their defiant attitude for the time being. But in the long run it seems unlikely that Soviet pressures will be successful; they do not take account of the pride which is the most essential characteristic of the old and the new China. Khrushchev by his tactless and insensitive bullying and disregard of Chinese interests has alienated, probably irreparably, a nation which only four years ago talked of Russia's ' selfless aid ' and believed that by ' leaning to one side ' in world affairs it had found its way of salvation. The consequences may not be immediately manifest, but in the long run they must be profound. The disillusionment with Russia might even undermine the foundations of the communist regime in China; if the regime remains and cannot be reconciled with Russia, it will have sooner or later to make an ' agonising reappraisal ' of its foreign policy. To bring China back into friendly relations with America would be too much to undertake for a long time to come, but there are large possibilities of political readjustment in relation to Japan. An epoch of history in which China has come into enmity, first with America and then with Russia, may yet produce, in a form undreamt of by its original Japanese sponsors, the ' Greater East Asia ', which seemed to have been expunged from the realm of practical politics with the conclusion of the Pacific war seventeen years ago.

REVISIONISM AND YUGOSLAVIA

Ernst Halperin

A PART from the name, contemporary communist revisionism seems to have nothing in common with the social-democratic revisionism of the nineties. However, it is a question of the same phenomenon. Now, as then, the call for an adaptation of Marxist dogma to the reality and demands of current politics is raised. Now, as then, this demand rouses the opposition of cadres of officials, who feel disturbed in their habits of thought and offended in their belief.

In the dispute between Bernstein, the first revisionist, and Kautsky, the first dogmatist of Marxism, the dogmatist won. His teaching suited the broad mass of the party officials, who were anything but revolutionaries. It gave their activity a religious consecration, for Kautsky taught that they were serving the salvation of mankind and were bringing the day of deliverance nearer by diligently attending their committee meetings, administering their funds, and distributing their newspapers and pamphlets.

Since then reality has prevailed over ideology, and today almost all social-democratic parties follow the policy which in his forgotten writings Bernstein recommended to them sixty years ago. But this development took place in opposition to dogma, in innumerable hotly disputed individual steps, each one of which appeared to be a betrayal of sacred principles. In the course of this process ideology crumbled away.

The history of modern communist revisionism begins in the spring of 1948. At that time the central committee of the CPSU, in a letter to the Yugoslav communists, made the accusation that their leaders were adherents of the 'erroneous views' of Bernstein and Vollmar. The reproach was unjustified. In fact at that time the communist regime of Yugoslavia differed from the regimes of most of the other 'People's Democracies' in greater harshness and not greater leniency towards the peasantry and the middle classes. Moreover, it was not really ideological differences which concerned the Russians. Underlying their conflict with Yugoslavia there were quite practical differences of interest. After the Yugoslavs were expelled from the Cominform, Moscow soon renounced further ideological subtleties and proceeded to more massive accusations. The Cominform resolution of November 1949 was the culminating point of the Soviet propaganda campaign. In it the Yugoslavs were no longer labelled followers of Bernstein and Vollmar, but 'hirelings of the imperialists', 'clique of hired murderers and spies', 'Yugoslav fascists', and 'nest of spies'.

The Yugoslavs' counter-propaganda never sank to this level. At first they limited themselves to opposing Moscow's claim to hegemony with a demand for the equality of rights of all communist countries and parties and for the right to an 'individual road to socialism', and then proceeded in 1949 to the ideological counter-offensive. And the Yugoslavs in their turn accused the Soviets of revisionism! This 'Soviet revisionism' lay, in Yugoslav eyes, in the fact that Stalin recast and falsified Marxism-Leninism in order to use it as a justification for Russian power politics. In contrast to this, the Yugoslavs postulated, among other things, the right of every communist party to its own revolution, not controlled by the Soviet Union and the Soviet army. Their standpoint at that time was very similar to the present standpoint of the Chinese, characterising as 'revisionism' Khrushchev's attempts to make the policy of the world communist movement identical with the interest of the Soviet Union as a Great Power.

THE Yugoslavs could not for long justifiably pose as the guardians of Marxist-Leninist orthodoxy. The date of their own revisionist fall from grace can be exactly determined. It took place on 26 June 1950, which can be regarded as the actual birth date of modern communist revisionism. On that day Tito spoke in the Yugoslav Parliament in support of the law on the administration of enterprises by the Workers' Councils. Thus began an economic and administrative reform according to principles which were completely new to the communist world and which could no longer be harmonised with orthodox Marxism-Leninism.

The reform was the child of bitter necessity. The planned economy organised on the Soviet model had completely broken down in Yugoslavia. Supplies were disorganised and the gigantic apparatus of officials was far too costly for the country, which was then still entirely dependent on its own resources and was suffering from the Soviet economic blockade. So a drastic retrenchment of officials had to be carried out, the principle of profitability had to be forced on the enterprises, and the execution of numerous all too costly projects of the five-year plan had to be given up. However, the Yugoslav leaders decided to go even further, that is, as far as the grant of autonomy to the enterprises and the establishment of a market economy in place of the planned economy on the Soviet model. Only this reform must not be allowed to lead to the restoration of private property and should certainly not appear to the party cadres as a retreat, but rather as a step forward on the road to socialism! The problem seemed insoluble.

The solution was provided by the ingenious idea of transferring responsibility for the management of the individual factories and enterprises from the state to the workers themselves and their organs. In practice the competence of workers' control is limited in various ways. The management is carried out by the director and the party cell, and the local authorities, who provide capital, have important supervisory functions.

The essential feature of the Yugoslav system, however, is not the extent of workers' control, and not even the workers' chance to share in profits, although this represents a real incentive. The essential point is the restoration of the independence of the enterprises. The Yugoslavs have succeeded in refuting Wilhelm Roepke's dogma that private property is the indispensable pre-requisite for a market economy. They have understood how to build the decisive advantages of the system of the market economy—competition, mobility, initiative, adaptation to the needs of the consumer—into an economy without private ownership of the industrial means of production.

Certainly the Yugoslav system can no longer be properly called Marxist. To be sure, Tito tried to pass it off as the first step to the 'withering away of the state' foretold by Engels and Lenin, but his argumentation was not valid. Numerous remarks of Marx and Engels show that their conception of the economy of the socialist future corresponded to the ideas of the Saint-Simonians : the direction of the whole economy by a central authority controlling production and distribution. Moreover to them the 'withering away of the state' certainly did not mean the decentralisation of the direction of the economy but merely the decay of the 'organs of repression', of army, police, and judiciary. And the formula 'management of production by the producers' used by Tito is not Marxist but syndicalist. The whole conception behind the Yugoslav economic system is similar to the views of the non-Marxist guild socialists. Thus, from the ideological point of view, this system represents a revision of Marxist-Leninist teaching through the introduction of elements of syndicalist and guild-socialist thought.

Soon the Yugoslavs were obliged to make a further revision of Marxism-Leninism in quite a different field. In the years 1950–1951 the continuous Soviet pressure had forced them to accept first Western economic aid and then also American military aid. This had to be ideologically justified, and so the Yugoslav ideologists suddenly discovered that in the West, alongside imperialism, there were quite other phenomena which could be quite positively appraised. They advanced the thesis that the West already contained socialist elements and the possibility of a gradual, peaceful development towards socialism existed. At the same time the Yugoslav ideologists now discovered that the Soviet Union was already so 'bureaucratically degenerate' that it was almost or perhaps quite impossible to call it socialist. This discovery was necessary to justify Yugoslavia's increasingly friendly relations with the Western powers.

SINCE the Yugoslav economic order had been differentiated from that of the Soviet Union through the introduction of Workers' Councils, the Yugoslav ideologists could risk a really radical, basic criticism of the Soviet system. Now they could openly name all the internal and external evils of this system and also attribute them with some degree of credibility to one cause, the centralisation of the Soviet economic and administrative apparatus which inevitably led to bureaucratic degeneration.

Certainly this analysis still had an important flaw : it failed to mention the dominating role of the totalitarian party in the Soviet system. Criticism by the Yugoslav ideologists of the totalitarian party dictatorship in the

Soviet Union was hampered by the fact that Yugoslavia was ruled by an equally totalitarian party organised on the Soviet model. This not only caused ideological difficulties but also hampered rapprochement with the West, particularly with the social-democratic parties and trade unions, with which the Yugoslavs would gladly have co-operated. In 1952, when any reconciliation with the Soviet Union and the world communist movement seemed unthinkable, the Yugoslav leaders decided to follow up the changes in the economic system with a transformation of the political system as well. The Communist party was gradually to sink into the background and begin to ' wither away '. Its place as the political body supporting the state was to be taken first of all by the ' Socialist Alliance ', a mass organisation without the rigid discipline and cellular structure of the Communist party. As the ' Socialist Alliance ' was dominated both locally and nationally by the same class of former partisans as supplied the cadres of the Communist party such a transformation would have involved no changes of personnel and hence no political shocks. However, it would be wrong to regard it as a mere trick to deceive the West. The transfer of the function of the state-sustaining political body from the tightly organised cadre party to a loosely organised mass party would have allowed a gradual transition to a milder form of authoritarian rule and the gradual participation of ever broader classes in the government. As a psychological preparation for this development, the Communist party was renamed the ' League of Communists ' at the Party congress of November 1952. This did not affect the structure of the party, but in a press conference at the end of the congress the leading party ideologist Milovan Djilas declared that the ' League of Communists ' was gradually to lose its political functions and be transformed into a mere educational union.

This promise was not fulfilled. Four months later Stalin died, and after his death the international situation gradually began to relax. In the summer of 1953 the first signs of a change in the Soviet attitude towards Yugoslavia became noticeable. Presumably it was this that induced Tito to postpone for the time being the planned internal reform and to await further developments. But Djilas pressed on.

In November and December of 1953 Djilas published in the party paper *Borba* a sensational series of articles in which he demanded that the political monopoly of the communists be ended and suggested that the totalitarian party discipline and even the regular party cell meetings should be abolished. ' There are certainly enough people in the world ', he wrote, ' who get along without such meetings, who lead the normal life of normal people and are not for that reason ruined, but are even good and honest—and socialist.'

Thereupon Djilas was expelled from the central committee and relieved of all party offices. Later, as is known, he had to spend many years in prison on account of his journalistic activity for Western periodicals and the publication of his principal work, *The New Class*, in America. *The New Class* describes how the totalitarian party dictatorship develops into the unbridled despotism of a new exploiting class, which collectively owns the means of production and degrades the rest of the population to a complete absence of rights. It is the most radical, most coherent ideological proclamation of the new, communist revisionism. For that reason the book is disputed even in revisionist circles. In Poland and Hungary even those revisionists who have completely broken with the party both inwardly and outwardly question the correctness of Djilas' thesis, because it only incompletely corresponds to their own experiences and observations. This is due to the fact that in those countries the party was too weak to completely penetrate and remodel society; as a result the old non-communist intelligentsia still plays an important social role there in spite of its loss of political power. On the other hand, in countries like Russia and Yugoslavia, the phenomenon of the ' new class ' is clearly observable.

To the extent that it was sociological and critical in its dispute with the Soviet system, Yugoslav revisionism stagnated after the elimination of Djilas, its most vital and aggressive ideologist. On the other hand it still achieved a most important further development in another field— the theoretical foundation of Yugoslav foreign policy. Once again this development took place in the course of an adaptation to changed external circumstances and to the needs of practical politics. In the first years after Stalin's death the attitude of the Soviet rulers towards Yugoslavia became noticeably milder. From this resulted the possibility of normalising relations with the Soviet Union and the Eastern bloc as a whole, and of re-establishing the economic relations broken off in 1948–1949. Obviously the Yugoslav leaders did not for a moment think in this context of giving up their good relations with the West and forgoing American economic aid. Instead, they tried to maintain good relations with both camps, something which in those years of slackening international tension seemed by no means hopeless.

It was, however, impossible to deal with both the parties, between which Yugoslavia wanted to stand as a neutral, at the same time. The Western powers were used to Yugoslav criticism and continued to put up with it. They kept their eyes on the essential point, which was that Yugoslavia was not giving up its national independence and did not enter into any military agreements with the Soviet bloc. In contrast, the communist world does not tolerate any criticism or any deviations. Every objection which the Yugoslavs expressed against the foreign policy or internal conditions of the Soviet Union would disturb relations with the Eastern bloc. For this reason it was necessary to assent unconditionally, at least in words, to the Soviet Union's foreign policy and to stop public criticism of conditions within the Soviet Union.

The thesis that internally the Soviet leaders were on the way to correcting Stalin's errors, and that in foreign policy they had already completely abandoned Stalin's policy of aggression in favour of a genuinely peaceful policy, served as an ideological prop for the justification of this attitude. This naturally made it possible to represent Yugoslavia's support of

Soviet foreign policy as something which served world peace, helped the peoples to live together peacefully, and furthered the co-existence of different social systems.

It is easy to scoff at the Yugoslav policy of ' active co-existence ' and dismiss it as a typical Balkan horse-trading trick. However, one should not overlook the fact that it is a case of a very serious heresy against the spirit and letter of Marxism-Leninism. The Yugoslavs, that is, have by no means returned to the orthodox view of the West as imperialism in the last stage of decay, but maintain that a lasting co-existence of the two social systems which is not to be regarded merely as a tactical manoeuvre is possible. This, however, is no longer compatible with orthodox Marxism-Leninism. It is classical revisionism, just like Bernstein's. That is why the section of the Yugoslav party programme of 1958 dealing with foreign affairs gave the greatest offence to the dogmatic ideologists of the Soviet bloc and contributed most of all to the fresh breach with Yugoslavia.

THESE, then, are the two essential points in the programme of Yugoslav revisionism with which the communist world has to come to terms today:

First, Yugoslav economic teaching, which recognises the independence of enterprises officially managed by the Workers' Councils, the market economy, and the principle of free competition, even if in practice there are more or less substantial limitations. The great importance of this system for the communist world derives from the fact that the Soviet total planned economy is not capable of satisfying the material demands of the large new middle class of intellectuals and highly-skilled and specialised workers. Sooner or later a radical economic reform will become unavoidable in the Soviet empire. Partial reforms like that of 1957 yield no more than a temporary alleviation; only the grant of autonomy to the enterprises and the introduction of a market economy can really help. And at the moment the Yugoslav system represents the only practicable alternative to a return to private ownership.

Second, the foreign policy doctrine of Yugoslav revisionism. Its importance for the communist states lies in the fact that it would represent an appropriate basis for a genuine policy of peaceful co-existence. No state can afford persistently to base its foreign policy on erroneous basic assumptions. Yet the Marxist-Leninist dogma that the West is rotten and is advancing towards its downfall is false. The Soviet Union is faced with a set of extremely vigorous states. Sooner or later it will have to accommodate itself to a durable arrangement with them if it is not to exhaust itself in an armaments race or perish jointly with them in a war. But orthodox Marxism-Leninism does not extend far enough to provide the ideological foundation for such an arrangement. This is the strength of Yugoslav revisionism : its importance extends far beyond the frontiers of its own country because it corresponds to a real need of the

Soviet Union—the need for a comprehensive economic reform and a new orientation of foreign policy.

In addition there is the *third*, treasonable, aspect of Yugoslav revisionism which the party authorities themselves condemn—Djilas' criticism of the totalitarian party dictatorship. The direct development of the revisionist Djilas from a politburo member and a leading party ideologist into an anti-communist democrat shows what dangers to the rule of the totalitarian party are concealed in revisionism. Born of the rulers' need to adapt the theory and practice of the system to altered circumstances, it inevitably leads by way of criticism of the defects of Stalinism to the denial of the party dictatorship as a whole. By expelling Milovan Djilas the Yugoslav leaders succeeded in halting this development for the time being and in freezing party ideology at a stage in which it could still be reconciled with communist dictatorial rule.

In Yugoslavia revisionism served the communist regime; in Poland and Hungary it was a symptom of decay of this regime. Accordingly in these two countries it concentrated right from the beginning on criticism of the party, its practice and its moral theory—that is, on precisely those subjects which were forbidden it in Yugoslavia. To those numerous revisionists for whom freedom of thought and of speech and inner party democracy were of primary importance, the Yugoslav example had little to say. Some of them, like the members of the *Po Prostu* group in Poland, actually thought they were Titoists, but they did not understand Titoism correctly.

In Poland and Hungary almost the only people to give evidence of a real understanding of Yugoslav teaching were the theoretical economists at the Universities—a group which is assigned only slight political importance in the communist system. In Hungary there was also the practically-oriented interest of a set of leading politicians in friendship and co-operation with Yugoslavia; they hoped by this means gradually to liberate their country from its political ties with the Soviet Union. Essentially, though, the revisionism of both Hungary and Poland was autochthonous, that is, it arose on account of concrete political conditions in its own country and was not to be attributed to foreign Yugoslav influences.

IN Poland and Hungary the communists were a tiny minority which had only come to power thanks to the Soviet Union and only maintained itself with Soviet support. In the Stalinist period they had tried to break the will of the people by police terror, but in this they did not succeed. The non-communist population responded with a moral counter-pressure whose strength and effectiveness cannot be imagined by anyone who did not himself visit those countries at that time. The communists were shunned like lepers, surrounded by a wall of contempt, and as they were not numerous they were daily and hourly made freshly aware of their isolation. Some communists reacted with defiant hatred, but many felt an increasingly strong need to fill in the gulf between

themselves and the people and to free themselves from their social isolation. Polish and Hungarian revisionism was to a large extent an
expression of this need, which became overwhelming after Khrushchev's
anti-Stalin speech had robbed the already unsettled communists of the
last moral convictions about their own dogma.

This tendency can be best followed in the literature of the Polish
revisionists, who in any case were able to publish more or less freely for
a much longer time than their Hungarian political friends, so that their
output is much more abundant. On rereading it one is at once struck
by the demonstrative, extraordinarily personal and self-centred character
of most of these writings. One is faced with endless confessions of
remorse, self-recrimination, and attempts at excuses and justifications.
At the same time these writers assiduously demonstrate that even though
communists, they share with their non-communist readers a negative
opinion of the Soviet Union, their own communist party, and Marxist-
Leninist moral teaching.

Free from this frequently disagreeable egocentric note, and yet typical
of Polish revisionism, are the writings of Leszek Kolakowski, who outside
Poland is its best-known representative. His arguments are often
ingenious, the reasoning is consistent and the logic compelling, but the
final result, reached with a great expenditure of effort, is always some
commonplace long familiar and self-evident to any decent liberal-minded
bourgeois; for instance, that the end does not justify the means, or that
the party would be protected from errors and tyranny if within its own
ranks it permitted freedom to express opinions and form groups. Here
one has the appealing case of a really honest, convinced communist who
one day somehow grasped the meaning and significance of liberal views,
and then took the greatest pains to prove this point by point to himself
and his party comrades with the application of Marxist methods of
analysis.

In spite of all these weaknesses, one must not overlook the fact that
the political programme of both Polish and Hungarian revisionism was
truly revolutionary. It included the introduction of full freedom of
thought and freedom for the spoken and written word within and outside
the party, and its realisation would doubtless have led to the party
dictatorship's collapse.

In Poland this was prevented at the last moment by Wladyslaw
Gomulka, the man who is often regarded abroad—and also in the
communist countries—as the true leader of the Polish revisionist movement. In reality, however, Gomulka is not a revisionist. He belongs
rather to a much older alignment within the world communist movement
and is an admirer of A. Warski, the leader of the right wing of the
Polish communists in the twenties. This right wing, which was later
proscribed by Stalin as a 'Bukharinist right deviation', was naturally not
a purely Polish phenomenon but an international grouping within world
communism. Its programme for the post-revolutionary period was
gradual and cautious development, no experiments, no intensification

of the class struggle, and above all no conflict with the peasants! That is precisely Gomulka's present internal policy.

As far as world policy was concerned, the right wing view in the twenties was that capitalism had moved into a period of stabilisation and could not be expected to collapse soon; therefore the Soviet Union would have to conduct a defensive foreign policy and, while exploiting contradictions within the capitalist camp, look round for allies. Everything indicates that even today this is still Gomulka's view; hardly knowing the West, he seems not to doubt the correctness of Lenin's thesis that imperialism is the last stage in the decay of capitalism. A further factor in Gomulka's case is the personal trait of pronounced Polish nationalism, but this does not have anti-Soviet implications, for Gomulka continues the old tradition of those Polish politicians who looked for support from their eastern neighbour against their German neighbour in the west.

Basically, then, Gomulka's political views, at least by communist standards, are conservative. The almost fortuitous agreement in views and temporary community of interests with the revisionist hotheads just sufficed to make a short-term alliance possible in the autumn of 1956. After power had been taken over, the contradictions between the conservative Gomulka and the revisionists who were pressing for comprehensive political reforms and ideological revisions soon became unbridgeable. He then allied himself with the centrist group of the party apparatus which was much closer to him, in order to get rid of the revisionist allies who had become inconvenient.

THE case of Imre Nagy is similar. His internal programme, like Gomulka's, also coincided with the programme of the Soviet right wing in the twenties. His character had fewer facets than Gomulka's, but his views were just as conservative, and for this reason his revisionist allies had their difficulties with him in the months of the struggle against Gero. Only on one point did Nagy go far beyond Gomulka and the views of the old right wing: his decision on a neutral Hungary detached from the Soviet system of alliances was, in contrast to Gomulka's foreign policy, no longer compatible with orthodox Marxism-Leninism and it was this one point in Nagy's programme that, conflicting with the military interests of the Soviet Union, brought him to his end before the firing squad.

Nagy is dead, but up to now, thanks to continuous close contact with Khrushchev, Gomulka has maintained himself at the head of the Polish party in a surprisingly assured way. Since the 22nd congress of the CPSU there have been signs of a rapprochement between the party secretariats of Belgrade, Rome and Warsaw. Gomulka, however, as an entirely defensively inclined politician, will not go one step further in a rapprochement with Tito and co-operation with Togliatti than is agreeable to Khrushchev: he could only be expected to take up any sort of position opposed to Moscow as a last desperate step if his internal programme was seriously threatened by a political change in the Soviet Union.

This brings us to the question of the attitude of the Soviet Union itself towards revisionism. This is by no means unequivocal. Developments in the Soviet Union since the 20th party congress convey the impression that strong revisionist forces are at work there, but that again and again they are checked by equally strong conservative counter-forces. In this context it would be hazardous to state that Khrushchev himself or any other leading Soviet politician is a conscious revisionist; it is also possible that the party leadership is induced by the force of circumstances to take apparently revisionist steps, but that these contradict their own views. In any case, observation of Soviet internal and external policy reminds one of a swimmer who again and again takes a run to plunge himself into the cold water of revisionism only to stop at the last moment at the furthest edge of the pool.

Such a start, and a very promising one, was attempted at the 20th party congress. Then not only the myth and personal reputation of Stalin, but also the authority of his teaching were destroyed. Afterwards even Walter Ulbricht had to say of Stalin: 'He was not a classic author of Marxism-Leninism'. The road to a comprehensive ideological revision and to every possible practical reform seemed to have been opened up. What is more, such a reform movement seemed unavoidable, for the ideological vacuum left after the devaluation of Stalin's teaching had somehow to be filled up again. Even such a sober and competent observer as Palmiro Togliatti then reckoned with a far-reaching reform; indeed, as he explained in *Vie Nuove*, he supposed it would take the form of ' decentralisation ' and ' participation of the masses in the direction of the economic and social organism ', that is, on the Yugoslav model. However, there was no reform, but instead the resolution of the Soviet central committee of 30 June 1956. In this Togliatti was reprimanded and the necessity for any radical practical reforms or ideological revisions was denied, while the problem of Stalinism was said to be settled by the condemnation of the ' personality cult '.

Further measures smacking suspiciously of revisionism were the dissolution of the machine tractor stations and the conversion of their equipment from state property into kolkhoz property in the spring of 1957, and the decree, issued later, on the formation of ' inter-kolkhoz ' industrial enterprises, in which several kolkhozes were supposed to participate. The two together represented a completely new, most interesting development in Soviet society· as it meant that co-operative property, which was now being extended by the ' inter-kolkhoz enterprises ' from agriculture into industry as well, was being strengthened at the expense of state property. However· no ideological reason for these measures, which were incompatible with the old doctrine of the superiority of state property, was forthcoming, and this was no accident, for the strengthening of co-operative at the expense of state property cannot be given any but a revisionist justification.

In exactly the same way the revision of the ideological foundations of Soviet foreign policy started at the 20th party congress stuck half-way. At that congress, the two Lenin theses on the inevitablity of war and of violent revolutions were disavowed, but the new theses were not ideologically underpinned by a fresh appraisal of the opponent, a revision of the Leninist thesis of imperialism's predatory nature. Instead they were justified solely and exclusively with the statement that the imperialist beast of prey had become weaker.

THIS refusal to revise the orthodox Marxist-Leninist picture of the world was paid for later in the discussion with the Chinese. For as long as the Soviet ideologists accepted the basic Chinese thesis of imperialism's predatory nature they were at a disadvantage right from the start. A man cannot enter into any lasting agreements with a beast of prey. In order to justify them a revision of the picture of the world similar to that which the Yugoslavs had long ago completed in their foreign policy doctrine would be necessary.

The hesitation of Soviet politicians and ideologists on the brink of revisionism is doubtless due to serious differences of opinion and conflicts of interest within the ruling class. But besides this another factor probably also plays a part—naked Russian nationalism. It so happens that the Yugoslavs marked out the revisionist path. It would be extremely humiliating for the leaders of the Soviet empire if they had to accept economic and ideological lessons from the representatives of a small Balkan state. Moreover, it would automatically mean that Moscow would lose its position of ideological leadership in world communism, a position which is in any case seriously challenged.

The Yugoslav leaders, above all Tito himself, have still not given up the hope that one day the Soviet Union will still be forced to take the road of revisionism. Abstract logic is on their side. To be sure the ancestor and originator of all Marxist revisionism, Eduard Bernstein, had to learn that in politics things do not go according to the laws of logic and reason.

POLAND

K. A. Jelenski

IN October 1956, special planes brought the top ranking figures of the Soviet Communist party, headed by Khrushchev, Molotov, and Voroshilov, to Warsaw in a desperate attempt to save the monolithic character of world communism by threatening Polish 'revisionists' with Soviet armed intervention. In October 1961, communist monolithism was destroyed by Khrushchev himself, attacking Chinese, Albanian, and 'anti-party' dogmatists, while Gomulka appears to be one of his most trusted supporters inside the bloc. No wonder that the 22nd CPSU congress was hailed by the Polish Communist party with self-congratulating satisfaction.

After October 1956, Poland was the boldest 'revisionist' experiment inside the Soviet camp. Its position inside the bloc gradually gathered strength, while Gomulka liquidated the ideological and cultural conquests of the October upheaval, and the Soviet Union was becoming convinced that events in Hungary would not be repeated in Poland; still, the character, if not of heresy, at any rate of an experiment limited in time and place, remained. Since the 22nd congress the Polish model has acquired, in the framework of European communism, certain potentially general characteristics. Five years ago, and in spite of Khrushchev's speech at the 20th congress, the Soviet Union still represented 'dogmatism' in the eyes of most Poles. Since then, Khrushchev has become, in the purely pragmatic sense, the first 'orthodox revisionist' of world communism. Dogmatism, aggressiveness, the threat of war, administrative methods, institutional marxism, *partiinost* in philosophy and science—all the stalinist heritage has now been schematically and symbolically carried over to the new scapegoats—China, Albania, the 'anti-party' group. Might not the Poles begin to consider Khrushchev as an ally, facing his own 'Natolin' opposition on a world scale?

Naturally enough, the ninth plenum of the Polish Central Committee, following the 22nd congress, and the theoretical articles in the official party organs, *Trybuna Ludu* and *Nowe Drogi*, stressed this aspect of the question, recalling that the Polish party accomplished 'a genuine turn of events' in October 1956, which has only now come to full fruition in the Soviet Union. Official Polish party voices are echoing Khrushchev's thesis, but louder and with more precision.

In one point only did the Polish party go further, but it is a crucial point: in the assessment of the origins and social character of Stalinism. For obvious reasons, Khrushchev, while condemning stalinism anew and more forcefully, could not undertake any deeper analysis of its origins, effects, and social implications. With—for a marxist—incredible impudence, he continued, as he did at the 20th congress, to attribute the crimes of stalinism solely to the character of the late tyrant, stubbornly looking for ' Cleopatra's nose ' in Stalin's moral profile. *Pravda* (11 November 1961) states unequivocally: ' The cult of personality was a superficial boil on the perfectly healthy organism of our party.' Polish communists were often the victims of stalinism rather than its accomplices, and they do not have the same grounds for such discretion. Incidentally, while the euphemistic ' cult of personality' is still the semantic rule in Russia, Poles have reverted, since the 22nd congress, to the more straightforward term ' stalinism ' (they had avoided calling that particular spade by its name for the last three years at least).

IN his report to the ninth plenum, Gomulka attempted to trace stalinism back to conditions existing before the capture of complete power by Stalin and, characteristically, he attributed its development to the forced collectivisation of agriculture. The economist Oskar Lange acknowledged, in his speech at the plenum, that Gomulka had given ' an outline of a marxist analysis ' of stalinism, but went on to say: ' As Marxists we know that the symptoms of the worship of personality cannot be regarded exclusively as a question of the character of one man or of a small group of people.' He attacked believers in the ' historical necessity ' of stalinism as a short-cut to industrialisation : ' The worship of personality and everything it involves does not constitute some kind of unavoidable stage in the process of the building of socialism, which all countries, and in particular underdeveloped ones, would have to follow, as various bourgeois and rightist social-democratic critics of socialism think. This is an erroneous view, and marxist analysis can prove it is erroneous.' The same position is stated with even more precision in the December 1961 issue of *Nowe Drogi*, in an unsigned leading article (which means that it represents the views of the Central Committee): ' There is need for a marxist analysis of the period of the cult of Stalin, for an explanation of the conditions and circumstances in which the cult could develop and on which it was based, and of its social, political, economic, and moral effects. The need for this analysis arises not only from ideological reasons. It is also of great political importance : it should arm the communist movement for a struggle against such conditions, in order to overcome the contradictions born of the movement itself and which, as they developed, created fertile soil for the spreading of the cult of personality.'

Characteristically, *Nowe Drogi* backs Lange's warning against interpreting the objective causes of stalinism as its historical justification : ' Marxism is alien to all historical fatalism. The uncovering of the sources and objective causes does not mean that things had to develop the way they did. There is no situation in which there is no possibility of choice, no contradiction which cannot be solved in several fashions, at a lesser cost, avoiding much unnecessary suffering and undesirable effects '. Finally, the Polish official party organ gives the CPSU a mild but pointed lesson : ' Today particularly, when the objective causes have begun to disappear, when, as a result of the activity of the Party and the Soviet people the entire aspect of the Soviet Union has changed profoundly, the cult of Stalin and the entire system connected with it has been suspended in a vacuum, in the historical sense. It must finally be unmasked and overcome '.

SINCE the attitude of the Polish Communist party towards stalinism, so different from that of the Soviet party, has a definite ' polycentric ' look, let us now pass on to the theory of polycentrism itself. *Trybuna Ludu* was the *only* newspaper inside the Soviet bloc to quote Togliatti on polycentrism. In his report to the ninth plenum, Gomulka condemned the slogan of polycentrism, but seemed to approve of the realities behind it :

> Some comrades in fraternal communist parties consider that in existing conditions, when international communism has become widespread under diverse circumstances, the differences in the kind of political activity and methods of work impose the necessity of accepting the idea of polycentrism, which they fail to define with any degree of clarity. The differences in the kind of political activity and the methods of work of various communist and workers parties do not always follow from the actual conditions in which a given party is working. They can also be the result of the dogmatic or revisionist tendencies from which a party may be suffering.

But, after having pointed to Albania and Yugoslavia, he added : ' There is now no centre which would direct the activities of the individual communist and workers parties. Nor is one necessary '. Ignoring the ' wishful thinking ' element, what can be the alternative to a ' nonexistent ' and ' unnecessary ' monocentrism?

Where the 22nd CPSU congress met with unreserved support in Poland is on the peaceful coexistence issue. Gomulka said at the ninth plenum : ' The most important problem of our time is the problem of war and peace. The historical mission of the communist movement is to bar the way to war and to save mankind from a nuclear catastrophe '. The resolution of the plenary meeting was emphatic: ' The Polish party is in full solidarity with the analysis of the international situation and the general line of international policy of the 22nd congress of the CPSU. It is a Leninist policy of coexistence. . . . This policy has as its aim the saving of mankind from the catastrophe of a thermonuclear war, which has become the historical mission of the communist movement. This policy expresses the most vital interests of all nations and has the universal support of the Polish people '.

There is no need to doubt the sincerity of these statements. Whatever the differences between the Polish and Soviet societies, they have in common the desire for greater material welfare and for peace. The CPSU would certainly find it far from easy today to change its posture

of peaceful coexistence even in the name of ' ultimate socialist victory '.
It is difficult to accuse China openly in the Polish press of ' warmongering ', but there is persistent criticism of dogmatic attitudes in this field.
Thus the popular weekly *Swiat* writes (3 December 61): ' What caused
the dogmatic, sectarian ideas in international policy?   Without doubt
they were closely connected with the overall internal policy, with the
belief—even if it were not clearly formulated—that since two world wars
brought in turn the creation of one socialist state and then the emergence
of a whole system of socialist states—war may be not only harmless but
even useful for the socialist cause, and at least that is not the greatest
tragedy of humanity '.

Indeed, the elements of the trend represented by the 22nd congress
which are bound to have a particular appeal to Polish public opinion are
those designed to adapt the Soviet party to the requirements of the new
industrial society and to ensure the international peace necessary to carry
out this transformation.   Paradoxically, these two pragmatic, non-
ideological elements of Soviet policy are considered by Polish communists
as likely to favour a sort of ideological revival in Poland.

The contrast between the pragmatic aims of the Soviet leaders
(rationalisation of Soviet life, construction of a new industrial society,
catching up with America) and their renewed insistence on ideology has
been stressed often enough.   The explanation is also well-known.   If we
assume that the principal aim of the Communist party is to perpetuate
its rule, then Soviet communism is committed to diffusing an ideological
smoke-screen which covers this essential fact and the realities of Party
rule.   The utopian accent of the new CPSU programme, its ideological
character, the stress it lays on a foreseeable but still distant future, are so
many answers to a pressing, if unformulated question : ' If all you are
really aiming at is a particular formula of the Welfare State, then would
not the rationalisation of our social life require also some degree of
political democratisation? '   In other words: While their main preoccu-
pations are of a pragmatic character, the Soviet communists need ideology
as a justification of their monopoly of power.

Now the Polish communists are in the strange and exceptional position
of not needing this ideological justification in practice.   The justification
of *their* monopoly of power is based on geopolitical arguments, to which
the Poles are traditionally accustomed.   This line of reasoning is also well-
known and combines negative elements (the Soviet Union would not
allow any other form of government in Poland), and their positive
rationalisation (the argument of the Western frontiers and of the German
danger).   In addition, most Poles would agree that since October 1956
Poland has the best possible form of communist government.

From October 1956 until 1961, Polish communism could not rest on a
genuine ideology, and those who would follow its logic were mistrusted.
Institutional marxism was so completely discredited in Poland during
stalinism that there was no hope of reviving it.   On the other hand, the

lively ideological turmoil of the young intelligentsia in the October period had a definitely revisionist character, and its political implications (workers councils, workers democracy, egalitarianism, etc.) were dangerous for the party's monopoly of power. Ideological disputes with revisionists were naturally taking place, but no one seriously believed that the Poles could again be made to take an interest in orthodox marxist ideology. Hence a certain relief in the party at the discovery that the post-October generation is no longer interested in ideology and that Polish social life is taking on a 'socio-technical pattern'. Characteristically, this discovery seemed to rejoice the whole Polish centre—from positivist catholics to communist technocrats. There were of course some critics on the fringes: Reactionaries—on the usual ground of nostalgia. Catholics—because the 'materialist' young generation was not concerned with 'the higher spiritual values'. Revisionists—because they were concerned not merely with welfare but also with freedom. The few honest orthodox communists—because they realised that even greater welfare does not lead to a classless society.

The satisfaction derived from the progressive character of the 'socio-technical generation' often had comical aspects. There was one issue of *Polityka* with two neighbouring articles: about America and about the Polish town of Szczecin. The United States was commented on with distaste: nothing but materialism, vulgar mass culture, dreams about a bigger car, a bigger refrigerator, stultification, indifference, reaction. Szczecin was described with approbation: what healthy, positive young people, thinking about their jobs, planning to buy scooters, wishing to earn more, integrated into the country's economic progress—no hooligans or revisionists, but good and progressive citizens.

CRITICISM of this 'socio-technical generation' became louder after the 22nd congress, as if the new turn of events in the Soviet Union deprived ideology of some of its dangers. Newspaper after newspaper began to discover that the socio-technical pattern does not satisfy socialist standards. Most of the criticism was based on an opinion poll concerning the attitude of Warsaw University students, undertaken in June 1961 by the sociology department of Warsaw University under Professor Stanislaw Ossowski and published last November. The same team had made a similar enquiry in 1958, so that the evolution of student opinion over three years can be traced. The proportion of students approving the present Polish social and political regime is much greater than in 1958; the great majority now believe that the socialist model will sooner or later be adopted everywhere; while, three years ago, all students unreservedly condemned the stalinist period in Poland, they now believe that it had some positive features; three years ago an absolute distrust was expressed towards all intervention of the authorities in the field of public liberties; today, while 'liberal' opinion predominates, it is no longer so allergic to government. On the other hand, the answers show a definite decrease

of interest in ideological, social, and political questions, in what the com-
mentators call 'the problems of socialism'. In the words of the authors
of the study, ' one of the factors in the growing acceptance of socialism,
which is combined with a decline of theoretical interest, is the growing
economic and political stability of the country. Because of this stabilisation, the centre of interest is shifting to the satisfaction of personal and
occupational needs, and turning away from problems of organising the
world according to one's own values'.

Commenting on the enquiry, the journalist Marian Czerwinski wrote
in *Przeglad Kulturalny*: ' Socialism is beginning to open up prospects of
individual welfare and benefits, rather than creating concern for the fate
of other people. This average young man—student or technician—might
tell us something on these lines: " You were so intent on this socialism—
well, you've got it! Don't bother us any longer, we're all right ".'
Czerwinski added: ' It is most probable that the only way out of the social
neurosis—frustration, shame, hatred, despair—which was left by the
stalinist period, was through this socio-technical pattern.'

The 22nd congress also started off a discussion in the Polish press
about the freedom of science, socialist humanism, the need for internal
party democracy. This new discussion was so lively and interesting that
at times it recalled the intellectual atmosphere of October 1956. However,
it was not initiated by young revisionists, but by communist intellectuals
of the older generation, who not only did not join the revisionists in
October 1956, but showed a strong ideological resistance to their ideas.

Those responsible were Adam Schaff, Oskar Lange, Professors Infeld
and Ehrlich, Stefan Zolkiewski, Putrament, Alicja Lisiecka, and others,
generally fairly close to party orthodoxy. They are representative of
what might be called ' orthodox revisionism '.[1]

THE role of orthodox revisionism in Poland since October 1956 has
been both important and ungrateful. Orthodox revisionists have
attempted to ' modernise ' marxist thought, to enlarge its field of interest
to include disciplines and methods of research hitherto considered
' idealistic ' or ' reactionary ', while claiming to remain entirely faithful
to marxism-leninism. Like the party's political leaders, they were striking
out on two fronts—against dogmatists accused of fossilising marxism, and
against revisionists accused of liquidating it. The position of orthodox
revisionism can be summarised by two quotations from Adam Schaff:
Against dogmatists: ' There is no thesis in marxism which should be
preserved if it is denied by facts. There is no thesis in marxism which
should be preserved from discussion if new facts and arguments appear.'
Against revisionists: ' But with all the tolerance and breadth of the

---

[1] On ' philosophical ' and ' orthodox ' revisionism, see Zbigniew Jordan's excellent
article ' Rewizjonizm w Polsce ' (Revisionism in Poland), *Kultura*, December 1961–
February 1962.

approach, there are limits which cannot be crossed without obliterating one's marxist position.'

Orthodox revisionism is important because it has often served to pick up previously condemned theses of philosophic or ' authentic ' revisionism and obtain the seal of party approval for them. Thus, one of the main fights of Polish revisionists after 1955 was directed against the notion of *partiinost* in philosophy and science (in the light of which ' academic objectivism ' was considered reactionary). Leszek Kolakowski devoted a number of essays to this question; but the decisive theoretical blow against the crude concept of *partiinost* was dealt by the orthodox revisionist Oskar Lange. Lange made a distinction between mystifying ideologies and ideologies tending to uncover reality. He added, following Max Weber, that both kinds have the character of ideal types, and are never realised in their pure form. Mystifying ideologies cannot entirely ignore the real character of social relations, or they could have no practical bearing. On the other hand, mystifying elements are creeping into ideo- logies designed to uncover reality (Lange pointed to revisionism, dogma- tism, and the cult of personality). On the strength of this reasoning he proposed to distinguish between two approaches to reality : a progressive and a conservative one. The progressive approach favours the advance of science, the conservative approach tends to restrain it. What was left of *partiinost* in this new conception was the notion that the progressive approach needs to be related to ' the workers movement and to the construction and development of socialism ', a notion obviously designed to secure official approval of greater scientific freedom.

In his article in *Kultura*, Zbigniew Jordan propounds a thesis of ' the logical inevitability of revisionism '. He arrives at this formulation on the basis of the well-known contradiction between marxism as the ideology of socialism and marxism as a social theory leading to positive knowledge about the world. Othodox revisionism tries to find a way out of this dilemma by distinguishing between a ' creative ' and a ' liquidatory ' revision of marxism. In practice this does considerably enlarge the field of application of various scientific and philosophical methods, and implies a break with the stalinist principle of *partiinost*. But—theoretically at least—orthodox revisionism continues to have one feature in common with dogmatism : it is the party which, in the last instance, decides what is ' creative ' and what is ' liquidatory ' revisionism.

We come here to a point which seems to have been decisive in the negative attitude of orthodox revisionists during the October upheaval and since the 22nd congress. Communists like Schaff and Zolkiewski belong to a generation which was completely seduced by the myth of party monolithism. Whatever their intimate hopes and sympathies may have been, they saw in revisionism a threat to the unity of the party and opposed it on those grounds. It may have been both a surprise and a relief for them to see that the monolithic character of communism is being destroyed not by 'revisionists' but by Khrushchev himself, fighting it out against 'dogmatists'.

In some measure, Polish orthodox revisionists like Schaff and Lange may consider themselves the pioneers of a trend which won at the 22nd congress, and which faces the scientific and social implications of the transition to an industrial society. Not long ago Professor Schaff was criticised in Soviet learned journals for his attempts to enlarge the methods of marxism by introducing new sociological methods of enquiry, by opening the door to questions raised by existentialism and by the logical analysis of language. But since the 22nd congress, Schaff has acted as mentor to an international meeting of communist ideologists in Prague, devoted to modern sociology, while the December meeting of Soviet and Polish sociologists in Moscow proved that the Soviet Union had at last resolved to borrow, through the intermediary of Poland, some of the new Western methods of sociological enquiry to achieve a more rational social and economic development.

MUCH has been said—since October 1956—about the influence which Poland does, may, or should exert on the evolution of the Soviet Union. It made a definite impact on the literary and artistic ferment in Russia, and, through the instrumentality of such orthodox revisionists as Lange and Schaff, helped to implant in the social sciences and economics new ideas and methods of research. But manifold obstacles continued to exist throughout these years: The animosity, if not the hatred of the Polish public towards the Soviet Union, and the ostentatious lack of interest in Soviet problems on the Polish side; on the Soviet side, a combination of the traditional national distrust of the Poles, and suspicion of Polish revisionism. The trend represented by the 22nd congress, however slow and hesitant its pace, may well reduce some of these obstacles. For the first time since its accession to power, Polish communism is benefiting from conditions which may enable it to influence the approach to Soviet internal contradictions (between the rationalisation of economic and social policy and the insistence on ideology as a justification for the party's monopoly of power) in a more liberal sense. But if Polish communism is to accomplish this, the kind of problems the Poles are dealing with must always be ahead of the kind of problems the Soviet Union is tackling, and the really new problems are invariably posed, not by orthodox revisionism, but by philosophic revisionism.

It is philosophic revisionism which provides the challenge necessary to the development of orthodox revisionism, which then in its turn is in a position to establish a dialogue with Moscow. To use concrete examples: the natural Polish partners in a philosophic, scientific, social dialogue with the Soviets are men like Schaff, Lange, Zolkiewski. But we know to what extent the contribution of these leading orthodox revisionists is due to their own debates with Kolakowski, Ossowski, Strzelecki, Chalasinski, Beylin.

The discussion raised in the Polish press at the time of the 22nd congress on freedom of scientific research and discussion was started by such orthodox revisionists as Schaff, Lange, Infeld, Ehrich, and has been widely reported in the West. It found an echo in a round-table discussion on the crucial theme of 'Ideology versus Sociotechnics' organised by *Nowa Kultura*. The economist Edward Lipinski was particularly outspoken:

> I once said in polemical fervour that the first duty of a real marxist is to fight for freedom, since I consider that when freedom is lacking mistakes accumulate, and around these mistakes forces crystallise which hamper progress. Even in fighting against evil, we create new elements of evil. There will always be people and groups in whose interest it will be to preserve evil. And here the basic condition is freedom to fight for one's own convictions. Had there been a greater freedom to express our thoughts and formulate criticism during the period of the cult of personality, the crimes of stalinism might have been averted.

It must be said, however, that most of the recent statements by Polish orthodox revisionists, however outspoken, are limited. While the 22nd congress brought new life into Polish discussions concerning freedom of science, economy, sociology, it seems to have had adverse effects on the Polish literary scene. Here the recent trend is disquieting. An apparently innocuous *vie romancée* of Julius Caesar by Jacek Bochenski was awarded the literary prize for 1961 by the jury of *Nowa Kultura*. But it seems—paradoxically—safer to criticise the cult of personality by referring directly to Stalin than by transposing the scene to classical times. The jury was instructed to select another book for its award, and its refusal to do so brought about, first a reshuffling of the editorial board, and, later, a governmental decision to abolish all official literary prizes. Bochenski's book was finally withdrawn from circulation. The prohibition on presenting two short plays by Leszek Kolakowski after five days on the stage is another indication of the renewed rigidity of the Polish censorship.

The young veterans of October revisionism joined eagerly in the new discussion now initiated by their elders; Pawel Beylin and Jan Strzelecki made brilliant contributions to the 'freedom of science' discussion, and the Warsaw 'Crooked Circle' club, which is the centre of liberal socialist opinion, organised a public discussion on the theme of freedom of speech. The famous poet Antoni Slonimski, one of the most courageous figures in Polish literary life, was quoted as saying: 'Let us press for freedom, then freedom of speech will come automatically'. But the distinction between the kind of freedom whose need is recognised by technocrats for the sake of efficiency, and the kind which is feared by ideologists eager to keep the party's monopoly of power unquestioned, appeared again. After a heated debate in which Professor Schaff argued—against a sceptical audience—that there is greater intellectual freedom in Poland than in the United States, the 'Crooked Circle' was closed down.

THE Sino-Soviet conflict, which came into the open at the 22nd congress, has been watched in Poland with intense interest.

Polish communist intellectuals entertained great sympathy for the Chinese revolution in Stalin's time. The picture of a ' spontaneous ' and ' authentic ' revolutionary movement which was so far away, and about which so little was known, had its obvious use as a justification of a regime which was only too well known. Moreover, they had a tendency to project the Polish tradition of revolutionary struggle for independence on to the wars of independence waged by the colonial peoples. During the ' Hundred Flowers ' period, Polish revisionists made great use of the Chinese example to argue their own case, just as, during the fateful days of October 1956, they considered Mao as their distant protector against the threat of Soviet intervention. However, the Chinese insistence on crushing the Hungarian revolution and their subsequent hostility to all revisionist tendencies put an end to any pro-Chinese leanings in Poland.

In supporting the Soviet line against the Chinese, Polish communists are sure of public backing. Is there a serious chance of transforming this negative support into a positive one? Were it not for the taboo attaching to ' Polish-Soviet friendship ', the enquiry referred to above might well have included a question on the Polish students' attitude towards the Soviet Union. It is likely that, just as the students' attitude towards the stalinist past was less unequivocally negative in 1961 than it was in 1958, so their dislike of Russia has diminished over the last three years, even if it is difficult to speak of a ' growth of friendship '. Over the last year, the Polish press has at last hit on the only formula for intelligent pro-Soviet propaganda : publishing the work of Soviet writers under official criticism in their own country. The Soviet press attacks Evtushenko's ' Babi Yar '? The very official and orthodox Polish *Polityka* immediately publishes it. What can be the reaction of the young Polish reader to Evtushenko's ' Prologue ', recently published by *Nowa Kultura*, with its longing for foreign travel, for ' art, just like myself, always different ', with its scorn for conformism and hypocrisy, if not one of true, newly discovered kinship? *Nowa Kultura* has made a regular feature of Russian non-conformist poems by Evtushenko, Voznesensky, Vinokurov. Thus the Russian revisionists are used by Polish communism to lure the young Polish intelligentsia back to ortho-doxy. Without any doubt, the image the Poles now have of the Soviet Union is much less one-sided and crude than it was some years ago. There is a growing realisation that new forces are at work in the Soviet Union itself, and open interest is slowly replacing blind prejudice.

Many sore points remained, of course. Some of them have been dealt with as a result of the condemnation of the ' anti-party ' group. Thus, the recently published Soviet *History of the Patriotic War* condemns Molotov for having publicly rejoiced, in September 1939, in ' the disappearance of Poland, that ugly bastard of the Versailles Treaty '. A more delicate problem is posed by the Katyn mass-murder of Polish officers, prisoners of war in the USSR. Theoretically, there is nothing to prevent the Soviets from ascribing ten thousand more victims to Stalin and Beria. Nobody in Poland doubts that the Soviets, not the Nazis, committed this particular crime, and it was whispered in Warsaw cafés, and perhaps even in ministerial couloirs, that admission of this by the Russians would eliminate another painful complex from Soviet-Polish relations. But, for whatever reasons, neither the Soviet nor the Polish Government is willing to go back on this lie. In his speech on 20 January 1962, on the occasion of the twentieth anniversary of the refoundation of the Polish Communist party, Gomulka even thought fit to refer to the Katyn massacre and to ascribe it to the Nazis, although for the last six years there has been an unwritten rule in Poland not to mention this subject.

IF polycentrism is now the central issue of the communist movement, superficial logic would suggest that its repercussions would strengthen the ' specific Polish road to socialism ' which has been, at several recent turning points, so closely associated with Gomulka.

' National communism ' is, after all, so recent a phenomenon that it still sounds almost like a contradiction in terms. For the Founding Fathers, for the early revolutionaries, even for the stalinist *apparatchiks* (at least at a certain level of their consciousness) there never was any doubt that the victory of communism on the world scale would mean the end of nationalisms, the realisation of the universal society and of Marx's vision in which society would replace the state. This is not the place to retrace the history of the gradual erosion of the internationalist features of the communist movement. But even after the Russian revolution, when it could be seen that communism was not going to be realised according to the predictions of Marx, an internationalist conception prevailed, in the form of the voluntary accession of each new communist state to the Union of Soviet Socialist Republics, which was conceived not as a geographically defined area, but as a federation of all the communist states of the world. This principle was even used to justify the annexation of the Baltic states. The first *theoretical* departure from this line was the post-war conception of ' popular democracies '. Still, the purely tactical character of this new form of ' national communism ' was obvious: the communist parties of the satellite states were merely given time in which to use nationalist feelings in order to lead their countrymen eventually into the Union. It was in Poland (after Yugoslavia) that it became clear what would happen to communist leaders who took the ' independence ' line too seriously.

The term ' the Polish road to socialism ' was first coined by Gomulka in 1948, when he wrote in *Nowe Drogi*: ' Both for the Polish Socialist party and for the Polish Workers' party, the independence of Poland is a supreme consideration to which all others are subordinated '. Indeed, the nationalist issue was—together with the attitude to collectivisation, —the main feature of Gomulka's conception of ' the Polish road to

socialism '. Like many Polish communists, he was led to analyse the
reasons for the failure of the communists to build a mass movement in
pre-war Poland. He attributed it to their insistence on internationalism
and their indifference to Polish independence, which they identified with
reactionary nationalism. This meant that among the left wing, all the
power of attraction which patriotism has for the Poles was exerted by the
Polish Socialist party (PPS), which had broken with the left-wing internationalists before the first world war precisely on the independence issue.
The merger of the Polish Communist party with the PPS in 1948, was
used by Gomulka as an occasion for reviving the ' patriotic argument ',
and he was quite explicit in his condemnation of the old Luxemburgist
tradition and in extolling the patriotic virtues of the PPS.

But Stalin did not like his local agents to take their tactical role too
seriously. The central committee meeting of August-September 1948
took Gomulka to task for his conception of ' the Polish road to socialism '
and denounced him as a ' national deviationist '. Between September 1948
and December 1949 three major purges were conducted in the Polish CP
under the slogan of eradicating the nationalist deviation, affecting more
than one quarter of the total membership. Even so, the reactions of the
rank and file in October 1956 proved that the purges had merely driven
the nationalistic majority underground.

The key to Gomulka's past and present policy is perhaps given by his
confession of his cardinal sin, concerning his attitude towards the USSR
and the CPSU, published in the September-October 1949 issue of *Nowe
Drogi*:

> The core of my rightist, nationalist complex must have been my
> attitude to the Soviet Union, to the CPSU. . . . My attitude could be
> reduced not so much to . . . the relationship between the CPSU and the
> Polish party as to the relationship between Poland and the USSR
> as states. . . . It never entered my head that Poland could progress
> along the road to socialism without being supported by the Soviet
> Union. . . . These things I understood, but . . . it was . . . difficult for
> me to shift my attitude as regards the Soviet Union to the ideological
> party plane.

In other words, Gomulka was, and remains, a good communist and a
faithful ally of the USSR. But he objected to the total dependence of the
Polish Communist party on the CPSU. That was a heretical attitude in
1949, but the very terms of his confession sound pretty orthodox now,
since it is the CPSU which has evolved towards acceptance of his position.

In fact, ' the Polish road to socialism ' appeared as a slogan when it
encountered Soviet resistance, and disappeared when the Soviet Union
recognised and admitted the realities behind it. The dramatic eighth
plenum of the Polish Central Committee in October 1956 gave express
approval to it, but later the slogan was dropped. The conference of the
Communist parties called by Khrushchev to Moscow a year later, under
the pretext of celebrating the fortieth anniversary of the October Revolution, was in itself a manifestation of the fact that Moscow recognised

the existence of some degree of polycentrism within the communist movement. Gomulka played back on this occasion and emphasised the need
for unity, solidarity, and cohesion in the Soviet bloc, while at the same
time opposing the revival of any international communist organisation.
The 22nd congress was a further important step on the road which seems
to be Gomulka's, and he has less to fear than ever from any eventual
Soviet pressure on the basic tenets of his policy—his own conception of
agriculture and of relations between Church and State. Khrushchev
himself went further than ever in his report to the 22nd congress in
giving indirect approval to Polish agricultural policy. Through a fortunate
coincidence, the Polish harvest for 1961 was a record one. As 87 per cent.
of the cultivated area in Poland is still in private ownership, this stands
out in contrast with the Soviet Union where Khrushchev, in spite of his
reforms, has not been nearly so successful. During his recent visit to
Poland, Demichev, secretary of the CPSU central committee, congratu-
lated the Polish communists on their agricultural successes, and shortly
after the congress *Kommunist* echoed Khrushchev's oblique approval.

In these conditions, Gomulka is certainly satisfied. He never had any
liberal leanings himself, and the appointment of the sinister General
Witaszewski, a former supporter of the Natolin group who, as head of the
Security Police, threatened Polish intellectuals with ' gas-pipes ', leaves
no doubt about his determination not only to forget the ' Polish road to
socialism ' verbally, but to prevent its following the path indicated not
merely by the young October revisionists, but also by the more enlightened
representatives of orthodox revisionism.

As Khrushchev's staunchest ally—along with Hungary's Kadar—
Gomulka seems to be moving on his own road towards what a French
commentator has aptly called ' le communisme des patries '.

HUNGARY

G. R. Urban

IN Hungary de-Stalinisation has posed more questions than the communist party or government seem able to answer. Among the most serious is the inability or reluctance of the local party official to fall into line, revealed most clearly in connexion with agriculture. The 22nd CPSU congress came at an awkward time for Hungary, shortly after the drive to complete collectivisation had antagonised a large proportion of the Hungarian population, and the local party official who had to coerce and browbeat the peasants into the collectives resented the instructions to apply the policy more mildly. In the popular mind collectivisation equals Stalinism, and Kadar's propagandists are hard put to it to explain why violence had to be done to such a large part of the Hungarian population when milder winds were beginning or continuing to blow elsewhere. From the experience which hindsight provides, one can see that the Hungarian party completed collectivisation not a moment too soon; it is to be doubted whether in the atmosphere prevailing in the country today a similar drive could be successful. This, one may assume, is a thought not distant from the minds of the peasants, and if they are dragging their feet they may well be contemplating the possibility of undoing some of the changes foisted on them shortly before the 22nd CPSU congress.

A quiet but widespread withdrawal of all but the most inescapable kinds of labour, combined with a serious drought and wholly inadequate investment, have played havoc with agricultural production plans. There are already signs that in many parts of the country collectivisation has been carried out in name only. Private plots and not the collectivised land continue to be the centre of the farmers' efforts and emotions. In a number of places ingenious ways have been found by the local communist officials, disturbed by the undermining of labour morale on the collective fields, to evade the party's advice. On some collectives private plots are allocated on paper only, and the farmer is paid the equivalent (in kind) of what his plot would yield had he been given one. Describing how some of the party's more hidebound agents are actually trying to eliminate private plots rather than follow the party's directive and support them, *Nepszabadsag* (3 March 1962) said:

> One wonders what the farmers themselves, the members of these collectives, say to all this? Do they vote for it? . . . It is inconceivable why this (nominal) form of private plots should be so strongly pressed in some places at a time when the membership is flatly against it. It may well be that those who are encouraging this trend are guided by the best intentions; nevertheless, they are wrong.

It is against this background that one has to see Kadar's tug of war with an army of bewildered local secretaries.

CONFUSION has been made worse by the party's decision to appoint outsiders to responsible positions. This, to give him his due, has been Kadar's policy since 1957, but it is only since the 22nd congress that the drive is being taken seriously. Today expertise is the decisive qualification for appointments other than those inside the party, and outsiders are encouraged to attend party meetings and make their views known. This encroachment upon their privacy has had an extremely unsettling effect on the party's local agents. Until quite recently communists have taken ill-disguised pleasure in belonging to a world inaccessible to the general public, and the change appears to detract from their prestige and leadership. Kadar is, or acts as though he were, confident that it is safe for the party to invest in the co-operation of the great mass of Hungarians. The local man, whose first experience of fear coincided with the 1956 revolution, may have a different view. Resistance to this innovation is accordingly fierce and widespread. Day after day the official press warns, preaches, and admonishes, and reports of local refusals to follow suit are equally frequent.

> There are still people who believe that their particular position entitles them to special rights and privileges. There are no special positions. Leaders and employees are equally subject to the statutes of the party and the laws of the State.[1]

The removal of these men and their policies carries an element of risk for the party—too little would not suit Kadar's books, too much might jeopardise the whole exercise. To impress a policy of this kind on a party conditioned by the dos and don'ts of an earlier age is a hazardous and sophisticated operation. The party never tires of warning members that between the Scylla of an unprincipled liberalism and the Charybdis of Stalinism there is a third and saving channel. What is not being said quite so clearly is how the local man is to hit upon these uncharted waters.

If knowledge, experience, and expertise alone determine a man's place in society, what is the party member's position vis-à-vis these outsiders? How does the party expect him to behave when given orders by men he has been taught to despise? Party-cells and local organisations have already produced surprising responses.

> Some people in the party-cells do not agree with the policy of the central committee. This disagreement has taken practical shape in despotism and a fettering of speech. . . . But now the atmosphere is clear, everyone talks freely so that it can be openly said that sectarian thinking is defeated.[2]

The number of party secretaries dismissed or routed in election is not known, but it seems clear that enough pressure has been brought to bear

---

1 *Delmagyarorszag*, 1 November 1961.
2 *Nogradi Nepujsag*, 5 November 1961.

from Budapest to encourage local organisations to get rid of some of their more unpopular leaders:

> The dykes were breached. . . . It was made crystal clear during the discussion that, at the height of his power, the party secretary was cold and extremely difficult to approach. . . . He liked to summarise his ideas in short imperatives: ' expel ', ' dismiss ', ' punish ' . . . How can a man with this attitude head the party-cell after the 22nd CPSU congress? [3]

That there is a gap between what Kadar wants to see done and what is actually carried out on the farms and on the factory floor, is admitted by some of the more enlightened local leaders: ' It is true that central leadership of our party is free from deviations which might distort their Leninism, but this in itself is no guarantee that in the basic party-cells, too, major or minor sectarian or right-wing deviations are automatically corrected '.[4]

The sectarians on their part appear to be arguing a case which has an instinctive appeal to purists and older hands. One complaint that runs through comment after comment both in the capital and in the provincial press, centres on the damage de-Stalinisation has done to party morale. To judge from some of the complaints, it also appears to have given fresh courage to revisionists and counter-revolutionaries:

> Since the 22nd congress a number of people have been increasingly vocal in saying that their time has come because the congress condemned the cult of personality. These people think that they should now be rehabilitated on the strength of their activities during the counter-revolution. Many of them have already applied for admission to our local party cells. . . . The courageous criticisms which followed the 22nd congress are being interpreted by many as a *carte blanche* for throwing mud at the people's system and the socialist camp.[5]

WHATEVER else the 22nd congress may have done, it has certainly created a taste for criticism. The government's purpose in its policy of relaxation is to increase efficiency and make local leaders and factory managers conscious of their responsibilities. If a certain amount of steam can be let off in the process, so much the better. But from the party machinery's point of view this operation has not much to commend it. Inevitably it is the most faithful (and vulnerable) servants of the establishment who find themselves at the business end of rectification. One need not be a communist to dislike the removal of pedestals if one happens to be comfortably established on one.

The official press and radio miss no opportunity of laying bare to their audiences hair-raising instances of dilettantism, wastefulness, despotism, nepotism, and other varieties of abuse and mismanagement. The new

[3] *Nepszabadsag*, 26 November 1961.
    Zalai Hirlap, 21 January 1962.
    Somogyi Neplap, 5 January 1962.

class feel that the ground is being eroded under their feet, and it would be less than human to expect them to hide their apprehension :

> [The man I spoke to] looked depressed and was full of complaints. He is himself manager of a large factory in Budapest . . . and he reeled off . . . a large number of recent articles all of which criticised the shortcomings of leading officials. Well, said my friend, taken one by one, these cases are true enough. He was, he said, opposed to such practices. . . . But, he added . . . when all these writings are read together, do they really help us? . . . Don't they create an atmosphere which is hostile to any kind of leadership? [6]

The official answer to this question is No, and there is nothing in Kadar's speeches or in the press to suggest that the experiment is considered too dangerous to continue.

Whatever the rights and wrongs of these cases may be, they are unique in Hungarian and probably communist jurisdiction. It is equally remarkable that they have been reported in the official press. These litigants appear to have taken the party's protestations of socialist legality at face value, and to have set out to test the impartiality of the law. To appreciate their courage one has to remember that in this field, too, the party speaks with several voices. On 6 January 1962 Tibor Vago produced in *Hungarian Law* [7] a spirited apologia of Stalinist juris-prudence, arguing that considerations of class will continue to be decisive in assessing the significance of crime.

> In our jurisprudence it is still indispensable that we should examine class roots and class interests. . . . It is our general principle that in a political case, or one which may have political repercussions, the clarification of class background is very important.

At the other end of the scale we have the first deputy of the Chief Public Prosecutor, Dr Csendes, putting in a plea for a more thoroughgoing de-Stalinisation. Seldom has the party's recent past been more heavily indicted, or confidence in its capacity to renew itself more crudely shaken :

> The personality cult was not only mortally dangerous to our lives and freedoms but—and this is more significant—it also jeopardised the ideals of our lives, depriving us of communist self-respect. . . . It robbed us of the ideals of our youth and trampled into the mud all our finest ideas. Under Horthy's fascism it was a difficult thing to be a communist, but for the difficulties we had to face and the sufferings we had to undergo we drew strength from the comradely solidarity which existed among us communists, the trust we had in each other, our friendship and the enthusiasm we had for our cause. These purely human motives gave beauty and content to our youth. . . . The personality cult was trying to rob us of all this. When we were young communists (and today's young communists are no different) we had great respect for our older comrades whose names we were often not even allowed to know, but whose teaching and

6 *Nepszabadsag*, 24 January 1962.
7 *Magyar Jog*, 6 January 1962.

behaviour we revered and were trying to emulate. These ideals, too, were taken away from us by the personality cult; we were told to respect idols and our minds were being gradually emptied of our memories.[8]

Dr Csendes goes on record with a number of attractive promises: no one will be prosecuted for his political views, nor will the courts juggle with their yardsticks to suit antiquated theories about class: 'Today all enjoy the same rights before the law and only crime will be prosecuted'. Moreover, confession and self-indictment will no longer suffice to establish a person's guilt. Defendants will be assumed innocent unless there is sufficient evidence (other than his own confession) to show that he is guilty. 'All men with a clear conscience may sleep quietly at night, and if the bell rings early in the morning they may be quite sure that it is the newsboy or the milkman.'

This is a far cry not only from Vago's words but also, and this is more important, from the views of Csendes' principal, the Chief Public Prosecutor, Szenasi. The spirit in which the latter's office is conducted may be gauged from a book he published under the slightly misleading title, *On the Watchtower of Legality*.[9] The Chief Public Prosecutor holds that 'social danger' arises either from the act itself or from the social position of the person responsible for that act. Of the second category he says:

> Social danger may arise from the person if his special position is such that his interests are . . . opposed to the growth of . . . socialist society. Such are, for instance, capitalists, landowners, kulaks, former senior civil servants, etc. The material and personal aspects of the crime from which a threat to society arises determine for those engaged in prosecuting and judging crime whether they will be lenient or rigorous, choose a serious form of reprisal, or punishment involving re-education. . . . It is possible that a crime is extremely dangerous to society but not the criminal (for instance, theft committed by a worker). In such cases the sentence may be more lenient. But it is possible that the crime is hardly dangerous to society but the criminal is (for instance, theft committed in the fields, by a kulak). The sentence then will be more rigorous.

Today collectivisation is nominally completed and there are no more 'kulaks'. Nevertheless, as Vago's article testifies, the spirit of illegality is still alive in the laws and practices of communist Hungary. But may Dr Csendes' revisionism (and there are others who share his views) not have won enough of the public's confidence to persuade them that they can now go to the law courts and expect (though not always get) justice? And if individuals can muster up courage to take *Nepszava* to court, why should they stop there? Why not report the policeman who opens your mail, or the party tough who bludgeoned you into the collective?

8 *Nepszabadsag*, 14 January 1962.
9 *A Torvenyesseg Orhelyen* (Budapest, 1958).

It would be difficult to find a more revealing case than 'The Dis-integration of Unity' [10] in the party-cell of the Railway Research Centre in Budapest. This is a story of feuds and counter-feuds, intrigues, gossip and malice. Since the 22nd congress, we are told, partisanship has 'poisoned the atmosphere of the Institute'. Two battle groups have taken up positions along lines which may be typical for party-cells throughout the country. Ostensibly the question was whether ideological considerations should be allowed to govern research, or whether scholar-ship and achievement should take precedence over *partiinost*. But one need not be particularly eagle-eyed to see that the quarrel was really between dyed-in-the-wool dogmatists on the one hand and those who would simply produce better engines or signalling equipment for the railways.

These phenomena are country-wide. As yet the conflict is limited to the party and the new class who have climbed on its band-waggon. The nation as a whole, although keenly interested in the strange malaise which has attacked the body of its rulers, is spectator rather than partici-pant. The people have learnt something from 1956—they are cautious, they are ready to exploit any change that may come their way; but by and large they are too sensible to allow the vagaries of doctrine to inter-fere with the serious business of living. This retreat from politics is new in Hungarian thinking and may be no more than transitory. But while it lasts, Hungarian fortunes will be willy-nilly tied to those of cliques and schools of thought within the communist movement.

THE contradictions in the Hungarian Communist party may suggest a 'good' Kadar surrounded by a host of wicked dogmatists. This is a misleading distinction. Kadar's long-term objectives have never been in doubt and his somersault on 4th November 1956 has shown how far he is prepared to go; the reforms he advocates and his denunciations of the past are clearly geared to promoting, not hindering, the growth of a communist society. Yet it is impossible to ignore Kadar's appeal for those who, having convinced themselves of the futility of liberation, are now content to back liberalisation. When, reversing Rakosi's motto, Kadar says that all who are not against the regime are with it, he is throwing the gates open to the majority of Hungarians whose influence in key positions is bound to reduce the speed, and may ultimately alter the course, of communist policy.

As Kadar sees it, danger lies in the crass forms of dictatorship and the repercussions they produce; to forestall these and take the public into his confidence, even at the risk of alienating numerous (some would say important) elements in the party is, for him, the least hazardous path. Kadar knows from experience that there is a critical mass of white-collar Hungarians who make or mar governments. By installing them in posts of responsibility he hopes to rivet their interests to those of the party.

10 *Nepszabadsag*, 6 February 1962.

For the party, there are obvious risks in this operation; its present emphasis on tolerance enjoys, as far as it goes, the support of an incredulous and often amused public. To play on the people's goodwill rather than on its fears, to remind the party that it is a small minority in a large mass of non-Marxist but perfectly respectable Hungarians, to warn party members that ' although we have a one-party system we must always assume in our work that we have 20 parties and secret elections every single day ', to condemn force, brow-beating, and ' moral pressure ', to warn hotheads that even such time-honoured appellations as ' reactionary' may boomerang if used carelessly, and, above all, virtually to write off the class struggle—these are sentiments with which the Hungarian public would have no reason to quarrel.[11]

If, therefore, Kadar is, broadly speaking, on the right track, there is still one question which remains to be answered : who, apart from the men at the bottom rungs of the party ladder, are his opponents?

Recently the party was told by Dezso Nemes, one of the duller of Kadar's back-room boys, that the ideological ripples of the Chinese communes had reached ' some of our own comrades '.[12] This is a vague hint, but is it conceivable that the complicated matters to which Nemes was referring could have made sense to, let alone confuse the thinking of, people other than those fairly high up on the hierarchy? The retirement in January of Istvan Friss from policy-making may have been one step in the party's campaign to remove its problem-children. The recent reshuffle of minor government posts, putting a large number of technicians effectively in charge of economic controls, was a demonstration of the party's determination that it will practise what it preaches. But the men these experts have replaced were, by and large, not heavily committed on the dogmatist side, so that the demotion-equals-dogmatism equation does not necessarily hold water.

There is at the present time no certain answer to this question. But its seriousness should not be underestimated.

> Should we artificially stir up political clashes at a time when socialism is decisively established in our country and in our economy and exploitation, too, has virtually ended? Would shadow-boxing and fighting windmills bring us closer to socialism or communism? *No, no and again no.*[13]

Who are the men who want to ' stir up clashes ', and why this impassioned No? There is a good deal in the theoretical writings of Hungarian communists to make even some of Kadar's trusted exegeta slightly suspect.

[11] Kadar talking to workers of the ' Ikarus ' factory, *Nepszabadsag,* 4 March 1962. ' Remember that many sorts of people with many different pasts and views live together with us in our people's system. They live and work honourably, each in his own field. . . . Should we now start a war against them? But *why*? They do not harm us—we only fight those who attack the people's power. The great majority of these people have found their place in our system, have accepted our system. This they show by their work, thus putting themselves, objectively, on our side.'
[12] *Tarsadalmi Szemle,* February 1962.
[13] ' The Real Class-Struggle ', by J. Szanto, *Nepszabadsag,* 10 March 1962.

Some of the orthodoxies one detects in Szirmai and even Nemes are no more than stylistic, but others go deeper. Szirmai's attack on literary revisionism, Nemes' formula that the class-struggle goes on though in abated form, would seem to be out of tune with Kadar's pronouncements. Apro, one of the oldest Stalinists, is strangely silent, nor have Kiss and a number of others shown their hands since the 22nd congress.

Kadar and his supporters have considerable understanding for 'old comrades' who find it easier to 'break heads' than to keep them whole and fill them with new meaning. But it is not so certain that the understanding is reciprocated. If holy Russia and the class-struggle drop away, what is left, for these veteran fighters, of communism?

The dogmatic wing is restive but without a head and powerless to do more than delay. But will it be quite so powerless if polycentrism is allowed to run its full course? The absence of a controlling party allows for various shades of independence. Given a renewed crisis in agriculture or in the country's balance of payments, might Kadar's hidden detractors not decide that for them polycentrism means freedom to pursue a harder course?

AT the moment Kadar is on the offensive and he is increasingly impatient with men he considers incorrigibly committed to the self-defeating ways of Stalinism. To safeguard party unity he has to tread more carefully than his protector in the Kremlin, yet such has been the opposition to his policies that early in April his axe fell, removing Imre Dögei from the ranks of the party.

Dögei's expulsion cuts into the Sino-Soviet dispute no less than into agriculture, of which he was minister in Kadar's first Government. The first and most brutal wave of the collectivisation campaign (1958–1959) was carried out under his stewardship, earning the party the hatred of millions of peasants who had just settled down to the most prosperous life they could remember since the end of the war. By rusticating this old communist, the party is washing its hands of coercion, serving notice on lesser men that resistance to Kadar's agricultural functionalism will no longer be tolerated.

But this may also be the opening shot in a campaign to put agriculture on a more rational footing. Using Dögei as a scapegoat, a case may be gradually worked out for the rehabilitation of some of the most aggrieved sections of the farming community by enlarging the area of private plots and allocating them more permanently to their operators, establishing family farming on a national scale and offering more generous incentives and enforcing them nationally. All this would give a fillip to Hungary's lagging agricultural production, but it would also change the nature, although not the name, of the 'socialist' dispensation.

Dögei's flirtation with Chinese ways of thinking also centres on his own *métier*. When, after the middle of 1957, Chinese flowers began to be mown down and 'rectification' replaced horticulture, the Hungarian communists were quick to voice their approval.

The intensification of the class struggle, the setting up of communes, the leap-forward movement, and the subjugation of Tibet were all given maximum publicity, but it was at no time suggested that Hungary could usefully emulate any of China's internal innovations. The regime's official view of the agricultural communes was that of a friendly spectator, admiring but aloof. But there appears to have been an unofficial view, too.

What we know now of Dögei's position at that time makes it seem highly probable that, together with some Bulgarian comrades he, too, and possibly others besides him, saw a good deal of virtue in the communes experiment. It would appear that in them the ideological ripples of which Nemes spoke had found ready recipients.

Dögei fell into disgrace in May 1960, when he was removed from the Central Committee for pursuing 'sectarian, pseudo-leftist views and activities'. But although he was given a 'final warning' to desist, his expulsion from the party in April 1962 was, apparently, made necessary because he continued with his 'official and unofficial tours to the provinces, spreading views opposed to the policy of the party and making declarations defamatory of it '.[14] The piquancy of this double ostracism is that between his fall as Minister of Agriculture in January 1960 and his expulsion from the Central Committee in May 1960 (not then made public) Dögei was appointed Ambassador to China, and that the resolution expelling him from the Central Committee also cancelled his appointment to Peking (which, incidentally, he never took up) implying that his deviations to the left, particularly in 'forcing the middle peasants to join the co-operatives ahead of schedule ', made him ineligible for this sensitive post.

Seen against this background, Dögei's fall is the clearest practical condemnation of dogmatism we have yet had in Hungary, and an indirect avowal that it survives not only at the grass-roots of the party, but also amongst people in high and influential places. Also, it shows that these men are in spiritual, if not actual, league with the Chinese, and that Kadar is alive to the temptations Peking's militant evangelism presents to a good many of his followers.

But Kadar's worries can hardly be said to be over, for if Dögei was successful in 'concealing his disagreement with party policies ',[15] how many others may still be successful in concealing theirs? Kadar is obviously anxious to do as little damage to his party's facade of unity as he possibly can. But can he avoid doing more?

14 *Partelet*, April 1962.
15 *Ibid.*

THE BALKANS

J. F. Brown

AFTER the second world war the Balkan states and nations, with the narrow exception of Greece, found themselves once more under the shadow of a great imperial power. In Yugoslavia, Tito's partisan movement, dominated by a Communist party bound to the Soviet Union by ideology and personal devotion, had emerged triumphant. In its turn, this movement controlled the Communist party of Albania. In Bulgaria and Rumania the position in 1945 was not so well defined. Though Russian troops had overrun both countries and it was obvious that the respective Communist parties would play a major role in the post-war proceedings, they had of necessity first to operate as parts of coalitions formed from a wide range of anti-fascist parties and politicians. But whether in Bulgaria, where the Communist party was strong and the bulk of the population pro-Russian, or in Rumania, where the Communist party was weak and the population violently anti-Russian, the Soviet Union was confident that its well-laid plans for domination would meet with little or no effective opposition from Britain or the United States. Her confidence was justified and the Communist take-over got swiftly under way.

In the space of three years the situation had changed greatly. The Yugoslav Communist party, second only to the CPSU in strength and prestige among the ruling Communist parties, and second to none in dedication, had been expelled from the communist company amid a chorus of opprobrium and vilification. Only four months after the masterstroke of the Czechoslovak coup d'état, the Cominform meeting of June 1948 tacitly revealed that the Soviet camp was not monolithic, that communist power was not indivisible, and that national communism had made its debut on the world's political stage. Like every great event in history, the break with Tito has been subjected to intensive scrutiny from both scholars and journalists. Its beginnings have been pushed back to the early days of the partisan movement. With the wisdom of hindsight it is, of course, possible to see potential significance in Stalin's impatience at not being continually consulted about Tito's military intentions, or in Tito's bewilderment about the failure of the Soviets to give him full diplomatic support. After the war the differences became more sharp, but in fact, ' any man who, prior to January 1948, would have predicted a break between Tito and Stalin would be entitled . . . to be honored as a prophet with occult powers of predicting the future but certainly not as an expert basing his prognosis upon factual evidence '.[1]

---

[1] Adam B. Ulam, *Titoism and the Cominform* (Harvard, 1952), p. 106. Mr Ulam gives, I think, still the most convincing interpretation of the underlying causes of the break with Stalin.

The spirit behind this sensible warning might also be applied to the origins of the conflict. Today, with the phrase 'national communism' ringing in our ears, there is an automatic inclination to attribute every case of deviation within the Soviet bloc precisely and exclusively to this factor. In the Tito case 'national communism' is certainly what the Yugoslav leaders made it appear, it is the way the Yugoslav people and the rest of the world took it, it is essentially what it developed into; and there was something more than Balkan sentiment or skilful propaganda in the famous Yugoslav plea: 'No matter how much each of us loves the land of socialism, the USSR, he can, in no case, love his country less'.[2] But in the last (or the first) analysis the question was more narrow, boiling down in the main to whether Tito, Rankovic, Djilas, Kardelj and company were to have control in Yugoslavia or not. The fact that the Soviets wanted to exploit Yugoslavia, had just frustrated Tito's expansionist schemes, and regarded Belgrade as a satellite pawn, was not as important to Tito as the fact that the Soviets were undermining his control over his party and state apparatus by dealing directly with whichever of his subjects they chose, and were encouraging Yugoslav officials at every level to look upon the Soviet ambassador in Belgrade almost as the *de facto* leader of the country. In the early stages of this typically Soviet behaviour Tito had been genuinely shocked and had made his feelings known to the Soviets, apparently believing that they would rectify a situation which must be unknown to them. It seems clear that, up to the beginning of 1948, the Yugoslav leaders, despite the considerable weight of evidence piling up to the contrary, genuinely thought that the King in Moscow could do no wrong. This belief had been the cement with which Tito had rebuilt the Yugoslav Communist party after he took it over in 1937. It had been the basic inspirational tenet of the communists within the partisan movement. It was only later that Tito realised that by making these respectful complaints in all good faith he was digging his own grave as far as the Soviets were concerned. Just as Djilas had irrevocably blotted his Moscow copybook by a chance remark in 1945 comparing the behaviour of Soviet and British officers,[3] so Tito by the beginning of 1948 was at the point of no return. Continued and successful defiance of Moscow by himself and his faithful band was essential for political and perhaps personal survival. Even had he backed down and recanted, both he and his lieutenants would have been finished.

THE question arises whether Tito would have made his complaints in the first place could he have foreseen the consequences. Very possibly he would not. It is often argued that the underlying reason for the Yugoslav, Chinese, and Albanian deviations from Moscow is that in these three countries the communists came to power by their own exertions,

---

[2] *The Soviet-Yugoslav Dispute: Text of the Published Correspondence* (London, Royal Institute of International Affairs, 1948), p. 19.
[3] Ibid., p. 13.

largely independently of and, in China's case, in spite of the Soviet Union. Consequently these parties were proud and self-conscious, had their own way of looking at things and would, by their very nature, fail at some time or other to go along with the Soviet Union. This is a valid argument but it can be overstated and become a facile explanation for a very complex series of problems. In the case of Albania, for example, the ' bootstraps ' theory has certainly been overplayed. The Albanian Communist party was the creation and creature of Tito. Immediately after the war the communist regime could not have survived without Yugoslavia. In 1948 Hoxha simply changed protectors and in 1960-1961 he did the same again. This is not to detract either from the heroism of the Albanian partisans or from the desperate courage of Enver Hoxha. It is simply to say that the Albanian state and its ruling circles have always been dependent on some protector or other.

In Yugoslavia there is no doubt that the partisans won through largely by their own exertions. But it was precisely in the Yugoslav party that the notion of the country becoming a Soviet republic was very strong, not only in the rank and file but also among the leaders.[4] To offend the Soviet Union was a mortal sin, and if Tito had not been so naive until it was too late he might well have refrained from provoking the enmity of Stalin in spite of the most extreme provocation. Where the argument about indigenously based parties holds completely true is when the conflict breaks out. Then the unity forged during the lonely struggle gives a party the will, strength, and character to hold out, although, again, had Yugoslavia been an occupied country this would, of course, have been impossible. The dazed Yugoslav party remained united and jumped together into the dark. Without its wartime inspiration it would probably have disintegrated in disastrous factionalism. That the rank and file had always needed Tito had been an accepted fact. In 1948 Tito and his lieutenants needed them and the Yugoslav people in their struggle for power with Stalin.

It is never very difficult to project a personal struggle or consideration on to a wider plane. In Tito's case, given the nature of his complaints against Stalin, the fact that they implied the domination of his country by the Soviet Union, that in political terms in 1948 his interests were those of the Yugoslav state, and that here the nation as well as the party were behind him, the transition from a power struggle to a national struggle was a smooth, almost automatic one. Something personal became something national, and Tito became the eponymous villain who gave his name to every act of defiance against the Soviet Union and to every communist who put his own country's interest before the interest of the Soviet Union. ' Titoism ' and ' national communism ' became synonymous.

---

[4] This was not confined to eventual traitors like Zhujovic. Kardelj, for one, apparently entertained the idea. See Ulam, op. cit., pp. 128–129, and *The Soviet-Yugoslav Dispute*, p. 38.

Thus the first crack in the cohesion of the Soviet bloc came in 1948 and was caused by a Balkan country. Was there anything essentially Balkan in this fact, or in the mental and psychological approach which made it happen? It is difficult to give a wholly affirmative answer to the first part of the question convincing enough to stand the test of serious enquiry. But some valid historical allusions can be made. Historically, the Balkans have been a prey to the ambitions of great powers, foreign penetration being facilitated by convenient communication routes through the difficult mountain terrain.[5] In late medieval and modern times the dominant power in the Balkans was, of course, the Ottoman Empire. This domination was preceded by a period when the Bulgarians, Serbs, and Rumanians in turn carved out great empires for themselves. The Ottoman yoke did not affect national feelings nor interfere with religious belief, and it at least gave the peoples the freedom to dream about their past national glories. In the nineteenth century the struggle for deliverance against the common oppressor encouraged an aggressive national selfconsciousness. In Serbia and Montenegro, as well as in Bulgaria, there also grew up the image of Russia as the Slav messiah, the liberator of the enslaved Slav peoples, and here, of course, the bond of a common Orthodox religion played an important part. Coupled with these factors, and in part bred by them, were the irrationality, the extremism, and the violent temperament of the people, their readiness to take the most appalling and often senseless risks.

Tito and his closest followers were fanatical communists who had self-consciously renounced their heritage. Some of them, of course, as Croatians (Tito) or Slovenes (Kardelj) had little connection with it. But the heritage could not be renounced completely; to take a single but not unrepresentative case, the turbulent career of Milovan Djilas shows him to be a true son of Montenegro. As for irrationality, it can, of course, be argued that Tito's desire to save himself from Stalin's wrath was hardly an irrational one, but the Yugoslav's readiness to go naked into a hostile world recalls the heroically ' senseless ' action of the reactionary General Simovic in defying Hitler only seven years before. It was also the extremism of character which caused the sudden and violent reversal of feelings towards Russia so soon after the break. If ever there was a god that failed it was the Soviet Union in the Balkans.

Even if Tito and the top ranks of the Yugoslav party were not greatly influenced by these factors, a large proportion of the relatively new communists and the masses of the population were. And Tito certainly knew this and relied on it. Hence in June 1948 he had more popular support than he ever had before or has had since. The communist hero became a national hero.

IT is when discussing the aftermath of the 1948 break that the history and the character of the Balkans play an important and definable role.

[5] Cf. Robert L. Wolff, *The Balkans in Our Time* (Harvard, 1956).

If the Balkan area has been fairly easy to control from the outside, internally it lends itself to the most serious type of fragmentation. A number of causes, geographical, historical, ethnic, and religious, have generated separatisms and enmities which have given the Balkans an unenviable notoriety. Always conscious of their past glories and intoxicated by the joy of delivery from servitude, each new state tended to see itself as the direct heir of its medieval forerunner. Such aspirations were impossible to achieve completely and led after independence to disastrous clashes. Nor did the interference of the great European powers, whether in direct self-interest or the desire to preserve a balance of power, help matters. The state boundaries which emerged in the 20th century left a trail of bitterness and resentment, and the still unsatiated territorial demands of some of the larger Balkan states created genuine fear amongst the smaller.

The smallest state in the Balkans is Albania. By no one in the Balkans or the Adriatic had the Albanians ever been taken seriously, and it is true that, despite strong folk traditions and the possession of a worthy national hero in Scanderbeg, they seem to have found it much easier to absorb themselves into a foreign pattern than their Balkan neighbours.[6] The Albanian state was created in 1913 only because Austria wished to check Serbian designs on the area. When liberation finally came, the Albanian patriots not only had to begin stirring up the dormant national consciousness of their people, they had to evade the greedy demands of their more powerful neighbours that their territory be divided. Indeed, Albania barely survived the first world war; it was only Wilson's insistence on national self-determination that prevented the secret treaty of London of 1915, authorising a partition of the country, from being implemented.

But the danger persisted, most obviously from fascist Italy. Albania's ' natural ' enemy, however, was Serbia, now the conscious master of the new Yugoslavia which included some 700,000 Albanians of the Kossovo-Metohija region. This area had been ceded to Serbia by the Treaty of Bucharest in 1913. Palpably dependent on foreign support for its very survival, Albania's problem was how to take the money without rendering the service. In 1924 the north Albanian landlord-chieftain Ahmed Zogu rode into Tirana on a white horse provided by the Yugoslavs, with promises of financial support from the same source. But, mainly because of internal economic and financial difficulties, the Yugoslav pump dried up. Zogu (soon to assume the throne) next turned to Rome and there submitted to the fatal embrace which, though it benefited Albania a good deal materially, was to end on Good Friday 1939 with Italian troops in Tirana.

6 For a most perceptive and stimulating explanation relating the traditional internationalism of the Albanians with the causes of the current dispute with the Soviet Union, see William E. Griffith, ' An International Communism? Peiping, Tirana and Moscow: Polycentrism in Practice ', *East Europe*, July 1961.

After the war the players were different but the game was very much as before. The Italian danger had gone but communist Albania was now the puppet of communist Yugoslavia. Despite the common ideology which both countries now at least superficially shared, there were understandable reasons for Albanian hatred and fear of Yugoslavia. The Belgrade regime was now quite clearly the strongest in the Balkans, and there was no longer an ambitious power across the Adriatic against which she could be played off. Tito was regarded as Stalin's favourite protégé and the Soviet Union was the overlord of the whole area. Moreover, Tito was dizzy with success. Under the guise of a plan for Balkan federation, he was seeking to bring Albania, Pirin Macedonia, and even the whole of Bulgaria under his control. Balkan federation looked like Serbian chauvinism writ large.

For Albania there was both a greater will and a greater need to resist Yugoslav domination than ever before. In the first place a more than embryonic Albanian national political consciousness had now come into being, fostered by King Zog who, for all his concessions to Mussolini, had done much to further the notion of Albanian unity. This consciousness had been tremendously strengthened by the wartime struggles not only of the communists but of other resistance movements like the Balli Kombetar and Legalitei. At the end of the war most Albanians were ready to resist Greek claims to Northern Epirus and resented Yugoslavia's re-acquisition of the Kosmet with its preponderantly Albanian population.[7]

I T was this question of the Kosmet which after 1945 brought a new element into the Albanian regime's fear of Yugoslavia. The Albanian people are divided into Ghegs and Tosks, differentiated by the two principal dialects of the Albanian language,[8] separated roughly by the River Shkumbini. Historically, the Ghegs north of the Shkumbini had dominated the Tosks. Primitive, with a society organised on closely knit tribal lines, they had lorded it over the slightly less primitive Tosks who, rather more numerous than the Gheg, consisted largely of a few great landowners and many exploited peasants. Educational standards in this area were higher, and some students went abroad to study. Many came back convinced radicals. The first break with the traditional Gheg predominance came in 1924 when the Harvard-educated Orthodox bishop Fan Noli, himself a good example of the first radical wave of returning students, assumed power for a few months.[9] His government was soon swamped by Zog, himself a Gheg chieftain, and the country settled down to another 15 years of Gheg predominance. During this period the Albanian communist movement was slowly evolving and most of its

---

[7] In 1941 the Kosmet had been placed by the Axis powers under the administration of the Albanian puppet government.

[8] On this fascinating question of Ghegs and Tosks see R. V. Burks, *The Dynamics of Communism in Eastern Europe* (Princeton, 1961), pp. 144–149.

[9] Bishop Fan Noli is now head of the Albanian Orthodox Church in America and lives in Boston.

leading members were Tosks. Enver Hoxha, the young man who was to become their leader, spent the six years from 1930 to 1936 as a singularly unsuccessful wandering scholar in France and Belgium. He himself was a Tosk from Djinokaster and the Tosk majority in the upper echelons of his regime after liberation has been striking.[10]

In 1945, therefore, the Tosks had, for almost the first time in the nation's history, a political as well as numerical predominance. They meant to keep it that way and cowed the Ghegs by resorting to the most severe oppression. But the fear of Gheg predominance has persisted, now transferred largely to the Ghegs in the Kosmet in Yugoslavia. All the Albanians under Tito are Ghegs.[11] If these ever combined with the Ghegs in Albania, the Tosks would lose their numerical and political domination and many of them would lose their heads as well. Hence the gripping fear of Tito's ambitions, no matter how they may be hidden in the ' internationalism ' of the Balkan Federation scheme. The Cominform denunciation of the Yugoslavs gave the Albanians their chance of throwing off Yugoslav domination and danger, established during and after the war.

When the tough and experienced Yugoslav emissaries came into Albania at the beginning of the war they found the communists there (or at least the people who called themselves communists) riddled by factionalism. With professional skill and ruthlessness they reduced the chaos to manageable dimensions and got the Albanian Communist party off the ground on 8 November 1941. They agreed to Hoxha's leadership, but never really trusted this cosmopolitan dandy who had picked up too much education and too many bourgeois habits during his years in Western Europe. Their man was Koce Xoxe, a worker like most of them were. Xoxe became the Yugoslavs' principal agent within the Albanian party and as Minister of the Interior after the war he was probably the most powerful man in the regime. With Yugoslav support he built up an impressive apparatus and seems to have pursued a steady policy of isolating Hoxha.[12] By 1948 both Tito and Hoxha were looking at the writing on the wall. In Tito's case the writing was Stalin's, in Hoxha's case it was Tito's.

Personal considerations of power and the struggle to retain it did, therefore, play an important part in Hoxha's first act of ' national communism '. Even in the broader issues of Tosk versus Gheg the reason for the fear of Yugoslavia was not so much national as sectional. This is not to deny that here, too, as in the case of Yugoslavia, nationalist concern was not the main general reason for the action taken but again

---

10 ' Of 27 key communist leaders of the post-war period some 19, or two-thirds, came from south of the Shkumbini.' Burks, op. cit., p. 147.

11 It is true that the Albanians in the Kosmet have come to some extent to regard themselves as a third Albanian group and many call themselves Kossovars. But in the last analysis they are Ghegs and the Tosks certainly regard them as such.

12 It was during this period of Xoxe's influence that Mehmet Shehu, typically outspoken in his anti-Yugoslav attitude, and Liri Belishova, later to become a pro-Soviet ' traitor ' were in disgrace.

it was the case of the nationalism being preceded and stiffened by reasons of a very pressing personal or sectional nature.

TITO'S expulsion from the communist camp in 1948 caused serious convulsions among all the ruling communist parties in Europe. Practically all the victims of these convulsions had Titoism or 'national communism' included in the fantastic indictments presented against them. In Rumania Lucretiu Patrascanu was imprisoned, Traicho Kostov was hanged in Bulgaria, and, of course, Koce Xoxe met his death in Albania. After June 1948 there was a conscious and successful effort on the part of the Soviets to tighten their grip on the satellites and to standardise their political, economic, and social development. Stalin had realised this need even earlier and the establishment of the Cominform in September 1947 was designed to meet it. The Tito incident only served to intensify these efforts towards *Gleichschaltung*. Purges in the parties threw to the top or to the positions of real influence people of whom Moscow could be absolutely sure.

In Albania Enver Hoxha became the biggest Stalinist of them all. Now a Soviet satellite of full status, he revelled in the anti-Tito onslaught, and could afford to ignore the disturbing rumour that Stalin had once offered his country to Yugoslavia.[13] The situation had now changed and he knew it. He was safe, his Tosks were safe, his country was safe. But situations have a habit of changing more than once. In 1953 Stalin died, and no one watched the ensuing struggle in the Kremlin more keenly than did Enver Hoxha. The man who emerged victorious exceeded his worst fears. In intra-bloc policy Khrushchev immediately showed himself a fence-mender. His first object was to improve relations with the two communist countries where 'national communism' had done most harm, China at the far eastern end of the communist world and Yugoslavia at the far western. In 1954 he visited Peking and much more generous terms of alliance were drawn up; in May 1955 he visited Belgrade. His aim was to bring Yugoslavia back into the fold and to do this he was prepared to make a number of concessions. At the Tito-Khrushchev meeting the Yugoslav leader made part of his price the removal of some of his enemies, Rakosi, probably Chervenkov, and, of course, Hoxha. It needed no great perception on Hoxha's part to realise that something like this was brewing. The following eighteen months were probably the most tense he had spent since coming to power. Two of Tito's arch enemies, Rakosi and Chervenkov, were removed, Stalin was denounced at the 20th CPSU congress, the whole foundation on which he had built his power seemed to be crumbling. Finally, the Hungarian revolution spread its tremors to Albania. But Hoxha survived, not because he had behind him a determined and united party, but through a combination of traditional Albanian clan nepotism, patronage, terror, and great skill, plus his fortunate geographical isolation from the rest of the socialist camp.

13 Vladimir Dedijer, *Tito Speaks* (London, 1954), p. 320.

The Belgrade meeting of 1955 was, therefore, the beginning of an entirely new situation for the Albanian communist leaders. Tito was being courted by Moscow and was agreeing to the courtship only on certain conditions which were highly dangerous to them.

AGAIN, as in 1948, the question of power was involved as well as national considerations. The circumstances of the Albanian differences with Moscow beginning in 1955, and the Yugoslav differences with Moscow prior to 1948, were, of course, not the same. But, in the last analysis, the bones of contention were similar. With both sets of leaders it was a question of power and survival. In the case of Hoxha and company it was probably even more a question of survival. One must assume that after 1948 the Soviet ambassador in Albania did not consider the feelings of Hoxha or Shehu when he wanted any information or wanted to summon an Albanian official directly to his Embassy. Hoxha was cheerfully prepared to accept this affront to his dignity so long as his clique stayed in power and his country was protected from the Yugoslavs. After 1955 he was not sure of either. Once he had survived the Hungarian disaster in October 1956 he was probably glad that it had occurred, hoping that it would keep Khrushchev away from any further dalliance with the Yugoslavs.[14] In fact the Khrushchev-Tito courtship was broken off in 1957, and after the Yugoslav party's programme in April 1958 there seemed little hope of reconciliation. During this period Hoxha may have persuaded himself that Khrushchev had been cured of his lunacy, and Khrushchev for his part occasionally found Hoxha's constant and virulent attacks on the Yugoslavs useful. But in 1959 the Soviet leader, in the context of his international policy, evidently decided that he needed Yugoslav support, and his trip to Tirana in May of that year was probably an attempt to forestall dangerous repercussions. With his disillusion complete, Hoxha soon fell into the arms of Mao, who was similarly unconvinced by Khrushchev when visited by him later the same year. And, what was more important for Hoxha, Mao had since 1957 been second only to himself in opposition to the Yugoslavs.

Hoxha, whose interest in the range of ideological questions which have come to divide Moscow and Peking was wholly secondary compared with his views on Yugoslavia (and Greece), saw Mao as a suitable saviour. Whereas China's hostility to Yugoslavia sprang from her approach to a wide range of ideological and political problems, Albania's approach to a wide range of ideological and political problems sprang from her hatred of Yugoslavia. Mao represented the second greatest power in the communist bloc; he and his party had tremendous international prestige. China was the only force which might be able to make Khrushchev

[14] The first camp onslaught on Tito after the Hungarian revolution was in an article by Hoxha in *Pravda* (8 November 1956) ostensibly written to commemorate the 15th anniversary of the founding of the Albanian party.

change his mind. China, too, was able to supply Albania with the
economic help necessary at least to keep her going, and Chinese moral
support would, it was thought, protect Albania from any serious consequences of Soviet anger. Hoxha was shrewd enough to realise that the
Soviet bloc had changed greatly since Stalin's day. Much more freedom
of action was now possible and the emergence of China put power relations within the bloc in an altogether new light. All these calculations
were right. Where Hoxha did miscalculate was the extent to which
Khrushchev was prepared to gamble to get his way. He found out at the
22nd CPSU congress. Hoxha is a poker player of some repute but
Khrushchev called him on 17 October 1961.

It would be irrelevant to relate the course of the Albanian-Soviet
dispute here, but as it developed, the nationalistic viewpoint of the
Albanians became more clear.[15] The fear of Yugoslavia became if anything more intense. A new element in this fear were the developments,
alarming from the Albanian point of view, in the Kosmet. There Tito had
carried out a liberal policy of autonomy, had improved the standard of
living far beyond anything in Albania, and had built a quite impressive
educational system with a university at Pristina. He had not done this
for nothing. The glitter of the Kosmet was to serve as a reminder to the
Ghegs of northern Albania that they would be better off under Yugoslav
rule, while the educated elite being trained there were to be the cadres in
case that rule ever became an actuality. In 1960, to add to this permanent
threat from Yugoslavia, came what must have seemed to Hoxha a serious
threat from the south. This was the statement by the Greek Liberal
leader, Mr. Sophocles Venizelos, that he had brought up the question of
autonomy for Northern Epirus in a conversation with Khrushchev and
that Khrushchev had promised to look into the matter.[16] Hoxha must
have felt here, quite rightly, that in the interest of his own policy of
coexistence and disarmament Khrushchev was prepared not only to
ignore Albania's national interests, but positively to injure them. This was
another and quite valid reason for Hoxha to beat the nationalist drum.
He has been beating it with an even greater frenzy since the break with
the Soviets came and there is no reason to think that he is not evoking a
genuine response from his countrymen.

IF, then, one agrees that the Albanian leaders' reasons for defying the
Soviet Union were both personal and national, with the one easily
merging into the other, then one can see a basic similarity of origin
between the Yugoslav and Albanian deviations. To the populations of
the two countries the causes must have seemed, and were certainly made

[15] See Griffith, loc. cit., and J. F. Brown, ' Albania, Mirror of Conflict ', *Survey*, January
1962. On Albania and the Sino-Soviet dispute, see Donald S. Zagoria, ' Khrushchev's
Attack on Albania and Sino-Soviet Relations ', *The China Quarterly*, December 1961 ;
Richard Lowenthal, ' Duel with a Shadow ', *Encounter*, February 1962.
[16] *Deutsche Zeitung*, 5 July 1960.

by skilled propaganda, to be much more nationalistic than they actually were, and hence, with Balkan romantic irrationality they strongly supported their regimes. There were other similarities. Both beleaguered parties held surprisingly firm, and even in the few defections there are in fact striking parallels; the Yugoslavs Hebrang and Zhujovic have their Albanian counterparts in Belishova and Tashko: Admiral Teme Sejko was the Albanian Arsa Jovanovic. Both parties were, before the break, 'left extremist' deviationists vis à vis Moscow. Albania is, in fact, likely to remain that way much longer than Yugoslavia. Hoxha's Stalinism had little or nothing to do with his dispute with Khrushchev. Like Gomulka in the other direction, Hoxha could have pleaded specific local conditions and have got away with as much Stalinism as he liked. What brought on the wrath of Khrushchev was Albanian defiance of the Soviet Union on foreign policy and the building of a Chinese bridgehead in an area which the Soviets regard as their exclusive domain. After the break, of course, both Tito and Hoxha were vilified for the repressiveness of their internal policy and a wide variety of ideological charges were made, many of them justified and some probably quite sincere. But this was not what caused either dispute. Mikoyan was much closer to the truth when at the 22nd CPSU congress he charged the Albanian leaders with departing from internationalist positions. 'What nationalism can lead to,' he continued, 'and separation from the socialist camp, is shown by the experience of the revisionists of Yugoslavia.' [17]

There are, of course, many differences in the situation of Yugoslavia in 1948 and of Albania in 1961. One is particularly relevant here. On 29 June 1948 the Yugoslavs were completely alone in the world. Historically it was not a new situation for them, and they faced it with a sort of high-spirited equanimity. On the other hand the Albanian tradition of cleaving to something greater has been maintained in the dependence on China. Furthermore, the Albanians even now insist that they are still members of the camp, as do the Chinese on their behalf, and protest at their exclusion from Comecon or Warsaw Pact sessions. Despite their castigations of Togliatti's polycentric notion, they are acting in a true polycentric fashion. They are building socialism and are therefore, they argue, members of the socialist camp and its organisations. They are allied with China, also a member of the camp. The club is a loose one and they disagree violently with most of its members but they are, they argue, still in it, supported by the second most powerful member.

In the case of Yugoslavia, the camp was much less flexible than it is now, and there was no China. Tito had to go it alone and make an agonising reappraisal of his relations with the West. And here there may be a final and potentially very significant similarity between the two situations. Hoxha, for all the aid and support he is getting from Peking, must realize that China is too far away to be a real protector, and has already been making discreet overtures to the West for the establishment

17 *Pravda*, 21 October 1961.

of diplomatic relations and economic help. Italy has already shown itself
more than willing to be approached. But this willingness has caused a
ruffling of feathers in Belgrade and Athens. The old Balkan-Adriatic
rivalries may be stirred up again because of the new heresy of national
communism.

IN the two other Balkan communist countries, Rumania and Bulgaria,
the story is much shorter and less dramatic. Indeed, in Rumania it
is practically non-existent. Here the conditions necessary for a strong
'national communist' movement were almost completely lacking. The
party for several years after 1945 was woefully weak; if ever a regime was
imposed by force on a country from outside it was the Rumanian. At the
end of the war it numbered fewer than 2,000 members, was demoralised
and torn by factionalism, and had no record of success or achievement.
Furthermore, it was bordered by the Soviet Union and until 1958 had
Soviet troops stationed on its territory.

Probably more than in any other East European country, communism
was regarded as something specifically un-Rumanian. The radical creed
which had attracted many Rumanians was fascism. The loss of Bessarabia
and Northern Bukovina to the Soviets, though it caused indignation
amongst the population, probably caused little opposition in the party,
and, even if it had, this would have counted for little, given the situation
in which the party and country found itself after the war. It is just possible
that, if Hitler's Vienna Award had not been reversed after the war and
Northern Transylvania not handed back to Rumania, even in the supine
Rumanian Communist party there would have been some rumblings.
The situation, however, never arose.

The subjective and objective factors militating against 'national communism' in Rumania make the case of Lucretiu Patrascanu so untypical
for the Rumanian party. On his arrest in February 1948 he was accused
of nationalist deviations on the questions of the Magyar minority, and
there are some grounds for believing that he resented the blatant Soviet
economic exploitation of Rumania. There may, of course, have been
others who thought like him, but if there were, Patrascanu's case acted as
a grim deterrent, and 'national communism' became a dead issue in
Rumania.

The situation of the Communist party in Bulgaria was markedly
different. There it had always been strong and mainly Bulgarian
ethnically. It was the oldest and most powerful Communist party in the
Balkans and had given a whole galaxy of talent to the international
movement. It was, therefore, a self-confident party and many of its members had a considerable record as partisans in the second world war.
Their achievements were, of course, nothing like those of the Yugoslavs,
but there was a good deal of similarity between the Bulgarian and the
Yugoslav parties at the end of the war. They were also similar in their
rather naive devotion to the USSR.

It was precisely because of their traditions and their devotion to the Soviet Union that many Bulgarian communists must have begun to feel disillusioned well before the end of the war. They now saw themselves pushed aside as the Soviet favourite in the Balkans by the Yugoslav party. This was apparent in several ways, but it hurt most in the change of the Soviet attitude toward Macedonia, the hottest of several hot potatoes in the Balkan area. The Bulgarian communists were true nationalists in that they considered the whole of Macedonia to be Bulgarian, and at first the Soviets had supported their cause. But the growing successes of Tito's partisans and the reluctance of the Bulgarian communists to agree to an armed uprising early in the war [18] caused the Soviets to change their minds. By 1945 Tito's partisans controlled Vardar Macedonia and the Yugoslav party had the greatest power and reputation in south-east Europe. Since 1943 the Soviets had regarded them rather than the Bulgarians as controlling Macedonia. This must have been a bitter pill indeed for many Bulgarian communists to swallow; both their national and their communist pride had been assaulted. Nor could many of them have felt much enthusiasm for the Balkan Federation plan which Tito was pushing at the time with Moscow's blessing. Certainly not the way that Tito envisaged it—with Bulgaria being the seventh federal state along with the six Yugoslav states, Albania to be thrown in later. It is true that the Bulgarian Dimitrov was also pushing the plan (if not quite as Tito saw it), and when Stalin scotched the scheme and humiliated Dimitrov in January 1948 many Bulgarian communists must have been relieved. When Tito was denounced in 1948 many must have been enthusiastic.

If this analysis is correct there must have been a good deal of 'Titoism' or 'national communism' in the Bugarian Communist party between 1944 and 1948. In many ways it was strikingly similar to the Albanians' national communism in 1960-1961, being based on fear of Yugoslavia and disillusion over the Soviet Union's policy of favouring her. Had Tito not suddenly changed from favourite son to whipping boy, national communism' might have loomed very large in the Bulgarian party.

As it was, it produced one true martyr in the person of Traicho Kostov. Until his dramatic fall in March 1949, Kostov, though number three in the hierarchy after Dimitrov and Kolarov, was probably the man who actually ran the country. He was a fanatical communist, a believer in rapid industrialisation and the collectivisation of agriculture. But he was very much a Bulgarian communist. He had opposed the Balkan Federation plan at a time when the Soviets were supporting it. This, of course, made him a marked man. But this was by no means all, for, in what he

[18] As recently as October 1961 this question was the subject of an angry exchange between Yugoslavia and Bulgaria. It was initiated by a series of articles in the Skoplje daily *Nova Makedonja* and taken up by the Macedonian party secretary, Lazar Kolishevski, in a speech in Prilep on 11 October. *Rabotnichesko Delo* of 16 October gave a furious answer to Kolishevski but never addressed itself to the Yugoslav charge that the Bulgarian communists had shied away from an armed uprising in Macedonia in 1941.

considered to be the interests of Bulgarian communism, he used to worry the Russians for more economic help than they were prepared to give and, more seriously, had the courage to express openly his resentment at the looting of his country by the Russians. This was indeed ' national communism ' and he paid for it with his life in December 1949.

Georgi Dimitrov died a few months before Kostov was executed and Vassil Kolarov died shortly afterwards. The deaths in quick succession of the three top Bulgarian communists left the way open for the Muscovite Chervenkov who became Bulgaria's ' little Stalin '. Chervenkov ruled the country from 1950 to April 1956; in March 1954 he gave up the nominal leadership of the party to Todor Zhivkov, in a deferential gesture to the collective leadership principle enunciated after Stalin's death, but this did not affect his real power. Chervenkov's demotion in 1956 (he retained his Politburo seat and was made a vice-premier) was due to a number of interrelated causes, among them his antipathy to Tito. There is little evidence to connect Chervenkov in any way with ' national communism '. His hatred for the Yugoslav party was mainly that of a well-trained Stalinist dogmatist for revisionism. This also explains his antipathy towards Khrushchev, which seems to have been accompanied by a growing fascination with the dazzling militancy of Mao both in domestic and particularly in foreign policy. His attitude may have had a fair measure of support in a party which has always taken its Marxism-Leninism seriously, and for other reasons too. There was probably dislike of Khrushchev's persistent attempts at rapprochement with Belgrade not because Tito was a revisionist but because he was a Yugoslav. If the main reason for the Albanians' deviation was their fear of Yugoslavia, then it would follow that there must exist a number of grounds for a Bulgarian deviation. In 1955, when the Soviets made their first approach to Belgrade, it was only eight years since an ebullient Tito had been hoping to make Bulgaria the seventh Yugoslav state, only eight years since it had been agreed in principle to concede even Pirin Macedonia to Yugoslavia. If a Belgrade-Moscow rapprochement ever became a fact, what concessions might not a self-confident Tito force on an unpredictable Khrushchev?

But Tito, as well as Hoxha, has his admirers in Bulgaria. The picture of every Bulgarian as a flaming irredentist with the name of San Stefano engraved on his heart is overdrawn. Opposed to this attitude is another which, for many years, has favoured some form of association with Yugoslavia (on equal terms) and has worked constantly to bury the old enmity. This was Stamboliski's policy after World War I; it received a set-back with his murder in 1923, but it persisted. No doubt Dimitrov, out of touch though he was with Bulgarian opinion in 1945, had support for his policy of union. Moreover, Tito's independence, and the relatively fortunate position he has carved out for his country, have aroused envy, reflected in the steady persistence of a small, but potentially powerful, ' revisionist ' wing in the party. It was submerged in 1957 when Chankov,

Terpeshev, and Panov were dismissed from the central committee. But in the spring of 1961 this group appeared again, and, though derided by the regime as ' piteously small ', was obviously important enough to cause considerable concern.[19] Certainly, for many citizens in Bulgaria, 17 years of communist rule have created a state of mind in which anybody who stands up to the Russians is something of a hero, and it is this that accounts for the admiration not only of Tito but also of Hoxha. The present Zhivkov leadership is, therefore, faced with an opposition inspired by a number of often wildly conflicting motives. Its only comfort is that most of it is passive and much of it almost purely instinctive.

* * * *

What has happened in the Balkan communist world since 1948 has happened in societies where the old systems of economic and social relationships had been or were in the process of being broken down. The events were brought on by leaders or groups of men who were completely different from the governing classes of the pre-war days, and who were firmly dedicated to an ideal which proclaimed that it made such happenings impossible because it rendered the motives which prompt them irrelevant and obsolete. Yet what has emerged from this analysis is a situation surprisingly similar to that which prevailed in the pre-communist era. The communists have a ready-made and simple explanation of why these things went on previously, and Moscow, with its accusations of ' bourgeois nationalism ', has a ready-made and simple explanation of why they persist. This is quite true. But to use such formulations is to make the mistake of thinking, or implying, that this ' bourgeois nationalism ' is just a piece of capitalist wreckage floating about in a smooth socialist sea. The truth is that throughout the world, and nowhere more so than in the Balkans, ' bourgeois nationalism ' buttressed by personal self-interest is still a most powerful driving force of political action. This certainly emerges from the study of development in communist Yugoslavia and Albania and, to a considerable degree, in communist Bulgaria. In the Balkans, more than elsewhere in Europe, nationalism did not mean achievement, stability, and security. It meant frustration, bitterness, and fear, and the new communist leaders shared these passions. This did not mean they were unaffected by ideological considerations. The ideological arguments they used against each other and against Moscow were not artificial, but they were largely a rationalisation of more primitive drives, the superstructure built over them. This is the most ironical feature of a situation full of ironies and paradoxes. A creed predicated on internationalism has not produced cohesion in the Balkans; it has simply added a new dimension to the very many differences which have tragically divided the area.

[19] See *Partien Zivot*, March 1961, and *Novo Vreme*, April 1961.

EAST GERMANY

Evelyn Anderson

EAST GERMANY's position in the Soviet orbit is marked by a series of striking paradoxes. Among the satellite leaders (not counting the Albanians) Walter Ulbricht is today the most typical Stalinist; yet he is also one of Stalin's earliest public critics and one of Mr Khrushchev's most dependable supporters. Within the Soviet camp the GDR plays a decisive part as the ' westernmost bastion of socialism '; yet, as one of the visibly most oppressive and most crisis-ridden of all Soviet outposts, it is for the Soviet leaders also a source of chronic political embarrassment. Industrially, East Germany is far more advanced than the rest of the satellites, and yet it suffers from more severe and more frequent economic setbacks and crises than all the others. It is nowadays the USSR's biggest and most valued trading partner; yet, at the same time, also one of its costliest economic liabilities. East German wages and living standards are considerably above those of the Russian people; yet the Soviet Union must continue to support East Germany with large amounts of economic aid. Perhaps most important of all—the GDR is a fully developed totalitarian state; yet it is in no sense a nation and not even half a country.

In view of all these contradictions, and the dilemmas which they pose, it would not have been surprising if Moscow's policy vis-à-vis the GDR had been rather more wavering and inconsistent than it has actually been. Yet, in recent years at least, the frequent impression of Soviet hesitations and inconsistencies seems to have been created by changing Soviet propaganda needs rather than by actual changes in policy. No doubt there are many ways in which Khrushchev may yet modify his attitude to the Ulbricht regime, but on the most vital issue there is no longer any hesitation. We cannot know for certain precisely when the Soviet leaders decided finally to abandon the project of German reunification and to give their full backing to Ulbricht's policy of East German separatism, but there cannot be much doubt that this had ceased to be an open question long before the Berlin wall went up in August of last year.

OPTING FOR SEPARATISM

Most likely the final decision in favour of separatism was taken during or just after the international communist conference in Moscow in November 1957. It was immediately after that conference that the Soviet Union first launched its drive for a summit conference with a flood of notes and Bulganin letters to the statesmen of the West suggesting a final settlement of East-West conflicts. It was also immediately after that conference that Ulbricht felt at last free publicly to announce that his opponents in the SED (communist party) leadership—the Schirdewan group—had been ousted for deviations in which the re-unification issue played a decisive part. Re-unification was not the only issue at stake, but it was central, just as it had been in the case of the most prominent earlier anti-Ulbricht faction, the Zaisser-Herrnstadt group, expelled in 1953. Ulbricht himself has drawn attention to this connection on more than one occasion. He did so again only a few months ago, at the SED central committee meeting in November 1961, where he spoke at enormous length about the 22nd CPSU congress and its lessons for the SED. Both his speech, and the resolution adopted by the meeting, repeated the charge that the Zaisser-Herrnstadt faction had taken up Beria's policy [1] of opposing the building of socialism in the German Democratic Republic and of favouring capitulation to the German Federal Republic, while the Schirdewan-Wollweber-Ziller group was once again accused of having failed to understand that the 'national question' could, in existing conditions, be solved only by strengthening to the utmost the power of the 'Workers and Peasants State' and by concentrating on the building of socialism in the GDR. [2]

Ulbricht's own decision to forsake re-unification for the policy of 'building socialism' in a separatist East German state is easy enough to understand. It was the only possible course to provide him and his regime with a chance of political survival. But for several years after its first proclamation, in May 1952, he could not feel sure that this policy would in the long run have Soviet backing. And without Soviet backing, as the rebellion of June 1953 demonstrated, his regime could not have survived for a day.

Soviet policy on this issue seems in fact to have remained undecided right up to the autumn of 1957. Among other indications, this is suggested by the secret minutes of the SED central committee meeting in October 1957, extracts from which have since been published in the West. [3] It was at that meeting that Ulbricht criticised SED leaders who favoured a policy of relaxation and a slowing down of 'socialist construction' so as to keep the door open for re-unification. But although he stressed that this was a basic issue, he did not elaborate the theme because, as he explained, he was making only an interim speech. The subject would have to be taken up again at the next central committee meeting, and by then it would probably be possible to spell out things which so far had been left unsaid and to draw practical conclusions.

This speech suggested that Ulbricht, at that time, was still very unsure how far he could go without a fresh mandate from Moscow. He left for Moscow almost immediately afterwards, and by the time the next central committee meeting was convened, in February 1958, he had clearly

[1] That this was also one of the unpublished Soviet accusations against Beria has since been reported by several independent witnesses. Cf. Wolfgang Leonhard, *Kreml ohne Stalin*, p. 109 ff.

[2] *Neues Deutschland*, 28 November, 1961.

[3] *Frankfurter Allgemeine Zeitung*, 15 January, 1958.

secured all the backing he still required. He had evidently been given a free hand to deal with his opponents, the Schirdewan group. They were promptly removed from the leadership because, as the official indictment explained, they had failed, among other things, to understand how dangerous it was to pursue the goal of German re-unification at all costs. So far as East Germany is concerned, the quest for re-unification—or, as the SED usually puts it, re-unification at all costs—rated from that time onwards as revisionist deviation Number One. If Hungarian, Polish, and Yugoslav communists were denounced as heretics because they wanted to pursue national policies of their own, East German communists henceforth were heretics if they persisted in their desire to re-create their nation. Like other national communists elsewhere in the Soviet orbit, they were also advocates of an all-round thaw and of more liberal and more humane policies in all fields—policies which in East Germany are usually described as the policy of the safety-valve. In fact, in the East German version of revisionism, the two goals, re-unification and the liberalisation of GDR policies, have always been inextricably mixed.

Most likely it was the shock of the Hungarian and Polish events in the autumn of 1956 and of the revisionist infection which, after the 20th CPSU congress, had spread through all parts of the Soviet empire, that made Khrushchev more willing than he had hitherto been to give Ulbricht his full backing for his separatist East German policy. Ulbricht, it is true, had been one of those out-and-out Stalinists whom Khrushchev seemed determined to dislodge from power. There were even indications that Ulbricht had gambled on Molotov's victory at the time of the crucial power struggle in the Kremlin between Khrushchev and the anti-party group.[4] But Ulbricht had chosen his moment well. Revisionism, right then, was the 'main danger', and if, in East Germany at least, it could be kept under control only with the aid of Ulbricht's methods and Ulbricht's policies, then this course had to be adopted. Other considerations arising from the Soviet Union's overall strategy in the great East-West contest seem to have reinforced rather than weakened Ulbricht's case, and he was evidently able to convince Khrushchev that, provided only he was backed in the GDR, he in turn would serve Khrushchev with the same unswerving loyalty with which he had served Stalin.

So far at least this bargain has been scrupulously kept by both sides, and there is nothing to indicate that it will not also be kept in the future.

ULBRICHT BACKS KHRUSHCHEV

On every important controversial issue up till now Ulbricht has promptly and publicly sided with Khrushchev, even though he did so in some

---

[4] A former member of the Harich group, Manfred Hertwig, who after a term of imprisonment in the GDR escaped to the West, has reported that during his interrogation in the spring of 1957 the East German Attorney General Melsheimer told him with perfect candour: 'You seem to have bet on Khrushchev, and then you discovered too late that the man of the future is Molotov.' *Unteilbares Deutschland*, No. 4, 1960.

instances with an obvious lack of enthusiasm. But the private misgivings he may have had, and presumably still has, about the whole de-Stalinisation campaign did not prevent him from supporting it fully in public. And that, after all, was what mattered. After the 20th CPSU congress Ulbricht was in fact the first communist leader outside the Soviet Union publicly to criticise Stalin's personality cult and to inform the astonished East German communists that it would from now on be quite wrong to count Stalin among the classics of Marxism-Leninism.[5] After the 22nd CPSU congress he was equally prompt to order the renaming of the streets, factories, and cities which had been called after Stalin and to express his full support for all that had been said and resolved at the Soviet Party congress, including the renewed denunciations of Stalin and the anti-party group.

No doubt, during the period when the 'main danger' was revisionism, Ulbricht's championship of Khrushchev was rather more wholehearted than before and since. But even after the anti-revisionist campaign had died down and other issues had come to the fore, he never withheld his support. As soon as the Soviet-Albanian dispute had reached a point where reconciliation could no longer be expected, i.e. after the international Moscow meeting of November 1960, Ulbricht immediately went on record with an attack on the Albanian leaders for their 'dogmatic and sectarian concepts'[6]—a full ten months before Khrushchev himself did so in public. More vehement denunciations of the Albanians followed in Ulbricht's SED central committee report on the 22nd CPSU congress. And, to leave no doubt at all about his unconditional loyalty to Moscow, he also launched another attack on those who doubted or denied the Soviet Union's and the CPSU's 'leading role'.

Only on the Sino-Soviet conflict did Ulbricht, for a short time at least, seem to hesitate or waver. In October 1959, when relations between Russia and China were already visibly strained, Ulbricht made a speech commemorating the tenth anniversary of the Chinese People's Republic in which he specially emphasised that the Chinese Communist party, and Mao Tse-tung personally, had enriched Marxism-Leninism—a speech which might well have conveyed the impression that among the living masters Mao counted for rather more than Khrushchev.[7] Nor was that all. At about the same time the SED journal *Einheit* published a highly appreciative article on the controversial Chinese communes by Paul Wandel, Ulbricht's Ambassador in Peking (and one of Ulbricht's former revisionist opponents). Soon afterwards two important SED delegations, both headed by Politbureau members (Hermann Matern and the late Heinrich Rau) visited Peking in quick succession, and Matern, too, praised the Chinese communes, while Moscow continued to treat them with eloquent silence.

5 *Neues Deutschland*, 4 and 18 March, 1956.
6 *Ibid.*, 18 December, 1960.
7 *Ibid.*, 2 October, 1959.

These flirtations with the Chinese, however, stopped once the latent Sino-Soviet conflict had become manifest. After the Peking WFTU congress in June 1960, at which Soviet and Chinese delegates had advanced openly conflicting views on basic issues, Ulbricht fell into line with his Soviet patrons. But although, from that time on, the relevant anti-Chinese articles in the Soviet press on peaceful co-existence and related themes were promptly and prominently reproduced in the GDR, there still occurred some mishaps. In June 1960 the *Thüringische Landeszeitung* approvingly quoted the Chinese representative at a current agricultural exhibition in East Germany who had claimed that the system of communes had universal validity and that the communes were in fact 'the highest form of collective farming'. Shortly afterwards, on 21 June 1960, the day of the opening of the Bucharest conference, the (East German) *Berliner Zeitung* published an article by Professor Heymann, Chief of the Press and Information department of the GDR Foreign Ministry, which not only echoed, in general terms, all the current Chinese views on war and peace and imperialism, but approvingly quoted Mao's description of the imperialists as 'paper tigers'—a term which also appeared in the headline of the article.

Whether these were the ingenuous aberrations of people who had not yet grasped how the wind was blowing, or deliberate attempts to spread pro-Chinese propaganda, they were quickly corrected and do not seem to have been repeated since. The main SED organ, *Neues Deutschland* (17 June), promptly took the *Thüringische Landeszeitung* to task for publishing the Chinese speech on the communes without critical comment, and reproved those who 'attempt to create the impression that China's way from agrarian reform via agricultural co-operatives to the people's communes is valid also for other countries'. And, after Ulbricht's return from the Bucharest conference, the *Berliner Zeitung* published an authoritative sharp rejoinder to Heymann's pro-Chinese article. Ulbricht's own report on the Bucharest conference left no doubt whatsoever that he was firmly on the Khrushchev line, and a *Neues Deutschland* editorial (26 July) on the same subject openly and indignantly hinted at the quarrels during the Bucharest conference, which at that time had not yet been publicly revealed anywhere else in the communist world. After the 22nd CPSU congress Ulbricht's support for Khrushchev's anti-Albanian and anti-Chinese policies became even more emphatic. He not only denounced the Albanians but also criticised the Chinese for their failure to support Khrushchev against Albania.[8]

KHRUSHCHEV BACKS ULBRICHT

While the Chinese demonstrated their displeasure with Ulbricht's open criticism by staying away, for the first time in eleven years, from this year's Leipzig spring fair, Khrushchev recompensed Ulbricht more than generously for his consistent support. He did so in a three-fold way—

[8] *Ibid.*, 28 November, 1961.

in the realm of foreign policy, through repeated economic aid, and by giving Ulbricht a free hand to pursue, and even intensify, his own Stalinist course at home, always provided that this could be combined with keeping in step with Khrushchev's de-Stalinisation and anti-dogmatism campaign in the Soviet Union and in the bloc as a whole.

To an old hand like Ulbricht, the juggling between de-Stalinisation abroad and Stalinism at home presented no insuperable dilemma. In his SED central committee report on the 22nd CPSU congress he solved the problem very simply by asserting that, while the open discussion of the crimes committed by Stalin and the anti-party group had not only been necessary but was symptomatic of both the CPSU's ideological maturity and Khrushchev's 'consistent Leninism', there was no need for the SED to emulate this example. For the SED had already eradicated all vestiges of dogmatism and the personality cult a long time ago. With his undeniable gift for twisting arguments, Ulbricht even managed to suggest that it was the very repression of all revisionist opposition groups which most clearly reflected the SED's consistent stand against dogmatism because—he argued—the typical dogmatists in East Germany were revisionists like the Schirdewan group who had refused to admit that the conclusions of the 20th CPSU congress could not be 'mechanically' applied in the different national conditions of the GDR. The argument about the SED's premature de-Stalinisation was also taken up in *Neues Deutschland* (12 November 1961), which boasted that the SED had never been guilty of 'such grave and tragic violations of internal party demo-cracy and of socialist legality' as were manifested, for instance, in the Rajk or Kostov trials.

Ulbricht's pseudo-dialectical arguments about dogmatism and revisionism are not likely to have fooled anyone, least of all Khrushchev. Yet, from the Soviet point of view, Ulbricht's personal interpretation of the different national roads to socialism was not really more intolerable than, for instance, Gomulka's. And if Poland can be kept within the camp while enjoying a certain degree of internal autonomy, there was no reason why the GDR, at the other extreme, should not be given a similar licence.

The Russians, however, gave Ulbricht not only a free hand in con-ducting his domestic affairs as he thought best, they provided him, over and above this, with massive diplomatic and economic support. Their diplomatic aid centred of course on the deliberate creation of the Berlin crisis on which they first embarked in the autumn of 1958. In retrospect, it is easy to recognise that this whole campaign was from the beginning designed to achieve two inter-related but distinct objectives, i.e. that of putting the GDR once and for all into the ranks of the internationally recognised, established states, and, secondly, that of eliminating the manifold threats with which a free West Berlin menaced the economic and political stability and the ideological security of the GDR.

Both these objectives clearly served not only the interests of Ulbricht and the SED but also those of the Soviet bloc as a whole, and the persistence with which Khrushchev has pursued them is not surprising. It is true that, at least so far as the elimination of a free West Berlin is concerned, it is not easy to see how he can achieve his goal. It is also likely that the repeated postponement of the deadline for the signing of a German peace treaty has been bitterly disappointing and, at times, acutely embarrassing for Ulbricht. But it would be foolish to conclude from this that the various postponements and withdrawn ultimatums reflect Soviet vacillation on basic objectives or serious policy disagreements between Khrushchev and Ulbricht. On the contrary, all the evidence suggests that Khrushchev's intermittent retreats and conciliatory gestures to the West on the German question during the past three-and-a-half years have been strictly temporary respites, given either because the Soviet leaders were momentarily preoccupied with other pressing problems or because the East-West conflict over Berlin threatened to take too dangerous a turn. The long-term strategy, so far as one can see, has never been affected by these interludes. They were instances merely of *reculer pour mieux sauter.*

If there remained any doubts about this, they must have been finally dispelled by the erection of the Berlin wall on 13 August 1961. Of course, the wall, as has often been pointed out, had the primary function of stopping the flow of refugees. But it was also meant to demonstrate that both the GDR's separatist statehood and its vital role as the Soviet camp's westernmost bastion had become irrevocable, and that any further negotiations with the West would have to proceed from that basis.

The Soviet leaders had perhaps not really much choice in this matter. Any alternative looked from their point of view far too perilous. They must have known all along, better perhaps than anyone else, that the absorption of the GDR in a re-unified Germany, neutralised or not, would inevitably result in a blatant exposure of Ulbricht's total lack of popular support; and it does not require exceptional imagination to visualise the possibly disastrous effect which such an exposure of political bankruptcy could have on the precarious stability of the Soviet camp and on communist prestige in the world at large. Khrushchev simply could not afford to let the GDR regime founder just because—and this is perhaps the profoundest paradox in the East German situation—it has so singularly failed to master any of its problems.

THE GDR CRISIS

This failure has by now become notorious even though the GDR has in some respects made very substantial economic progress. Its propagandists claim that industrial output is now three-and-a-half times as large as before the war. This grossly exaggerates the successes achieved, but even Western economists estimate that, compared with the prewar period, industrial output has almost doubled. In the Soviet bloc economy as a whole, moreover, the GDR has in recent years played an increasingly important part as the chief supplier of heavy engineering goods. The

USSR alone now depends for over 40 per cent of all its imported machinery on exports from East Germany. All these are symptoms of a notable industrial advance; but it is an advance that has been achieved by debilitating all human and material resources in so ruthless a manner that constant breakdowns, dislocations, and emergencies of one kind or another have by now become the rule rather than the exception. As a result, planning targets as well as planning methods have had to be constantly revised. The second five-year plan, for instance, which was to cover the period from 1956 to 1960, was adopted only in the spring of 1958. After a run of only a few months, it was scrapped to make room for the new seven-year plan. The seven-year plan, which officially began in January 1959, was adopted only in the autumn of that year, and the planning targets for the years 1959 and 1960 were changed several times. The plan for the calendar year 1961 was not even discussed by the SED central committee before March 1961, and the factories which were supposed to follow its instructions did not receive their detailed production targets before the middle of the summer. Then, in July 1961, the whole planning machinery was once again completely reorganised.

All this would suggest that planning in the GDR follows rather than precedes and directs actual economic development. And to a considerable extent this appears in fact to have happened and to be still happening. Shortages of every description, from labour, power, and essential raw materials to all sorts of special machinery and spare parts, have compelled an increasing number of enterprises to live from hand to mouth, to muddle through with improvisations, and to put up with intermittent total breakdowns.

In a state so heavily dependent on external trade as East Germany, planning is in any case far more difficult and chancy than in more self-sufficient countries. To the extent that the GDR authorities have sought to direct their foreign trade, by trying to reduce their dependence on Western imports generally and West German imports in particular, they have only aggravated their own problems, because they found themselves suddenly short of essential and not quickly replaceable raw materials, specialised machine tools and spare parts. Even more crucial, probably, has been the over-ambitiousness of the goals they set themselves under the slogan of 'building socialism'. With their declining population of working age and their extremely scanty raw material base, the ruthless determination to achieve these goals at whatever cost, and achieve them in record time, was in any case bound to produce an intolerable degree of overstrain. The millions of refugee workers, peasants, and specialists who escaped from this overstrain (and from much else besides) made it infinitely worse.[9] Then, on top of all this, came the upheaval of the

9 Up to 13 August 1961 the grand total of GDR refugees registered in the West had risen to the huge figure of 3,700,000. Approximately half of them were under 25 years of age. Among the professional specialists who have fled from the GDR since 1954 were 17,082 engineers and technicians; 16,724 school-teachers; 752 University teachers; and almost 5,000 doctors, dentists, and veterinary surgeons.

final collectivisation campaign, which in the first few months of 1960 was rushed through like a military operation.[10]

Small wonder, then, that during the past two years or so things have gone from bad to worse. Output in almost all the important industries has begun to lag more and more behind the plan targets. Between mid-1960 and mid-1961 the rate of industrial growth fell by almost half. The increasingly poor performance of certain key industries—especially the power, building materials, heavy engineering, and electro-technical industries—has started a chain reaction with at times disastrous effects both on other domestic industries and on exports. Many important food-stuffs as well as industrial consumer goods have become even scarcer than before, so that the government in 1961 had once again to resort to partial rationing and to the cancellation of previously existing facilities for the hire-purchase of durable consumer goods. Even in Leipzig at the time of the fair this spring, where the authorities always try their utmost to impress foreign visitors with the nearest equivalent they can muster to a Potemkin village, it was impossible, Western correspondents reported, to buy an electric bulb and next to impossible to obtain such things as ordinary nails. Fresh fruit was practically non-existent; green vegetables wholly unobtainable, while hotels and restaurants, except a few VIP establishments, were unable to provide potatoes more than twice a week.

This is not to suggest that ordinary East German workers must now go hungry or make do without the barest necessities. That would be a gross exaggeration. Even today their standard of living appears to be still considerably above that of their opposite numbers in most other communist countries, including the Soviet Union. But the comparisons which they themselves make are not with the rest of the communist world, but with their own pre-war past and even more with current conditions in the non-communist part of their country. What is more, in contrast to the Soviet Union, living conditions in the GDR have in recent years, except for very brief interludes, not improved, and in some respects they have even deteriorated, and this, added to the relentless physical and mental strain, has produced something like an all-pervading sense of hopelessness.

Yet it is less than four years since Ulbricht, at the SED congress in July 1958, promised the East German people that by the end of 1961 they would have more food and more consumer goods per head than West Germany. This seemed a fantastic undertaking even at the time, especially as the priority needs of the basic industries continued to be heavily emphasised in all the economic plans. Nevertheless, until a year ago, Ulbricht's propagandists went on proclaiming that the goal of over-taking West Germany before the end of 1961 in per capita consumption was to be considered the GDR's foremost task. This propaganda was officially dropped only in March 1961, when Ulbricht explained to the

---

[10] At the end of 1959 more than half of all agricultural land was still in private hands. By April 1960, collectivisation was completed.

SED central committee that an increase in living standards now depended exclusively on a further increase in labour productivity.

For once he had spoken the approximate truth. The GDR had come to the very end of its resources and had no reserves left. Any further economic advance or, indeed, even the maintenance of existing living standards and existing rates of economic activity could only be achieved either with the aid of massive outside help or by somehow forcing or inducing each individual worker and collective farmer to increase his individual output. Ulbricht tried both. The slogan for East Germany's workers from that time onwards was to produce more in the same time and for the same pay. The principal method advocated to achieve this result was the raising of working norms—the very measure which in similarly critical circumstances in the past had been the signal which started the 1953 rebellion. But, as it turned out, even after the last escape routes had been blocked by the Berlin wall, the slogan of more output in the same time and for the same pay was not at all easy to translate into practice. In many cases more output was simply not possible because the raw materials were lacking or because essential machines were not available or could not be repaired for lack of spare parts. In other cases managements (in conspiracy sometimes with local party bosses) circumvented instructions to raise norms for fear of losing key workers to other enterprises. Elsewhere the workers' resistance to still higher norms seems to have been cautiously encouraged by local trade union officials, especially in those industries, such as building, where the industrial accident rate and the rate of fatal accidents had risen sharply. In his speech at the SED central committee meeting last November Ulbricht himself hinted at some of these difficulties. He admitted that some of the decrees passed in the interest of the economy as a whole ran counter to the interests of individual workers. Some workers, he said, did not seem to understand the need for changing norms. They did not understand that wages were no use unless there were also goods in the shops, and that it was essential to maintain a balance between prices and wages. In view of this defective understanding on the part of the workers it was not surprising that trade union officials were now facing difficult problems. However, as he also assured his listeners, now that the escape gap had been closed it should become easier to force the pace.

No doubt it did become easier. But the problems nevertheless remained. And in the winter of 1961-62 they threatened, despite the wall, to become even more intractable At that very critical moment Khrushchev came once again to Ulbricht's rescue. He provided the necessary minimum amount of grain (while Poland's non-collectivised peasants had to help out with potatoes), and in February, after prolonged negotiations, the Soviet Union agreed to grant the GDR a huge additional special credit for its imports from Russia. This new aid agreement was one which the Soviet Union could ill afford. It was much larger than any comparable assistance given by the Soviet Union for many years to any other country, and more especially to any other satellite state. But that only accentuated its significance. The fact that Khrushchev, despite Russia's own pressing needs, nevertheless felt impelled to provide this additional aid shows more clearly than anything else how very serious the GDR crisis has become and how determined Khrushchev has remained to save it in all circumstances from open collapse.

The GDR crisis is of course even more a political, moral, and cultural than a merely economic one. Since the wall went up the cultural Waste-land seems to have become even more desolate, and repression appears to have been further intensified. So far as one can judge from East German newspapers, prison and hard labour (now euphemistically called educational labour) sentences for often quite trifling so-called counter-revolutionary or anti-state activities have become both longer and more frequent. People who, after 13 August 1961, continued to tune in to Western radio or television programmes were dubbed 'ideological frontier-crossers' and savagely persecuted. In an organised campaign, characteristically called ' Blitz contra Nato transmitters ',[11] youth brigades were sent round to hack off the offensive ' West aerials ' because, as one of the organisers of the campaign explained at the time, it had been established that nearly all the spies, saboteurs, and traitors in the GDR had been launched on their criminal career by listening to or watching seemingly innocent music, sports, and entertainment programmes from the Nato stations. Perhaps even more sinister as a portent of things to come is Ulbricht's recent assertion at the Madgeburg peasant congress in March that many of the collective farm failures were due to the activities of former Nazis who, on the instructions of Western radio stations, were now trying to cause harm.

Worse, however, than all these detailed facets and aspects of the East German crisis is the fact that the German Democratic Republic has become a state in which the last spark of hope seems now to have died. There must have been quite a few of its better educated subjects who felt it to be of symbolic significance that among the last to desert them for the West, when the wall went up, was the author of *The Principle of Hope*, the veteran Marxist philosopher Ernst Bloch.

It seems difficult to believe, in view of this deep-seated malady, that the Soviet leaders can still feel confident that Ulbricht, even with con-tinued Soviet backing, can ever succeed in lifting the GDR out of its state of crisis. Most likely they feel no such confidence. Most likely they persist in backing Ulbricht for the simple reason that they think they cannot afford to do otherwise.

[11] SED propaganda language bears an increasingly close resemblance to the peculiar jargon formerly associated with the Nazis.

ALBANIA

The November 1960 Moscow Meeting: A Preliminary Reconstruction

William E. Griffith

ONLY very rarely does extensive evidence of a secret Communist meeting become available to the non-Communist world; when it does, as in the cases of the July 1955 Soviet Central Committee plenum [1] or of Khrushchev's " secret speech " at the Twentieth Soviet Party Congress,[2] it gladdens historians' hearts and adds greatly to our comprehension of Communist history and current developments. Such evidence was not always unavailable; before Stalin totally dominated and terrorised the Comintern, material on developments in the international Communist movement and even within the Soviet Party itself occasionally would appear in the publications of other European Communist Parties.

Since the public outbreak in 1960 of the Sino-Soviet dispute,[3] the availability of such evidence has again rapidly increased; given the likelihood that the dispute, whether or not it leads to an open Sino-Soviet rupture, will not be solved soon or completely, it may well increase even more rapidly in the future.

[1] See the account by a Polish defector who saw a full stenographic record of the July Plenum: Seweryn Biaĺer, ' I Chose Truth," *News From Behind the Iron Curtain*, V, No. 10, October 1956, pp. 9–16. This account has been generally accepted as reliable; see Zbigniew Brzezinski, *The Soviet Bloc*, 2nd ed. (New York: Praeger, 1961), p. 495, note 43, and Leonard Schapiro, *The Communist Party of the Soviet Union* (New York: Random House, 1959), p. 558, note.

[2] For annotated texts, see Bertram D. Wolfe, *Khrushchev and Stalin's Ghost* (New York: Praeger, 1957) and Boris I. Nicolaevsky, " The Crimes of the Stalin Era," *The New Leader* (undated supplement).

[3] Donald S. Zagoria, *The Sino-Soviet Conflict 1956–1961* (Princeton Un. Press, 1962) and " Sino-Soviet Frictions in the Underdeveloped Countries," *Problems of Communism*, X, No. 2, March–April 1961, pp. 1–13 ; Zbigniew Brzezinski, *The Soviet Bloc*, 2nd ed. (New York: Praeger, 1961), especially the epilogue, " The Impact of the Sino-Soviet Dispute," pp. 409–442, " The Challenge of Change of the Soviet Bloc," *Foreign Affairs*, XXXIX, No. 3, April 1961, pp. 430–443 (also in his *Ideology and Power in Soviet Politics* (New York: Praeger, 1962), pp. 141–161), " Patterns and Limits of the Sino-Soviet Dispute," *Problems of Communism*, IX, No. 5, September–October 1960, pp. 1–7, and " Deviation Control: A Study in the Dynamics of Doctrinal Conflict," *American Political Science Review*, LVI, No. 1, March 1962, pp. 5–22; Kurt L. London, ed., *Unity and Contradiction* (New York: Praeger, 1962); G. F. Hudson, Richard Lowenthal and Roderick MacFarquhar, eds., *The Sino-Soviet Dispute* (New York: Praeger, 1961), " Schism Among the Faithful," *Problems of Communism*, XI, No. 1, January–February 1962, pp. 1–14; David A. Charles, " The Dismissal of Marshal P'eng Teh-huai," *The China Quarterly*, No. 8, October–December 1961, pp. 63–76. For a summary of unpublished documents, concerning the Moscow 1960 meetings and before, which, in spite of initial allegations of their being forged (Branko Lazitch, " Une nouvelle mystification," *Est et Ouest*, XIII, No. 253, March 1–15, 1961, pp. 1–4, and Paul Wohl in the *Christian Science Monitor*, February 14, 1961), I would consider (with Harsch, *Christian Science*

The part of this material which is most important for the study of current and recent developments in the Sino-Soviet dispute and in the international Communist movement is that contained in statements and ideological declarations by the smaller Communist Parties, both within and without the Communist camp. Within the camp, probably the Polish and Albanian[4] Communist Parties have originated the most interesting material; without, the Italians, the French, the Belgians,[5] and the Indonesians. However, only exhaustive coverage of material from all Communist Parties can provide either a general appreciation of the state of the international Communist movement[6] or enable, once considerable new material concerning it has become available, the reconstruction of a specific episode.

The purpose of this article is to offer a provisional historical reconstruction, based upon material which became available in early 1962, of the Communist meetings in Moscow from September to December 1960. Most of this material consists of official documents and statements of the Italian, French, and Belgian Communist Parties; briefer material from other parties has also been used. The meetings themselves were entirely secret; only the final declaration was published. The first detailed account of their proceedings was published by the British Soviet expert Edward Crankshaw in *The Observer* (London) in February 1961.[7] The Italian, French, and Belgian material confirms much of the Crankshaw account; it never contradicts it; and it adds much more.

Contrary to some initial Western views[8] that the meeting had resulted in some kind of *modus vivendi* between Moscow and Peking, and, as

---

Monitor, February 15, 1961, and Brzezinski, *The Soviet Bloc*, 2nd ed., p. 512) reliable and reflecting in general the actual course of events, see Edward Crankshaw in *The Observer* (London), February 12, 19, 1961, and May 6 and 20, 1962; for his analysis, " Khrushchev and China," *Atlantic Monthly*, CCVII, No. 5, May 1961, pp. 43–47; their material is now confirmed and expanded in the extremely revealing Italian and French communist documents on the meetings, *Interventi della delegazione del P.C.I. alla Conferenza degli 81 Partiti comunisti e operai* (Rome: Sezione centrale di stampa e propaganda della Direzione del PCI, January 15, 1962) (Joint Press Research Service (JPRS) 12461, February 14, 1962) and *Contribution de la délégation française à la conférence des partis communistes et ouvriers, Moscou, Novembre 1960* (n.p., n.d. [Paris: PCF, November 1961]), and in several articles in the Belgian CP newspaper *Le Drapeau Rouge*, by Jean Terfve, January 5, 8, 9, 10, 11, 15–17, 1962 (JPRS 12759, March 2, 1962); by Ernest Burnelle, January 19–29, 1962 (JPRS 12615, February 23, 1962), both pro-Soviet; and the pro-Chinese one by Jacques Grippa and the pro-Soviet answer by the Belgian CP Politburo, February 22, 1962 (JPRS 13314, April 4, 1962, pp. 10–91). For summary and analysis of the Italian, French and Belgian documentation, see " Documents sur la crise de l'Internationale communiste," *Est et Ouest*, XIV, No. 275, March 16–31, 1962, pp. 1–11, and " Nouveaux documents sur la crise du movement communiste international," *ibid.* XIV, No. 277, April 16–30, 1962, pp. 5–11.
[4] The author is now preparing a book on Albania and the Sino-Soviet rift.
[5] Cited in footnote 3, *supra*.
[6] See the excellent one by Alexander Dallin, " Long Divisions and Fine Fractions," *Problems of Communism*, XI, No. 2, March–April 1962, pp. 7–16.
[7] Cited in footnote 3, *supra*.
[8] *e.g.*, Brzezinski, *The Soviet Bloc*, 2nd ed., pp. 427–429.

illustrated by the preponderance in the final statement of Soviet ideological and policy formulations, represented substantially a Soviet victory, and despite the fact that Sino-Soviet ideological polemics declined thereafter, it is now clear that, on the contrary, Sino-Soviet (and Soviet-Albanian) relations deteriorated during and after the meetings.

The Moscow meeting of the eighty-one Communist Parties [9] opened in November and lasted several weeks; its final declaration was published in *Pravda* on December 6. It was preceded by the meeting during September and October of a preparatory commission presided over by Suslov, who submitted a CPSU draft of a declaration. The commission's discussions, which lasted three and a half weeks,[10] were inconclusive on the key issues of the Sino-Soviet dispute.

When the 81-party meeting opened, according to the Crankshaw account,[11] the Russians held confidential briefings of the other delegates, based on a 127-page circular letter and a commentary on it by Suslov. They declared that the conference had been called earlier than had been originally planned because of the Chinese violations of the 1957 Declaration. These included, according to the Russians, disruptive campaigns within " certain foreign parties " (certainly the Albanian, probably some of the East Asian), and an attempt to denigrate and unseat Khrushchev personally,[12] by incorrectly denouncing his travels in the West and his " peace " policies. Instead, as Suslov put it in his opening speech to the 81-party meeting, " the Chinese nominally support coexistence; but at the same time they say war is inevitable." [13] The Russians also made clear their intent to force other parties to choose between them and the Chinese. As Crankshaw paraphrases their position:

> . . . Some Parties wanted to patch up a compromise " for fear that similar differences might arise in their own Parties," but this would not do. It was impossible for the two views to be reconciled. A choice had to be made, a clear verdict given. " As a result of the actions of the Chinese Party the fate of *all* Communist Parties is at stake." [14]

The main issues discussed at the meetings were, as Thorez described them, four:

> . . . the character of our epoch, problems of war and of peace, paths of transition to Socialism, and unity of the international communist movement and rules which regulate the relations among fraternal parties . . .[15]

---

9 For analysis of the conference, see especially Zagoria, *op. cit.*, pp. 345–369, which, however, must be supplemented by the Italian, French and Belgian material.

10 Matern in *Neues Deutschland*, February 12, 1961.

11 *The Observer*, May 6, 1962.

12 This is also in " Intervention de Maurice Thorez," *Contribution*, pp. 31, 34.

13 Crankshaw, *The Observer*, May 20, 1962.

14 *The Observer*, May 6, 1962.

15 " Déclaration de la délégation du parti communiste français," *Contribution*, p. 37.

The meetings were dominated by an intensified Soviet counterattack, begun the previous June at Bucharest, against the Chinese Communists. In the best Leninist tradition, the Russians challenged the Chinese on the organisational issue, insisting that they must accept democratic centralism and therefore a ban on " fractionalism " within the international Communist movement. The Soviet draft declaration submitted to the preparatory commission included a ban against fractionalism.

The Italian documents enable the reconstruction of the Soviet draft on this point. Already perhaps modified somewhat under Chinese pressure, it emerged in the draft declaration presented to the meeting as a statement which, had the Chinese agreed to it, would have required them to accept all majority decisions of international Communist meetings, and specifically to cease their support of the Albanian defiance of Moscow, their anti-Soviet activities within other Communist parties, and their " fractional " activity within international Communist front organisations.

The Italian documents speak of " the reference to the ' inadmissibility of fractionalism ' [i.e., the binding character of a majority vote] in the draft declaration." [16] In his first speech, Luigi Longo, head of the Italian delegation, paraphrased the preparatory commission's draft provision:

> . . . we hereby state our complete agreement with the text of the new declaration, where it reminds us that the interests of the communist movement require the constant and united application, by all communist parties, of the decisions taken collectively by the fraternal parties in their conferences. Furthermore, for the maintenance of good relations among communist parties, and in order that the authority and autonomy of each of them be respected, every party must refrain, and order its members to refrain, from all fractional activity among the rank and file and within the bodies of the other parties. All exchange of information and all critical observations between one party and another must be channelled through the responsible bodies of each of them . . .[17]

Thorez gave substantially the same version.[18] The Italian and French documents indicate that such a ban on fractionalism was included in the original Soviet draft presented by Suslov to the preparatory commission, that the Chinese refused to accept it there, that it was reintroduced by the Cuban and Brazilian parties in the 81-party meetings, that the Chinese still refused to accept it and refused to sign the declaration unless it were omitted, and that it was therefore replaced by a general reaffirmation of the necessity for unity.[19] The same was also the case with the issue of

16 " Lettera," *Interventi*, p. 77.
17 " Primo intervento," *Interventi*, p. 68. The first sentence of this quotation was in the final declaration; the rest of it presumably represents the substance if not indeed the actual text of the original Soviet draft and of the Cuban-Brazilian amendment.
18 " Intervention de Maurice Thorez," *Contribution*, pp. 32–33.
19 " Primo intervento," *Interventi*, p. 68, and " Lettera," *ibid.*, p. 77; " Intervention de Maurice Thorez," *Contribution*, pp. 32–33. The final general reaffirmation may have been taken from an Italian amendment (see *Interventi*, p. 77).

the validity of the CPSU Twentieth and Twenty-first Congresses as a
" model " for the international Communist movement; here the amendment was Polish.[20] The Chinese also refused to accept this; the final
Declaration merely repeated the 1957 formulation.[21]

The new documentary material gives little indication of what else
Khrushchev and the other Russian representatives at the conference said,
but since the final statement is so much in favour of Soviet positions there
is no reason to assume that they made any major concession to the
Chinese views. Khrushchev formally abjured the " leading role " of the
Soviet Party,[22] a move he made public the following January.[23] He also,
according to Crankshaw,

> . . . gave an impassioned evocation of nuclear war and insisted that he
> was absolutely sincere about disarmament (" the only true humanism ").[24]

Both Thorez and Longo, and therefore, one assumes, Khrushchev as
well rejected the proposal by " several delegations " that an international
secretariat be set up.[25] No specific evidence is available concerning the
identity of these delegations. Since Thorez opposed the idea, it could
not have been favoured by Khrushchev. One may perhaps assume that it
was proposed by either the Chinese and Albanians or the " neutralist "
balancing East Asian parties, or both, with the motive of hindering such
unilateral initiatives as Khrushchev's counterattack against Mao.

Although Liu Shao-ch'i was the head of the Chinese delegation, Teng
Hsiao-p'ing, secretary-general of the Chinese Party, made the two main

---

20 " Intervention de Maurice Thorez," *Contribution*, p. 30. (The Polish amendment in
my view did not, as stated in *Est et Ouest*, XIV, No. 277, April 16–30, 1962, p. 8,
deal with the question of the USSR's leadership of the camp.) " Primo intervento,"
Interventi, p. 46.

21 The Albanians stated in early 1962 that the Russians promised at the meetings not to
use this formulation to " impose " the XX Congress's decisions on other parties.
(" Deeper and Deeper into the Mire of Anti-Marxism," *Zëri i Popullit*, January 9,
1962.)

22 *Ibid.*; *cf.* the Belgian CP Politburo statement, *Le Drapeau Rouge*, February 22, 1962,
and " Intervention de Maurice Thorez," *Contribution*, pp. 30–31. The Thorez material
indicates that the Chinese supported the maintenance of the CPSU as " the head "
of the movement. See Hoxha in *Zëri i Popullit*, November 8, 1961, for the Albanian
and presumably the Chinese position on this point. The 1957 Declaration, signed
only by the ruling parties, spoke of the camp of Socialism " headed by the Soviet
Union "; it seems likely that the Chinese, wishing to repeat this formulation, were the
ones who proposed that the 1960 Declaration also be signed only by the ruling parties
(see " Intervention de Maurice Thorez," *Contribution*, p. 41). Among the twelve
ruling parties, the Albanians would have supported the Chinese, and the North
Koreans and North Vietnamese would probably have been neutral; the Chinese
numerical inferiority would therefore have been much less than among all 81 parties.

23 N. S. Khrushchev, " For New Victories of the World Communist Movement,"
Kommunist, No. 1, January 1961, pp. 3–37, and *World Marxist Review*, IV, No. 1,
January 1961, pp. 3–28.

24 Crankshaw, *The Observer*, February 12, 1961; the Chinese denounced his use of the
term " humanism " (*Le Drapeau Rouge*, February 22, 1962).

25 " Primo intervento," *Interventi*, p. 69; " Déclaration de la délégation du parti communiste français." *Contribution*, pp. 42–43.

Chinese speeches at the conference; they were the most bitter Chinese attacks yet against the Russians. According to Crankshaw, Teng charged that

> . . . The Soviet party was opportunist and revisionist; it lacked any deep knowledge of Marxism; its ideas about disarmament were absurd; its help to Nehru and Nasser only helped imperialism and was an " opportunist mistake "; peaceful coexistence could mean nothing, except as a tactical weapon to deceive the enemy; the Soviet idea of a division of labour among the countries of the Socialist camp was wrong, and China must go her own way . . .[26]

The Italian, French, and Belgian material now makes possible a more complete reconstruction of Teng's speeches. The essence of Teng's position, according to Longo, was that the Soviet Central Committee, Khrushchev personally, and almost all other Communist Parties (*i.e.*, those not pro-Chinese)

> . . . have strayed away in spirit and in substance . . . in the most obvious manner, from the proper road of Marxism-Leninism, and from the [1957] Moscow Declaration . . . [27]

The Belgian Communist Politburo's paraphrased summary [28] gives more detail on what Teng said concerning the Soviet Twentieth and Twenty-First Congresses and other points:

> . . . First thesis: We must stop referring to the Twentieth Congress of the CPSU as if its teachings were valid for the entire world Communist movement . . . ever since the Twentieth Congress of the CPSU, that party has led the majority of the Communist parties along the road of surrender to the imperialists. The Albanian Workers' Party believed it was clarifying this reasoning when it accused the CPSU of revisionism.

The Belgian account continues, in probably not too exaggerated a version:

> . . . there is a blanket denial of the validity and the usefulness of the criticism of the cult of the personality; there is anger at the idea that it is possible and useful to prevent the start of a third world war; there is doubt as to the political advantage to be gained by upgrading the different paths to socialism; there is scorn for the " utopian " belief in the theory of bloodless ways for the working class to rise to power in some countries, and under given conditions. Furthermore, the necessary unity of the workers' movement against the dictatorship of the capitalist monopolies and of the forces of war [i.e., with the Social Democrats— W.E.G.] is down-graded to a secondary position, yielding its place to the *verbal* excoriation of the Social Democratic leaders and their mistakes . . .

Turning to the Chinese objections to the Soviet version of peaceful coexistence, the Belgian summary goes on, Teng declared that

[26] Crankshaw, *op. cit.*
[27] " Primo intervento," *Interventi*, p. 48 ; " Secondo intervento," *ibid.* p. 72.
[28] *Le Drapeau Rouge*, February 22, 1962 ; *cf.* the briefer but similar version in " Primo intervento," *Interventi*, pp. 56, 59.

. . . the struggle for peaceful coexistence can be considered only as a tactical manoeuvre, a means of moral disarmament of the peoples of the capitalist countries and of material disarmament of those same countries. World disarmament and true peaceful coexistence will only be possible when there are only socialist countries left in the world . . .

Again the Belgian account comments:

. . . it goes back to the old view that a third world war is inevitable and that our first duty is to get ready to win it, at no matter what cost in human lives and destruction. Several theories logically follow from this. One is that of the necessary harmless and safe nature of " local wars," in so far as world peace is concerned. Another is the foolishness of the efforts made by many Communist parties in capitalist countries to work out plans for action whose object is to develop democracy, to limit the power of the monopolies, and profoundly to change the policies of their respective countries. And yet another puts the revisionist stamp on the Rome Conference of the 17 Communist parties from the capitalist countries.

Teng also strongly defended the permissibility of fractionalism within the international Communist movement:

. . . In the world Communist movement, the minority is not bound to adopt the general political line adopted by the majority. It has the right to devote its full attention to a continuous . . . action, without any limitation . . . [29]

As Longo paraphrased him:

. . . you claim the right to maintain and propagate, even after the conference, all your own views, which will not be embodied in the closing declaration, and call upon History for the final judgment . . . History will tell which was right . . . [30]

According to Crankshaw, Teng gave an illustration which could only have made totally clear to Moscow the totality of Peking's defiance:

. . . Lenin, he said, by splitting the Social Democratic Party into Bolsheviks and Mensheviks, had formed what was at first a minority fraction in order, successfully in the end, to win a majority . . . [31]

The Belgian account also states that at the meetings the Chinese and Albanians

. . . took up arms against the principle of fraternal equality among the parties and went all-out for the mistaken concept of the " leading party " . . .

As the Belgian version added, this had been the CPSU " until the new order came into being "—*i.e.*, until Khrushchev formally repudiated the

[29] Belgian CP Politburo, *Le Drapeau Rouge*, February 22, 1962.
[30] " Primo intervento," *Interventi*, pp. 69–70; *cf.* " Intervention de Maurice Thorez," *Contribution*, pp. 31–32, which gives the same summary of Teng's position.
[31] Crankshaw, *op. cit.*

114 WILLIAM E. GRIFFITH

concept. The Belgians clearly intimated that the Chinese held to this view because they hope some day to assume this role themselves:

> . . . actually, the minute you consider that the " leading party " can be ideologically and politically wrong, you begin to wonder who can take its place, and consequently if perhaps it mightn't be you . . .

The Chinese most likely have no such ambitions for the present; in the long run, however, they probably do. They therefore are opposed to polycentrism; they want the international Communist movement kept rigidly united, with themselves having much more to say about its policies than they now do. Specifically, Teng criticised Soviet-Chinese " state relations " (probably the withdrawal of Soviet specialists and the cut in Soviet economic aid), denounced the Soviet support of India in the Sino-Indian border dispute, and demanded that the World Peace Council be narrow rather than broad in its membership.[32] Furthermore, he denounced Khrushchev's flattery of imperialist leaders:

> . . . This is intolerable; no considerations of protocol can explain away Khrushchev's tactless eulogy of Eisenhower and other imperialists . . .[33]

Finally, he attacked the low level of Soviet aid to China, which had been no more than what China herself had given to other parties, and which in any case was a duty which " gives no grounds for presumption or bragging." [34] Teng also bitterly condemned the " soft " Soviet attitude towards Yugoslavia.[35]

Thorez spoke after Teng but before Hoxha.[36] As one would have expected, his speech was quite as strongly anti-Chinese but considerably more pro-Soviet than Longo's; in no instance did it deviate from the current Soviet line. Thorez totally rejected Teng's speech:

> . . . We have now acquired the certitude that it is not a matter of disagreements limited to two or three points of the Declaration proposed to this Conference, but of an entire line opposed to that of the international communist movement.
>
> We have at the same time the confirmation that it is not a matter of divergencies between the Chinese Communist Party and the Communist Party of the Soviet Union, but of a profound disagreement of the Chinese comrades with the whole international communist movement . . .[37]

32 " Intervention de Maurice Thorez," *Contribution*, pp. 5, 11, 14–15. Teng's line on the WPC was the same as the Chinese one at the December 1961 Stockholm WPC meeting; see the speech of Liao Ch'eng-chih in *Peking Review*, IV, No. 51, December 22, 1961, pp. 12–14. Teng's attack on Khrushchev's pro-Indian policy is also in Crankshaw, *The Observer*, May 6, 1962

33 Quoted by Crankshaw, *The Observer*, May 6, 1962.

34 *Ibid.* This seems to have been one of the most serious Chinese grievances against Khrushchev; see Longo to the PCI CC, *L'Unità*, December 23, 1961.

35 *Ibid.*

36 " Intervention de Maurice Thorez," *Contribution*, pp. 5–36.

37 *Ibid.* p. 6.

Thorez endorsed all aspects of the Soviet position: on peaceful coexistence, on the Twentieth and Twenty-First CPSU Congresses, on the necessity of a broadly rather than a narrowly drawn peace movement, on the danger of thermonuclear war and the necessity and possibility of avoiding it (here his formulations were quite as strong as Longo's), on the peaceful transition to Socialism (here he spoke less of democracy than did Longo but fundamentally took much the same position), and on the temporary nature of the dictatorship of the proletariat.[38] Unlike Longo, he did not take anything like a pro-Yugoslav position; on the contrary, he declared that the PCF

> . . . has not ceased to denounce the theories of " national communism " developed particularly by the Yugoslavs, at the same time that it has unmasked their splitting activities . . . [39]

It was now Hoxha's turn.[40] Although he had not gone to Bucharest in June or to New York in October, both he and Shehu went to Moscow in November. (By this time they had crushed the pro-Soviet Albanian opposition, including Belishova and Tashko.) The meeting which occurred in Moscow between Khrushchev and Hoxha was more of an exchange of denunciations than of views. According to a probably correct later Albanian account [41] the meeting, at Khrushchev's initiative, was scheduled for November 9. Immediately preceding it, however, with no previous warning to Hoxha, the Russians distributed to all the delegates a " long official document " which denounced the Albanian leadership, *inter alia* for " anti-Soviet policies and activities " and " undertook the defence of anti-party elements " (*i.e.*, the pro-Soviet Belishova and Tashko, purged the previous summer). Even so, the Russians still pressed for a meeting with the Albanians which finally occurred on November 12. As might have been expected, and as Khrushchev later declared,[42] it came to nothing; according to the Albanians, the Soviet leader at its conclusion declared that he could reach a better understanding with Macmillan than with the Albanians.

On November 16 (after Teng but before Longo), Hoxha delivered a philippic against Khrushchev which ended all chances of a reconciliation between Moscow and Tirana. His speech contained all the major themes of the Albanian attack upon Khrushchev which he made public a year

38 *Ibid*. pp. 13–14, 16, 24–25, 27.
39 *Ibid*. p. 34.
40 For a detailed analysis of Soviet-Albanian relations, see the author's forthcoming book on Albania and the Sino-Soviet rift, from which this is in part taken.
41 " Khrushchev Has Been Devoting His Time to Aggravating the Divergencies with Our Party and State Instead of Solving Them," *Zëri i Popullit*, March 25, 1962. As of June 1962 Moscow had not challenged this version.
42 Khrushchev to the XXII CPSU Congress, *Pravda*, October 29, 1961.

later.[43] Hoxha repeated the Chinese position on the ideological issues: the nature of the epoch, peaceful coexistence, and peaceful transition to Socialism. On the organisational issue, he denounced Khrushchev for having accused the Chinese Party at Bucharest at short notice and for having demanded that the other Parties support him in this, a procedure to which the Albanians had properly objected. Hoxha generally approved of the draft declaration, except for the ban on fractionalism. He declared that " the cult of personality does not apply only to Stalin . . . who had world-wide renown and was the follower of Lenin." He was predictably violent against Yugoslavia. Khrushchev, he declared, had gone to Belgrade in May 1955 without informing the Albanians and had thereafter disregarded their protest. In 1956 he had spread " false information . . . concerning the physical liquidation of Yugoslav agents including a pregnant woman " (i.e., Liri Gega). Khrushchev's analysis of the political causes of the Hungarian counter-revolution and of the events had been wrong[44]; he and Suslov had had confidence in Tito in spite of the latter's desire " to co-ordinate the counter-revolution in Albania and Hungary." Khrushchev had incorrectly taken the sole initiative of intervening in Hungary. Only Czechoslovakia " has held a correct attitude towards the necessity of unmasking Tito." Referring to Khrushchev's interview with the Greek leader, Hoxha declared that " we have put Sophocles Venizelos in his place "[45]; that " we shall make no territorial concessions," and added:

. . . We do not want a rectification of the Albanian-Yugoslav frontiers . . . but we demand the protection of the Albanian minority in Yugoslavia, one million strong . . .

Hoxha's most violent charges against Khrushchev dealt with Soviet-Albanian relations: Khrushchev had in August 1960 sent a letter to the Albanian Party asking them to " join a *bloc* " against the Chinese Party,[46] thus making themselves guilty of fractionalism. The Soviet Union had brutally intervened in the Albanian Party in an attempt to force some of its leaders " to choose between the 200 million Russians and the 650

---

43 The only detailed available official communist documentation concerning this Hoxha speech are the attacks on it in " Primo intervento," *Interventi*, pp. 48–51, and in " Déclaration de la délégation du parti communiste français," *Contribution*, pp. 38–40. There also exist three apparently reliable but incomplete summaries of the Hoxha speech; the most extensive is in BBC European Service, C.R.U. Talk No. 2,098, June 9, 1961, from which all the following quotations are taken; see also Victor Zorza in *The Guardian* (Manchester) and David Floyd in *The Daily Telegraph* (London), June 9, 1961. " Primo intervento " and " Déclaration " have largely confirmed these three, as has " Marxism-Leninism Will Triumph," *Zëri i Popullit*, November 1, 1961. The report Hoxha made to the December 19–20 PPSh CC Plenum (*Zëri i Popullit*, December 21, 1961) has remained unpublished. See also Hoxha, speech, November 7, 1961, in *Zëri i Popullit*, November 8, 1961.
44 Cf. *Interventi*, pp. 45–71, at pp. 48–49.
45 *To Vima* (Athens), June 28, 1960.
46 This has now also been alleged in " Khrushchev . . .," *Zëri i Popullit*, March 25, 1962.

million Chinese "; Belishova had " capitulated to the dishonest threats of the Soviet Union." The Soviet ambassador in Tirana and his staff were continuing their pressure, which had " gone so far as to precipitate a revolution in the army." Marshal Malinovski attacked Albania at a Warsaw Pact Chiefs of Staff meeting; Marshal Grechko threatened to exclude Albania from the Pact; Khrushchev had threatened to expel Albania from the Socialist camp, but this would not depend upon him.[47] Khrushchev told Teng Hsiao-p'ing " We shall treat Albania like Yugoslavia "[48]; on November 6 Khrushchev said, " Russia has lost an Albania; the People's Republic of China has gained an Albania." Hoxha then emotionally described the Soviet economic pressure on Albania:

> . . . Albania has suffered earthquakes, floods and a drought of 120 days and has been threatened by famine. Only 15 days' supply of wheat remained in stock. After a delay of 45 days, the USSR promised us 10,000 tons of wheat instead of 50,000 tons or—in other words—15 days' supply of wheat to be delivered in September or October. These are unbearable pressures. The Soviet rats were able to eat whilst the Albanian people were dying of hunger; we were asked to produce gold.[49]

He also reportedly attacked the Poles violently, declaring that Foreign Minister Rapacki, a PZPR Politburo member, was an imperialist agent.[50] A week later, before the end of the meetings, Hoxha and Shehu, perhaps taking fright at their own boldness, precipitately returned to Tirana via Budapest [51] and Italy.[52]

Some time after Teng and Hoxha, Longo, the head of the Italian delegation spoke. (The absent Togliatti, the old Comintern fox, was presumably far too experienced to participate personally in so potentially hazardous an international meeting.) In addition to the points of his speech which have previously been covered, Longo violently attacked the Albanians. " Words fail us," he said, " for proper denunciation "; the Hoxha speech was " beneath contempt " both as to content and to method.[53] Its method was that of " hypocritical double talk," its personal attack on Khrushchev and the Soviet leaders " dishonest and childish." [54]

[47] This is particularly interesting in view of the November 1961 statement by the Indonesian CP head, Aidit, in Djakarta that membership in the camp is determined by whether or not a country is " objectively " building socialism, and therefore Albania cannot be expelled from it, since even Khrushchev admits she is building it. (*People's Daily*, December 1, 1961.)

[48] *Cf.* " A Year of Historic Proofs," *Zëri i Popullit*, December 6, 1961.

[49] *Cf.* my forthcoming book on Soviet-Albanian relations.

[50] Brzezinski, *The Soviet Bloc*, 2nd ed., p. 432, footnote.

[51] *Pravda*, November 26, 1960; Radio Budapest, November 27, 1961, in B.B.C. *Summary of World Broadcasts*, Part 2, No. 501, p. 3 (summary), November 29, 1960.

[52] Peter Florin, " Zur abenteuerlichen Politik der albanischen Führer," *Einheit*, XIII, No. 3, March 1962, pp. 14–26, at p. 24.

[53] " Primo intervento," *Interventi*, pp. 48–49.

[54] *Ibid.* p. 49.

In a clear reference to Hoxha's denunciations of Khrushchev's cut in Soviet economic aid to Albania, Longo declared:

> . . . we cannot disguise the ideological and political dissension of which we speak as a dispute involving nothing but relations among certain socialist countries. We do not want to intervene directly in international relations, but we cannot refrain from pointing out that certain insulting insinuations made by the Albanian delegate in connection with the policies of the Soviet government struck our ear as an insult to the entire assembly . . . all the more offensive the more it is masked behind oily assurances of friendship and fraternity, with epithets and turns of expression that one can conceive of addressing only to a class enemy . . . [55]

Turning to Teng's first speech, Longo, like Thorez, insisted strongly that the draft declaration's reference to the Twentieth and Twenty-First Congress be maintained. As to Teng's main thesis, that Khrushchev and the Soviet Party were anti-Marxist-Leninist, Longo declared:

> . . . this accusation is false and even slanderous, in that it is utterly unfounded, and in that it transcends the bounds of admissible criticism . . . [and] undermine[s] the value and the scope of the policy implemented, in recent years, by all the parties . . . [56]

Longo strongly defended against Teng's attack the "democratic . . . Italian way to Socialism." [57] In so doing he came very close to making "democratic struggle" a permanent rather than temporary and tactical phase of Italian Communist activity and used phraseology whose similarity to Yugoslav ideology is striking:

> . . . we must use these democratic institutions as tools for furthering the real power and effective influence of the working masses, we must integrate these institutions with new forms of democracy, including that of direct democracy . . . particular importance is vested in . . . the struggle for what we call structural reform: . . . measures that tend to place effective restrictions on the power of the great monopolies over the nation's entire life, to nationalise certain industries, to establish forms of democratic control over certain sectors of the national economy, and, first and foremost, over the public sectors of the economy, to bring about far-reaching agrarian reform, and so on. These aims . . . were once generally defined in the Communist movement as aims of a transitional character. Lenin considered it allowable and necessary for the Communist Party, under certain circumstances, and particularly in periods of revolutionary crisis, to adopt such aims as these. . . . We believe that in the present phase of history, and particularly in certain countries, such as Italy, the planning of the struggle for such goals as these is an important and permanent task of a Communist party . . . [58]

[55] *Ibid.* p. 50.
[56] *Ibid.* pp. 48, 50.
[57] *Ibid.* p. 59.
[58] *Ibid.* pp. 59–60.

In his discussion of the issue of " fractionalism " Longo made clear the relatively right-wing Italian position. While strongly defending the draft declaration's provision against " fractionalism," he also asserted that

> . . . All the Communist parties are independent, with equal rights, and are responsible for working out their own policies in relation to actual conditions in their respective countries . . . any formulation that might imply subordination of some Communist parties to another is incorrect, as Comrade Khrushchev observed . . .

In his second speech, Thorez' denunciations of Hoxha were quite as strong as Longo's. He declared:

> . . . our delegation condemns categorically the intervention . . . of comrade Enver Hoxha . . . The members of our delegation have listened to it with a sentiment of shame. Communist militants, they had never heard such language, either in the assemblies of their party or in the meetings of the international communist movement . . .[59]

Like Longo, he denounced Hoxha for bringing up inter-state Soviet-Albanian relations and for attacking Khrushchev personally, and declared that the Albanian leader was in fact opposed to the Twentieth CPSU Congress and to the totality of Soviet policy since 1953.

Like Longo, Thorez demanded that the Declaration officially endorse the Twentieth and Twenty-First CPSU Congresses and insisted that the Twentieth Congress had not (as the Chinese had presumably maintained) furthered revisionism and opportunism. He rejected a proposal, presumably made by the Chinese, that only the twelve ruling parties should sign the declaration, defended the Soviet position on support of " national bourgeois " leaders in underdeveloped countries, rejected the presumably Chinese proposal for an international secretariat, and again denounced Chinese policies and actions with respect to the World Federation of Trade Unions and other international front organisations as set forth in a memorandum on the subject which the Chinese had distributed. (In this memorandum the Chinese had apparently demanded that membership be narrowly limited and that the WFTU should denounce the anti-Communist ICFTU more violently.)

Presumably most if not all of the other pro-Soviet Party representatives denounced the Albanians. Reports of only three are available at this writing. The Spanish Communist leader Dolores Ibarruri (" La Pasionaria ") called Hoxha's speech " provocatory and unfit to be uttered by a militant proletarian,"[60] and " contrary to Communism and Marxism-Leninism." Hungarian First Secretary Kádár declared that

---

[59] " Déclaration de la délégation du parti communiste français," *Contribution*, p. 38.
[60] " Secondo Intervento," *Interventi*, p. 71.

> . . . each of us to whom our unity and the interests of socialism and free-
> dom are dear can do only one thing: oppose these false views with
> principled impatience . . .[61]

The Outer Mongolian First Secretary Tsedenbal later said that his Party
had warned the Albanians that

> . . . unless they seriously revise their incorrect position it is only logical
> that they may finally find themselves in the company of their former
> adversaries—the revisionists.[62]

The Chinese, however, refused to disavow or take exception to the
Albanian tirade.[63]

One can deduce something of the positions of the other Parties from
the texts of the greeting messages sent by them to Moscow on the
anniversary of the October Revolution, the ostensible occasion for the
81-Party meeting. From the formulations on the possibility of avoiding
war it is clear that the Chinese, Albanians, North Koreans, and North
Vietnamese did not explicitly endorse the positive Soviet line on this
issue. The fact that they were the only ones which used the formula
"the camp of Socialism headed by the Soviet Union," as subsequent
events made clear, did not indicate a pro-Khrushchev attitude but the
opposite. (When one remembers that Mao insisted on this at the
November 1957 Moscow meeting, *inter alia*, to prevent the Yugoslavs
from signing the declaration, one can realise that the phrase was perhaps
even by then far from being pro-Khrushchev.)

Teng's second speech at the conference was just as unyielding as the
first. According to Crankshaw, Teng, although admitting that the
majority of the delegates were against the Chinese views, declared this
was only because of "misunderstanding which had been aggravated by
slanderous lies." Furthermore, he added, Khrushchev had indirectly
attacked Mao in his speech, "evidently talking without knowing what he
was saying, which he frequently does."[64] Longo said that he

> . . . showed no signs of wishing to take account of the arguments and the
> exigencies set forth by the spokesmen for their brother parties . . .[65]

Thorez declared that Teng

> . . . had rejected, in an absolute and haughty fashion, all the criticisms
> addressed to the Chinese Communist Party. Either those who had made
> the criticisms "had not understood" the Chinese comrades, or their
> parties had themselves left the correct line formulated in the 1957
> declaration . . .[66]

[61] Quoted in Florin, *op. cit.*, p. 25.
[62] Tsedenbal to the II MPRP CC Plenum, *Pravda*, February 3, 1962.
[63] Belgian CP Politburo statement, *Le Drapeau Rouge*, February 22, 1962.
[64] Crankshaw, *The Observer*, May 20, 1962.
[65] "Secondo intervento," *Interventi*, pp. 72–73, at p. 73.
[66] "Déclaration de Maurice Thorez," *Contribution*, p. 47.

Nor did the pro-Soviet majority take a more compromising line. In his second speech, replying to Teng's second one, Longo declared:

> ... It was the Chinese comrades, with their articles and their positions, which they have developed within international bodies, who brought the Moscow Declaration and the great ideological and political victories that have been achieved on that basis, by the individual parties and by the international communist movement as a whole, under discussion again. The Chinese comrades have, by their actions, sown the seeds of doubt, uncertainty and confusion within the international communist and workers' movement and have made the task of many parties far more difficult ...

He also reiterated that

> ... as a consequence of the attitude taken by our Chinese comrades, we feel it more than ever necessary that our conference confirm, and forcefully, in its concluding resolutions, the inadmissibility of any party's opposing the general line agreed upon in this conference, or in any other international conference ...

and concluded with a plea that the Chinese

> ... delegation and the Central Committee of their party reflect on the consequences that their stand may have for the international Communist movement ...[67]

Thorez took an equally serious view of the Chinese:

> ... An abnormal situation, full of dangers, has thus been created: if this situation has to be prolonged, it could result in considerable harm for the world revolutionary movement. Imperialism, although weakened, would doubtlessly look to benefit from it.
>
> Reflect once more, comrades of the Chinese Communist Party. It is not possible that you will take no account of the opinion of the overwhelming majority of the parties represented at the conference. It is not possible that you will remain obstinate in an attitude so prejudicial to our common cause ...
>
> We ask you to communicate to the Central Committee of your party this present démarche which we are making to you ...[68]

There is as of this writing (June 1962) no detailed material available concerning the attitude taken by other Communist delegations during the meetings. However, in view of their earlier and later declarations (notably during and after the CPSU Twenty-Second Congress in October 1961) it would appear that in addition to the Albanians only the East Asian Parties even in part supported the Chinese.[69]

For Hoxha the time for reflection had passed. For the Chinese it had not; the very fact that the conference adopted an agreed statement

---

[67] "Secondo intervento," *Interventi*, pp. 72–73 .
[68] "Déclaration de Maurice Thorez," *Contribution*, p. 48.
[69] Crankshaw (*The Observer*, May 6, 1962) reports that "only the Albanians, the Koreans, the Indonesians, the Siamese, the Vietnamese, the Burmese, the Malayans, and the Japanese spoke up for China."

indicated that some kind of compromise was still possible. In editorials on November 21 and 23 [70] the Chinese and Russians made clear that their positions remained far apart. The Chinese declared:

> ... Any view that overestimates the strength of imperialism and under-estimates the strength of the people is contrary to the Moscow Declaration and is completely incorrect ...
>
> Those views which oppose the revolutionary struggles of the various peoples to the struggles for defending world peace are, therefore, very wrong ...

Moscow asserted:

> ... The CPSU firmly upholds the principles of creative Marxism-Leninism. Guided by these principles it drew major theoretical conclusions and made generalisations at its 20th and 21st Congresses ...

Yet the same editorials also indicated willingness to change some emphases. The Chinese gave way somewhat, but not much, on " creative Marxism ":

> ... New historical developments and new experiences in class struggle constantly demand that we, basing ourselves on the fundamental principles and methods of Marxism-Leninism and on scientific analysis of objective things, make new summations to guide revolutionary struggles and enrich the contents of Marxism-Leninism. But, in the course of studying new experiences, we should, under no circumstances, depart from the fundamental principles and methods of Marxism-Leninism and disregard the facts. Otherwise, it would be a fundamental violation of Marxism-Leninism ...

So did the Russians (while still calling it a " general line ") on " peaceful coexistence ":

> ... The Communist Party of the Soviet Union has always regarded the Leninist principle of the peaceful coexistence of states with different social systems as the general line of the Soviet Union's foreign policy. This principle does not deny the struggle of classes, nor does it mean the reconciliation of socialism with capitalism. Rather, it presupposes an intensification of the struggle for the triumph of socialist ideas, for the complete victory of socialism ...[71]

During the last days of November the conference was in recess and a " drafting committee " was at work, of which presumably the Soviets and Chinese were members. The only evidence concerning the contents of the draft statement at this stage is in a letter of the Italian delegation to Khrushchev.[72] What, if any, reference should be made to the Twentieth

[70] "Give Full Play to the Revolutionary Spirit of the 1957 Moscow Declaration," *People's Daily*, November 21, 1960 (excerpts: Hudson, Lowenthal, and MacFarquhar, *op. cit.*, pp. 171–173); "Unity Under the Banner of Marxism-Leninism," *Pravda*, November 23, 1960 (excerpts: *ibid.* p. 173).

[71] Quoted from Hudson, Lowenthal and MacFarquhar, *op. cit.*, pp. 172–173.

[72] "Lettera," *Interventi*, pp. 74–77, at p. 74. This PCI letter was written to Khrushchev so that he would receive it " before the end of the work of the drafting committee."

Congress was still a matter of controversy; the Italians opposed " any compromise or any retreat on this point." [73] This letter also gives the only evidence, aside from Crankshaw's brief reference to the hostile Chinese attitude and Hoxha's philippic, on the Yugoslav issue. (There were probably Soviet-Chinese differences roughly parallel to those between the 1948 and 1949 Cominform resolutions, but no evidence is available on this point.) The Italian letter reveals a significant element for the general position of the Communist " right wing ": the Italian attempt to tone down the condemnation of Yugoslavia.

The draft declaration had probably contained, in order to assist in a compromise with the Chinese, a somewhat stronger condemnation of Belgrade than Khrushchev himself would have wanted. Even so, the Italians submitted an amendment which, they maintained,

> . . . does not stray from the substance of the concepts expressed in the draft declaration. However, it is couched in less bitter and offensive terms . . .[74]

The amendment, the Italian letter continued, would prevent the Yugoslav leaders from arousing public opinion against the declaration, was more realistic about Yugoslav influence, and, most importantly, would eliminate the provision that all Communist Parties must " isolate Yugo-slavia from the workers' movement "—a provision which would implicitly condemn the Belgrade Declaration and stop all contacts with Yugoslav organisations (which the Italian Party was intensifying) thus hindering rapprochement with other leftist organisations. (The December declara-tion did not contain this final provision; it follows that this Italian and Soviet initiative [75] towards deleting it was successful.)

The Sino-Soviet struggle in the drafting committee must have been bitter; exactly how it was resolved we do not know.[76]

THE MOSCOW DECLARATION

Even this incomplete account of what actually occurred during the Moscow meetings makes clear that the final declaration, as Mr. Zagoria has written, was

> . . . not a real compromise of Soviet and Chinese views, but a collation of them. While the document, in its broad outlines, must be regarded as a Soviet " victory," its ambiguities and qualifications were so numerous that it could hardly serve as a guide for any of the Communist parties. Both Russia and China could and did derive different conclusions from it. The ostensible Soviet victory was thus bought at the very heavy

73 *Ibid.* p. 75.
74 *Ibid.*
75 That the Russians also favoured this is clear from Florin, *op. cit.*
76 Ho Chi Minh, according to at least one Indian press report, mediated. (K. V. Narain in the *Hindu Weekly Review*, February 6, 13, 1961.)

price of an unworkable compromise which served clearly to demonstrate that the Russians were no longer able unilaterally to dictate law for the entire international Communist movement . . .[77]

Mr. Zagoria's negative judgment of it was later confirmed by the Belgian Communist Politburo, which publicly referred to the statement as

. . . so " loaded " . . . that it was possible to quote from it to support the statement, the defence, and the application of political views diametrically opposed, and often outrageously divergent . . .[78]

On the fundamental question of authority and legitimacy within the international Communist movement no decision was reached. The final statement contains no reference to " fractionalism," but only to " jointly " reached decisions (*i.e.*, there was no clear unanimous decision as to whether a majority vote was binding or a unanimous one was required) and to bilateral and multilateral discussions. But in an 81-Party meeting, the only world-wide authority, the Russians were bound to have a majority, as was the United States in the early days of the United Nations General Assembly. By 1960 Peking was no more ready than either Moscow or Washington has been since 1945 to allow its interests to be determined by a majority in a group many of whose members are even less powerful than Albania.

On all other issues the statement leaned strongly towards the Russian position but usually was sufficiently ambiguous so that the Chinese could (and did) interpret it in their favour: on the " nature of the present epoch," on the relative danger of dogmatism and revisionism, on local war (where Khrushchev after the conference recognised the justness and inevitability of " wars of national liberation " but condemned " interstate " wars [79]), on the destructiveness of world war (where in general the statement took the Soviet position), on disarmament, on underdeveloped areas (where the compromise ideological concept of a " national democracy " was outlined), on peaceful transition to Socialism, and on Communist strategy in capitalist countries (which reflected primarily the Soviet view), and on Yugoslavia.

Although the formulation on Yugoslavia was a compromise, and probably went farther than Khrushchev would have wished, it was far from an adoption of the Chinese-Albanian view. Nowhere did it include the 1949 Cominform formulation that the Yugoslav leadership has become an *agentura* of the imperialists. Nor did it even declare that " objectively " they aid the imperialists; their " subversive " operations were not ascribed to anyone's benefit. Furthermore, it did not declare that Yugoslavia was no longer a Socialist country; it only said that " it

---

[77] Zagoria, *The Sino-Soviet Conflict*, pp. 367–368. See *ibid.* pp. 345–365 for a detailed analysis of the statement, on which the following is in part based.

[78] Belgian CP Politburo statement, in *Le Drapeau Rouge*, February 22, 1962.

[79] Khrushchev, *op. cit.*

is in danger of losing the revolutionary gains " (*i.e.*, Socialism). Finally, as we have already seen, it omitted any mention of "isolating" Yugoslavia from the international Communist movement.

CONCLUSIONS

The official Communist accounts of the Moscow meetings are consistent internally and with each other. The Italian, French and Belgian ones also confirm in large part, and never contradict, the Crankshaw version. To date, at least, one can therefore be fairly confident of the authenticity although not of the completeness of the reconstruction given above.

The reconstruction increases still further one's estimate of the bitterness, the all-inclusiveness, and the lack of agreement which characterised this Sino-Soviet encounter. It demonstrates that the key issue, as the whole course of Communist history would *a priori* have enabled one to forecast, was the organisational one : the issue of " fractionalism." On this issue the Russians launched the main thrust of their counter-attack against the Chinese efforts within the international Communist movement to thwart Moscow's policies and subvert its satellites. On this issue the Chinese remained adamant. Since, as all Lenin's theories and actions so clearly demonstrated, the organisational issue is the decisive issue in any bureaucratic élitist movement, it follows that on this key issue the Russians were unsuccessful at the Moscow meetings, and the Chinese, although they did not win on it, succeeded in maintaining the *status quo ante*.

The above reconstruction also demonstrates the significance of the issue of Yugoslavia, not only for the Albanians but for the Russians, Chinese, and Italians as well. Ever since the 1948 Soviet-Yugoslav break, Moscow's attitude towards Belgrade has always been an integral part and a faithful reflector of its general foreign policy line. When it favours *détente*, it favours *détente* with Yugoslavia as well; when it intensifies tension, Soviet-Yugoslav relations also worsen.

Finally, the reconstruction highlights that the Moscow meetings themselves were more " polycentric " than initial reports had indicated. The Italian position on such issues as the peaceful transition to Socialism and on contacts with Yugoslavia demonstrated that even in 1960 the international Communist movement was not divided into a Chinese-Albanian " left " and a Soviet " right " but, rather, in a far more complex manner.[80] On policy issues the Russians were in the centre, the Chinese and Albanians were on the far left, most of the other Asian Parties were close to the Chinese, several of the European Parties (East German, Czechoslovak, French) also had leftist policy sympathies but submerged

[80] *Cf.* Dallin, *op. cit.*

them in favour of organisational loyalty to Moscow, and some other European Parties (Polish, Italian, and in part Hungarian) were to the right. On the organisational issue, the degree of control by Moscow of other parties, the extent and kind of Chinese influence, and the degree of polycentrism in the international Communist movement, the Soviet Party was completely supported by those Parties which by tradition, leadership, financial support, or Soviet economic aid or military presence or threat have consistently been faithful to Moscow; it was strongly opposed by the Chinese, who aspire first to more influence and eventually to predominance in the world movement, and by the Chinese ally, the Albanians. It was less strongly opposed, but still not endorsed, by the " Communist neutralists ": those Asian Parties, in and out of power, which gain from balancing between the two Communist giants. Finally, it was endorsed, but far from totally, by the right wing parties, in particular the Poles and the Italians, which did not desire a break with Moscow but preferred more autonomy than they now have.

The Moscow meetings confirmed and deepened the rifts and feuds which had become public in 1960. They were followed by a continuing decline in Sino-Soviet relations and within the year by the Soviet-Albanian break.

ITALY

Giorgio Galli

IT was after the 20th Congress that Togliatti first enunciated the famous formula of polycentrism:

> The Soviet model should no longer be obligatory . . . . The complex of the system is becoming polycentric, and in the communist movement itself one can no longer speak of a single guide . . . . The criticisms of Stalin give rise to a general problem, common to the whole movement.[1]

This last statement was criticised by the Soviet leaders,[2] and the serious crisis which developed in the East owing to the events in Poland and Hungary caused Togliatti to abandon any autonomous attitude and support the Moscow line in every respect. This brought about a crisis in the PCI, as shown not only by the exit from the party of some well-known leading figures such as Giolitti, Reale, and Onofrio, but also by the situation described as follows by the PCI's Central Committee before the party's 9th congress (January 1960):

> There has been a falling off in the number of our registered members, from 2,035,353 in 1956 to 1,787,338 in 1959. The greatest decrease occurred in 1957, of 217,197 . . . This fall assumes more serious proportions in some federations and regions, where it runs the risk of affecting the character of the party.[3]

Until 1956 the Italian Communist party (PCI) had maintained and consolidated its strong position, first shown in the 1946 elections, when they obtained over 4,000,000 votes (nearly 20 per cent. of the total) about 400,000 fewer than the Socialist party, which later split, on the issue of collaboration with the communists, into a left wing (PSI) and a right wing which took the name of Social-Democratic party (PSDI).[4] The PCI–PSI pact on unity of action gave the communists substantial advantages, enabling them to avoid isolation both in politics and in the trade unions and, profiting from the prestige of the USSR as a great power, to influence over 20 per cent. of the electorate in favour of Soviet policies in international affairs. But though its policy had brought the PCI these gains, the reaction among other parties had in a sense forced the Italian working classes on to the margin of Italian society, in which they exercised less power than the working classes enjoyed in other western industrial countries. It was the realisation of the subordinate

---

[1] Interview in the periodical *Nuovi Argomenti*, also published in *L'Unità*, 17 June 1956.
[2] See *Pravda*, 30 June 1956.
[3] *Rapporto di attività del Comitato Centrale e Progetto di tesi per il IX Congresso* (Rome, 1960), p. 71.
[4] *Trent'anni di vita e di lotte del PCI*, Ed. Rinascita, 1951, pp. 146–7.

and defensive role being forced on the workers that aroused doubts in the PSI, first shown at its 1955 congress, about the advisability of its alliance with the PCI; this was one of the factors in the communist reaction to the 1956 events.

If the PCI succeeded in overcoming this crisis without much difficulty, this was due as much to the USSR's prestige successes after 1956 (e.g. in space flights, links with the anti-colonialist revolutions) as to the fact that no effective progressive alternative to the policy of the PCI was put forward in Italy, where the possibilities of agreement between the PSI and the anti-communist left wing were blocked by the strong resistance of the conservative forces. This resistance found expression in April 1960 in the formation of a Christian Democrat Government led by Tambroni and openly supported by the neo-fascists, which provoked a combination of anti-fascist forces in which the PCI played an important part. The resulting tension led to clashes in June and July 1960 (originating in the neo-fascist MSI's attempt to hold its congress in Genoa, an action regarded as a challenge to anti-fascism), after which the Tambroni Government resigned. But a phase of compromise ensued, in which the new political line advocated by the PSI, the PSDI, the PRI, and the Christian Democrat left wing had once again to mark time.

IN the meantime, however, divergences were developing between China and the USSR, of which the PCI became aware at the Peking meeting of the General Council of the World Federation of Trade Unions in June 1960, and more definitely at the Moscow conference of the 81 communist parties in the following November. At the beginning of 1962 the PCI published a pamphlet containing the texts of the first and second speeches made at that conference by the party vice-secretary, Luigi Longo, in the name of the Italian delegation, as well as the memorandum of the Italian delegation to Khrushchev and to the CPSU delegation after the Italian standpoint had been excluded from the final document. The speeches and memorandum demonstrate explicit opposition to the Chinese thesis not only concerning peaceful co-existence but also concerning the non-violent transition to socialism and the attitude to the Yugoslavs. A communist publication, commenting on these texts, speaks of the ' frank and energetic attitude of criticism hitherto adopted by the PCI in relation to the Albanian Communist party ' and of ' lively discussion between the representatives of the PCI and the Chinese Communists concerning the relation between peaceful coexistence and the class struggle.' [5]   And elsewhere:

> It is possible, in a number of countries, to realise the transition from capitalism to socialism by peaceful means, advancing continuously on the road of development of democracy, without a prior revolutionary rupture and civil war . . . The Chinese comrades ask us to

[5] *Vie Nuove*, 25 January 1962.

indicate what country is advancing along this road. We reply in all tranquillity and firmness that the PCI itself has been moving for some time in this direction . . . The draft declaration presented to the conference represents in some respects, in our view, a step backwards in relation to the clarity of the preceding conference [i.e. of November 1957] . . . We wish to emphasise here that what often escapes some comrades who are not operating in capitalist countries is that the tone we adopt in speaking of our disagreements with the League of Yugoslav Communists constitutes one of the yardsticks whereby the Social-Democratic parties and trade unions and more generally, public opinion as a whole can estimate the sincerity of our unitary policy and our capacity to collaborate even with forces which are politically and ideologically distant from us.[6]

With these statements the PCI, though it subscribed in the final document to a position much closer to that of the Chinese, took up a stand to the right of the world communist movement. And it should be noted that the PCI, far from advancing continuously if peacefully towards socialism, had as we have said contributed towards putting the Italian working class in a less favourable position than that of the working classes in other industrial countries. But these facts were not at that time known to the party as a whole. A first public indication of the position adopted was given a few months later in an article by Togliatti on the problems of democracy and socialism following on the congress of the Albanian Communist party in February 1961. In connection with a letter of criticism sent on 20 March by the CPSU Central Committee to the Albanian leaders, Togliatti wrote:

When, for example, we learnt from our representative at the Albanian party's congress that at that congress questions of party life and internal debate had been posed in a way which seemed to us mistaken and dangerous, we made known our views, but the direct responsibility and the correction of mistakes are not our concern.[7]

But in the course of the spring and summer the USSR's new success in space, the violent debate with the West concerning Berlin, and the launching of the CPSU's new programme completely diverted the attention of the communist rank and file from the question of possible differences of attitude between the various communist parties, and in particular between the CPSU and the Chinese party. When, at the 22nd congress, the debate departed from the programme to embark on a violent attack on the Albanian Labour party and the anti-party group, and on thinly-veiled polemics with the Chinese, culminating in the public removal of Stalin's body from the mausoleum in Red Square, amazement and dis-orientation within the PCI quickly reached a pitch equal to that of the autumn of 1956. This state of mind found expression at the meeting of

6 *Interventi della delegazione del PCI alla conferenza di Mosca degli 81 partiti comunisti ed operai* (Rome, 1962), pp. 40 and 71.

Rinascita, April 1961.

the PCI's Central Committee on 11/12 November. The debate at that meeting must also be seen in relation to the internal situation in Italy which, in view of the imminent congress of the Christian Democrat party, due in January 1962, had once again begun to move in the direction of a converging action by the PSI on the one hand and the PSDI, PRI, and left-wing Christian Democrats on the other, in favour of a centre-left Government with a programme of reforms that might win socialist support.

Thus the PCI found itself faced with the problem of a further weakening of the links between itself and the PSI, in addition to the problem of relations with the USSR and the communist movement as a whole which had been the main theme of the Central Committee's meeting in November. Togliatti's report began with a lengthy and positive evaluation of progress in the USSR and of the CPSU's new programme, but later on it touched on more controversial points. In relation to the attack on the 'anti-party group' and the fresh condemnation of Stalin's methods he said:

> One asks oneself whether it was really necessary to reopen the story of the denunciations and concentrate the attack against a group of old collaborators of Stalin who had been expelled from the Central Committee in 1957. To this question it is not easy to give an exhaustive answer, since we are not *au fait* with all the internal life of the Soviet party and its directive organs . . . The violations of legality and the crimes committed at the highest levels of the party, the armed forces, and the state on Stalin's responsibility constitute a terrible tragedy which now weighs upon the minds of both old and young generations, and from which we are not yet freed. . . . The problem of Stalin is a grave and profound one transcending individual denunciations of inhuman actions, and impinging on fundamental questions of the working-class and communist movement which inescapably have to be tackled. For this reason we regard as mistaken and misguided what the Albanian communists are doing, with the partial support of the Chinese comrades. The Albanians counter the Soviet comrades' denunciations by a mere superficial outburst of words lacking in any critical sense.

But the reasons for the dispute with the Albanians were of course deeper, and connected with the attitude of the PCI to the Chinese and Yugoslavs:

> The thing for which the Albanian communists cannot be forgiven, apart from their violation of all the normal standards of democratic centralism, is that in their relations with the Soviet Union and the other socialist parties they have gone so far as to abjure and set at naught proletarian international solidarity. The objection raised by comrade Chou En-lai to comrade Khrushchev's criticism of the Albanian leaders concerned only the form of relations between the parties, but even with those limitations I do not think it was acceptable, because his public criticism in this case came after all the questions had been raised and discussed in secret without arriving

at any result. We have had, and we maintain, reciprocal friendly
relations with the Yugoslav communists too. . . . We have criticised,
and still do, the programme approved by the last congress of the
League of Yugoslav Communists. But . . . it is a mistake to treat
Yugoslavia and her regime as one would treat an enemy; on the
contrary the Yugoslav communists should be able to feel that while
there may be disagreements with them there is no preconceived
hostility towards them.

Finally, Togliatti made a point of reiterating that Stalinist methods
had never been used in the PCI:

> We have been particularly careful to maintain and develop the
> democratic character of our party, constantly promoting debate and
> a comparison of ideas within it, and at the same time accepting
> debate and comparison from any opponent.[8]

Apart from this last, obviously inaccurate, statement, Togliatti
reaffirmed the position of the PCI to the right of the communist movement, reverting to some of the themes of 1956 (the problem of Stalin
involves questions that are basic for the movement), and striving to
minimise the Sino-Soviet dispute. But for the first time the Central
Committee showed that it did not accept his view of the situation, and
certain divergences of standpoint came to light which had for some time
been latent in the PCI. Togliatti found himself forced to mediate between
the various different trends which can to some extent be discerned even
within a monolithic party such as the PCI.

THERE is, in the first place, a group linked sentimentally to Stalin
and politically to the views of the Stalin period which Togliatti has
described as ' sectarian ' and ' dogmatic '. The chief exponent of this
group is Mauro Scoccimarro, an old colleague of Gramsci and Togliatti
who was in prison or confinement under surveillance throughout the
fascist regime. The group is a kind of ' old guard ', always ready to
denounce the dangers of revisionism. Another group mobilised against
the same danger consists of a new left wing which has a strong position
in the communist youth organisation (the Italian Young Communist
Federation, or FGCI), and which is represented in the Central Committee by the editor of the FGCI newspaper *Nuova Generazione*, Achille
Occhetto, who comes from the university student organisations. At the
time of the November meeting of the Central Committee that paper
published a photograph of Trotsky, ' one of the most original personali-
ties of the October Revolution, whose ideas have recently come under
discussion again '.[9] This phrase, which the paper itself subsequently

---

[8] All the above quotations of Togliatti are from *L'Unità*, 11 November 1961. The
writings of Togliatti on the subject have been published in a collection of his articles,
Problemi del movimento operaio internazionale, 1956–1961 (1962). The position of
Pietro Nenni on these questions is given in his recent book, *Le prospettive del
socialismo dopo la destalinizzazione* (1962).
[9] *Nuova Generazione*, 10 November 1961.

described as infelicitous, at once caused the word 'Trotskyist' to be applied to the group. In point of fact, in the debate within the party this group puts the accent on the need to tackle the problems of socialist revolution in countries of advanced capitalism now that the end has been reached of the phase of isolation and backwardness in the USSR which prompted both the Stalinist standpoint and Trotskyist criticism. It is significant that both the old and the new Left see in the new political formula of a centre-left government an attempt on the part of the Christian Democrats and the main capitalist groups to rationalise Italian capitalism with a view to adapting it to the present phase of development and capturing within the new system that part of the working-class movement represented by the PSI.

At the other end of the scale is the group which can be said to be represented by Giorgio Amendola, son of a Liberal politician murdered by the fascists, who joined the PCI in the 1930s when in his early twenties and lived abroad during the fascist era. In the 1956 crisis, according to the evidence of Fabrizio Onofri, 'many comrades believed they had found in Amendola the key man of the situation',[10] but after the Hungarian crisis he ceased to urge 'renewal', or the adoption of fresh standpoints, within the party, in which he was responsible for organisation up to the 9th congress, early in 1960. Subsequently he was in charge of the 2nd (May 1961) conference of communist factory workers, from which it emerged that there had been a considerable weakening of the PCI's position in factories which the party was unable to remedy, as various admissions in subsequent months confirmed. The official thesis of the PCI, that a peaceful and democratic way to socialism exists in Italy, has in Amendola one of its apparently most convinced supporters; he regards the centre-left policy not so much as a mere manoeuvre of the big monopolies to satisfy their own interests, but rather as a dialectical factor in the evolution of Italian society which might have favourable developments for the working class if the PCI can contrive to guide it wisely.

Bearing in mind this situation, it seems likely that Amendola seized the opportunity of the 22nd congress to propose a far-reaching 'renewal' within the PCI on the basis of an open confrontation of the various policies. He declared :

> The 22nd congress represents . . . the end of a formula of fictitious unanimity, which had nothing to do with real ideological and political unity. . . . Even in our own party, discussion must develop, if need be up to the point of forming, from time to time, majorities and minorities on various problems. This does not mean the formation of different trends . . . but the constantly widening development of an internal democratic debate.

[10] Fabrizio Onofri, *Classe operaia e partito* (Bari, 1957), p. 107.

He added that ' polycentrism has become necessary ', whereas Togliatti did not use that term in his report but preferred to speak of a multiplicity of centres of direction ' [11]

The scene of the confrontation urged by Amendola should be, he said, an ' extraordinary ' party congress, and this was formally proposed by Aldo Natoli, politically a close colleague of Amendola, with whom others present also associated themselves. The suggestion was strongly opposed by Scoccimarro :

> I do not propose to speak at length since at this point of the debate the speech I would have made is no longer possible, because there would be too many things to say which cannot be said in a short time, and also because it is better that certain questions basically affecting the life and action of the party should be first discussed within the Directorate. . . . In this debate too many questions have been poured out pell-mell. . . . I shall later have the opportunity to say fully what I think about all the new problems before us today. For the moment I will confine myself to saying that I do not agree with the proposal to call a congress which would be, objectively speaking, extraordinary. An extraordinary congress can be justified only by extraordinary and exceptional reasons and motives. As to the problems before us today, the Central Committee and the Central Control Commission have full authority to deal with them and to decide on the immediate needs of the party. (*L'Unità*, 12 November 1961.)

As can be seen, Scoccimarro, although ' deciding not to speak ', managed to say a good deal, including the fact that it was better to terminate the Central Committee's meeting in order to embark on discussion within the more restricted framework of the Directorate. Togliatti's reply, which was not published, seems also to have been very stiff, especially in relation to Amendola, and definitely hostile to the convocation of an extraordinary congress. This subject was discussed in the PCI Directorate in the following weeks. But in the meantime the debate within the PCI aroused considerable repercussions abroad.

IN the first place, Hoxha's speech of 8 November became known; in this speech, made on the twentieth anniversary of the foundation of the Albanian communist party, he attacked the PCI Secretary in person :

> I think of those who speak of internal party democracy and respect for its standards, and in particular of Togliatti. What does he think of the way in which the 22nd congress attacked us? He knew nothing about the evolution of our relations with the CPSU, whose Central Committee had taken no decision to condemn our party, nor had it ordered its representative at the 22nd congress to do so, at least so far as I know. But Togliatti excommunicated us and accused us of dividing the international working-class movement. But it is not for him to say that, seeing that only five years ago he

attacked the Soviet socialist system, demanding polycentrism and multiple spheres of influence within the international communist movement. The Albanian party neither can nor will ever be accused of this. With his anti-Marxist theses Togliatti has rendered a great service to the revisionist Tito. It is strange that no one has attacked the revisionist operation of Togliatti.[12]

In fact, as will be recalled, *Pravda* had done so. But now Hoxha could not be allowed to say that standpoints such as that of the PCI were left unanswered. Therefore once again the Soviet daily explained that 'the personality cult was an excrescence foreign to the healthy organism of Soviet socialist society, which was denounced and effectively eradicated from our party thanks precisely to the fact that the bases of the social structure of the state were and remain healthy'. (*Pravda*, 21 November 1961.)

This judgment implicitly refuted that of Togliatti, according to which Stalinism was 'a terrible tragedy which still weighs upon us' and 'impinges on fundamental questions of the working-class and communist movement which inescapably have to be tackled'. Simultaneously, in the Central Committee of the Polish party Gomulka, the most open-minded of the communist leaders, was taking up a position against polycentrism, affirming that 'today there is no centre capable of directing the activity of the individual communist and working-class parties and . . . there is no need of such a centre. . . . Every party is . . . fully autonomous and independent' (*L'Unità*, 23 November, 1961).

But the most direct attack on the attitudes which had emerged within the PCI came from Thorez, speaking at the Central Committee of the French Communist party (25–27 November). The attack was facilitated by another article which had appeared in the meantime in *Nuova Generazione* (17 November 1961) by Michelangelo Notarianni, secretary of the communist youth movement in Milan, entitled 'Bureaucratic Degeneration in the Socialist State'. The attack also linked on to another dispute which had developed since 1956 between Togliatti and Roger Garaudy, of the French Communist party's political bureau, following on the PCI's 8th congress, and which constitutes one aspect of the divergence observable for some time between the narrow and rigid French party and the more flexible and open-minded PCI. Togliatti, in his report to the Central Committee, had tried to make the French party appreciate the 'multiplicity of centres of direction', referring to the 'great success' of the Rome meeting of representatives of the Western European Communist parties in November 1958, at which the French played an important part (and in fact the outcome was a very rigid and narrow document) and from which, according to Togliatti, 'a platform emerged which still retains its value'.[13] But despite this, Thorez' attack was direct and decisive:

[12] *Est et Ouest*, 15 February 1962.
[13] *L'Unità*, 11 November 1961.

The thesis of polycentrism is surprising and disquieting. There is no longer a single centre of direction: so why talk of setting up several? According to what we have read ... the 22nd congress has also been presented as a sort of corrective to the Declaration of the 81, as putting an end to a ' fictitious unanimity '. On the plane of party organisation, the formation of a majority and a minority is regarded as possible—in other words, a return to trends and fractions and the abandonment of the Leninist conception of the new type of party. A national communist youth organisation has brought out a paper in which we find blazoned across a whole page the heading ' Degeneration of the Socialist State '. There is even talk of giving Trotsky back his place! ... Comrades, in fighting revisionist and opportunist trends, we cannot neglect sectarian and dogmatic deviation which might become the greatest danger of all if we cease to fight it.[14]

As can be seen, Thorez attacked Amendola for his ' right-wing ' attitude, *Nuova Generazione* for its ' left-wing ' standpoint, and in the last analysis Togliatti for his polycentrism and because he allowed expression to such attitudes. Here is the PCI's reply:

Concerning the problems of the international working-class and communist movement, our party's resolution . . . leaves no doubt as to the decisive importance attributed to the unity of the movement, nor does it allow of any interpretation of ' polycentrism ' as a multiplicity of centres of regional direction. The term is used to emphasise the necessary and indispensible autonomy of each party within the framework of proletarian internationalism. . . . In our party's Central Committee . . . international problems have been treated in this same spirit and also in new terms corresponding to the new problems of today. For example, the opportuneness of a public debate between the communist parties has been discussed, unlike what has been thought suitable in previous international gatherings: but on this point presumably the French Communist party does not disagree, since it is taking the initiative in promoting a public dispute with our party. Similar considerations apply to the internal life of the parties: no one in the Central Committee of our party has questioned the Leninist principle of ideological unity, within the framework of a debate and confrontation which would be perfectly free and which for that reason would not become crystallised either by divisions into trends or by an opposite bureaucratic conception of centralism or a formal conception of unity.

Togliatti added that:

In 1956, during the 20th congress, at a meeting at which there were present the representatives of all the parties adhering to the Information Bureau (Cominform), the proposal was made to try out a certain organisation of a ' regional ' type, that is to say on the basis of closer contacts for information between parties operating in similar circumstances. This proposal was not, however, made by our party. It was agreed to as an experiment, not without some

[14] *L'Humanité*, 27 November 1961.

heart-searching. Some attempt was also made to carry it out, especially by the French and ourselves, but it produced no useful result; it was eventually abandoned, and has never been discussed since. What I say can be confirmed by Comrade Scoccimarro, who was with me at the meeting that took place during the 20th congress.[15]

The young communists, in their turn, replied with the report of the national secretary· Rino Serri, to the central committee of the FGCI on 5 December:

> Concerning the debate opened in *Nuova Generazione* . . . it is not a question of rehabilitating Trotsky, as Comrade Thorez, who has been misinformed, fears; it is a question of scrutinising, discussing, and re-examining the whole Soviet experiment. This does not mean that the debate will not draw attention to defects: we cannot fail to make some critical mention of the emergence, in some articles, of attitudes that are mistaken and sometimes even frivolous and unconsidered.[15a]

This amounted to a partial retraction on the paper's part, further emphasised by Togliatti with the assertion that ' some public interventions by *Nuova Generazione* . . . are mistaken, confused, and unacceptable '.[16] The paper clarified its own position as follows:

> Comrade Thorez . . . has also expended some words on *Nuova Generazione* [which] published . . . ' The Degeneration of the Socialist State ' . . . In point of fact the title was ' The *Bureaucratic* Degeneration of the Socialist State ' . . . On the alleged ' rehabilitation ' of Trotsky . . . the bourgeois press has expended whole columns of print. . . . We are not Trotskyists and have no sympathy with Trotskyism. . . . The readers of our paper are aware that the same issue which contained the alleged ' rehabilitation ' also included an attack on ' The Temptations of Trotskyism and Neo-Trotskyism ' arising here and there.[17]

IN the meantime the party vice-secretary, Longo, who had gone to Moscow after the Central Committee meeting in November, probably brought back to Rome the negative impressions of the Soviet leaders. Togliatti, who had always been opposed not only to opening a debate but also to informing the whole group of party leaders about what had been happening in Moscow from 1953 down to the Beria crisis,[18] was able to seize the opportunity to close a discussion which during the preceding weeks had begun to percolate even to the party's local and peripheral organisations. In agreement with Scoccimarro and the old guard, he disowned, as we have seen, the attitude of *Nuova Generazione*, and also routed the Amendola group, since there was no further talk of holding

15 *L'Unità*, 28 November, 2 December 1961.
15a Ibid., 6 December 1961.
16 *Ibid.*, 7 December 1961.
17 *Nuova Generazione*, 15 December 1961.
18 *Cf.* in this connection *Togliatti e Stalin*, by Giulio Seniga (Milan, 1961). Seniga was at that time second in command of the National Vigilance Commission of the PCI

an extraordinary party congress or of the legitimacy of forming majorities and minorities. Indeed, the disputed question of the date of the next congress was settled by an evasive if unanimous decision to hold it 'within the statutory period' (*L'Unità*, 24 December 1961).

The decision was taken at a fresh session of the Central Committee whose tone was very different from that of the earlier one. As if to confirm the re-establishment of normality, the report was made not by Togliatti but by a minor figure, his trusted young colleague Enrico Berlinguer, who had replaced Amendola as the man responsible for party organisation and who spoke on the theme of 'the strength, development, and tasks of the party at the present time'. He referred in the following terms to the debate just concluded:

> The debate was lively, and was always based—but for a few exceptions—on a sound party spirit . . . there were also some negative factors and aspects. . . . At times there was confusion, disorder, and even excitement, though this was largely understandable especially in the earlier stages. . . . Sometimes, on the other hand, there were real misunderstandings of a sectarian and conservative nature concerning the significance of the 22nd congress. The discussion enabled a good many of these misunderstandings to be cleared up, though some still persist. . . . On the other hand, there were also at times misunderstandings in the other direction: a tendency to depart not only from our political line but also from the very foundations of our ideology, our international spirit, and our conception of the party. . . . The recent meeting of the FGCI's Central Committee must be regarded as completely satisfactory both for the seriousness, enthusiasm, and spirit of investigation with which the problems were tackled and also for the answer given to the negative trends which had emerged in some articles in *Nuova Generazione*.[19]

Togliatti, for his part, while to all appearances mediating between Scoccimarro and the Amendola group, reduced the whole problem to the need for the Directorate to keep the Central Committee more closely informed:

> Comrade Scoccimarro said something which is formally perfectly correct, namely, that if there is a profound disagreement within the Directorate, the latter should itself decide to take it to the Central Committee. But the comrades want something more than that. Those of them who argued with comrade Scoccimarro want all the details of the line of policy proposed by the Directorate to the Central Committee to be made known. . . . Now, this demand has a legitimate foundation. This does not mean that the minutes of the Secretariat and the Directorate should be published in all the newspapers; that would be simply absurd. But it does mean that the comrades in the Directorate . . . ought to make all the relevant facts available to the Central Committee. Naturally, both the Directorate and the Central Committee work from the same point of departure and with the aim of achieving unity.

[19] This and the following quotations are from *L'Unità*, 4, 21, 22, 23 December 1961.

138   GIORGIO GALLI

After these brief introductory references, both Berlinguer's report and
Togliatti's speech ignored the problems of international communism
which had come up during the debate of the preceding weeks, and dealt
instead with the situation of the party in general and the internal political
prospects. But the way in which the discussion had ended emerged clearly
from the sharp tone of Scoccimarro's speech (in agreement with Togliatti)
as compared with the cautious and self-defensive character of that of
Amendola. Scoccimarro said:

> After the 22nd congress there was renewed talk of ' polycentrism ',
> as an affirmation of the autonomy of the communist parties. But this
> is not correct. Polycentrism has never signified either an affirmation
> or a limitation of the parties' autonomy. The fact is that with the
> present relations between communist parties polycentrism can only
> assume the meaning of international fragmentation. This explains
> the anxieties expressed in the criticisms voiced by some communist
> parties from other countries. But such was not at all our intention.
> Therefore there is no need for any further discussion of poly-
> centrism. The question has been raised of the continued validity
> of the international resolutions of 1957 and 1960 after the disagree-
> ment which has arisen with Albania and the dispute with China.
> Those documents still retain their full validity. There may be debate
> between the parties, but . . . it is possible to discuss in order to
> strengthen the unity of the international communist movement, not
> to break it.

Amendola said:

> As to the problems of internal party democracy, I would refer to my
> speech at the last Central Committee, which has clearly lent itself
> to various misunderstandings and wrong interpretations. . . . The
> question of the majority and minority . . . is an instrument which
> can be useful and necessary in preventing the formation of a fictitious
> unanimity and in achieving the real political unity of the party. . . .
> A discussion . . . based on already existing documents, which allow
> of amendments being presented and discussed in open debate and
> eventually voted on, can make it possible to improve on ambiguous
> formulas, clarify the terms of possible dispute, and thus achieve a
> real and substantial party unity.

But if discussion of the great problems raised by the 22nd congress
was closed, the questions themselves remained open, as was clear from
Longo's speech, the most significant one made at this meeting of the
Central Committee, which also began with a proposal to abandon the
term ' polycentrism ':

> It is proposed . . . to give up using the term ' polycentrism ' if it is
> likely to give rise to misunderstanding and confusion. . . . In our
> talks with the Soviet comrades we put the question, why was the
> denunciation of the personality cult and condemnation of the anti-
> party group revived at the 22nd congress. The reply was that it had
> been found possible to carry out the liquidation of the personality
> cult only by means of a stern struggle against the anti-party group. . . .

Some parties, and in particular the Albanian party, made use of the defence of the cult of Stalin's personality to conduct a shameful struggle against the CPSU and its leading group. The Soviet comrades told us that the cult of Hoxha's personality was an internal problem for Albania and did not concern us. Nevertheless, they added, they could not permit the distribution among their active cadres of the Albanian leaders' documents, articles, and speeches directed against Khrushchev and the other Soviet leaders. . . . Up till now the Chinese comrades have not made known their views on the merits of the Albanian leaders' standpoint . . . they have preferred to intensify their manifestations of sympathy towards Albania and her leaders and to reproduce in their own press Tirana's calumnies and lies about the USSR. In Longo's view, the dispute between the CPSU and the Chinese party goes beyond the questions of peaceful coexistence, the inevitability of war, and the personality cult. At the basis of this dispute there is perhaps a different conception of the march towards socialism and communism in the countries of the socialist system. This march, according to a certain conception, should take place as a single whole; the more advanced countries should adapt their pace to that of the more backward ones, placing all their material advantages at the disposal of the latter to accelerate their advance. It is clear that, setting out from a conception of this kind, it is no longer possible to agree with the economic challenge launched by the USSR to the capitalist countries, with the strategic and tactical plan of peaceful coexistence, or with Soviet economic aid to the ex-colonial countries, still less with the programme for a transition to communism and the relevant measures for the democratisation of Soviet institutions. . . . The Chinese comrades do not conceal their reservations about these aspects of Soviet policy. We, on the other hand, consider that the Soviet policy . . . is the most useful for the general advancement of the socialist camp.

This speech, after the inevitable homage to ritual expressions such as the ' personality cult ', brings out clearly the profound problems of an economic and general political nature which are today causing differences of substance in the international communist movement. If these differences were to continue or become accentuated, the PCI could not fail to experience their repercussions. They would call into question one of the cardinal points of the policy of the past thirty years, based at it has been on the premiss of the monolithic unity of the whole communist movement. These repercussions could especially make themselves felt at the various levels within the PCI if at the same time Italian internal politics were to move into a phase no longer dominated by conservatism, but directed instead towards changes and reforms for the benefit of the working classes, in which the PSI would participate, while the PCI would be pushed out to the fringe. Were this to happen, yet another of the cardinal points of communist policy of the past thirty years would be called into question: the premiss that in Italy no serious initiative can be taken in the direction of reform without the participation of the PCI and that party's collaboration with the PSI and the Catholic and Social-Democratic popular masses.

The continuity and results of communist policy in the past decades have been based on two premises: on the prestige gained by the PCI through belonging to the ranks of world communism guided by the USSR, and on the advantages accruing to it from its long alliance with the socialists in the common struggle against the forces of conservatism. And it is obvious that if these two premises were to be simultaneously called in question, it would not be easy for the Italian communist leaders to shelve problems and reduce discussion to a minimum as they succeeded in doing in November-December 1961.

FRANCE

Pierre Fougeyrollas

FOR thirty years Thorez has been the leader of the French Communist party (PCF). Between 1930 and 1939, he succeeded in transforming an extremist proletarian movement into a Stalinist party with a rigidly monolithic structure. By 1945, the PCF was the largest party in France and the most powerful communist organisation in the West.

Two kinds of period alternate in the history of the PCF: those in which Soviet diplomacy coincided with French national interests, e.g., between 1935 and 1938, and between 1941 and 1946, and those in which it was directed against major French interests, e.g., between 1939 and 1941, and between 1947 and the present.

Thorez' strategy always strictly followed Soviet policy. His tactics varied according to the period. When Soviet and French interests coincided, he tried to strengthen the PCF's position with the masses and made alliances which involved support of the popular-front government in 1936 and participation in the first government of the Fourth Republic. When Soviet and French interests clashed, Thorez was less concerned with rallying the masses than with preserving the cohesion of his party machinery, with a view to future periods of expansion.

After Stalin's death in March 1953, the omnipotent secretary general of the PCF was compelled to face two new series of difficulties: those created by the modernisation of French society and the far-reaching changes in the condition of wage-earners, and those connected with the crisis of international communism, i.e. the process of destalinisation, and it is possible to explain the strategy and tactics of the PCF between the 20th and 22nd congresses of the CPSU, in terms of those two series of problems. There is no doubt that the duration and intensity of the Algerian tragedy and the phenomenon of Gaullism helped to make Thorez' position more difficult, but they did not play a decisive part in shaping PCF activities. After the 20th congress, the intellectuals and the few leaders who opposed Thorez were excluded or relieved of their posts, and Thorez' authority among the rank and file is still as great as in the past.

His strategy and tactics also involved some disagreements with the leaders of the Italian Communist party, displayed openly during the 22nd CPSU congress, and they have not been overcome. An analysis of these disputes suggests some hypotheses on the future of communism in Western Europe.

The profound and rapid changes that have taken place in French industrial life since about 1950 brought with them not only a gradual improvement in the living standards of the wage-earners, but a trans-formation in their way of life and their attitudes to work. Yesterday's proletariat living on the edge of society was replaced by a progressively Americanised class of wage-earners, integrated into and transforming social life.

Whether or not he understood these changes, Thorez felt that the influence of the PCF was endangered by this process of modernisation. The PCF as an ideological party was threatened by this new stage in industrial society in which its ideology was losing its appeal. Because he was aware of these dangers rather than because he misunderstood the new economic trends, Thorez in 1954 insisted on the preservation of the Marxist theory of the absolute and relative impoverishment of wage-earners in a capitalist system. He did not fear a new period of détente between communist countries and the West. He had become accustomed under Stalin to adapting to such turns in communist strategy. But he did fear the social and political effects of economic modernisation in France. Thorez also feared a revision of Stalinist ideology that went beyond questions of economic doctrine.

His economic policy was bound to arouse opposition in the trade unions of the CGT (trade union federation) and in the apparatus of the PCF. In the CGT, a minority led by Pierre Brun advocated a constructive economic programme. They wanted trade unionists to participate in the process of modernisation in order to obtain the maximum advantages for the wage-earners. They wanted to support Mendès France's experiment and help modernising elements in management in their struggle against those who benefited by an outdated economic structure. They hoped to achieve a rapprochement between the CGT and the other trade union federations who were in favour of such a policy.

In Italy, the CGIL (communist-controlled trade union federation) adopted a more constructive economic programme, and its leaders, communists included, decided to go along with what they termed the representatives of neo-capitalism. In France things were otherwise. The communist majority of the CGT strictly applied the directives of Thorez and rejected a positive economic programme, the minority being condemned for its betrayal of the basic interests of the proletariat.

Meanwhile the workers as a whole remained indifferent to these discussions. Tired of the purely political orientation of the CGT, they struck only for material benefits and for reasons of solidarity. A call for a strike from the CGT alone is now insufficient to bring out the workers in any numbers; it requires agreement with the Christian and / or socialist trade union federation before an effective strike can take place. The CGT retained most of their votes in the elections to the factory committees, as the PCF retained its votes in political elections. But both of them lost some of their capacity to engage in direct action.

Some of the PCF leaders, aware of this new trend, endeavoured to modify Thorez' policy. Pronteau and the staff of the review *Economie et Politique* made some attempt to analyse the development of western economy and advocated more flexible methods of action for wage-earners, assuming that these would be better adapted to new living conditions.

They were supported by Kriegel-Valrimont, former member of the political bureau of the PCF and to a lesser extent by Casanova, leader of communist intellectuals, and by Servin, organising secretary of the PCF and considered as the heir presumptive to the Secretary Generalship. Since open discussion on these matters was out of the question, plots and stratagems were resorted to.

It seems that Casanova and Servin obtained some support against Thorez from Togliatti and the leaders of the Italian Communist party. Early in 1961 the opposition hoped that Casanova would replace Thorez as Secretary General, with Khrushchev's blessing. Attacked by Stalinists in the Soviet apparatus, and by Chinese leaders with their Albanian allies, Khrushchev sought the support of the European communist parties. Thorez controlled the machinery of the French communist party and Casanova did not; therefore Khrushchev was bound to appeal to the former for support.

In November 1960, a compromise was reached in Moscow between the two conflicting trends. This is expressed in the famous *Declaration of 81 Communist Parties*, and Thorez was rewarded for supporting Khrushchev, or rather the Soviet-Chinese compromise.

Thorez was then in a position to get rid of Casanova, Servin, Pronteau and Kriegel-Valrimont on the pretext that they favoured neo-capitalism and Gaullism which was 'the political expression of the dictatorship of monopolies'. This was achieved without trouble at the 16th congress of the French communist party.

Within the framework of international communist bureaucracy, the strategy of Thorez was coherent and consistent, whilst that of Togliatti and his supporters in the PCF was less so. Countries such as France and Italy are being modernised under the impact of technical and economic necessity and this has many social repercussions. Those elements in management who are better placed economically and who are at the same time the most dynamic and skilled, co-operate with their staff, workers included, and with the more dynamic elements in agriculture and trade against those who stand to benefit by the outdated structure, whether employers or employees. Those Italian and French communists who wanted to support modernisation, at least partially, were attacked by Thorez in the name of Marxism-Leninism and the class struggle. This orthodox position appealed to the diehards of the party with their rejection of any revisionism. Thorez was also prompted by political fears that any collaboration with capitalist elements would serve to strengthen those elements. By advocating the union of workers and smallholders, small tradesmen and small factory owners, Thorez appears faithful to the dogma of the class struggle and at the same time seeks to slow down modernisation. If his political strategy was followed by the masses, the development of Western society would be retarded and their resistance to the communist bloc weakened. If a greater participation of their parties and trade unions in the transformation of industrial society seems to be in the interest of French and Italian workers, the strategic interests of

world communism dictate the opposite. This is the political strength of
Thorez.

Even with the loss of some of its members and some of its aggressiveness, the communist party holds to its main object, which is to capitalise
on discontent, to weaken Western society, and to preserve its apparatus
until the eventual occupation of its territory by the Red Army. Whereas
if the CP tried to modernise, it might become a reformist party like the
Labour Party.

If one admits that the true social revolution is taking place now
through modernisation, communism seems fated in the West either to
disappear or to remain only as an instrument of Soviet imperialism. On
this fundamental issue, the subtlety of Togliatti can do nothing against
the brusque but coherent intransigence of Thorez.

THE evolution of French society has created some problems for
Thorez' strategic thinking. It is the task of any communist leader
to solve the problems connected with his region. However, since 1953,
and particularly since the 20th congress of the CPSU, he has also had
many difficulties connected with the evolution of Soviet communism.
Destalinisation served the higher interests of the CPSU and the political
interests of Khrushchev. Stalin's regime was characterised by such
despotism and cruelty that some degree of liberalisation was necessary in
order to maintain the dictatorship of the party. The denunciation of the
' cult of personality ' enabled Khrushchev to give some guarantees to the
Soviet people, especially to the new strata of technicians, economists, and
administrators, and at the same time it enabled him to consolidate his
own position against the ' anti-party group '. For such an operation to
be successful it had to be controlled and limited. It had to be explained
within the party as a political necessity without being allowed to degenerate into a revision of totalitarian principles. This is reflected in the
simultaneous attacks on dogmatism and revisionism.

Khrushchev as master of the party machinery and of all means of
mass communication and propaganda in the USSR was able to carry it
out, but it created difficulties for Western communist leaders, who had
of course no control over the non-communist press in their countries and
could not prevent a more fundamental criticism of the ' cult of personality ' or suppress the questions about the fundamentals of communism to which it led.

The French and Italian leaders reacted quite differently. Togliatti,
in an interview with the review *Nuovi Argomenti*, asked whether the
crimes committed under Stalin did not affect the socialist character of
the infrastructure in the Soviet regime. Thorez, on the contrary, took
the stand that the ' cult of personality ' did not apply to his party. The
bloody crimes of Stalin became in the official terminology of the PCF
' errors ', the product of arbitrary violations of Marxist-Leninist principles. Since the famous report on the cult of Stalin's personality read

by Khrushchev at a closed meeting of the 20th congress was never published officially in the USSR, it became for the leaders of the PCF ' the report *attributed* to Comrade Khrushchev '.

In June 1956 the leaders of the CPSU, worried by the development of revisionism in the communist world, rejected Togliatti's statements in *Nuovi Argomenti* and forced him to retract them.

The return of Gomulka to the leadership of the Polish Communist party and the Hungarian revolution and its repression by the Red Army enabled the leaders of the PCF to reassert their control over the disturbed and doubting rank and file. The explanation given by Thorez and Fajon was quite clear: ' At the very moment when Anglo-French imperialism and its Israeli ally launched the Suez adventure, American imperialism used all kinds of former nazis and fascists in an attempt to overthrow the people's government in Hungary. Fortunately, by its determined intervention, the Soviet Army saved the Hungarian workers from fascism. Objectively, the revisionism of Nagy, Gomulka, and Tito had served imperialist designs and had become a vehicle for bringing fascism back to Central Europe '.

The Italian communist leaders, whilst not going to the verbal extremes of the French, also condemned the Hungarian revolution and justified Soviet intervention as a ' painful necessity '. Thorez could in fact be said to have followed a more correct line than that attempted by Togliatti. Between the 20th and 22nd Soviet congresses the PCF was abandoned by several intellectuals, or, what came to the same thing, they were expelled. In the Italian party, in spite of Togliatti's flexibility, things were not much better. And, whereas Thorez preserved the homogeneity of the party machinery, Togliatti had to reckon with the opposition of revisionist elements. It is true that his party retained more members and a greater influence on the masses than the PCF, but the political situation in the two countries could not be compared. For instance, the alliance with Nenni's Socialist party served the interests of communists in Italy whilst the PCF was isolated, Mollet and the French socialists rejecting any form of cooperation.

After 1956, the attempts made in French communist circles to get rid of Thorez were weakened by the fact that his opponents were neither representative nor consistent. They were hardly ever recruited among workers or peasants who, when they disagreed with Thorez' policy, did not attend cell meetings and dropped out of the party. The opposition was limited to Parisian intellectuals, discreetly encouraged by some of the leaders. The second weakness was their failure to stand firm on the issue of destalinisation and its theoretical and political implications. Anti-Thorez intellectuals were torn between horror at the Soviet repression in Hungary and fear that the communist power in Budapest might completely collapse. One of their unofficial organs, *L'Etincelle*, condemned the execution of Nagy and his friends, but did not dare openly to criticise the Russian armed intervention. In a book which caused his expulsion from the PCF in 1961, Baby justified this intervention as a cruel necessity and condemned the handful of communist intellectuals who broke with the party because of it.

The opposition's third weakness lay in a lack of ideological and political unanimity. They disagreed with Thorez' intransigent economic views and acknowledged that capitalism could still raise the living standards of the masses. In doing so they appeared as a *right* wing opposition. Yet, from a political point of view, they criticised Thorez for his softness towards Gaullism and his moderation about Algeria. They would have preferred an alliance between the PCF and the FLN in an illegal campaign against the Fifth Republic. In this they appeared as a *left* wing opposition. It is easy to understand how Thorez was able to treat this confused ideology as a mixture of economic neo-Bukharinism and political neo-Trotskyism and to defeat it easily. The most active faction of this opposition finally joined up with the Parti Socialiste Unifié, in which there is a comparable mixture of economic moderation and political extremism.

Another of the opposition's weaknesses was their uncertain and changing attitude towards China. Between the communist victory in 1949 and up to about 1958, China was at the height of its popularity with the Parisian extreme left. Chinese leaders, as opposed to their Soviet counterparts, were said to be subtle, urbane, adaptable, and patient, and their technique of government to lack the patent brutality of Stalinist Russia. China was considered the leader of the underdeveloped countries in the struggle against western imperialism and colonialism, and all the revolutionary hopes previously vested in the proletariat of industrialised countries were transferred to her. For some time the opposition exaggerated the 'liberalism' of the Chinese as against the narrow dogmatism inherited from Stalin. The belligerence and dogmatism of Peking during the 1958 debates on peaceful co-existence caused a change in these opinions.

During the 22nd congress, Leduc, one of the leaders of this opposition, published in *L'Express* an article on peaceful co-existence supporting Khrushchev and denouncing the Chinese as deviationists. Thorez moved with the times. For obvious geo-political reasons he supported Moscow against Peking and stole Leduc's thunder by taking the credit for the denunciation of China and Albania.

On his return to his constituency in the Paris suburb of Ivry, Thorez hastened to rename Avenue Staline Avenue Lenine. Shortly after, Marcel Prenant, former member of the Central Committee, who resigned from the PCF, founded a ' Society of former members of the PCF faithful to Marxism-Leninism ', in the hope of re-shaping PCF policy. This seems as utopian a plan as that of an unfrocked priest attempting to change the policy and rites of the Catholic Church.

FOR several years the membership and influence of the PCF have been steadily declining, and this trend is likely to continue. But the long-term prospects of communist organisation are shaped by the party machine. This is why the opposition of Leduc and Prenant was so ineffectual.

De-stalinisation has shown that a communist party in a free country faces the choice between a monolithic structure assuring rigid discipline in its ranks, and controversy which threatens its survival as a Marxist-Leninist party. The PCF lost some members and some influence on the masses, some intellectuals and leaders were expelled, but Thorez succeeded in retaining the monolithic structure. He only has to wait for a more favourable historical situation.

In Italy, fewer members were lost to the party, whose aggressiveness and impact on the masses are consequently greater. But the division between a dogmatic majority and a revisionist minority threatens the unity of the Italian Communist party. In order to avoid its disruption, Togliatti may have to go back to the original monolithic structure and to adopt a somewhat modified Thorez position.

De-stalinisation would probably not have been brought to the fore again had it not been for the Soviet-Chinese dispute. For some time the existence of this dispute, which now seems to affect the whole destiny of world communism, was denied by the communist press. In France it was not only party militants who said that Moscow and Peking were in complete agreement; certain leftist elements in Paris, fascinated by communism, rejected the idea of tensions between Russia and China as absurd. Nevertheless the leaders of the PCF knew that Soviet-Chinese relations were deteriorating and that international communism would soon be faced with a major crisis. This prospect raised a series of ideological, political, and strategic problems.

Some leaders (Casanova, Servin, Pronteau, and Kriegel-Valrimont), aware of economic and social changes in Western Europe, and encouraged by the attitude of some of their Italian counterparts, wanted the PCF to support Khrushchev against Mao, Enver Hodza, and Molotov. They believed that peaceful co-existence, de-stalinisation and a modernisation of communist political methods in France could only be effective if the new trend represented by Khrushchev triumphed over Chinese aggressiveness and over stalinist dogmatism in the CPSU. They assumed that their stand would embarrass Thorez, whose ideological sympathy with the Chinese and the Albanians was well known.

Other leaders, including Billoux, Guyot, and Feix, were mainly concerned with the Algerian problem. They wished the party to adopt a more radical policy on the issue of Algerian independence. They were prompted to favour Mao Tse-tung against Khrushchev by a whole series of circumstances, such as Chinese intransigence towards colonialism, China's prestige with the uncommitted nations, and their own distrust of de-stalinisation. They hoped to rally Thorez to their views and to convince the party cadres, among whom sectarianism and dogmatism prevailed.

Thorez, wishing to remain master of his party and free to manoeuvre, refused to join either faction. He distrusted de-stalinisation on ideological grounds and had some affinity with Enver Hodza, whom he had visited several times in Tirana. He tended to consider the revisionism of Tito and even that of Togliatti as a more serious threat than the dogmatism displayed by Mao and Hodza. But he was not in favour of an extremist policy on Algeria. He feared that his party might be forced into illegality, he distrusted the FLN, and disliked Tito and Nasser, with whom the Algerian nationalists had connexions; he believed that a prolongation of the war in Algeria weakened France and the whole West. All these reasons inclined Thorez to adopt a prudent and circumspect attitude. Ideologically, he was close to the Chinese point of view, but politically he was nearer to Khrushchev's diplomacy.

In late 1960, the meeting of representatives of the 81 communist parties proved very satisfactory for the Secretary General of the PCF, since the triumph of Soviet policy was balanced by ideological concessions to the Chinese. Thorez was presumably too careful to show any solidarity with Enver Hodza or to commit himself in favour of Molotov, Malenkov, and Kaganovich.

During 1961, the Secretary General expelled Casanova, Servin, Pronteau, and Kriegel-Valrimont from the party, because of their attempts to overthrow him. He may have felt that the pro-Chinese trend within the political bureau would be satisfied with the Moscow compromise. At the same time, Waldeck Rochet, who had previously entertained some sympathy for the anti-Thorez opposition, became Deputy Secretary General of the PCF. This post was created for him, obviously in connexion with the Moscow compromise and in order to reinforce the internal cohesion of the party structure.

At the 22nd congress of the CPSU, Thorez gave his approval to Khrushchev's policy, deploring and condemning the Albanian position. Back in France, he imposed this attitude on the leadership of the PCF. Only one member of the central committee, the former deputy for Corsica, Giovonni, refused to follow Moscow's lead and protested his friendship for the Chinese and the Albanians. So far he has not been rebuked.

SOME observers were astounded by the swift readjustment in Thorez' policy in relation to the Soviet-Chinese conflict. In fact, it is understandable that he should have supported the Soviet point of view, sacrificing his ideological preferences to the political requirements which he equated with the interests of communism. He might have preferred a continuation of the Moscow compromise, which had only been in existence for one year. However, faced with the fact that there was a dispute between the Soviet Union and China and that it was no longer a secret, he conformed to what one might call ' geo-political ' requirements. If the PCF can only be put in power by a foreign communist army invading

France, elementary geography indicates that it would be a Soviet rather than a Chinese army.

One can understand why Enver Hodza prefers to turn Albania into a Chinese bastion in Europe rather than face a destalinisation which would lead to his downfall. In his particular case, considerations of internal policy shaped a foreign policy which is in direct contradiction with geo-political dictates. The position of the PCF is entirely different, since it is not in power and could only gain power, in the foreseeable future, as the result of foreign invasion. In such circumstances, it would be an aberration to support Peking against Moscow.

By subordinating ideology to geo-political considerations Thorez has thrown some light on the true nature of the Soviet-Chinese dispute and of world communism. Indeed, the real disagreement between Moscow and Peking is neither about the historical role of Stalin's crimes and merits nor about the ideology of peaceful co-existence which can be interpreted in a variety of ways. In truth, behind the facade of Marxism-Leninism the old game of power politics continues and Chinese power with its satellites is opposing Russian power and its satellites.

Lenin and Trotsky envisaged the Soviet state as a means of promoting communist revolution in the whole world. Stalin had come to consider the international communist movement as a means to an end, which was the reinforcement and expansion of the Soviet state's empire. In this respect both Mao Tse-tung and Khrushchev are Stalinists, although the former has shown what some call a neo-Trotskyist aggressiveness and the latter has denounced the ' cult of personality '.

Prompted by the current interests of Chinese imperialism the Peking government relies heavily on the theme of China's leadership of all under-developed countries and adopts an extremely aggressive attitude towards the West. The interests of Russian imperialism, however, press Khrushchev to develop his country technically, to raise living standards in the Soviet Union, to avoid a war with the West whilst seeking to weaken it, and to restrain Chinese imperialism which hampers his strategy today and may in the near future threaten Russian interests in the Soviet East and Far East.

Communism was revolutionary and internationalist in 1917; it has become imperialist and nationalist since. While Russia was the only great communist power all communist parties were the instruments of Russian imperialism. When communism was established in a country which is bound to become a great power and is a potential great power today rivalry between the two imperialisms and a split in the communist world could not be avoided. The ideological dispute between Moscow and Peking conceals and reveals at the same time the antagonism which opposes Chinese imperialism to Russian imperialism.

AFTER the 22nd CPSU congress an argument started between Thorez and Togliatti as soon as they returned to their countries. The leaders of the PCF presented the congress as ' a stage in the march towards communism ', the new wave of destalinisation as ' evidence of the incomparable maturity of the peoples of the USSR ', Albanian opposition as ' a dogmatic and sectarian error ', and the Chinese attitude as ' a regrettable encouragement given to the Albanians '. As usual, Thorez made the necessary adjustments without allowing dangerous controversies.

Within the Italian Communist party acrimonious discussions took place. Some leaders demanded that the critical survey of Stalinism be continued in the Soviet Union and asserted their intention to outline their future strategy and tactics without any direction or influence from Moscow. This attitude, amounting almost to rebellion, was particularly marked in the communist youth movement. Togliatti himself recalled his interview of 1956 in *Nuovi Argomenti* and stated that the debate about the past of the Soviet regime should go beyond the issue of Stalin's personality. He also said that communist parties should no longer be directed from one centre and that the international communist movement should have several centres, in other words that it should become *polycentric*. The Italian communist press attacked the leadership of the PCF and criticised as schematic, superficial, and inadequate the explanations given by the leaders to the rank and file on the questions of the 22nd congress. Thorez answered that his party had never slavishly followed the orders of the Moscow centre. He emphasised the fact that in 1946 he had developed the idea of ' new roads ' to socialism, taking into account national characteristics as an element in each country's historical evolution towards communism. He added that no unique centre of the world communist movement existed, as the Communist International had been dissolved in 1943 and the Information Bureau of Communist Parties in 1956.

In this debate Italian and French communists do not speak the same language, even when texts are translated from one language into the other. To simplify the issue, one might say that Togliatti acknowledges his former obedience to Moscow but denies the value of obedience for the future, whereas Thorez refuses to recognise that he ever was subordinate to Moscow and remains in fact as obedient as ever.

Togliatti hopes to retain as many members and as much influence on the masses as possible. To that end he practises a tactic of adaptation to Italian social life and its evolution. He is compelled to tolerate some revisionist trends in the party and uses them to serve his policy of adaptation while controlling them in order to limit their dissolving influence. He fears single leadership of the whole of international communism, since it would compel him to accept either the extreme rigidity of Mao or the heavy and flat ideology of Khrushchev. This is why he is bent on retaining some freedom of movement and manoeuvre for his party.

Thorez cannot expect an evolution in French politics which would bring him back into the government. He is relying on rigidity, cohesion, and a monolithic structure in the expectation of a shift in the balance of power in Europe in favour of the Soviet Union. Consequently he fears any relaxation of his links with Moscow, since it is on them that his policy is based.

Once more national rivalries underline ideological controversies. The debate between Togliatti and Thorez is evidence of a struggle for national leadership within the orbit of Western communism. It seems unlikely, however, that polycentrism as advocated by Togliatti can be achieved in Western Europe. There is already a polycentrism limited to two centres, since both Moscow and Peking have their satellite parties. This situation reflects the existence of a Russian and a Chinese power. Their adherence to Marxist-Leninist ideology can no longer conceal the fact that they are both imperialist powers, with all the disagreements and antagonisms which are traditional in the relations between empires.

Both the Soviet Union and China will be tempted to use the communist parties of their spheres of influence in order to manoeuvre against the West and against each other. If the French or the Italian Communist party is granted a measure of control over minor communist organisations, it will merely be delegated by Moscow and applied on its behalf, as it has always been in the past. For geo-political reasons, the two parties appear to be reduced to the role of instruments of Soviet imperialism, unless they rebel against the masters of the Kremlin. In this rather improbable case, they would themselves be transformed into political organisations which could no longer be defined as Marxist-Leninist.

*   *   *

AT PRESENT the PCF is weakened but still retains its strong party machine, and is still capable of immobilising several million left-wing votes by capitalising on dissatisfaction. Under Thorez' leadership it has proved that in France communism must of necessity be totalitarian. Genuine participation in the task of democratic modernisation, pursuit of destalinisation, including moral and intellectual re-thinking, the adoption of democratic mores with free and frank discussions would sooner or later have been fatal for this party. By destroying its own totalitarianism it would have destroyed itself.

THE U.S.S.R. AND THE DEVELOPING COUNTRIES

Leopold Labedz

IT is forgotten today that during the war, when Wendell Willkie was challenging Roosevelt in a Presidential contest, there was much talk about One World. The world that emerged from the war was divided in two. But Stalin was quite candid in his *Conversations* with Djilas (much more so than with the Western statesmen in Teheran and Yalta): ' Whoever occupies a territory also imposes his own social system.' He did not, however, pay much attention to the possibility of the emergence of a third world.

It would not be quite correct to say that it was only after Stalin's death that his successors discovered *le tiers monde*. After all, Soviet interest in the underdeveloped countries dates back to the 1920 Congress of Baku. But there is little doubt that it is only since the death of the old dictator that a new determined effort, political and economic, has been made to influence the policy of the newly emergent states, to play a new, global role in the post-colonial era. What had previously been the concern of the Party was now taken over by the state, adding, from the Soviet point of view, a new dimension to international relations.

The general picture, as seen from Moscow today, is conveniently summarised in a survey of ' The Upsurge of the Workers' Movement in the Countries of Asia and Africa ' (*Kommunist*, No. 6, 1962). It acknowledges that ' as a result of the relative numerical weakness and inadequate organisation of the proletariat in Asia and Africa during the struggle for political independence, the national bourgeoisie has established its hegemony in the liberation movement of many countries '. However, ' at the present stage of the liberation movement, when the majority of Asian and African countries have won their independence and the task of establishing an independent national economy comes to the forefront, the role of the proletariat becomes much more important . . . a real basis emerges for strengthening the unity of the working class and for consolidating its union with all the toilers, and with the peasantry in the first place '. While exaggerating the numerical growth of industrial workers in the countries of Asia and Africa (by lumping together in the total statistics countries like Japan and Guinea), and stressing the important part played in the political struggle there by the trade unions, the review firmly emphasises that ' for the countries of Asia and Africa, where peasants form up to 80 per cent of the population, the agrarian and peasant problem always was and remains one of the most important questions of the national revolution '. During the struggle for independence the peasants supported the national bourgeoisie, but now they are getting disappointed and looking for an alliance with the working class. This alliance should be ' the nucleus of a wide national democratic front, uniting the working class, the peasantry, the national bourgeoisie, and the progressive intelligentsia '. Its purpose will be to establish the state of national democracy, which constitutes a form of transition to a non-capitalist path of development for the countries of Asia and Africa, a form which 'will eventually open the prospect of the establishment of socialist society'. This, the review concludes, 'is the main task of the communists'.

What is the relation of this general scheme to the more intricate specific local conditions in various underdeveloped countries and what political consequences follow from it?

THERE is a curious parallel between the processes which led to the loss of political innocence by the Americans, and those by which the Russians, in the course of their policies towards the developing countries, are losing some of their doctrinal ignorance. General schemes of economic aid are no longer regarded in the West as the cure for all post-colonialist ills, independently of local social and political conditions. But although this particular Point Four for underdeveloped intellectuals is now largely accepted, the need for a systematic association between economic aid and social reform is far from being generally recognised. The Alliance for Progress is a step in this direction, but the means to implement it are not yet clear. If the Russians have difficulties with the 'national bourgeoisie', so have the Americans. Local vested interests, relying on the nationalist panacea ('aid with no strings attached'), and on a certain degree of blackmailing (by pointing to a communist danger or the possibility of *rapprochement* with the Soviet bloc), can both effectively extort aid and prevent its sensible use. Generally speaking, in all the underdeveloped countries, a viable political order depends no less on the present agricultural policy than on the future rate of industrialisation, and the chances of subversion are inversely proportional to the degree to which local political elites are ready to act upon this rather obvious observation.

This is not to say that the complex circumstances of so many different countries can be reduced to a single factor, the understanding of which will make a political solution of the problem easy. Wisdom, including political wisdom, depends, as we know from the time of Aristotle, on the ability to differentiate. Indeed, the very concept of 'underdeveloped countries' may by now be an obstacle to understanding, by focusing our attention too exclusively on just one characteristic, however important, of 'the revolution of rising expectations'. In doing so, the social, cultural, and historical backgrounds of different societies disappear behind a cloud of economic generalisations.

This is probably the greatest handicap for Soviet policy in these areas. It is not just bound to a cliché; it is tied to a dogma and has to live up to a scheme which is of very limited relevance to the particular countries with which it has to deal. Admittedly, it starts with certain advantages: it has a revolutionary theory, it can play upon social discontents and post-colonialist frustrations, it offers a myth of accelerated industrial development. But it also suffers from grave deficiencies: it does not understand the sociological or anthropological elements of the real situation and consequently misjudges the behaviour-pattern of social groups and political elites in these countries.

The Russians are presumably slowly learning to be more subtle. By now they have had their share of experience, in Guinea and elsewhere, of the perils of the policy of subversion-cum-economic aid. Moreover, the Soviet programmes of African, Oriental, and Latin American studies are getting into their stride and a greater degree of political sophistication is only to be expected in the future. Even so, Soviet policies are on the whole unlikely to lose their schematic flavour.

IT has been pointed out in these columns that the Soviet image of the national bourgeoisie has been vague, contradictory, and subject to constant modification.[1] Paradoxically, the Soviet attitude to it was hostile when, according to the more recent interpretation, the national bourgeoisie was ' progressive ', leading the struggle for national liberation, and became more friendly more recently, when it is ceasing to be ' progressive ', or at least is becoming less so.

Political realities and the need to support, for reasons of state, the leaders of the national movements of the new countries, do not, however, preclude allusions to their pernicious or at least contradictory role. In particular, it is categorically stated that their socialist pretensions must not be accepted as the real thing; they can be genuine only if they have the communist stamp. The local brands of socialism are rejected as fraudulent deceptions of the masses. Thus Yuri Popov, writing in *Asia and Africa Today* (December 1961), explained that ' pro-imperialist circles hiding behind talk about " real African socialism ", are attempting to castrate the class content of the proletarian struggle and to force the African working class to betray the principles of proletarian internationalism, as well as to drag into the African working-class movement the narrow nationalist slogan that " all Africans are brothers ". However, this false bourgeois thesis will become less and less popular on the African continent . . . The day is not far off when the all-conquering teachings of scientific socialism will triumph on the African continent '. No less emphatic is the Director of the Soviet African Institute, I. I. Potekhin, who declared in the *World Marxist Review* (November 1961), that ' there is a lot of talk about socialism in Africa, and the ideas of socialism are fairly widespread, but these ideas are not those of scientific socialism ', and elsewhere explained that ' the theory of " African Socialism " is being used to deceive the toiling masses in the interest of the capitalist development ' (*Narody Azii i Afriki*, No. 1, 1962). This, according to him, is the more easy, not only because of their ' petty-bourgeois mentality ', but also because of their persistent tribalism, which, as he now admits, cannot be entirely blamed on the pernicious influence of the imperialists (*Vestnik Akademii Nauk SSSR*, No. 2, 1962).

[1] W. Z. Laqueur, ' Soviet Doctrine and the New Countries ', *Survey*, No. 37.

There are other statements of this kind. In the November 1961 issue of *Mirovaya Ekonomika i Mezhdunarodnie Otnosheniya* G. Mirsky and V. Tyagunenko criticised the concept of 'Arab, Indian, or African socialism', and the May 1962 issue of the same magazine declared:

> The situation is changing. . . . The movement of national liberation is acquiring a new character. . . . Life is putting in first place in the independent countries the task of internal social transformation. . . . These demands inevitably create sharp social conflicts, since they affect the interests of the ruling groups.

The latest of such pronouncements was made by Khrushchev himself.

Speaking in Sofia on 18 May, he said that many Asian and African countries announce that socialism is being built there, and that one could only rejoice that the liberated peoples were tying their future to socialism. 'But what kind of socialism do they mean?' he asked. 'How do they interpret it? On what forces do they intend to rely in building socialism?' And he pointedly added that the present nationalist leaders would have to understand that 'it was only by relying on the working class that victory could be achieved and correct solutions found to vital social problems, or else other people would come after them who would better understand the demands of life' (*Pravda*, 20 May 1962).

But the Soviet leaders speak a different language when they are dealing directly with the African leaders. Thus Mikoyan declared during his visit to Accra that Ghana 'had made great progress in building socialism in the country' and enlarged further on the point:

> Our parties operate under different conditions; they have a different history and different tasks. What brings us nearer to each other, however, is your effort to build socialism. In the foreword to the Russian edition of his autobiography, your outstanding leader Dr Nkrumah wrote: 'The creed of our party is socialism.' Your party has assumed the task of stirring all people to attain and build socialism under African conditions (*Pravda*, 13 January 1962).

However, when Modibo Keita of Mali, and later Mamadou Dia of Senegal, visiting Moscow, proclaimed that the building of socialism is the official goal of their countries, their hosts carefully refrained from speaking on the subject, and limited themselves to diplomatic flattery and general references to the economic progress of these African countries. This probably reflects their frustration at not being more successful in inducing the African leaders to sever their economic and technical relations with the West, and particularly the association of some of them with the European Common Market. As Khrushchev put it with acerbity, instead of turning to their 'true friends', some 'honest leaders get themselves involved in bargains with imperialism'.

In praising his hosts, Modibo Keita went very far in exalting their ideology and even declared—rather like Fidel Castro—that the activists of his Sudanese Union Party 'had been guided since 1946 by the invaluable teachings of Marxism-Leninism' (*Pravda*, 22 May 1962). But he also discreetly added that 'the conditions in our country are somewhat different from yours, and so are our methods' (*Pravda*, 23 May 1962), and stressed its unchanging attachment to non-alignment:

> We have chosen the road of co-operation with all countries without exception. We are for non-alignment with the blocs and this is in our view the best way to maintain our independence by assuring our country a harmonious development (*Le Monde*, 1 June 1962).

Mamadou Dia was even more explicit:

> Our choice is to build socialism in our country, to build it not in the abstract, but concretely, not according to theoretical schemes, but in line with our own social and economic conditions. And we also say that we do not want to be dogmatists. I must tell you, as I should be frank here, that we do not pretend to be Marxists-Leninists (*Pravda*, 6 June 1962).

While not giving up its long term ideas, the Soviet attitude to the nationalist movements and to the national bourgeoisie in the developing countries depends for the moment on purely opportunist considerations, more particularly on the degree of political benefit it can derive from using them against the West. This explains both the vehemence against the countries 'governed by reactionary pact-makers' and the indulgence and continuous aid for neutralist countries where the communists have been suffering local reverses. It is precisely in the latter category that the economic aid given by the Soviet Union is proportionately the greatest.

This does not however preclude the pursuit of the strategic line aiming at the formation of states of 'national democracy'. Among the countries considered to be in the transitional stage towards the 'road of non-capitalist development' are Indonesia, Ghana, Guinea, and Mali, while Cuba has already reached that stage. Although Moscow must have realised by now that its possibilities of control are limited, and many surprises may be in store even within the ideologically kindred movements, its overall strategy has hardly changed. In Asia it gives diplomatic and military help to Soekarno, while the Indonesian communists who are represented in various organs of his 'guided democracy', are trying, as *Kommunist* (No. 6, 1962) points out, to transform it into a 'national democracy', a prospect considered realistic in view of the fact that 'the strong Indonesian Communist party, with its almost two million members and great authority over the masses, undoubtedly influences the policy of the government' (*Mirovaya Ekonomika i Mezhdunarodnie Otnosheniya*, No. 4, 1962, p. 78). In Latin America, it relies on the alliance with *fidelismo* and is ready to sacrifice for it the interests of the 'old cadre' communists. As the Escalante affair has shown, for the Soviet leaders 'Havana vaut une messe'. In Africa they probably reckon that the real chances of a communist challenge will arise only in a decade or so, and that by then the Moscow-trained cadres will be cured of their pan-African or Afro-communist leanings, and the influence of Western education will play a lesser role. It is precisely because of this that present prospects are limited, as is recognised in the case of Nigeria. It is emphasised that, at the moment, of the ' Nigerians in the governmental machine, holding high positions, 80 per cent. received their education in Britain. This has undoubtedly impressed its stamp on their way of thinking and behaving ' (*Asia and Africa Today*, No. 4, 1962).

THESE calculations almost certainly underestimate the centrifugal pull of national sentiment, as well as of local interests, ambitions, and conditions; but the spectre of polycentrism does not prevent the Soviet Union from going vigorously ahead with its effort to train the pro-Soviet cadres and to use the ruble offensive to strengthen its positions in the developing countries, even though so far neither has been an unqualified success.

The training of cadres receives particularly great attention. The Lumumba University (formerly People's Friendship University) received a good deal of publicity, but there are many other institutions, less well-known, in which future political elites are being prepared from among the present semi-intelligentsia. Of particular importance are the schools for trade unionists (such as ' The Trade Union School of the World Federation of Trade Unions' in Budapest, or the Fritz Heckert trade union school in East Germany).[2] This is especially relevant for Africa, where the trade unions will play a crucial part in the political development of the continent.

The role of the intelligentsia is recognised, although in theoretical analyses it is still the spectre of the ' national bourgeoisie ' that dominates the scene. The intelligentsia (or semi-intelligentsia) does not fit smoothly into the class scheme, although it can easily be coupled with the adjective ' progressive '. To apply it to the elements of the ' national bourgeoisie ', the old theoretical game of distinguishing between its different strata is being played.[3] Thus the ' national bourgeoisie ' is said to consist of three layers, the big, the middle, and the small bourgeoisie, and the differences in their political attitudes becomes more marked with the achievement of independence. Before then, the whole bourgeoisie is progressive, because it suffers under the imperialist yoke of foreign capital; afterwards it is only ' certain groups of the national entrepreneurs who are capable of undertaking resolute anti-imperialist action ', while it is only the small bourgeoisie which shows progressive leanings. But, as Khrushchev reiterated in his speech in Sofia, the national bourgeoisie ' under contemporary conditions has not yet exhausted its progressive

---

[2] For this and other information on the subject cf. ' Der Ostblock und die Entwicklungsländer ', Quarterly reports, published by the Friedrich-Ebert-Foundation, Bonn.
[3] Cf. N. Savelyov, ' On the role of the national bourgeoisie in the national liberation movement ', *Mirovaya Ekonomika i Mezhdunarodnie Otnosheniya*, No. 5, 1962. Various other schemes, basically similar, were put forward at a conference on ' the problems of national liberation movements and social and economic development in the newly liberated countries ', held under the auspices of the same journal. Cf. Ibid., Nos. 3, 4, and 5, 1962, and a series of articles on the subject by Jerzy Kleer in *Politika* (Warsaw) 28 April, 12 and 26 May, 1962.

role'. In practice, the three-tier analysis of the 'national bourgeoisie' resembles a similar analysis of the Soviet peasantry during the time of collectivisation. While there can be no doubt that there were rich, middle, and poor peasants in Russia at the time, the label *kulak* was attached to all of them, whatever their actual station, if they refused to join the kolkhozes. Similarly the 'national bourgeoisie' is branded 'reactionary' when it refuses to follow Soviet injunctions and becomes 'progressive' when it joins the 'anti-imperialist front', whatever the actual social position it occupies within its own country. There are no attacks on the Imam of Yemen as a feudal reactionary, but it is said that 'in the Philippines, for instance, the destinies of the country are in the hands of the reactionary bourgeoisie, linked by common interest with the big landowning aristocracy and the foreign imperialists'. Nasser's 'Charter of National Action' indicating 'the Egyptian way to socialism' has not yet been commented upon, but no doubt it will present a rather involved problem for the Soviet theoreticians, who find it difficult enough to explain how 'the internal class contradictions can sometimes find their expression in action which seriously limits the rights of landlords, and even result in such governmental measures as the nationalisation of big capitalist property which has recently taken place in the United Arab Republic'.[4] The Indian 'national bourgeoisie' is commended for 'solving such national tasks as the liberation of Goa'. In Africa, Potekhin stated authoritatively, 'The antagonistic character of the contradictions between the national bourgeoisie and the working class is overshadowed by the unity of interests in the fight against imperialism.'[5] In Latin America, too, the attitude towards the 'national bourgeoisie' is a function of its position vis-a-vis 'Yankee imperialism'.[6]

But, on the whole, despite the doctrinal schematism, the Soviet Union is gradually coming to realise in practice the politically relevant distinctions of the local scene, even though it cannot always exploit them.[7] It would be paradoxical if the Western political analysis, unencumbered by doctrinal blinkers, failed to recognise them at a time when the new political elites in the developing countries are becoming more sophisticated about Soviet policies and purposes.

MARXISM AND ASIAN CULTURAL TRADITIONS

Emanuel Sarkisyanz

IN both the United States and Western Europe, the present power conflicts over Asia have stimulated new interest in the Eastern peoples. As the fashionable term 'underdeveloped countries' indicates, this interest has been concentrated upon industrial plants, population explosions, educational planning, problems of credit availability and so on. However, these constitute only one of the dimensions in the relationship of Asian peoples to the West and to communism. This essay deals with only one factor in the relationship between oriental traditions and communism, but it is one which is rarely discussed. It is designed to supplement the more customary writings about the politics of Asian societies, from the angle of the history of ideas.

It is true that Marx and Engels occasionally commented upon Asian political and economic problems, particularly those of India and China. Yet the idea of appealing to the dependent colonial peoples of the East to rise against the capitalist West was originally quite alien to Marxism, as can be seen from the attitude of the Second International. The social-democratic parties of the metropolitan countries held an extremely moderate if not ambiguous position about independence movements in their colonies or protectorates. Marxism was originally anti-nationalist but definitely occidental. Not before it developed in its radical Russian variety did it become nationalist and anti-occidental.

Russia was the first among the underdeveloped countries; that is, Russia was the first agrarian state of non-occidental culture that found itself confronted by the overwhelming technological superiority of western neighbours, the earliest non-industrial country whose rulers therefore, most notably Peter I in the early eighteenth century, engaged in forced modernisation and compulsory westernisation from above. Thereby they broke with their established cultural traditions for the sake of the military power and competitive strength of their state. The Eastern version of enlightened absolutism began by forced rationalisation and the enforced secularisation of the idea of the state. With this compulsory creation of a ruling elite, a social abyss opened between the traditionalist, medievally-orientated peasant majority and the relatively enlightened ruling minority, a situation characteristic of underdeveloped countries to this day. It was a contributory factor in the Russian Revolution of 1917. The revolutionary sentiments of Russia's westernisers evolved out of the rationalist heritage of Peter I, but with the victory of the Bolshevik minority, Russia turned away from the western homelands of Marxism. Nevertheless, for a long time communism preserved an outwardly westernising appearance.

Russia's turn towards the East out of antagonism to the West had been anticipated by Russian nineteenth-century thinkers, both radical and conservative. Alexander Herzen became disappointed in both the European middle-class and the proletariat, and rested his hopes for the future on the agrarian peoples of the East. Herzen believed in the liberating mission of the oriental peoples of the Russian Empire, who possessed those social institutions in which he saw assurances of Russia's start over Western Europe on the road to democracy: agrarian collectivism, which was to protect the individual against proletarianisation and depersonalisation. The anti-revolutionary Dostoevsky urged Russia to free itself from the fear of being considered Asiatic. He claimed that Russia's erroneous estimate of itself as purely Western and not Asian (or rather Eurasion) had to be paid for by the futility of her policies in Western Europe. By contrast, Russia's greatest philosopher of religion, Vladimir Soloviev, saw in Eastern Asia an apocalyptic danger, if Christendom were to abandon its ecumenical mission; if the West were to betray its mission of Christianity, it would have to succumb to the Asiatics. And before his death in 1900 Soloviev came to believe that Europe, including Russia, had failed in that mission, a failure from which he expected the end of history.[1]

Unlike Soloviev, the revolutionary poets Andrei Bely and Alexander Blok infused this apocalyptic vision of Eastern Asia as executor of Europe's destinies with a millennarian hope of a utopian future. They welcomed the rising of Eastern Asia as a prelude to world revolution; it was to end the class struggle and thereby history would find its chiliastic fulfilment. This faith in a political millennium derived from primitive Christianity and entered into the spirit of the Russian intelligentsia from the peasant masses who had carried their semi-medieval attitudes into the twentieth century. Both the German sociologist Karl Noetzel and the Russian philosopher Nikolai Berdiaev saw in the ideologies of the Russian revolution the impact of late Muscovite religious utopian (Old Believers) thought.[2] This ' Old Belief ' became associated with almost all Russian peasant revolts up to the end of the eighteenth century. In secularised form, the fervent expectation of an approaching millennium provided the dynamite for that spark which came from Western-imported Marxist materialism.

THESE aspects of continuity between traditional Russian ideas about a perfect society and the communist utopia present a problem of intellectual history, but its elucidation has, unfortunately, been hampered by their political implications, and similar tendencies can be observed in the case of China. The conventional refutations of attempts to investigate elements of ideological continuity emphasise aspects in which

---

[1] Cf. Herzen, *Sobranie Sochinenii* (ed. Lemke), vol. 8, p. 47; Dostoevsky, *Polnoe Sobranie Sochinenii* (Petersburg, 1891–92), vol. 11, p. 515; S. N. Trubetskoy, ' Smert Solovieva ', in *Vestnik Evropy*, 1900, p. 414.

[2] Karl Noetzel, *Die soziale Bewegung in Russland* (Stuttgart, 1923), p. 106 ff.; N. Berdiaev, *The Origin of Russian Communism* (London, 1937); ' O Kharaktere russkoi religioznoi mysli XIXvo veka ', in *Sovremenniya Zapiski*, 1930, p. 310.

communism differs from Confucianism, and the strange conclusion is sometimes reached that because not *all* aspects of the Confucian and the communist utopian goals are similar, there cannot possibly be parallels in *any* aspect. Yet mere common sense suggests that all revolutions known to history both destroyed some aspects of the previous tradition and preserved some others; no revolution has ever eliminated or preserved *all* aspects of the system which it overthrew. That the content of Chinese Confucian concepts of a perfect society did differ greatly from the blueprints of Marxist communism, with its modern western origins, has too often obscured the fact that the latter could and did find structural points of departure in the very existence of the former. That the communist sphere in Asia almost coincides with the Confucian cultural sphere in China, Korea, and Vietnam can hardly be merely an accident of political circumstance. The intellectual starting positions of Li Ta-chao, the founder of the Chinese Communist party, were decidedly Confucian. The Confucian dual principle of a political authority (which was ideally to be derived from universal, cosmic Reason) and the concept of Utopia as the social application of universal Reason (derived from the cosmic harmony) provided an intellectual point of departure in China for what was Hegelian in Marxist communism.[3]

A perfect social order was the main goal of the Confucian intellectual tradition. The decisive currents of Chinese thought were concerned with social ethics in a rationalistically utopian sense. Indeed, the belief in the possibility of perfection in the social order is typical of the Confucian tradition in Chinese thought. Among the great world-religions, Confucianism (if it can be called a religion) alone postulated a perfect society, not as a means to any other-worldly goal—as did medieval Christianity and Buddhism—but as an end in itself. What the Confucian tradition sought in religion was not spiritual salvation but a principle of reason which could be superimposed upon a harmonious world order as the Reason of the State.

> The forces of civilisation, of humanisation of the world, were conceived of as that Reason which allows Humanity to be discovered in Man. They are the reason of the celestial laws, to which everything earthly is to subordinate itself, the reason behind the world order, its volition. It endows with the mandate of Heaven; upon those most strongly penetrated by it it bestows authority over men.[4]

French domination over Confucian Vietnam was not legitimised by reference to a Heavenly Mandate, as had been the rule of its Chinese-inspired dynasties, but the collapse of French domination in 1945 had consequences which seemed to obey the signs of the Heavenly Mandate when the Confucian Bao Dai proclaimed the independence of Vietnam and then turned power over to a nationalist-communist coalition under

---

3 Cf. E. Sarkisyanz, ' Über den Modernismus der Hochreligionen Asiens ', in: *Geschichte in Wissenschaft und Unterricht*, pp. 487, 489; ' Communism and the Asian Mind ', *Yale Review*, Spring 1950; *Südostasien seit 1945* (Munich, 1961), p. 25 ff.
4 Paul Mus, *Sociologie d'une Guerre* (Paris, 1952), p. 255.

Ho Chi Minh. According to Paul Mus, Ho Chi Minh appeared to Vietnam's rural masses as ' executor of the Law of Heaven ' (Thien Min). In the ' Xâ Hoi Hoa ' slogan of communist Vietnam the word ' Hoa ' means that radical renovation of the universal order which follows upon a catastrophe in the Confucian concept of history. Semantically, the slogan derived from the agrarian collectivist institution of Xâ—village communities of northern Vietnam. These communities were also the ideological units of traditional Vietnam: they were guardians of the ancestor cult which under a Confucian rationalisation remained the core of the rural Vietnamese outlook. The affiliation of the north Vietnamese peasantry to the Xâ village communities was ideologically founded upon the cult of the Earth Spirits whose Chinese ideographic sign is ' Xâ '. And the communist Vietnamese village Soviets likewise claimed to continue the function of the Xâ communities.[5] Thus their revolutionary programme was not understood as a break with the past but as a resumption of traditional values threatened by Western domination.

Paul Mus, French Indochina's eminent historian of ideas, thought that the parallels between animistic and Confucian cosmology and Hegelian and Marxist dialectics, with its ' scientifically ' conceived Reason immanent in predetermined history, were basic factors in the communist success in Vietnam. He emphasised that it was precisely the philosophic totalitarianism of Marxist communism which embodied that dual principle familiar from the Chinese Confucian tradition but lacking in Western secularism: Authority emanating from universal Reason and dominating the principle which moves the world, an authority which enforces this cosmic rationality in society.

> Under Heaven (T'ien-hia) it appears as the Way (Tao), as the Cosmic Principle . . . The strictness with which Marxism subordinates to itself all spheres of life proves in this [Confucian] perspective that it is destined for power. The Confucian state provided in this background a precedent.

MUCH more radically than the Confucian state did the communist Chinese state suppress independent Buddhism and Lamaist Tibet. The Chinese communist suppression of Tibet was greatly facilitated by the (at least initial) collaboration of a considerable section of the Lamaist hierarchy. Thus the Tashi (Panchen) Lamas, incarnation of the Amitabha-Buddha and politically second only to the Dalai Lamas, have traditionally collaborated with China, and the present Panchen Lama passed over to the communist side as early as 1951, even before the Chinese occupation of Lhasa. Since the flight of the Dalai Lama, he has become the main Tibetan instrument of communist control. According to a belief apparently widely held in Tibet, in the Panchen Lama shall be reborn—at the time of the decline and impotence of Lamaism—the

---

[5] Bernard Fall, *Le Viet-Minh: La République Démocratique du Viet-Nam 1945–1960* (Paris, 1960), p. 76 ff.; P. Mus, ' The Role of the Village in Vietnamese Politics ', in: *Pacific Affairs*, September 1949.

' King of Shambhala '. This Shambhala is a mythical land, its imaginary
location somewhere to the north of Tibet. The legendary twenty-fifth and
last monarch of Shambhala is the subject of prophecies about a coming
millennium. He is expected to lead the Lamaist peoples into a decisive,
final combat against the foes of Righteousness.[6] The faithful pray to be
reborn as fighters of Shambhala against the enemies of Truth; with the
triumph of Shambhala's hosts, Buddhism is to win the entire earth. They
are to crush the forces of evil and to prepare the coming of the future
Buddha Maitreya, whom Lamaism also expects from somewhere north
of Tibet. This is to bring about a social utopia in the spirit of a chiliastic
millennium: ' Grain shall then flourish on the fields without the necessity
of ploughing.'

Such expectations also refer to the rebirth in Northern Shambhala of
Kesar (Gesar), the hero of Tibetan and Mongolian epics, who also is to
usher in Utopia. Before his departure from this world, Kesar is said to
have declared ' That among the mountains, there shall not be some that
are mighty and others low. That among men, there shall not be some
that are mighty and others deprived of power; nor some that abound in
riches whilst others lack them: may happiness prevail in Tibet!' When he
received the answer that, with universal equality, social relations would be
out of their proper order, Kesar is said to have replied : ' My words have
been uttered too soon. I shall come back to repeat them.' A Tibetan
Lama said in the 1920s of his advent:

It is from Mongolia that he will come again with his army to
exterminate all those who oppose the Reign of Justice. We have
slept long, while he, the Invincible, was resting; but we shall awaken
for his return. To the conquest of the world he will lead the millions
of Asiatics who, today, are drowsing. He will be reborn among us.
The power of our united thoughts will construct him. He will be
the Thought Product of the minds of all of us whom the Europeans
wish to make their slaves. The true faith will be preached, and those
who refuse to act justly, the masters who insist on remaining masters,
the slaves who persist in remaining slaves, shall be exterminated.

Alexandra David-Neel reported that after the first world war it was widely
believed in Tibet that Kesar has already been reborn and that his advent
was to take place within fifteen years.

For over a century these expectations had been associated in Lamaist
thought with notions of social revolution. This is shown by a letter of the
first Russian-educated Buriat-Mongol, Dordji Banzarov. Under the

6 Ekai Kawaguchi, *Three Years in Tibet* (Benares, 1909), p. 499; E. Sarkisyanz, *Russland und der Messianismus des Orients* (Tuebingen, 1955), p. 371 ff. On Shambhala
see: A. Grünwedel, ' Der Weg nach Shambhala ' in *Abhandlungen der Bayerischen
Akademie der Wissenschaften. Philosophisch-philologische und historische Klasse*,
vol. XXIV, iii (Munich, 1915), pp. 78–9; R. Bleichsteiner, *Die gelbe Kirche* (Vienna,
1937), pp. 228–29; E. Sarkisyanz, ' Communism and Lamaist Utopianism in Central
Asia ' in: *The Review of Politics*, 1958, p. 624 ff.; A David-Neel, *The Superhuman
Life of Gesar of Ling* (London, 1932).

immediate impression of the 1848 revolutions, Banzarov put their Lamaist interpretation into the following words:

> The inhabitants of the Occident are now undergoing a period of turmoil. They have expelled their lords and khans and have become hostile to one another. It seems such also were the times in which Kesar was born into this world. Judging by the character of the present epoch, will not Kesar appear again? Then we will have the chance to be among his thirty-three companions.[7]

To the Lamaist peoples of the Russian Empire, the Buriats and Kalmuks, the Tsars were potential Buddhas. At the beginning of the twentieth century a rumour spread in Tibet that Shambhala of the North was to be identified with Russia. The Buriat Lama Agvan Dordji(ev) is reported to have presented Russia as champion of the Buddhist universalist imperial ideal. Such notions were connected with the identification of Northern Shambhala with Russia and they were to play a considerable political role in the early years of Outer Mongolia's People's Democracy. The Roerich expedition to Outer Mongolia in 1926 and 1927 observed that the Mongol soldiers of Sukhe Bator, whose role in Mongolia had been compared to that of Lenin, composed songs about Shambhala. They were sung in the Mongolian Revolution: ' The song begins with the words " Jang Shambal-in dayin " or " The War of Northern Shambhala ", and calls upon the warriors of Mongolia to rise for the Holy War to liberate the country from oppressing enemies. " Let us all die in this war and be reborn as warriors of Shambal-in Khan " goes the song.'[8] Even in Tibet—and after the communist revolution in Russia—Alexandra David-Neel observed an identification of Shambhala with Russia and a belief that Kesar's warrior companions had already been reborn, mainly in Russian territory. And in 1953 she wrote: ' Would the idea of taking advantage of those remarkable messianic dreams that haunt the Tibetans not occur to the leaders of Red China, now that they have installed themselves among them? Perhaps it has already occurred to them.'[9] Such a communist utilisation of certain Lamaist notions was particularly natural before the Chinese atrocities in Tibet following the 1958 rising. In Russia Stalin's purge of the Buriat champions of a Lamaist-Marxist synthesis, and his policy of killing off the leading survivors of the Buriat intelligentsia, was designed to strengthen Great Russian domination over such nationalities as the Buriats. This north Mongolian people were to be isolated from the attractions of Japanese-sponsored Pan-Mongolism, which might have drawn them away from the Soviet Union.[10]

In 1924 the Darnata Pandita Hutukhtu, a Lamaist incarnated hierarch of Outer Mongolia, declared that Buddhist morality was equalitarian and

---

[7] D. Banzarov's letter to Bobrovnikov, dated 12 April 1848, in D. Banzarov, *Chernaya vera i drugiya stati* (Petersburg, 1891), p. 111.

[8] George Roerich, *Trails to Inmost Asia* (New Haven, 1931), p. 157, quotation abridged.

[9] A. David-Neel, ' Prophéties et Légendes thibetaines ', in *La Vie des Peuples*, May 1925, p. 160; *Le vieux Tibet face à la Chine nouvelle* (Paris, 1953), p. 24.

[10] Cf. Sarkisyanz, *Geschichte der orientalischen Völker Russlands* (Munich, 1961), p. 387; ' Kommunismus und die Geisteskrise Asiens ', in G. K. Kindermann, *Probleme der Entwicklungsforschung* (Freiburg i.B., 1962), p. 345 ff.

endorsed the Soviet system. In 1925 the People's Commissar of Agri-culture of the Buryat Autonomous Soviet Republic spoke of the 'socialist transformation of Lamaism', and some Lamaist Marxists in Buryatia even joined the League of the Militant Godless. They stressed that Buddhism, being atheistic, could not be considered a religion. On this basis, Tsybikov, a well-known Lamaist scholar and author of a Russian description of a pilgrimage to Tibet's sanctuaries, participated in the anti-religious work of the Buryat branch of the Militant Godless. In 1927 the chairman of the All-Union Congress of Buddhists, the Lama Agvan Dordji(ev), declared that Western civilisation had developed the illusory principles of the Ego (whose reality Buddhism denies), deriving from it the primacy of property which produced capitalism and imperialism. Dordjiev produced at that time a Lamaist endorsement of the remedies expounded by Lenin. That Buddha himself was a pre-decessor of Lenin was a claim frequently made by Soviet Buryat Lamas and even by some Buryat communists in the Leninist period. The outstanding Buryat historian and revolutionary theorist Zhamtsarano stressed that 'Gautama Buddha had given the world an accomplished system of communism', and wanted to see Buddhism developed according to 'Lenin's testament'. And an official Soviet obituary of 1924 quoted with satisfaction comparisons of Lenin and Buddha made in the Orient.[11]

Actually, socialist if not Marxist interpretations of Buddhist ethics antedate the Bolshevik Revolution; they were first advanced in British India, appearing in the context of Buddhist modernism, that is, of trends endeavouring to reinterpret religious tradition under the impact of Western rule. As British domination over India and Ceylon was largely rationalised by 'educating its natives for the responsibilities of demo-cracy', India's cultural revival, and the movement for national emanci-pation, produced the counterclaim that democracy and even socialism were part of the indigenous tradition, in this anticipating the 'progressive' Occident. Thus at the beginning of this century Dhammapala, a prominent figure in the modern Buddhist revival, described Buddhist ethics as socialistic and another Buddhist modernist declared in 1907: 'The spirit of Buddhism is essentially socialistic . . . the accumu-lation of capital in the hands of a few can have no ethical justification . . . How does this differ from theft? . . . Buddhism prohibits theft of every form, whatever may be the euphemistic name by which it may be known'. It was this political Buddhism with its anti-Occidental orientation which helped to decide the Ceylon elections of 1956 in favour of neutralism.[12]

11 M. Pavlovich, 'Lenin i narody Vostoka', in *Novy Vostok*, 1924, p. 13; *People's Law* (in Mongolian) (Ulan Bator, 1924), cited in *Ateist*, 1927, pp. 68–9; Mandjigine, 'Protiv propagandy natsionalisticheskoi ideologii v Buriat Mongolii', in *Revoliutsionny Vostok*, 1932, pp. 243–5; A. Oshirov, 'O buriatskom lamaizme i borbe s nim', in *Antireligioznik*, June 1930, pp. 67–8; March 1927, p. 48; Zhamtsarano, *Osnovy buddizma*, cited in B. Toglitov, 'Lamaizm i buriatski natsional-demokratizm', in *Antirelitioznik*, July 1930, p. 22.

12 P. Lakshmi Narasu, *The Essence of Buddhism* (Madras, 1907), pp. 45–6; cf. Sarkis-yanz, *Südostasien seit 1945* (Munich, 1961); W. H. Wriggins, *Ceylon: Dilemmas of a New Nation* (Princeton, 1960).

But the most effective socialist interpretation of Buddhist ethics was developed in Burma, contributing to the communist failure in that country.

IN Burma communism encountered, in the person of U Nu, a rival socialism that is not a purely Western importation but has deep roots in the Buddhist tradition. If such political implications of Buddhism seem contrived, it is largely because Indology has made only the abstract, monastic Buddhism of the Canon, and not the historical lay Buddhism of the medieval epigraphy of Burmese kings, familiar in the West. It is this latter Buddhist tradition of *social* ethos going back to India's ideal Buddhist ruler Asoka, of the third century B.C., that was expressed, for example, by Burma's king Kyanzittha in his inscription of 1098-99:

> Tribhuwanadityadhammaraja, with his right hand he shall give boiled rice and bread to all the people, with his left hand he shall give ornaments and wearing apparel to all men. Men who are not equal in body, speech, or in spirit, the king shall make them equal. . . . Even all the poor old women . . . they shall become rich. . . . Those who lack cattle shall have plenty of cattle. . . . The pious gifts the king made in . . . digging tanks or planting groves . . . *only in order that all beings might escape out of Samsara* [earthly existence] . . . might obtain happiness in the worlds beyond until they arrive in Nirvana. The bar of the gate of Heaven . . . by wisdom shall the king draw open . . . and shall bring all mankind into heaven. He shall empty the four painful states of existence. When the King of the Law shall preach the Law, the sounds of applause of all men shall be like the sounds of rainstorm at the end of the ear . . . that all beings may obtain . . . plenty and be free from famine in every place that lacks water and land, our lord the king digs water tanks, creates cultivation . . . the exalted mighty universal monarch, the omniscient one, the Bodhisattva, who shall verily become the Buddha that saves and redeems all beings, who is great in compassion for all beings, who is exalted above all other kings that dwell in the four quarters of the earth.[13]

In Theraveda (Hinayana) Buddhism, liberation from suffering caused by attachment to the world of impermanence can only be achieved by individual contemplation and meditation. It was precisely for this reason that, when it expressed political ideals, as in the above inscription, these were designed to create such social conditions as would permit the meditation that alone liberates. Therefore the state was to ensure that economic relationships would allow the leisure necessary for meditation on which the achievement of Nirvana depended. This inspired the Buddhist ethos of Burmese kingship, with its ideal of a social order permitting each being to save itself. Even after the monarchy disappeared, with the British conquest of Upper Burma (1886), these traditional ideals of a perfect Buddhist state were preserved by Burmese folklore, still alive

---

[13] Kyanzittha's inscription, transl. from the Mon language in *Epigraphia Birmanica*, vol. I, part ii. Edited by Ch. Duroiselle (Rangoon, 1920), pp. 117, 123, 142, 146, 166.

even in the cities. A perfect Buddhist ruler, closely associated with the future Buddha, is the subject of some of Burma's most popular prophecies, still being republished. Although the ' Buddha Raja Marvel Prince' is apparently not mentioned specifically in the English literature about Burma, the belief in him is almost universal among the Burmese people outside the English-educated minority, and in many cases it is found even among them. He is expected to establish a perfect society, without rich or poor, but with inexhaustible wealth for all, in a world united by peace and harmony by the Buddhist ethics of non-attachment. This utopia is to come at the end of the present cycle of decline, a cycle of degeneration which began, according to the Dighanikaya of the Pali Canon and the Burmese Manu-Dhammathat, when the Illusion of the Self caused men to appropriate the freely growing nourishment, originally held in common by all, as private property. As a result the means of livelihood ceased to grow without labour; this made it necessary to elect the first ruler, a future Buddha.

IN the mind of the rural Burmese, British rule had undermined the economic basis of the Buddhist monastic institutions and therewith the basis for the meditation which alone could for ever free them from the realm of Impermanence and Suffering. To this traditionalist majority, the Buddhist goals constituted a primary aim of the struggle against colonial rule (though for most politicians religion was a means of exerting mass pressure for political goals). The ' Naga-Ni' party song of the Thakin nationalist revolutionaries, from which Burma's present governing party emerged, postulated prosperity as one aim of the struggle ' so that the poor will be enabled to build monasteries'[14]; that is, economic reforms were regarded as means in the pursuit of Nirvana as the goal. U Nu declared that socialism is the teaching which can bring humanity back to the blissful past when nature satisfied all human needs, before greed had moved men to appropriate more than their necessities, before private property had caused want and misery.[15] This was an application to politics of the Agganna-Sutta of the Buddhist Canon. In 1948 he had described property as a purely functional means for the pursuit of Nirvana (through meditation), maintaining that it is the illusion about the inherent value of property that has produced the class struggle and bloodshed throughout history; its elimination would usher in a perfect society.

In his November 1959 election platform U Nu (whose Buddhist charisma produced folkloric identifications of his personality with the expected Burmese ideal Buddhist ruler of the future and bearer of a perfect society),[16] referred to the ideal of the perfect Buddhist ruler

14 The text of the Naga-ni Song was kindly supplied to the writer by the Burmese Broadcasting Corporation, in Rangoon.

15 Thakin Nu, *Mein gun: mya* (Rangoon, 1949), pp. 69–70 ; the typescript of the Burmese text was supplied by the courtesy of the Union of Burma Information Department.

16 U Po U, *Bodayaza Min Sedja*, p. 142, as interpreted, for instance by U Maung Gyi Daw Thein, the publisher of the corresponding prophecies, in an interview with the writer on 15 August 1959.

(which inspired the inscription of A.D. 1090 quoted above). In describing his Buddhist socialism he said that the acquisitive economy had developed out of the Illusion of the Self, which Buddhism aims to overcome, and that it obstructs a social order which would make meditation economically possible for all, thereby permitting universal liberation from impermanence.

The Buddhist doctrine of redemption was, and has remained, primary in U Nu's thought, socialist economics secondary. For U Nu's ideology, as for the social ethos of traditionalist rural Burma, a welfare state (providing the economic prerequisities for meditation) is only a means; the final aim is the overcoming of the Illusion of the Self and release from the bonds of attachment to transitory existence.

Socialism and the welfare state have remained for him, throughout every shift in terminology and emphasis, economic means for Buddhist eschatological goals. In this sense his former minister Ba Swe had called Marxism a lower truth, facilitating the achievement of the Buddhist higher truth, since ' reflections about Ageing, Disease, and the fact of Death cannot be clearly answered by the Marxist Abhidhamma [philosophy] '; it can give ' material satisfaction, while at the present time men, being lost in concerns about food, concerns about clothing, and concerns about shelter, cannot meditate about the phenomena of impermanence . . . they cannot free themselves from the fact of Death. But having obtained satisfaction for the corporeal frame through material well-being, they shall be able to meditate over Ageing, Disease, and the fact of Death. The Buddhist Abhidhamma would give them clear answers, Release and Liberation.' [17]

Although the Burmese communists borrowed Buddhist philosophical terminology for translating Marxist dialectics into Burmese (for example, the communist theorist Thakin Soe),[18] they were not content to have their Marxism accepted merely as a particular methodology of liberation from economic suffering within the far more universal Buddhist methodology of liberation from all suffering. They refused to be content with the acceptance of Marxism as a limited economic truth within U Nu's Buddhist socialism. The Burmese communists were not content with Buddhist-Marxist ideological partnership, just as they refused to be satisfied with a coalition partnership in Burma's Anti-Fascist People's Freedom League government. In vain U Nu tried to convince them (by quotations from Marx and Lenin) that Burma provides no reason for the use of force to achieve a revolution, that among the Burmese people there are few economic contradictions, and that therefore Burma provides few sociological presuppositions for the class struggle. This did not deter them from starting civil war in 1949; their victory would have

[17] U Ba Swei, *Bama to hlan yei: hnin bama lou-tha: lu-du* (Rangoon, 1955), pp. 44-5.
[18] Thakin Soe, *Bama to hlan hmu* (Rangoon, 1934). This is examined further in my forthcoming book, *Buddhist backgrounds of the Burmese Revolution.*

transformed Marxism from an economic sub-structure for the Buddhist quest into an ideology monopolising power, thus endangering Burma's cultural traditions. Though U Nu did not abandon Marxist economic goals, he has (since 1958) rejected Marxist political and ideological doctrines. In the elections of 1960 the crypto-communists (United National Front) suffered a crushing defeat, obtaining only about 4 per cent of the popular vote. Their more revisionist Marxist rivals were also rejected by the electorate. U Nu's Buddhist charisma triumphed over the efficiency of a bureaucratic party machine and Burmese tradition over imported slogans. He was recently turned out of office by professional soldiers and bureaucrats, not in the name of democracy but in the name of efficiency. And the superior efficiency of communist dictatorships for purposes of forced modernisation does not cease to attract Asia's uprooted modernisers and managers who have no patience with tradition.

MARXISM AND AFRICAN CULTURAL TRADITIONS

P. Alexandre

TO anyone wishing to study the influence of marxism in Africa, the former French colonies are a fertile field. Marxist influence in colonial territories was generally in direct proportion to its importance in the home country of the colonisers themselves. And marxian thought, in its philosophical as well as its political and economic aspects, plays a more important part in contemporary France than in any other European power with African colonial responsibilities, past or present.

An obvious example is the attitude of the French Communist party during the crucial years after the Second World War—1945 to 1948—and to a lesser degree in the following decade. Through its *Groupes d'Etudes Communistes* (GEC), created and animated by European officials, mostly from the Education service,[1] it succeeded in shaping both the structure and the methods of the *Rassemblement Démocratique Africain* (RDA), which became the pioneering force in the emancipation of French African colonies. When the RDA broke away from the Communist party in 1951, marxist influence (chiefly communist) continued to be relayed in French Africa through the left-wing trade unions organised by the communist-dominated trade union federation (CGT), and also through propaganda aimed at the African students in France.

This kind of influence is primarily of a political nature and likely to be far less in evidence in countries where the communist party had either no influence (Britain, Belgium) or is clandestine (Spain, Portugal). However, communism and marxism are not absolute synonyms: there are heretical communists, as well as non-communist or anti-communist marxists. On this count France is in a special position. First, marxism permeates the thought and doctrine of almost all the non-communist left, including part of the socialist party, which held prominent posts in most of the Cabinets up to 1958. Then, a knowledge of marxism is a necessity for all French intellectuals. Anybody in France who wants to study law, economics, history, or philosophy, just cannot afford to ignore Marx and the marxist thinkers. Even the curriculum of secondary education includes an introduction to philosophy which would not be complete without a section on historical materialism.

Finally, it must be remembered that, up to 1958, the political leaders of the Overseas Territories (the Territoires d'Outre Mer of the 1946 Constitution) were quite intimately mixed up with French politics, where marxism is an important and living factor. This, of course, had no parallel in British colonies and even less in Belgian, Portuguese, and

---

[1] Up to 1948 communist infiltration went far higher up in the administrative hierarchy: at least one governor and one governor-general were communists or fellow-travellers.

Spanish territories. One result is that French-speaking African politicians tend to consider marxism, and especially communism, more in terms of internal politics than in terms of foreign relations. Marxism is thus more integrated (hostilely or sympathetically) in the political life of the French-speaking than in that of the English-speaking states.

The direct influence of the socialist countries—the USSR and satellites, China, Yugoslavia, and even non-marxist Israel—is felt all over Africa through scholarships, technical assistance, etc. It seems strongest in Guinea and Mali, especially in the former, where an Africanisation of marxism appears to be in progress.

In religious attitudes and behaviour, the influence of the colonial powers is somewhat harder to define and describe precisely. There probably are distinctions to be made between colonisers according to the religious tradition dominant in their culture, and to the nature of the relationship between church and state in their constitution and public law, as well as in home and colonial politics, all these factors being apt to react in different ways upon the attitude of the colonial and later on the national administration in such matters as its policy towards Christian missions, Islam, etc.

On the whole Britain, with her indirect rule theory, seems to have followed a policy of *laissez faire* in religious matters. However, the educational system gave the religious missions a somewhat privileged position, but less so than in Belgian and Portuguese colonies. In the latter the Roman Catholic church could almost be considered a branch of the administration. Conversely, the constitutional religious neutrality of the French territories, in conjunction with the political anti-clericalism of many officials, often resulted in tension between the colonial administration and the Catholic missions. As for the Protestant missions in French, Belgian, and Portuguese colonies, they were frequently considered to be so many nests of suspicious foreign agents.[2]

Islam, rather favoured by British colonial authorities, was held in suspicion by the Belgians and the Portuguese. In French territories it was seen sometimes as a Trojan horse of foreign propaganda, and sometimes as an ally against the political interference of Catholic clericalism.

To sum up, it seems that the colonisers with a Roman Catholic culture, including the French, were more apt to endow religious phenomena with a political significance, according to their own political tradition. However, the expression of political and social frustration through syncretistic cults, sects, and heresies (*kitawala*, ethiopism, Congolese kimbangism, Gabonese *bwiti*, etc.) was the outcome of local conditions rather than of the relationship between politics and religion in the colonisers' home country.

WHEN speaking of marxist influence it may be useful to define what exactly is meant by ' marxism.' In the strict sense, the word ought to relate to dialectical materialism as expounded by Karl Marx a hundred

---

[2] Including the French Protestant mission, because of the high proportion of Swiss citizens in its personnel and of the position of Protestants as a minority in France.

years ago, with or without the later developments and interpretations of his more or less faithful disciples: essentially a philosophy, an explanation of the world from which derive a number of theories, political as well as ethical or economic. This is the meaning retained throughout this paper.

Nevertheless it must be stated that in its current usage this is only one of many accepted meanings. 'Marxism' has become the nucleus of a kind of semantic constellation whose extreme points can be ranged approximately as follows:

(a) Dialectical materialism;
(b) communist orthodoxy;
(c) diplomatic sympathy with USSR or hostility towards Western bloc;
(d) non-conformism in politics and/or social revendications;
(e) single-party system with socialist trend in economics.

It is evident that c and d may well have no direct relationship with a, yet the mere fact of their being disparagingly embraced under the same names as a and b (considered as synonyms) is not without some psychological consequences.[3] The extensive and abusive use of these terms results, by a natural reaction, in a new kind of marxist, or communist, propaganda, if only because of the interest in marxism it generates among the people who are accused of drawing their inspiration from it. It is widespread enough to explain why, in several states, the opposition is already more or less overtly sporting a so-called 'marxist' label, even when knowing little or nothing of marxian ideology.

Marxist influence is spread chiefly through the channel of European languages. In their present state of evolution most Negro-African languages are not sufficiently developed to permit an accurate and efficient translation of *Das Kapital* or any other important doctrinal work. The social context in Africa today remains too different from that of nineteenth-century Europe to allow an exact transposition of terminology and notions, and even in those urbanised areas where the social contexts differ less, the poly-ethnical composition of the African population as well as European technical and economic ascendancy still give French and English a socially and intellectually dominant position vis-à-vis the vernacular.

It might then be expected that marxist influence would be small among the uneducated masses, deprived of the knowledge of any European language; more important among the traditional elite, who have had some sort of education in the use of French or English; and maximal in the new intelligentsia who have benefited from a full-scale European education.

The reality is somewhat different: the pattern referred to is more or less true as far as a theoretical knowledge of marxism is concerned,

---

3 The communists themselves play up this confusion between 'marxism' and 'communism' just as some Roman Catholics do with the confusion between 'Christian' and 'Catholic'.

but not as regards its practical influence on the general public. In the former French territories, at least, this practical influence is high among the traditional elite, to which a majority of the politicians and leaders belong. Most of them are either self-taught or have had elementary instruction in marxist theory in some ' school for cadres ' on either side of the Iron Curtain. They understand the efficient use of agitation and propaganda, of mass organisation, parallel hierarchies and so forth. They may be scarcely aware of most of Marx's basic assumptions, and may even view some of them with hostility, but when it comes to action among, by, and for the masses, they do work efficiently along marxian lines.

The up-and-coming university-trained generation often seem rather out of touch with the masses and sometimes more or less divorced from the elite in power, which they criticise on theoretical and ideological grounds. While many of them can discuss competently the finest shades of marxian and post-marxian thought, it is doubtful whether they will succeed in adapting it to the actual problems of African development.

The lack of homogeneity in contemporary Africa is again underscored if one tries to place the new African states within the marxian model of history. Leaving aside the question of the validity of Sekou Touré's Guinean socialism, the situation might be described as the coexistence of bourgeois states, some of them reformist, with feudal,[4] slave-holding, and patriarchal [5] survivals. In the economic field the same heterogeneity is in evidence, ranging from predatory hunting economies to a few cases of state capitalism. The theoretical problems arising from this situation are not easy to solve in marxian terms, and this may be why the best trained African marxists are often the most reluctant in their approach to these questions. A possible answer would be to consider the colonial and post-colonial situation in Africa as an original, mixed one, in which none of the classical phases exists in its pure state because of the constant interplay between societies at different stages, still further complicated by the evolutionary short-cuts resulting from colonial intervention. This would of course completely upset the classical pattern of class relations and therefore the revolutionary process in Africa; which is exactly the conclusion reached by President Sekou Touré.

AS might be expected, there is heterogeneity also in the religious field. There, an ideal blueprint would show three levels with two critical transition points : one at the point of change from traditional ethnocentric to ecumenical religions (Islam, Christianity), the other at the point of change from these to agnosticism or atheism. Things are, of course, much more complicated and the transitions are not clear cut. Traces from the ethnocentric religions survive among Christianised and Islamised people and even among agnostics. Moreover there are the various syncretistic religions, which seem to constitute a category by themselves. Some of

4 That is Potekhin's label for the Ashanti social system.
5 Would the pygmies belong to the patriarchal or primitive communist stage?

these are to be considered progressive and some regressive (the words, of course, imply no moral judgment), in relation to the theoretical scale of evolution drawn before. A progressive religious movement would be one tending to break the ethnical frame of a tribal cult (e.g. the inter-tribal West African ' fetishes,' such as *atigali-tigari*, the ' man of San,' etc.); a regressive one would tend to ethnicise an ecumenical religion (e.g. some of the tribal sects stemming from Islam or Christianity).

The African religious palette has fine distinctions of shade rather than clear cut contrasts. Africa's capacity for integration, cultural assimilation, one might even say for digestion, is especially developed where religious subjects are concerned. It is not surprising to see the philosophical aspects of marxism subjected to processes of this kind which might eventually produce unforeseeable syncretisms.

Traditional religions remain the most important in Africa by the number of their followers, and still wield a great deal of influence among the Christianised or Islamised populations. It is not easy to define them both accurately and briefly in general terms. However, most seem to have one interesting sociological trait in common: that of being ethnocentric, that is to say, each one of them is particular to one social entity, such as a tribe.

At first sight an ethnocentric religion appears as a more or less complex system of rites, these rites being the symbols for an underlying system of socially significant beliefs. Rites and beliefs form an indis-soluble whole which can to some extent be compared to a language, their relationship being, in such an interpretation, akin to the relationship *signifie: signifiant* in Saussure's linguistic theory. If the analysis is pushed further, the religious system is found to be in its turn inseparable from the rest of the social structure, its own function being threefold, that is, to express the social structure, to explain it, and to keep it working, to perpetuate it, while, simultaneously, the other structural elements, the other partial systems explain, express, and perpetuate the religious system. The religious function is conditioned by the other social functions and conditions them.

The pervasiveness of rites in this closely integrated type of society makes it safe to replace the *sacred : profane* contrasts by an opposition of ritual to non-ritual. Innovations and foreign imports are likely to be very quickly ritualised, even in cases where a European observer would think them to be of a strictly technical nature. The religious system is a social integrator more than anything else.

Still, Africans are well aware that the world is not limited to their own society. Religion, ethnocentric as it may be, must also offer an explanation of the whole environment, of the global ecology, in other words a cosmology or *Weltanschauung*. Yet this *Weltanschauung* also remains ethno- or sociocentric [6]: the social structure, as symbolised in

---

[6] ' Ethnocentric ' or ' sociocentric ' to be taken in a fairly wide sense; the cosmologic system discovered by the late Professor Griaule in the Niger Valley covers a very large area inhabited by a number of tribes belonging to different linguistic stocks and quite distinct from one another in many other respects.

religion, is both the image and the condition of the cosmic structure. Thus any breach of the social well-being may cause harmonic trouble in the natural order: murder or incest, for instance, resulting in drought or epidemic. Ethics, although socially determined, transcend in this way the limits of single societies to reach cosmic dimensions.

All this description is necessarily theoretical. It is doubtful whether any living society has ever actually conformed to it in all points, outside the monographs of ethnographers. At any rate, this state of affairs cannot continue after the social disruption caused by colonial interference. Nevertheless many elements of the traditional religions survive today, more or less integrated, more or less functional within the frame of the new systems. Marxist influence began to make itself felt with some degree of intensity only when the pre-colonial social structures were already in various stages of disintegration, and it has been and is particularly active in those areas where the disintegration of the former systems has gone farthest. Marxism in Africa has probably never been confronted with traditional systems in good working order; it has only met with their vestigial elements. The question is, how do these harmonise or contrast with dialectical materialism?

IN answering this question one must avoid the temptation to give too much importance to superficial resemblances between particular traits of African culture and individual traits of marxian philosophy. This confusion, or self-delusion, has for some years been rife among the African intelligentsia in France. It stems partly from fashion, and partly from an insufficient knowledge of both marxism and African ethnology. Starting from a correct assumption, i.e. the collective character of most pre-colonial modes of production, they end up with a so-called traditional African socialism which they try to link to a kind of proto-marxist philosophy founded on a more or less biased reconstruction of some aspects of traditional cosmologies.

All the same, there *are* some points of resemblance, not so much between classical marxism and traditional cosmologies as between the modern African interpretation of the remnants of such cosmologies and marxism as re-interpreted by Africans.

Marxism and Islam share a common advantage over other imported ideologies: they are all-embracing, as were the traditional systems. They are concerned both with understanding the world and with acting in and upon it. In other words, marxism can, up to a point, lead to a return of a tribal-type *Weltanschauung*, at a higher level of integration and on a scale far better adapted to the necessities of the modern world. A capital difference is, of course, that marxism as such is not in itself a ritual system. It is not impossible, however, that it could give birth some day to a ritual superstructure more or less rooted in African cultural tradition. The rationalist and atheistic character of marxism is not an insuperable obstacle to such an evolution if we accept the theories of some anthropologists according to whom the traditional religions are non-theistic ritual systems, rather like Confucianism.

There have also been attempts to trace a kind of dialectic and even of dialectic materialism in the traditional systems. This is again a confusion, in some cases intentional, between two different stages of intellectual evolution within two contextual frames which are very different, even if they sometimes show a few superficial similarities. Indeed, the total and constant interaction between the various fields of human activity and between cosmos and society, as more or less clearly postulated by traditional cosmologies, does often have a markedly dialectical character. Many of these cosmologies are dualistic, founded upon the necessity of conciliating and balancing opposites. This is indeed a brand of dialectics, though very far from the hegelian and marxian varieties, since it is static and not dynamic. If there is a dynamics it is a dynamics of stability; it tends to ensure social well-being, harmony between society and cosmos through the perpetuation of an equilibrium, and to ignore the notion of a progressive evolution from crisis to crisis.

The marxian notion of history would have been completely foreign to traditionally-minded Africans. The very notion of a traditional history is questionable. Many societies had, of course, records of their past, but in most cases these records, started as genealogies, quickly became mythical and were then integrated into the religious systems, their main function being juridical. This type of history can be said to merge with constitutional law; it often aims at explaining and justifying the present by the past, but seldom opens any definite eschatological perspective. In the societies whose systems of beliefs were eschatological, it was mostly of the ' back to the golden age ' type.

There is, finally, the question of materialism. The point has often been made that the deep religious feeling of the Africans is an insuperable obstacle in the path of marxist propaganda, because of the materialistic assumptions of the doctrine. It is true that most if not all of the African religions described by anthropologists are of a theistic nature, very often embodying belief in a High God or Supreme Creator, and are hardly reconcilable with marxian atheism. For all that, it does not necessarily follow that traditional religious systems are to be defined in terms of idealism or of spiritualism. It is questionable whether the contrast *materialism : idealism* is relevant at all stages of cultural evolution. Rites, especially magical rites, are a means of acting upon the material world. In many cases they are conceived and explained in strictly material terms (' forces,' ' energy,' etc.). Some African intellectuals even go so far as to find in traditional cosmologies a kind of prefiguration of modern physics. In all probability traditional societies did not oppose ' faith ' to ' reason ', or, if they did, the tension between them was resolved by the conciliatory dialectical process alluded to before.

It can be said in conclusion that, despite fundamental discrepancies, an efficient marxist propaganda can be, and actually has been, based upon the superficial resemblances between the remnants of the traditional religious systems and an oversimplified presentation of the essentials of marxism.

ISLAM was historically the first non-ethnocentric religion to acquire a large following in Africa. Its expansion may be divided into two phases, pre-colonial and post-colonial.

The first phase was marked by a periodic series of extensions and retractions corresponding to the growth and decline of poly-ethnical areas of rule. The late Professor Richard-Molard referred to these as 'the pulsating empires of the Western Sudan', and called Islam 'a cyclical political ferment'. But to the present writer it seems that Islam acted as a means of social and political integration for these empires rather than as the cause of their imperialist expansion. As much as, or more than, a mere corpus of supernatural beliefs, Islam is indeed a total, all-embracing social system. Superimposed upon the tribal total systems it gave the Sudanese empires a kind of common constitution which pre-served in some degree the former tribal structures. When it receded, the pre-Islamic systems came back into pre-eminence, while some Moslem traits survived by becoming integrated into them with a new functional definition. Islam also persisted as a supra-tribal system closely linked with long-range trade; the Sudanese trader used it as a kind of passport, partly freeing himself in this way from tribal boundaries.

In the post-colonial phase the progress of Islam seems to be directly connected with the disintegration of the traditional social system under the impact of colonisation. Islam appears then as a mechanism of reintegration at a higher level.

In the first phase Islamic expansion was chiefly due to propaganda—persuasive or constraining—by some African conqueror whose technical culture was not wholly different from that of the conquered people. In the second phase it was rather due to an indirect reaction against the intrusion of a non-African invader with disproportionate technical superiority. While the process of Islamic acculturation occurred formerly at the tribal level, it now occurs on a pan-African scale, the tendency being towards one Negro-African Islam, rather than Fulani, Hausa, Swahili, and other varieties.

Islam has been considered by colonial authorities sometimes as a subversive factor just as dangerous as marxism, and sometimes, on the contrary, as a more effective obstacle than Christianity to marxist in-fluence. In fact an important percentage of Moslems are to be found in states where marxist influence is strongest (Guinea, Mali) as well as in states where it is quite weak (Northern Nigeria).

In theory marxism and Islam ought to be absolutely incompatible, being in fundamental opposition in nearly all their respective essentials. In fact this incompatibility exists only where and when one of the two is to be found in a purely orthodox, puritanical form, that is, almost nowhere and never in Negro Africa. In most places, and especially where one or both are novelties, there are compromises and mutual contamination.

In many parts of Africa, Islam is to be considered as objectively progressive (even in the marxist sense), first because of its function as a social integrator in a context of de-tribalisation; second, because of the role it often plays in the anti-colonial fight for national emancipation. Certainly, there still exists a conservative Islam, led by customary chiefs, heirs to historical conquerors and for long the most faithful supporters of the colonial administration; but in recent years many of their pagan subjects have both become Moslems and acquired a new social (and national) consciousness.

A number of nationalist leaders of strong marxist tendencies are Moslems, or rather *islamisés*, without any serious Arabic culture but still members of the *'umma*, and, through this membership, more conscious of belonging to the Afro-Asian world than are some of their Christian or pagan colleagues. (And since their real knowledge of marxism is almost as scanty as their real knowledge of islamism, they see no contradiction between the two.) A young Senegalese nationalist once told me : ' We shall use marxism as a political and economic technique in our fight against you, and Islam as an ideology for the masses '. Which is in fact what is actually being done to some extent in Guinea and Mali, where it is sometimes difficult to distinguish between Islamised marxism and marxised Islam. Yet the mixture proves effective where a stricter orthodoxy in either would probably have failed.

There lies the problem for the future : if one of the orthodoxies prevails, a conflict will become unavoidable, all the more so because of the few apparent similarities between the two systems. The *'umma* is no more the International than predestination is economic determinism; the two eschatologies are absolutely opposed to each other. The exploitation for propaganda purposes of the superficial resemblances will aggravate the conflict if and when the oppositions become manifest. Meanwhile, and except in the areas where an orthodox Moslem oligarchy turns it into a conservative force, Negro-African Islam comes easily to terms with marxism in its present state.

THE present wave of Christianisation in Africa began at the same time as modern colonisation, in the second half of the nineteenth century, that is, at a time when European societies had become quite secularised, even in countries with a state religion or established church. Missionary action was often in the hands of non-conformist or disestablished churches, or of missions belonging to a nation other than that of the colonisers.

Nevertheless the missionaries, whatever their differences and conflicts with the administration and traders, did consider themselves for quite a long time as bearers of *the* Civilisation. On the other hand, the Africans, because they interpreted colonial society according to their own native sociology, quite naturally supposed Christianity to have exactly the same social function as their own religions. Hence, at first, the initial resistance to evangelisation, and, later on, its acceptance, when the Africans, convinced that Christianity was closely linked with European material superiority, accepted or sought conversion in the hope of sharing in this superiority.

Now the very nature of the colonial relationship, as well as the secular character of modern European society, could only result either in frustration of this hope, or in partial disappointment. Christianity in Europe is no longer a total system; it has become restricted to a field of its own, largely divorced from other domains of social activity; it is but one of several disconnected aspects of European culture. Conversion, while it tends to promote the dislocation of traditional African society, does not, in the present state of the relations between church and state, offer an instrument of social reconstruction adapted to the economic and political necessities of our time.

Because of its long historical tradition, the Roman Catholic church was the first to become conscious of this shortcoming. All Catholic political clericalism, from the ' Christian villages ' of the colonial era up to today's demo-Christian parties and trade-unions, is the result of an effort to re-structure society around the church. This attempt has met not only with political obstacles but with cultural ones as well; these the church has recently tried to remove by adapting its discipline and rites, going to the limit allowed under canon law.

As for the Protestant churches, they, also because of *their* historical tradition, have fallen into political or social clericalism much less often, even when they have been conscious of the problem posed by the secular-isation of European society in an African context. The principle of free enquiry gives them more scope for the adaptation of dogma as well as of discipline and rites. One result is the proliferation of schismatic churches and syncretistic sects with a Protestant origin. These are very often marked with an obvious social clericalism, arising from the desire—conscious or not—to use religion as an instrument to re-structure the world and society.

The Roman Catholic church is as uncompromisingly anti-marxist in Africa as elsewhere. Lately the Roman hierarchy in many colonies have often followed a policy of encouraging and helping the nationalist move-ments, so as to beat marxism on its own anti-colonialist ground. Simul-taneously they tried, successfully in a few cases, to identify Marx with Satan; but this strictly hostile and negative attitude has been resented by many educated Africans as an attempt to conceal a potentially useful truth and to treat them as irresponsible children. This reaction is reinforced by the fact that the Catholic church, despite some outstanding efforts in the fields of social welfare and trade unionism (and, for example, the work of Father LeBret's *Economie et Humanisme* group in Senegal), has got nothing as apparently clear and revolutionary as marxism to offer in the realm of economics. Antagonism is also aroused among the African intellectuals by the anti-scientific bias of the most conservative of the missionary clergy: a number of priests maintain a negative attitude towards science, believing that it endangers faith.

Protestant positions are less one-sided, and therefore more difficult to summarise. They depend partly on the nationality of the missionaries and partly on their theological trends. American missions, especially those which support Moral Re-Armament, are as strongly anti-marxist as the Roman Catholic church; some fundamentalists are also anti-scientific. German, Scandinavian, and Swiss missions are anti-communist rather than anti-marxist. On the other hand, the personnel of the French missions and of some of the nonconformist British ones often have left-wing opinions. In most cases Protestant missions of all nationalities have kept away from the colonial authorities, to whom some of them have become a nightmare because of the support they willingly gave to all native grievances. While they did not as a rule present their converts with any kind of clerical formula for reshaping society, they went farther than the Catholics in giving them freedom for individual personality development. Consequently there is every variety of attitude towards marxism among Africans with a Protestant education: orthodox communism as well as rabid anti-communism, and, what is seldom found among Catholics, a number of non-communist marxists who remain Christian all the same. On the other hand a Protestant education is not conducive to sympathy towards the mass parties, whose cadres, at least in West Africa, are rather of Catholic or Moslem origin.

On the whole Christianity continues to be widely identified with the Western world, and this is often a handicap nowadays. The care taken by many Christian missionaries to protect their flock from marxist temptation often gives it the attraction of a forbidden fruit. Many Africans think the prohibition is arbitrarily designed to deprive them of the panacea which could free them from the economic and intellectual domination of the imperialist West.

THE multiplication of syncretistic cults is an important aspect of the sociology of contemporary Africa. In most cases these cults seem to be instruments for the resolution of contradictions generated by the colonial situation, and for the re-integration of society at a higher level than that of the collapsing tribal system. Their doctrine is often quite elaborate, with a rich and complicated symbolism. They combine two types of elements: some from the traditional religions, lifted out of their former social context and re-interpreted in the light of European teaching; others imported from outside.

A cargo-cult aspect is frequently in evidence: the use of modern technical apparatus (telephone, submarine, etc.) as liturgical symbols, the announcement of a coming age of plenty with free access to all kinds of prestige gadgets, the quest for, and initiation into the ' White man's secret ', the mysterious foundation of his material power; all adding up to the search for a magical short cut to technical and economic development.[7] It is materialism of a new kind, quite different from Europe's rationalistic materialsm and both a product and caricature of it. It is apt to play an important part, positive or negative, in the actual problems of development.

In the colonial era the syncretistic cults were generally organs of political opposition, either active (e.g. *kitawala*) or passive (*matsuanism*). Nowadays some are still in opposition to their national governments, even though they may have helped to bring them to power. This political opposition may take various forms, sometimes directly related to the kind of materialism mentioned before. This may lead to africanised versions of agrarianism, spartakism, etc. reminiscent to some extent of similar phenomena in the theological field: a sort of economic ethiopianism.

This combination of economic aspirations amounting to a kind of materialism with political subversion has led a few observers to trace a marxist influence—or the direct action of Soviet agencies—in some of the syncretistic cults. There have been lurid descriptions of NKVD witchcraft schools for the training of Mau Mau or UPC (Union des Populations du Cameroun) terrorist leaders. While the extent of Mr Jomo Kenyatta's or the late Ruben Um Nyobe's marxian convictions remains an open question, it is a fact that there were and are some people with good marxist training among their followers; yet these are the very people not likely to be found in the terrorist gangs. Communist support for these movements (especially noticeable in the case of UPC) is given from the outside rather than in the field. The initiation ceremonies, the gruesome magical aspects of the insurrections, take place among people who have not reached the level of political consciousness where marxian doctrines could be of significance to them.[8] Of course Marx advocated recourse to violence; but he meant violence by an organised and conscious proletariat. That anarchistic colonial and post-colonial rebellions may have their impact on the cold war does not mean that the rebels are necessarily marxists.

However, the adepts of syncretistic cults rarely resort to large-scale violence: the cult often seems to be in itself a substitute for it. If such is the case, syncretism is a typical example of ' opium for the people ', and as such to be rejected by the marxist. Indeed, the governments and parties under the strongest marxist influence have no connection with syncretistic cults, except to fight them.

Messianistic or millenarist syncretism seems to lead its adepts into

---

7 The less frequent symmetrically reverse tendency towards a refusal of modern technique and a return to a pre-technical golden age where, for instance, magic would replace European technology could, perhaps, be interpreted as an anti-cargo-cult, a cargo-cult with a minus sign.

8 What is known of UPC profanation rituals among the Bamileke is strikingly reminiscent of similarly oriented rites among the Mau Mau. Spontaneous diffusion through the whole breadth of Africa being improbable, this must be explained by sociological convergence. The hypothesis of a common training school probably belongs to the realm of whodunnits and spy-thrillers. Still, the European press may have played a part in the inspiration of UPC leaders.

blind alleys; it is generally more regressive than progressive. Insofar as it often has politically subversive aspects, it may be used as a convenient tool to aggravate contradictions and precipitate crises. But in the long run it is even less compatible with a marxist organisation than any other religious system. This, nevertheless, does not absolutely preclude the use of some drops of Marx as aromatic bitters in a syncretist cocktail.

THE lack of social and cultural homogeneity in today's Africa often seems paralleled in the minds of individual Africans, especially as regards religious feelings and beliefs. There are Christian priests and marxist leaders who still believe in magic, devout Moslems who still sacrifice to their ancestors, and so forth. The famous ' acceleration of history ' is giving rise to a degree of confusion that makes things difficult not only for the sociologists, but even more for the Africans themselves, many of whom are acutely conscious of it and groping to find a way out. The growing incidence of mental disease among them may be a by-product of this situation.

The phenomenon is, indeed, rather different from the general Western trend of historical acceleration, although a partial consequence of it. It is not quite true to say that Africa has run through four whole centuries of historical evolution within a space of one generation; African history has, in fact, taken short cuts, missed beginnings, jumped over revolutions and evolutions, left out details; it is not a digest of European history, neither are its decades worth more than centuries in other climates. Yet it is true that Africa knew the steam-engine before the windmill and the water-wheel, Dr Livingstone without the Constantinian era, marxism after the Russian revolution, and Marx at the same time as Mao Tsetung. Europe has been exporting ready-made systems and not bothering to tailor new ones for the special needs of Africa; it is up to the Africans themselves to attempt this adaptation—not by any means an easy task.

However, the novelty of European ideological systems may well be an asset in this reconstruction. To African eyes modern European ideologies do not appear so much the end products of protracted intellectual and socio-historical evolution, as the starting point of new and still unpredictable evolutionary processes. Not to have gone through the great ideological and social battles makes Africa freer than we can be from the momentum of tradition. Africa has been and is being showered with a stream of imported ideologies of widely differing bases, assumptions, ages, aims, and degrees of evolution and elaboration. These are being grafted on to a stock of native concepts at various stages of degradation. And the graft is taking place in a wholly unique and unprecedented political, social, and economic context. Finally, while the influence of those ideologies certainly reacts upon the evolution within the context (economic development, political organisation, international relations, etc.), their ultimate fate is, at the same time, conditioned by this context and its needs.

Any long-term prophecy would certainly be unwise today. For the time being, it seems that the dominant trend is towards a kind of original synthesis, particular to Africa, between certain corollaries of marxism in the field of political and economic organisation, and a continuation of non-materialist, non-rationalistic (in the European sense) attitudes where the *Weltanschauung* and philosophy of action are concerned. A number of Africans reject atheism, although they claim to be marxists and do, indeed, use dialectical methods of reasoning, try to construct a socialist economy in their countries, and favour a neutralism hostile to the Western bloc. China is often their ideal, because they admire its achievements in the economic field and also, and chiefly, because they believe that the Chinese have succeeded in acclimatising marxism and in assimilating it while retaining their own cultural originality in its integrity.

On the whole, the ideal of the contemporary African elite most often seems definable as the will to achieve a working synthesis of all positive imports—idealism *and* materialism, marxism *and* jeffersonism, and so forth—by africanising them into an original whole. It will be a welcome —and, perhaps, not quite unlikely—surprise if they can succeed.

THE LEFT WING IN JAPAN

Robert A. Scalapino

MARXISM is in serious trouble in Japan. It is probably unwise to insist that the Japanese extreme left has reached its high-point and is destined for gradual decline. Many signs point that way, but the variables involving both Japan and the world are such as to make predictions hazardous. There can be little doubt, however, about current trends: Japanese Marxism is involved in extensive fragmentation; it is being pushed further onto the defensive; and despite some sallies and efforts at invigoration, it is in a general state of retreat.

When one examines the political spectrum in Japan, these facts become evident. In academic and literary circles, it is generally an older generation that now guards the Marxian citadels. Most younger intellectuals have either abandoned their battle-stations, or, at the very least, have insisted upon the right to modernise the weapons and reorganise the troops. In political circles, similar tendencies are operative. The Japanese 'left' has always been deeply divided, but fragmentation has recently developed at an accelerated rate and *within* the extreme wing. Once again, differences of generation are important. The old stalwarts of the Socialist party may cling tenaciously to the traditional tenets that they have held for forty years, but a younger group is beginning to insist upon fresh approaches. While these approaches still, in most cases, bear the Marxian label, in fact they represent forms of revisionism, some of them with far-reaching implications. The current controversy over ' structural reform ' in the Socialist party should be read in this light.

Further to the 'left', the Marxist forces are also in a state of confusion. The young radicals who lead *Zengakuren,* the National Students' Federation, are deeply divided over major ideological issues. Actually, the importance of Zengakuren has been exaggerated. The militant activist group is small and generally confined to the leadership. Rank and file students in Japan, including many members of Zengakuren, are normally apolitical. The activists, however, are zealous and they gain headlines. Occasionally, moreover, they are able to influence or direct significant protest movements involving other elements.

At present, the ' main current ' or majority leaders of Zengakuren represent an angry young generation of Japanese Marxists who have rejected all international communist authority. For some years they have spoken and written against Stalin, Khrushchev, and Mao. They have charged both Russia and China with bureaucratism. In modern communism as it actually operates, they have recognised an undesirable and seemingly permanent statism. When one reads their fiery little journals or listens to their speeches, one detects certain similarities with the anarchist protests against Bolshevism that poured forth in the early years after the Russian Revolution. It should not be forgotten, incidentally, that anarchism in that era had a substantial impact upon the Japanese ' left ', an impact never entirely lost.

The opponents of the ' main current ' leaders, however, charge them with ' Trotskyism ', not anarchism. Here too there are some parallels, both in the anti-stalinist position of the main current, and in their antipathy to the kinds of compromises involved in any ' two-stage revolutionary theory ' or united front tactics. These young men want to be known as militant revolutionaries. They are dedicated to the immediate march toward world socialism. Most of them, however, have declined the Trotskyite label and show no interest in the international Trotskyite movement.

A minority of the Zengakuren leadership is affiliated with the Japanese Communist party, but this party itself is deeply divided. In 1961, for example, Shojiro Kasuga and six other members and candidate members of the Central Committee left the party in the midst of violent charges and countercharges. The Kasuga group was charged with various ' crimes ' by the party regulars: Kautskyism, petty-bourgeois revisionism, and—naturally—anti-party and anti-class activities. In fact, Kasuga and his followers in certain respects are ideologically related to the old *Rono* group of pre-war Japanese Marxists, once led by Yamakawa Hitoshi; in other respects, their theories parallel those of the ' structural revisionists ' of the contemporary Socialist party. Yet they fiercely proclaim their orthodox communism and struggle with the JCP to capture the movement.

WHAT lies behind this picture of fragmentation throughout the ranks of Japanese socialism and communism? Let us first seek out the origins of Japanese socialism, and, more especially, the reasons why Marxism had an appeal to the Japanese intellectuals. Japan was the first society in Asia to feel the Marxist impact. Marx was introduced to the Japanese intelligentsia at the end of the nineteenth century, along with other Western socialist writers. Small intellectual socialist study circles were formed among the *avant garde*. But in the period prior to World War I, Marxism enjoyed no special vogue, not even among the tiny community of Japanese socialists. The social-democrats of this early period generally derived from Christian humanist training. The radicals moved into anarchism or anarcho-syndicalism, and other theories then enjoying some popularity among European and American socialist circles. Japanese ' progressives ' have always scanned the horizon to discern the latest trends. How else, it might be asked, does one catch up?

Marxism made its first significant gains among Japanese intellectuals in the period immediately after World War I. Building upon that background, it had an even greater influence in the years immediately after World War II. Incidentally, the term ' intellectual ' is used here in the same sense that the Japanese use it, namely as an occupational designation. The Japanese intellectual is an academician, a journalist, a member of the *literati,* a professional man of certain categories, or a university student.

At no time did a majority of the Japanese intellectuals affiliate themselves to either academic or political Marxism. By a considerable margin, the intellectual community as a whole was apolitical, liberal, or conservative in the Japanese style. Yet it cannot be denied that a small ' vanguard ' of Marxists, flanked by those upon whom Marxism had had a definite influence, tended to dominate the Japanese intellectual world in many respects. It was this group that often occupied the strategic heights—whether of ' progressive ' politics, ' scientific ' methodology, or publication.

To understand the appeal of Marxism to the Japanese ' progressive ' is to explore many fascinating problems relating not only to Japan but to the whole emergent non-Western world. Japan partakes of both the unique and the universal, and both factors were involved in the Marxian appeal. Let us first recognise the enormous problems faced by an intellectual class born into that society and in those times. The Japanese intellectual had only about forty years (1880-1920) in which to be introduced to the whole range of Western thought. He made no less a forced march than his society toward modernisation. Ideas flashed across his stage in kaleidoscopic fashion and not always in proper sequence. The order in which Western thought reached Japan was centrally connected with the particular timing of the Japanese emergence into the world stream, but it was also related to the more trivial accidents of random discovery and translation. Burke followed John Stuart Mill. For a time Samuel Smiles competed for popularity with men like Rousseau. But all—Mill, Rousseau, Smiles, Burke, Darwin, Spencer, Marx, Lassalle, and hundreds of others—both giants and pygmies, made their debut in the Japanese intellectual world within a very short period of time.

One can scarcely over-estimate the difficulties faced by those Japanese who were seeking to break out of their intellectual isolation quickly, to conduct a one-generation assault upon all citadels of Western political thought. Diverse ideas poured in with a rapidity that made adequate understanding and systematisation almost impossible. More serious than this for the Japanese intellectual, however, was the fact that Western ideas did not necessarily relate to the nature and proclivities of contemporary Japan. What was one to do if the ideas borrowed from the advanced West and believed to be the wave of the future (' progressive,' ' scientific,' and ' true '), did not fit the capacities of one's society? It was easy enough to talk of adaptation or synthesis, but that was an extraordinarily complex task.

This problem, together with the cultural legacy that helped to produce it, did much to shape the nature, function, and ideological predilections of the modern Japanese intellectual. Speaking broadly, the function of the intellectual has been to be dissident and non-participant. By classic definition, the intellectual thinks; he does not act. Or if he does act, it must be with signs of great reluctance, as if he were doing a necessary but vulgar thing. Otherwise, self-respect and even status are threatened.

In modern times, the risks of action have in some respects increased. To move from thought to action requires a certain compromise with one's personal value system. It involves one in procedures and decisions not wholly of one's own choice. This universal problem has been especially acute for many Japanese intellectuals because of the wide gap between their value system (derived from the West) and the institutions and processes of their society. How could the modern intellectual support whole-heartedly the Imperial myth? How could he operate within the factional groupings that called themselves political parties? The basis for intellectual criticism and non-participation was thus strengthened. The intellectual was sustained in his seeming determination to be apart from, rather than a part of, his society.

Non-participation in turn underlined the Japanese intellectual penchant for theory. There is nothing unique about intellectual interest in theory; to proceed beyond mere description to analysis, conceptualisation, and model-building is a universal quest. In Japanese intellectual circles, however, there has been a tendency to avoid empirical research, to impose theory upon fact in such a fashion as to make the latter obedient to the former.

IN seeking to draw a rough profile of the Japanese intellectual, perhaps one additional feature should be added. In the modern era, he has generally lived a highly compartmentalised life. His ideas have been liberal or radical; his pattern of life traditional and conservative. It is by no means unusual to find a staunch Marxist maintaining a strongly status-conscious relation with colleagues and students and managing his family in paternal or authoritarian fashion. Perhaps, indeed, the word is a substitute for the act. In many ways, the intellectual writes or says what he does not dare do.

It is against this profile and the accompanying background of modern Japan that the emergence and growth of Japanese Marxism must be seen. A wide range of stimuli were involved. For some intellectuals, Marxism satisfied both negative and positive impulses. It was a response to both intellectual and emotional needs; it played upon both the rational and the irrational elements within this gifted, frustrated group, which found in Marxism an analysis of prevailing social ills that was comprehensive and easily understandable, and that not only contained within it significant elements of the truth, but also fitted in well with the proclivities of the modern Japanese intellectual. Both his new learning and his old function equipped him to be a part of the protest movement. Yet he could not accept the type of protest represented by the traditionalists of his society. These types were anti-modern and often anti-intellectual as well. Marxism, on the other hand, championed both modernity and intellectualism.

Clearly, in the process of Japanese modernisation, there was much against which to protest. The development of modern Japan represented one of the earliest experiments in the forced-march technique. Later, Soviet Russia utilised statism and mass mobilisation in much greater degree, but Japan, like all other societies intent upon a rapid industrial revolution, used the means conducive to that end: a great increase in centralised power, with a corresponding decline in local autonomy; a constant exhortation to discipline and sacrifice in the name of national unity and patriotism (with the imperial institution the central nationalist symbol); and the rise of new privileged classes, inheritors of wealth and power. Marxism provided a more basic challenge to these trends in Japan than any other force. In its Japanese form, Marxism played upon the themes of social and economic justice for the lower classes, the rapid and full consummation of democratic freedoms, and the realisation of popular sovereignty. Only Marxism openly attacked the Emperor system. Only Marxism did full battle with Japanese militarism, and the expansionist tendencies that grew with the maturation of modern Japan. Only Marxism questioned the fundamentals of Japanese constitutionalism as it operated in the period before World War II. Perhaps it is not surprising, therefore, when the events of that war seemed to prove the validity of some of the Marxist charges, that many intellectuals looked at Marxism with increased respect. Here was a form of thoroughgoing protest that had shown neither the ambivalence of Japanese liberalism nor the forlorn backwardness of the agrarian-military primitivists. The Marxist protest, moreover, was not confined to the Japanese scene. Like the nationalist movement with which it competed, Marxism attacked Western imperialism and promised its destruction in Asia.

Marxism, of course, was more than a mere method of protest. It was also a modern technique of revolution, especially when Leninism was added to it. Its cultivation and use of mass organisation, its skilful combination of military and political tactics, and its central emphasis upon all forms of propaganda, acted as heady wine on those intellectuals who had for so long been frustrated by their isolation, weakness, and seeming helplessness. Relying upon Marxian tactics, perhaps the intellectuals could become participants, even leaders in the great political upheaval that would produce a 'truly democratic society' in a new, twentieth-century democracy. This was especially important to men who were already becoming disillusioned with parliamentarism. Japan was the first country in Asia to experience failure in its efforts to make Western-style democracy work. The experiment with parliamentarism in Japan began in 1890. Within a few decades, in many minds, parliamentarism had become synonymous with corruption, political parties with privilege, and Japanese-style democracy with fraud. In intellectual circles, hopes remained high that universal suffrage might make major improvements possible, but in time these hopes diminished. The Japanese common man proved consistently to be more backward, more difficult to reach, and less rational than the 'progressive' intellectual cared to admit. Gradually, however, the 'progressive' became discouraged with democracy Western-style and began to search for some short cut, some method whereby his faith in democracy could be retained, but the procedures could be altered to fit the contours of his society. Somewhat unconsciously, the Japanese intellectual began to search for a system of tutelage, an elitist rule that would guide the masses towards what was good for them. This search for an appropriate system of tutelage, incidentally, is now almost universal throughout the non-Western world. A theory of tutelage is the one broad ideology that most nearly unites all emergent societies today.

THUS Marxism-Leninism spoke in the name of *avant-garde* democracy, but it operated in fact on the basis of a strict elitist tutelage over the masses. It used all the terms to which the intellectual was committed : progress, democracy, science and freedom. But in operation it was not impeded by these terms. It could aim at monolithic unity, and not be plagued by diversity. It could try to mobilise and solidify the masses for any national purpose, without being hampered by a recalcitrant individual or group. It could promise rapid progress on its own terms, and not be worried about an opposition. Was this not a suitable—even a necessary—system for societies that wanted to kindle a one-generation modernisation drive based largely upon the sacrifices of their own people? To be sure, in the case of Japan, modernisation was already in progress, and the tutelage was in other hands. The Japanese Marxist was thus in the position of rebelling against one form of tutelage while favouring another.

There are also certain other psychological aspects of the Marxian appeal which cannot be ignored. To the Japanese intellectual, Marxism was a philosophy of optimism. It was a doctrine of inevitable progress, a promise that societies like Japan would catch up with the West and join in the universal stream. Almost more than anything, this was a goal of the Japanese ' progressive.' He wanted desperately to be relieved of his isolation, of the sense of always being behind, of the feeling of inferiority towards the advanced West. Liberalism made no promises. Its doctrine in effect was: work as hard as you can and hope for the best. There was no assurance that salvation would come, or even relief. Indeed, liberalism in action seemed to generate a rising tide of criticism covering every aspect of the society, a kind of rolling pessimism within the intellectual world. The Japanese intellectual, in many cases, seemed to need a set of firm beliefs. Thus Marxism had an appeal as a faith. But this appeal is stated more accurately if one suggests that Marxism represented a combination of faith and science, or perhaps faith in ' science.' The Japanese Marxist stood his ' science ' against the superstition, the error, and the ' retarded ideologies ' with which he was surrounded. In the progressive world, ' science ' swept all before it. Like democracy, it was a concept that could not be challenged. And the science of society was economic determinism. Who could question the truth of Marxism as revealed in its scientific approach to man in society?

It is here that a very different aspect of the Marxist appeal should be introduced, namely, the appeal of Marxism as a methodology. In Japan, academic Marxism has always been at least as powerful as political Marxism. The Japanese intellectual did not enter the universal stream with any complex or sophisticated methodological apparatus. Essentially, he was dedicated to descriptive writing. It is important that the ' science' of Marxism is relatively simple, easily comprehended and applied. Moreover, it has its greatest validity when applied to a society in the early stages of industrialisation. Thus conditions conducive to the use of Marxism as an advanced and scientific methodology were present in greatest degree from the late Meiji to the early Showa periods, roughly from 1910 to 1940. And it should be added that in those years, methodo- logical developments in Western social science did not offer any major competition. What was posited against Marxism? Generally, rather formal and legalist concepts in the political field, and economic doctrines that were specially attuned to the nature and problems of advanced industrial societies. During this period, the limited degree to which Western social science theory encompassed the emergent societies, especially those having different cultural traditions, is striking.

BEFORE surveying the present, we must note a few of the basic weaknesses that Marxism betrayed in prewar Japan. First, it is significant that Marxism has succeeded in Asia only where it has been able to capture and use the nationalist movement. Where it has been forced to fight that movement, it has invariably been weak. In prewar Japan, Marxism had to fight nationalism, and this was a heavy burden, however ' correct' its position. Moreover, in fighting nationalism in their country, the Japanese communists of this period revealed themselves completely dependent upon the Soviet Union. Indeed, Soviet control of the Japanese communist movement proved so onerous that a consider- able number of ' progressives' became independent Marxists after 1925, and challenged the orthodox communist views. Thus the fragmentation of Japanese Marxism had begun long before the postwar era.

But why has that fragmentation been accelerated in recent years, and why have a younger generation of Japanese intellectuals begun to turn away from Marxism? There is no simple or single answer to these questions. In the immediate postwar era, indeed, Marxism achieved a new prominence in Japanese intellectual circles. As noted earlier, many of the Marxist theses about prewar Japanese society had proven to be correct. Moreover, the intellectual now had a new freedom. He used this freedom to explore hitherto dangerous subjects and to engage in intensive criticism of his society and the whole of its past. Once again, Marxism was convenient as a weapon of social criticism. Some inter- national factors also aided Marxism. The new prominence of the Soviet Union, the wartime and immediate postwar alliance between the ' old and the new democracies,' and the victory of Mao Tse-tung in China were all events that abetted the Japanese Marxist cause in some measure. At the very least, the wave of the future seemed to be rolling leftward. Within a few years, moreover, Japanese Marxism had obtained a weapon that it had never possessed in the prewar period, namely, nationalism. After a brief honeymoon period, American policy came under increasing attacks from the Marxists, who saw in it a direct challenge to the sovereignty and independence of Japan. Now Japanese Marxism had its first real opportunity to capture and use nationalism in the manner of other successful Marxist movements.

Meanwhile, however, other, less favourable trends were developing. Some of these trends pertained to Japan; others to the external world. There have been two internal trends of central importance: the reshaping of Japanese democracy and the extraordinary economic development of Japanese society. Under the aegis of the American occupation, the old Meiji Constitution was scrapped and a new Constitution providing all formal democratic safeguards was enacted. This new Constitution has survived for nearly fifteen years and gradually garnered strength, albeit not without serious challenge. Japanese society has never been so free in terms of its formal political institutions. The problems of Japanese democracy come primarily from those continuing organisational and behavioural patterns of Japanese society that contradict these institutions. Nevertheless, the stereotyped Marxian theses about a revitalised Japanese militarism and fascism have been too exaggerated to gain widespread intellectual support. The Japanese intellectual—especially the older intellectual—is still extremely sensitive to these dangers, but the consistently emotional hyperbole of the postwar Marxist movement has gone far towards destroying its claim to 'scientific analysis,' the credit that it had built up as a result of its opposition to militarism in the prewar period. In short, while Japanese democracy is far from perfect, there has been sufficient democracy to challenge the accuracy of Marxian analyses that in fact are geared entirely to the period before World War II. This is but one indication among many of the innate conservatism that has characterised Japanese Marxism in recent years. The professional Marxists continue to argue the same issues, employ the same conceptual devices, and hold the same positions as they did thirty or forty years ago. And in many cases they are the same men! It is not surprising that such exercises become tiresome to a younger generation.

Marxism is also placed on the defensive because of the rapid economic development that has occurred in Japan during the past decade. Once again, the more extravagant Marxian charges are refuted by the evidence, especially when comparisons are made between Japan and the communist societies. But more importantly, Japan is moving into an economic stage where Marxism is less relevant, and where intellectual interest can no longer be confined to such simple theories. Economic development in Japan has reached a point where the Japanese economist can engage in much more sophisticated, complex forms of analysis and conceptualisation than Japanese Marxism has been able to advance. Perhaps a new, creative Marxism could encompass this new stage in some degree. But it has not appeared. Instead, the Japanese economist is turning increasingly to the West, where economic development and economic methodology now offer more comparable opportunities than at any time in the past. Communication between Japanese and Western economists has become increasingly meaningful—and the historic quest for the universal stream is being attained by the Japanese intellectual via a non-Marxian route.

THIS same trend is emerging in other social science fields as well. Empirical studies are beginning to flourish in Japan, and methodologies more appropriate to them are much in evidence. Thus the old monolithic Marxian approach is faced with an unprecedented challenge in intellectual circles, especially from the younger generation. The young intellectuals see Japanese Marxism not as a science but as a dogma, not as dynamic but as stagnant, not as progressive but as old-fashioned. Some of them are now searching among the Marxist movements elsewhere to see whether a new and creative Marxism can be discovered that will breathe fresh life into the Japanese movement. But most are searching more broadly, surveying the whole field of methodology, with a keen eye towards empirical research.

In part, this development is a product of trends abroad. The Japanese intellectual of today is aware of the fact that both academic and political Marxism have suffered substantial losses among the intellectuals of the advanced world. He knows that Marxism is no longer the ideological base of the European socialist movement, and that Western social science is almost devoid of prominent Marxists at present. He is thus aware of the fact that among the nations at his own level of development, Marxism gives no current sign of being the wave of the future. It is still of enormous significance in the world—but essentially it is of political significance, and in terms of the late-developing world. It actually has a much narrower *intellectual* representation now than it had fifty or even twenty-five years ago.

In the field of political Marxism, moreover, there have been world events of great importance. Since 1950, the whole nature of the communist world has been altered. The Empire centred on Moscow has been shaken, and today a new Byzantium is emerging in the East. Marxism in its statist form no longer has a single Pope or centre of authority. Recent events, moreover, such as the Hungarian uprising, the destalinisation campaign in the Soviet Union, and the widening Sino-Soviet cleavage have had a profound effect upon the Marxist movement everywhere. The Japanese intellectual Marxists have been deeply shaken. Under the impact of these events, the process of fragmentation has been accelerated. Younger 'progressives' in particular are in a mood to challenge all international communist authority and to question many of their senior leaders as well. A struggle of the generations is going on in Japanese Marxist circles in an effort to find new paths to the future.

Perhaps, in the long run, this will provide Japanese Marxism with renewed strength. Perhaps a younger generation of Marxists who feel freer to criticise the old dogmas will have an appeal which those subservient to Moscow or some foreign theorist could not. In part, no doubt, that will depend upon future economic and political trends within Japan and in the world. But even if a new generation of Japanese Marxists manages to liberate their doctrine from the fetters of the past, they will face many obstacles. Marxism can no longer have the same appeal to the Japanese intellectual that it had even fifteen years ago. The nature and problems of Japanese society have changed. Thus it will be difficult, if not impossible, to re-create many of the old appeals: Marxism as ' science,' ' truth,' the only advanced methodology: Marxism as a necessary technique of rapid modernisation; Marxism as the most feasible method of change in Japanese society. In socio-economic terms, and perhaps in political ones as well, Japan in these respects has passed beyond the Marxist stage.

There remain, however, enough problems to make the future of Marxism uncertain. If Japan has passed beyond Marxism, the world has not—and Japan lives in a part of the world that is clearly going to be heavily influenced by the ' practising Marxism ' of China and Russia for the foreseeable future. Nor is the long-range future of Japanese democracy clear. There are enough weaknesses in the Japanese democratic system to lend strength to protest movements, and Marxism remains a likely weapon of such movements. Moreover, the emergence of a truly independent Marxist movement, shorn of international control, might enhance its appeal and abet its creativity. Finally, the Japanese intellectual continues to face many problems that make him susceptible to this kind of movement: he remains more apart from, than a part of, his political society; his main function is a negative one; and thus he continues to be essentially restless and dissatisfied with trends in his society. As long as these conditions prevail, Marxism will remain a force in the intellectual world of Japan. But it will not soon, and probably not ever, regain the prestige which it had in the period immediately after 1945. Asia today stands in various relationships to Marxism-Leninism. Nearly one-half of East Asia is under Marxist-Leninist rule. Another portion of this vast area might be considered pre-Marxist in terms of its stage of development and basic characteristics. But Japan is probably post-Marxist unless external forces intervene.

INDONESIA

Lenin, Mao and Aidit

Justus M. van der Kroef

THE international advance of Communism in our time is in no small measure due to the apparent flexibility with which Marxist and Leninist concepts have been applied—often with startling selectivity—to the problems of the newly emergent and underdeveloped countries of the world. While generally and carefully observing all strictures against "revisionism" and "subjectivism," Communist leaders in these new nations dip with ease into the reservoir of the thought of Marx and Lenin and its practitioners for a justification of their particular tactics, pointing out that Communist thought itself invites flexibility and adaptability. Stalin could quote with approval Lenin's dictum that " We do not regard Marxist theory as something complete and inviolable; on the contrary, we are convinced that it has only laid the cornerstone of the science which Socialists *must* further advance in all directions if they wish to keep pace with life." [1]

The word " creative " when applied to Marxism and Leninism has lately received an unparalleled emphasis in Communist pronunciamentos, *e.g.*, the 1960 Moscow statement reiterated the principle of the 1957 Declaration and Peace Manifesto that " Marxism-Leninism demands creative application of the general principles of socialist revolution and socialist construction, depending on the specific historical conditions in the countries concerned, and does not permit of a mechanical copying of the policies and tactics of the Communist Parties of other countries "; while in his eulogy of Mao Tse-tung, on the recent publication of the fourth volume of Mao's *Selected Works*, Lin Piao, vice-chairman of the Chinese Communist Party's Central Committee, declared that " Comrade Mao Tse-tung creatively applied and developed Marxism-Leninism," also with " the greatest ingenuity and dextrousness in the art of struggle. . . ." [2] Whatever the significance for the world Communist movement of the theoretical and tactical differences currently existing between Moscow and Peking the operative term " creative application " will hardly be ignored by Communist theoreticians in the underdeveloped countries.

[1] J. Stalin, *Problems of Leninism* (Moscow: Foreign Languages Publishing House, 1954, 11th edition), p. 792. Italics in original.
[2] *The China Quarterly*, No. 5, January–March, 1961, p. 33; Lin Piao, "The Victory of the Chinese People's Revolutionary War is the Victory of the thought of Mao Tse-tung," *China Reconstructs*, December, 1960, Supplement, p. 2.

That such " creative application " of Marxism-Leninism can meet with success is currently well illustrated again by the case of Indonesia, where the Communist Party has grown in the past decade to the largest in South-east Asia. Since 1948, when the Indonesian Communist Party (Partai Komunis Indonesia—PKI) attempted a disastrous coup against the revolutionary Indonesian Government and, as a result, saw its membership shrink to less than 10,000 members, Communism in Indonesia has steadily gained in power, with Party members now numbering close to two million, with additional thousands in labour, youth, women's and veterans' fronts, and with its voice assured in the new mutual co-operation parliament and at the higher levels of government such as the Supreme Advisory Council and the National Planning Council. The new Indonesian state policy of NASAKOM (meaning the unity of nationalist, religious and Communist groups) has given the Communists recognition as one of the three official political currents in the country, and at no time in its more than forty-year-old history has the Party been so strong as now.

The principal reason for the PKI's resurgence is Dipa Nusantara Aidit, since 1959 the party's Central Committee Chairman, and chief tactician, organiser and theoretician. Elsewhere the tactics of the Party and its policies under Aidit have been described in terms of the changing Indonesian political scene.[3] The following pages will focus on some of the ideological roots of Aiditism, especially in terms of those Leninist and Maoist concepts which have been evidently most useful to the PKI. Obviously a complete résumé of Aidit's ideological antecedents cannot be attempted here, since it would be tantamount to writing a history of modern Communist thought; nor is it possible to delineate the tactical application of Aidit's theories. For the latter the reader is referred to the material mentioned in note 3. But in view of their significance for the underdeveloped countries of the world today, and also in the light of the history of Maoism, the following concepts may perhaps be touched upon in some detail: (1) the theory of the two-stage revolution, and especially of the role of the bourgeoisie in it, (2) the role of the peasantry, and (3) the concept of the proletariat and the function of the party.

THE THEORY OF THE TWO-STAGE REVOLUTION

Since August 17, 1945, when Indonesians proclaimed their independence from the Dutch, Indonesia, according to Aidit, has been in the grip of a

---

[3] Cf. by J. M. van der Kroef: " Indonesian Communism under Aidit," Problems of Communism, Vol. VII (1958), pp. 15–23; " Communist Policy and Tactics in Indonesia," The Australian Journal of Politics and History, Vol. V (1959), pp. 163–179; " Agrarian Reform and the Indonesian Communist Party," Far Eastern Survey, Vol. XXIX (1960), pp. 5–13; " Indonesian Communism and the Sixth Party Congress," Pacific Affairs, Vol. XXXIII (1960), pp. 227–249; " Communist Theory and Practice in Indonesia," Orbis, Vol. V (1961), pp. 43–63.

revolution which has two stages. The first stage, which remains to be carried out to its completion, is referred to as the " bourgeois democratic " revolution and involves the elimination of imperialism (*e.g.*, the acquisition by Indonesia of Dutch-held West New Guinea, destruction of " counter-revolutionary " rebel movements in Indonesia, which the Dutch are accused of aiding, and the elimination of all imperialist capital in the big foreign enterprises in Indonesia), of feudalism (*i.e.*, promotion of land reform), and the establishment of democratic liberties (*i.e.*, expression of partisan political opinion). The second or Socialist stage, which cannot be completed before the first stage is finished, will see the establishment of a " just and prosperous " Socialist society in Indonesia. In mobilising support for the completion of the first stage the proletariat, with the PKI in the vanguard, must seek the support of various non-proletarian groups, including the peasantry and the bourgeoisie, *i.e.*, classes the richer strata of which are certainly capitalistic, but which, if carefully guided, can collaborate with the proletariat and the PKI in a united front to complete the bourgeois-democratic phase of the revolution.[4]

Though Party work among the peasantry must always be intensified since " the essence of the Indonesian revolution is the agrarian revolution," [5] it is especially the bourgeoisie which, in the first or " bourgeois-democratic " phase of the revolution, is of importance. Before describing Aidit's analysis of the bourgeoisie and its subdivisions it seems well to stress the long historic perspective of the potential revolutionary role of the bourgeoisie and of the concept of the two stage revolution in Communist thought.

Both Marx and Engels refer to the revolutionary potential of the bourgeoisie in conjunction with the proletariat. In his *The Class Struggles in France, 1848 to 1859*, Marx had described the " petty bourgeois, the middle classes in general, stepping alongside the proletariat " in defence of " democratic republican institutions," and shortly before, in the *Manifesto of the Communist Party*, Marx and Engels had already pointed out that the very dynamic of the class struggle forces the bourgeoisie to turn to the proletariat for help and, indeed, " a portion of the bourgeoisie goes over to the proletariat " as the process of disorganisation in the ruling class of a capitalist society reaches its zenith. Engels, in *The Peasant War in Germany*, noted how the liberal bourgeoisie of Europe on the eve of the revolutions of 1848 " was still revolutionary, called

4 *Cf.* Aidit's essay, " Masjarakat Indonesia dan Revolusi Indonesia," in D. N. Aidit, *Pilihan Tulisan* (hereafter DNAPT), (Djakarta : Jajasan Pembaruan [for Pilihan Tulisan], 1960), Vol. II, pp. 299–300, and Aidit's address before the " Assembly of the 1945 Generation," reprinted in *Harian Rakjat* (Djakarta), March 18, 1960.

5 B. O. Hutapea, " Beberapa Paladjaran dai Konferensi Nasional Tani Pertama PKI," *Bintang Merah*, Vol. XV (1959), p. 257.

200   JUSTUS M. VAN DER KROEF

itself Socialist and Communist, and clamoured for the emancipation of
the working class," while in describing the unrest in Algeria in 1848
for the English Chartist newspaper *Northern Star* Engels was to touch on
a specific dialectic basis to the concept of the two-stage revolution in the
underdeveloped countries today, when he indicated that "the modern
bourgeois with civilisation, industry, order and at least relative enlighten-
ment following him is preferable to the feudal lord or to the marauding
robber with the barbarian state of society to which they belong." [6]

While Marx's disillusionment with the bourgeoisie tended to mount
over the years (his *Eighteenth Brumaire of Louis Bonaparte* and *The
Civil War in France* well express his disenchantment) the notions that the
bourgeoisie, or at least a portion of it, can be an ally of the proletariat,
that its dominance is preferable to the old feudal order, but that the
wavering of the bourgeoisie might again make it into a reactionary force,
were all to remain influential. Lenin quite explicitly adopted the course
of bourgeois revolution as "precisely a revolution that most resolutely
sweeps away the survivals of the past, the remnants of serfdom (which
include not only autocracy but monarchy as well)," which is "why a
bourgeois revolution is *in the highest degree advantageous to the
proletariat*," indeed, why "in *a certain sense* a bourgeois revolution is
more advantageous to the proletariat than to the bourgeosie," since the
very inconsistencies in the position of the bourgeoisie even during its own
bourgeois revolution will become more clearly revealed. [7] "That is why,"
wrote Lenin, "the more consistent the bourgeois revolution is in its
democratic changes, the less will it limit itself to what is of advantage
exclusively to the bourgeoisie" [8]; but on the other hand the inconsistent
and the wavering nature of the bourgeoisie will also reveal the more
consistently democratic position of the proletariat all the more fully.
Thus, in a sense, the proletariat in its alliance with the bourgeoisie cannot
lose: a consistent championing of democratic principles by the
bourgeoisie can only benefit the proletariat directly, while if the bourgeoisie wavers and becomes inconsistent the antagonistic position of
the proletariat as the only champion of true democratic principles more
fully reveals itself.

Basic to the contemporary "two-stage concept" of revolution is that
the establishment of Socialism (the second stage) cannot be accomplished
unless the reforms of the first phase have been completed. As Aidit put
it in his May 23, 1960, address, commemorating the fortieth anniversary
of the PKI: ". . . we must complete our revolution, a revolution that

[6] *Marx and Engels. Basic Writings on Politics and Philosophy*, Ed. by Lewis S. Feuer
(New York: Doubleday Anchor, 1959), pp. 17, 315, 419 and 451.
[7] V. I. Lenin, *Two Tactics of Social Democracy in the Democratic Revolution* (Moscow:
Library of Marxist-Leninist Classics, 1950), pp. 64–65. Italics in original.
[8] *Ibid.*, pp. 67–68.

is national and democratic in character. . . . To talk about Socialism is a joke and deception of the people if action is not taken to completely eliminate the influences of imperialism and feudalism in economic, political, social and cultural affairs." [9] This position has, of course, its reference points in Marx and Lenin. Marx, in his " Contribution to the Critique of Political Economy," asserted his well-known dictum that " no social order ever disappears before all the productive forces for which there is room in it have been developed, and new, higher relations of production never appear before the material conditions of their existence have matured in the womb of the old society." [10]

Lenin shared this view when he excoriated those who were trying to leap at once from " the eve of the collapse of capitalism " to the " higher phase of Communism," without going through " the first steps in the transition from capitalism to Socialism, or the lower stage of Communism," and he equally upbraided those who refused to collaborate with the bourgeoisie in an attack on monarchical absolutism and feudalism.[11] In collaborating with the bourgeoisie Lenin even urged his followers to soften their Socialist demands for the sake of unity in the attack on autocratic institutions. That this meant a short range, tactical support by the proletariat of bourgeois capitalist interests, which would serve the double purpose of strengthening the forces seeking the overthrow of the old order, while at the same time ultimately drawing the future class antithesis between proletariat and bourgeoisie in starker colours, was clearly in Lenin's thought. But this tactical approach also meant a liberation of capitalism—however temporary—as the old feudal order was overthrown. It is on this basis that Aidit has championed " national " capitalism in Indonesia today, i.e., as part of the bourgeois-democratic phase of the revolution which will see the end of imperialism and feudalism.[12]

But the liberation of bourgeois capitalism from the confines of feudal autocracy is not designed to create a traditional bourgeois capitalistic order, for the party and the proletariat must direct the anti-feudal and anti-imperialist revolution beyond this stage. It is this which gives the first or bourgeois-democratic phase of the two-stage revolution its peculiar character. Both Marx and Lenin commented extensively on the fact

[9] D. N. Aidit, *Peladjaran dari Sedjarah PKI* (Djakarta: Jajasan Pembaruan, 1960), p. 24. Compare *DNAPT*, Vol. II, pp. 299–300:
  " Our Party has a double task in leading the Indonesian Revolution. First, under the slogan ' Complete the demands of the August Revolution in their entirety ' we carry out to their completion the tasks of the bourgeois democratic revolution; secondly, *after the first task has been carried out*, we carry out to their completion the tasks of the revolution, which is proletarian and socialist in kind." (My Italics.)
[10] *Marx and Engels. Basic Writings, op. cit.*, p. 44.
[11] V. I. Lenin, " *Left-Wing* " *Communism, An Infantile Disorder* (Moscow: Library of Marxist-Leninist Classics, 1952), pp. 45, 89, 90, 92, 95.
[12] *Harian Rakjat*, March 18, 1960; *DNAPT*, Vol. II, pp. 284–300.

that a bourgeois liberal revolution may turn reactionary and contrary
to proletarian interests once it has succeeded, and that is why the
proletariat must guide and force the bourgeois-democratic process onward
toward the second or Socialist phase. In the bourgeois-democratic phase
proletarian interests must therefore predominate. Mao Tse-tung, basing
himself on Stalin and Lenin, thus speaks of a "new type" bourgeois-
democratic revolution to distinguish it from the old type bourgeois
revolutions in Europe which culminated in the establishment of a liberal
capitalist order, and this "new type" bourgeois-democratic revolution
is therefore part of the "proletarian-Socialist word revolution." [13] Aidit,
explicitly follows this view: "... the Indonesian bourgeois-democratic
revolution of today ... is no longer of the old out-dated type, but is something special, a new type. This new type bourgeois-democratic revolution
is ... a part of the world proletarian revolution which firmly opposes
imperialism. ..." [14]

It was not Mao but Lenin who first called attention to the revolutionary role of the bourgeoisie in underdeveloped countries, especially in
the context of what since has come to be known as the "national
liberation" movement. As the "Theses and Statutes" of the Comintern,
approved at its second congress in 1920, put it: "For the overthrow
of foreign capitalism, which is the first step towards revolution in the
colonies, the cooperation of the bourgeois nationalist revolutionary
elements is useful." In his article on "Democracy and Narodism in
China," published in 1912, Lenin pointed to the fact that "The Western
bourgeoisie is in a state of decay; it is already confronted by its grave-
digger—the proletariat. In Asia in contrast there is *still* a bourgeoisie
capable of championing sincere, militant, consistent democracy. ..." [15]
For Lenin, Sun Yat-sen's programme was essentially that of the dynamic
bourgeois-democratic and capitalistic forces, which, also agriculturally,
were seeking to demolish the medieval and feudal old order in China.
Revolutionary bourgeois interests and the interests of the peasantry were
thus brought together, argued Lenin. [16] This junction of forces in China
is by definition anti-imperialistic, for it seeks to eliminate the hold of
Western imperialism and capitalism on Chinese society. The liberation
of indigenous bourgeois capitalistic forces thus parallels the political
liberation of the nation from foreign control and hence the "national
liberation" movement in Asia partakes of the nature of the bourgeois
democratic phase of the two-stage world proletarian revolution. For

[13] Mao Tse-tung, *On New Democracy* (Peking: Foreign Languages Press, 1954), pp. 10–12, 18.
[14] *DNAPT*, Vol. II, p. 297.
[15] V. I. Lenin, *The National-Liberation Movement in the East* (Moscow: Foreign Languages Publishing House, 1957), p. 43. Italics in original.
[16] *Ibid.*, pp. 44–47.

Lenin, commenting on "The Junius pamphlet" in 1916, "National wars *against* the imperialist powers are not only possible and probable; they are inevitable, *progressive* and *revolutionary*," and in his "Report of the Commission on the National and Colonial Questions" to the second congress of the Comintern in July, 1920, Lenin again underscored the bourgeois and inherently capitalistic character of the "national liberation" movement: "There need not be the slightest doubt that every national movement can only be a bourgeois-democratic movement, for the overwhelming mass of the population in backward countries consists of peasants who represent bourgeois capitalist relationships." [17]

Lenin regarded it as "utopian" for proletarian parties to pursue Communist tactics in these underdeveloped countries without giving effective support to the peasant movement, *i.e.*, without supporting the bourgeois capitalist relationships which the peasantry represent. To make sure that under these circumstances Communists would not end up by supporting pseudo-reformers and reactionaries—the ever-present danger in the class dynamic of the bourgeoisie—Lenin recalled that the Comintern's "Commission on the National and Colonial Questions" proposed that the term "national revolutionary" be substituted for the term "bourgeois-democratic" and that only "genuinely revolutionary" bourgeois "liberation" movements be supported "in the colonies." It need hardly be pointed out that nowadays Communist theoreticians have been wont to combine the two terms and use the term "national democratic" alongside with "bourgeois-democratic." For Mao, as for Aidit, the bourgeoisie in their respective countries has never been free from a dualistic character, revolutionary at times, reactionary at others, as has indeed the peasantry, among whom feudal and capitalistic interests may also be present. [18] Yet, even so, the proletariat led by the Party can guide them effectively in a common anti-imperialist front. The unity of bourgeoisie, peasantry, and proletariat, forged and directed by the Communist Party is therefore not only essential to the bourgeois-democratic phase of the revolution, but is particularly indispensable to the success of the "national liberation" movement—part and parcel of the bourgeois-democratic phase—in the underdeveloped, colonial or semi-colonial areas. For example, the principle of class unity under party guidance is basic to the tactics of the national liberation movement in Asia as described by Liu Shao-ch'i to the "Trade Union Conference of Asian and Australasian Countries" in Peking, in November, 1949.

Class unity under Party guidance not only will prevent the bourgeoisie from wavering and becoming reactionary, it will also insure the intimate

[17] *Ibid.*, p. 170, 266. Italics in original.
[18] *Cf.* Mao Tse-tung, *Analysis of the Classes in Chinese Society* (Peking: Foreign Languages Press, 1960), p. 2, 5, and *DNAPT*, Vol. II, pp. 290–292.

linkage between the first and the second stage of the two-stage revolution. Stalin, in defending Lenin's version of the two-stage revolution, condemned the leaders of the Second International for thinking that between the first and second phase there would lie a chasm, during which capitalism fully developed itself and the proletariat would gather strength for the final assault on the newly liberated bourgeoisie. Rather the " bourgeois-democratic revolution, in a more or less developed country must . . . verge upon the proletarian revolution . . . the former must pass into the latter," and the proletariat, Stalin declared, citing Lenin, would " immediately " take advantage of the liberation of the bourgeois from the Tsarist feudal order in Russia " to bring about the socialist revolution in alliance with the proletarians of Europe." [19] It is perhaps of interest that Chinese theoreticians have recently again stressed this intimate linkage between the two phases of the revolution.[20] But the degree of accommodation to be accorded to bourgeois capitalistic interests in the first stage of the two-stage revolution, let alone in the early period of the second stage, is a matter dictated by variable circumstances. At one point in his *On New Democracy* Mao Tse-tung speaks even of " several stages " (apparently not just two) [21] in the course of the revolution, and elsewhere emphasises that " contradictions still exist in a socialist society," *i.e.*, in the second phase of the revolution, and that " contradictions " between the national bourgeoisie and the proletariat or even within the ranks of the national bourgeoisie must be considered as expected contradictions among " the people," *i.e.*, are not of a fundamental or reactionary character.[22] The latter view is also shared by Aidit. This would suggest some room for expression of the capitalist orientation of the bourgeoisie even in the early period of the second or Socialist phase of the revolution.

A somewhat related view appears in the work of Tan Malaka, probably the most important Indonesian Communist theoretician before Aidit, who around 1925 introduced the two-stage revolutionary concept in Indonesia. Malaka did not think it possible to establish Communism overnight in Indonesia. A preparatory phase was necessary

---

[19] J. Stalin, *Problems of Leninism, op. cit.*, pp. 39–41.

[20] See, *e.g.*, Shih Tung-hsiang, " The Distinction and Link-Up between the Two Stages of the Chinese Revolution," *Peking Review*, January 20, 1961, pp. 9–18.

[21] Mao Tse-tung. *On New Democracy, op. cit.*, p. 12. It seems hardly necessary to stress the Leninist basis of this contention. In the " supplementary theses " to the " theses on the national and colonial question " adopted by the second congress of the Comintern as part of the *Theses and Statutes of the Third (Communist) International* (Moscow: Comintern Publishing Office, 1920) in 1920 " successive periods of development of revolutionary experience " in the colonial countries are emphasized, as is the concept that " the revolution in the colonies is not going to be a Communist revolution in its first stages."

[22] Mao Tse-tung, *On the Correct Handling of Contradictions Among the People* (Peking: Foreign Languages Press, 1959), pp. 9, 23.

he maintained, in which non-proletarian elements in society would have to be rallied to the PKI banners. This meant that the Party would have to make allowance for the capitalist interests of society and Malaka deemed the Soviet New Economic Policy inaugurated in 1921 as particularly important for Indonesia, because the NEP had given renewed recognition to private property interests.[23] Eventually, however, these bourgeois political remnants would give way to the political order of the workers, *i.e.*, complete Socialism would be established. Because the PKI shortly after Malaka's formulation had to go underground, and because Malaka himself subsequently incurred the wrath of the Comintern, these ideas were not to be implemented in Indonesia until after the Second World War. It need hardly be pointed out, however, that Malaka's thought here closely parallels that of Bukharin and the Comintern directives toward the Chinese Communists at this same period in the mid-nineteen-twenties.[24] For Aidit, accommodation of capitalist interests in the first phase of the revolution is an accepted fact, as we have seen, though he has had no reason thus far to comment on the extent of such accommodation in the socialist phase.

For Mao, as for Aidit, the logic of the two-stage revolution is based upon a recognition of the semi-feudal or semi-colonial condition of their respective countries.[25] This recognition is not new with Mao, of course; Lenin had already said as much, and in their acceptance of Lenin's premise Mao and Aidit also endorse the implications of the essentially anti-feudal and anti-imperialist character of the bourgeois-democratic phase of the revolution. The importance of the national bourgeoisie in China's economic reconstruction had been explicitly acknowledged by

---

23 Tan Malaka, *Naar de " Republik Indonesia"* (Tokyo: 1925) and Harry J. Benda and Ruth T. McVey, eds., *The Communist Uprisings of 1926–1927 in Indonesia: Key Documents* (Cornell Un., South-east Asia Programme, 1960), pp. 129–134.

24 Bukharin, " Perspektiven der Chinesischen Revolution," *Die Kommunistische Internationale*, 1927, pp. 669–671, and " Theses on the Chinese Situation," by the Seventh plenum of the Comintern's Executive Committee, in Xenia J. Eudin and Robert C. North, *Soviet Russia and the East, 1920–1927: A Documentary Survey* (Stanford Un.: 1957), pp. 356, 359–362.

25 Mao Tse-tung, *New Democratic Constitutionalism* (Peking: Foreign Languages Press, 1960), pp. 1, 7 and *DNAPT*, Vol. II, pp. 276–277. In the " Supplementary Theses " to the " Theses on the National and Colonial Questions," part of the *Theses and Statutes of the Third (Communist) International adopted by the Second Congress, July 17–August 7, 1920* (Moscow, Publishing Office of the Communist International, 1920; reprinted by the United Communist Party of America, s.a.e.l.), Lenin—who was mainly responsible for these theses and statutes—indicates that the " revolution in the colonies " will have several stages, reflecting the interests of the peasantry, the petty bourgeoisie. etc. Both Mao and Aidit faithfully adhered to this fundamental Leninist principle, announced as early as 1920 as the tactic of international Communism. Ho Chi Minh, writing in 1926, praised Lenin for his insight " into the conditions of the most complex tasks peculiar to the East " and declared that Lenin " was the first " to realise the importance of a correct solution to the colonial question as " a contribution to the world revolution." Ho Chi Minh, *Selected Works* (Hanoi, Foreign Languages Publishing House, 1960), Vol. 1, pp. 140–141.

Mao (" Our present policy is to control not to eliminate capitalism "),[26] and earlier he had declared that " it would be sheer illusion to try to build socialism on the ruins of the colonial, semi-colonial, and semi-feudal order " without, among other things, the development of " private capitalist " enterprises, that is " without pushing to its end the democratic revolution which is bourgeois in character. . . ." [27] In Aidit's writings, as in the present party programme of the PKI, there is less explicit mention as such of the economic importance of the national bourgeoisie, but the protection and development of national capitalist enterprises and the concept of the participation of the national and petty bourgeoisie in the Communist-led united front of " the people " are recurrent themes in and are basic to PKI theory today.[28]

According to Aidit, the bourgeoisie is divided into three groups: (1) compradore, (2) national, and (3) petty bourgeois. The first " serve the interests of the big foreign capitalists," e.g., they are representatives of the big foreign trading and mining companies, and as stooges of imperialism they are targets of the revolution. But even the compradore element, strange as it may seem, can be an ally of the Party under certain specific circumstances, e.g., " when the Party's policy at a given time is only directed against one particular imperialism." Yet even so the reactionary character of the compradore element makes it generally the enemy of the proletariat. The national bourgeoisie also has a dual character : on the one hand it is a victim of imperialism and feudalism and so can be an integral element in the Communist-led united front; on the other hand the national bourgeoisie " does not have the courage fundamentally to fight imperialism, because economically and politically it is weak and it has class ties with imperialism and feudalism." Thus the national bourgeoisie must be under constant scrutiny and guidance of the proletariat, and Communists must remember that " it is not very difficult to pull this class to the left to make it stand firmly on the side of the revolution. . . ." Finally, the petty bourgeoisie (" the urban poor, the intellectuals, the small traders, the handicraft workers, the fishermen, the independent workers ") have a status, according to Aidit, almost the same as the " middle " peasantry, i.e., they too " suffer from the oppression of imperialism, feudalism and the big bourgeosie " and, therefore " they are one of the forces pushing the revolution forward and are a

---

[26] Mao Tse-tung, *On People's Democratic Dictatorship* (Peking: Foreign Languages Press, 1959), p 17.

[27] Mao Tse-tung, *On Coalition Government* (Peking: Foreign Languages Press, 1960), p. 49.

[28] *DNAPT*, Vo. II, pp. 297–300; *Material for the Sixth National Congress of the Communist Party of Indonesia* (Djakarta: Indonesian Communist Party, Central Committee [Agitprop Dept.], 1959), pp. 94, 98, 99.

reliable ally of the proletariat . . . they can only attain their freedom under the leadership of the proletariat." [29]

In his application of this class typology Aidit and PKI pronouncements tend to be particularly concerned with the national bourgeoisie. It is " the establishment of a united front with the national bourgeoisie " which " opens up possibilities for the development and building of the Party," Aidit has said, and in the reconstruction of the PKI since the dark days of the disastrous Madiun coup, stress was especially placed, according to Aidit, on indoctrinating cadres with Leninism, particularly with Lenin's " Left Wing Communism, an Infantile Disorder," that is, precisely the treatise which emphasises the necessity of the Party's tactical co-operation with the bourgeoisie.[30] The PKI's Politburo has indicated that " at the present stage it is in Indonesia's national interest to develop and raise the output of private national enterprises," and a policy of active support for private national enterprise, by providing technical and financial assistance and protection against competition from abroad, has been recommended by the PKI's " National Economic Seminar." [31] If we disregard the similar earlier theory of Tan Malaka, it could be said that this policy has, in effect, been with the Party since August, 1948, when the veteran Indonesian Communist Muso reintroduced into the PKI and won approval for the two-stage revolutionary concept subsequently embodied in the Party's " New Road for the Republic of Indonesia " resolution.[32] The Madiun coup, which cost Muso his life, and which threw the PKI into a period of steep decline, prevented the implementation of this policy until the ascendancy of Aidit and his associates in the Central Committee of the Party early in 1951. Since 1951 cultivation of the national bourgeoisie has been the PKI's unwavering policy.

But of late a new threat has presented itself to this policy. With the transformation of large foreign-owned (many formerly Dutch-owned) big private enterprises into state enterprises—a policy which the PKI has strongly supported on principle—there has emerged the problem of " bureaucratic capitalism " in the management of these state enterprises, i.e., the military and civil official managers are " chasing after profits no less than private enterprise," [33] and the Party alleges that these profits

29 *DNAPT*, Vol. I, pp. 248–249; Vol. II, pp. 290–292.
30 D. N. Aidit, *Peladjaran dari Sedjarah PKI, op. cit.*, p. 13, and D. N. Aidit, " Lenin and Indonesia," *Bintang Merah*, Vol. XVI (1960), p. 110.
31 " Consolidate Unity to Defend Democracy and Struggle for an Improvement in the Living Conditions of the People " (New Year's Message of the Politburo of the PKI, December 30, 1959), (Djakarta: 1960), p. 3, and *C.P.I. National Economic Seminar: Documents* (*Review of Indonesia, Supplement*, April–May, 1959), p. 7.
32 The resolution went through various editions and revisions, the last probably being *Djalan Baru Untuk Republik Indonesia* (Djakarta: Jajasan Pembaruan, 1953, 7th edition).
33 *Review of Indonesia*, March, 1960, p. 3; August, 1960, p. 9. See also *DNAPT*, Vol. II, pp. 554–555.

have benefited the managers to an unconscionable extent. Thus the emergent state capitalistic structure—a continuation from the colonial era [34] —has presumably tempted the national bourgeoisie toward a reactionary direction and in its celebrated July 8, 1960, statement on the performance of the government, as well as in many previous statements, the PKI's Politburo has excoriated this reactionary development. Yet the problem here confronting the PKI is not novel. Mao Tse-tung had already signalled the danger of the "bureaucratic capitalists" as ancillaries of feudalism and imperialism and the necessity of dealing with them in the context of an "antagonistic contradiction." [35]

The position of what Marx and Engels called the "intermediate" classes (i.e., the petty bourgeoisie) and their relationship to the proletariat has always been subject to considerable reinterpretation in Communist thought and even today the debate goes on.[36] For Aidit, as for Mao, the concept of the national bourgeoisie serves to enlarge the area of those intermediate classes which can be allies of the proletariat in its revolutionary struggle, i.e., the national bourgeoisie is by way of being an underdeveloped country's extension of the more orthodox Marxist concept of the petty bourgeoisie, and indeed, the native small trader, shopkeeper or industrialist in a colony who would ordinarily have been designated as petty bourgeois becomes—after the colony's political independence—a "national" bourgeois concerned with the elimination of the remaining privileged positions of the big foreign-owned enterprises in his country. The revolutionary potentials of the petty bourgeoisie, especially of the petty traders, Marx acknowledged explicitly on a number of occasions (see, e.g., again Marx's *Germany: Revolution and Counter-Revolution*), and the modern application of this concept in underdeveloped countries today has immensely strengthened the preliminary base of operations of the Communist movement.

THE ROLE OF THE PEASANTRY

Proletariat and bourgeoisie supply two elements of the *troika* of the national united front in the first stage of the Communist revolution; the third element comes from the agrarian society. Together these three constitute what Mao often calls "the people," a concept which was not invented by Mao, however, but by Lenin; and Aidit, like Mao, fully subscribes to Lenin's detailed analysis of the "advanced class," i.e., the

---

[34] See J. M. van der Kroef, "Colonial Continuity in Indonesia's Economic Policy," *The Australian Outlook*, Vol. XIV (1960), pp. 5–14.

[35] Mao Tse-tung, *On the Correct Handling of Contradictions among the People, op. cit.*, pp. 10–11.

[36] Donald C. Hodges, "The 'Intermediate Classes' in Marxian Theory," *Social Research*, April 1961, pp. 23–36; *World Marxist Review*, May 1961, pp. 71–84, June 1961, pp. 75–82.

proletariat fighting " for the cause of the whole of the people " and being " at the head of the whole of the people." [37] The " people " then, led by proletariat and Communist Party, make up the national united front which is the dynamic force of the first phase of the revolution, and of the " national liberation " movement today. Since underdeveloped nations tend to be overwhelmingly agrarian, it follows that in those countries the rural mass is in the numerical majority in the national united front and the PKI has recently pointed with pride to the fact that most of its members today are from the peasantry.[38] The agrarian character of the Chinese revolution has, of course, also generally been stressed by the present leadership of the Chinese Party, e.g., one recalls Mao's assertion in " On New Democracy " that " the Chinese Revolution is virtually the peasants' revolution." [39] This is but an amplification of the Comintern line (of the " Resolutions and Theses " of the fourth Comintern congress, 1922) that " the revolutionary movement in the backward countries of the East cannot be successful unless it is based on the action of the masses of the peasantry."

In relating the class structure of rural society to Communist action, however, it is Aidit who has been particularly flexible. But before describing Aidit's views, those of earlier theorists should briefly be considered. Both Marx and Engels, while recognising the conservative inclinations of the peasantry, had earlier acknowledged the revolutionary potentials of the peasantry, especially in the context of anti-feudal, bourgeois revolutions, and Engels' *The Peasant War In Germany* has served more than one Marxist historian and theoretician as an instrument with which to analyse the religious-egalitarian and revolutionary-Communistic overtones of other peasant insurrections in Europe.

Despite his well-known tactical vacillation—now rejecting the proprietary-capitalistic interests of the peasantry, then again explicitly catering to them by favouring a kind of nationalised system of land distribution among them—Lenin always remained wedded to the principle of the importance of peasant support for the success of the revolution generally, and especially in the demolition of the feudal order. (" The agrarian question is the basis of the bourgeois revolution in Russia," he wrote, " and determines the national peculiarity of this revolution. The essence of this question is the struggle the peasantry is waging to abolish landlordism and the remnants of serfdom in the agricultural system of Russia,

[37] V. I. Lenin, *Two Tactics of Social Democracy in the Democratic Revolution*, *op. cit.*, pp. 169–170; Mao Tse-tung, *On People's Democratic Dictatorship*, *op. cit.*, pp. 11; *DNAPT*, Vol. II, pp. 294–295.

[38] *Material for the Sixth National Congress of the Communist Party of Indonesia*, *op. cit.*, p. 62.

[39] Mao Tse-tung, *On New Democracy*, *op. cit.*, p. 54.

and consequently, also in all her social and political institutions.")[40] But Lenin made plain in his article " Socialism, Petty Bourgeois and Proletarian " (1905) that " to the Marxist the peasant movement is not a socialist but a democratic movement," and that the revolution furthered by the peasant movement is not anti-bourgeois but anti-feudal in character.[41]

In underdeveloped countries, therefore, especially those in Asia, where the peasantry had grown equally restive under the feudal yoke, the same appeal was to be made by Lenin and his associates to the peasant's proprietary bourgeois inclinations as was done in Lenin's agrarian programme for Russia. And so, along with emphasis on the organisational unity of workers and peasants in the colonial or semi-colonial countries of Asia, a programme of land distribution—or " land to the peasant " as the Communist slogan has ever since had it—for the benefit of the small farmer, the tenant and sharecropper, was to become part of Communist policy in underdeveloped lands. In these lands the small size and the comparative weakness of an industrial proletariat rendered the strategic value of the peasantry all the greater, and in accordance with Leninist policy the characteristic of the Communist cadres was and is not their class origin but their Marxist political consciousness,[42] which translates itself as " practice " into the ability to effectively mobilise the " national liberation " movement. The concept of the peasantry as representing " the main army of the national movement," that is as representing the chief force of the " national democratic " or " bourgeois-democratic " revolution was, of course, also accepted by Stalin.[43]

For Mao " the strength of the peasants constitutes the principal force of the Chinese revolution," [44] and the path along which the agrarian sector of the anti-feudal bourgeois-democratic revolution will develop in order to reach its culmination in the socialist phase Mao has described thus [45] :

> The agrarian revolution we have carried out is already and will be a process in which the landowning landlord class becomes a class deprived of its land, while the peasants, once deprived of their land, become small holders of land . . . Under Socialism the peasants' private ownership will in turn become communal ownership in Socialist agriculture; this has already taken place in the Soviet Union and will take place throughout the world.

[40] V. I. Lenin, *The Agrarian Programme of Social-Democracy in the First Russian Revolution 1905–1907* (Moscow: Library of Marxist-Leninist Classics, 1954), p. 343.
[41] V. I. Lenin, *Alliance of the Working Class and the Peasantry* (Moscow: Foreign Languages Publishing House, 1959), p. 124.
[42] *Cf.* Karl A. Wittfogel, " The Legend of ' Maoism,' " *The China Quarterly*, No. 1, January–March 1960, pp. 77–78.
[43] J. Stalin, *Marxism and the National and Colonial Question* (London: International Publishers, 1947, 4th ed.), p. 202.
[44] Mao Tse-tung, *On New Democracy, op. cit.*, p. 55.
[45] Mao Tse-tung, *On Contradiction* (Peking: Foreign Languages Press, 1960), p. 49.

Mao's principal views on the peasantry are wholly derived from Marx and Lenin, as is apparent also from his attempt to identify the peasantry with the Marxist-Leninist class antithesis. Thus in Mao's essays on the classes of Chinese society, the " middle " peasants, *i.e.*, those with sufficient land for their own needs who also till their own soil, are subsumed under the class of " petty bourgeoisie," along with small traders, lower government officials, intellectuals, and so on, while the category of " the semi-proletariat " for Mao includes " the overwhelming majority of the semi-tenant peasants " and the " poor peasants." In addition, Mao identifies a " rural proletariat " of peasant labourers and a " lumpen proletariat," consisting in part of peasants who have lost their land, and groups them with the proletariat generally. Moreover, " the industrial proletariat is the leading force in our revolution," although " all sections of the semi-proletariat and the petty bourgeoisie " (*i.e.*, presumably including " middle " peasants, tenants, " poor " peasants and farm labourers) " are our close friends." For Mao, landlords and compradors are often though not always undifferentiated and, as the enemies of the revolution, " represent the most backward and most reactionary production relations in China and hinder the development of her productive forces." [46]

Aidit's thought is in this respect an elaboration on Mao's theme.[47] Agrarian production relationships according to Aidit, considered in their political setting, involve five categories: (1) " imperialist " landlords, (2) " patriotic " landlords, (3) rich peasants, (4) middle peasants, (5) poor peasants and agricultural labourers. The predominantly rural character of Indonesian society dictates that the peasantry be the " basic force " of the Indonesian revolution, indeed, " without the active participation of the peasants the Revolution cannot possibly succeed."

In order to enlist the support of the peasantry, especially of the poor peasants and agricultural labourers who, before the contemplated agrarian revolution, " comprise the majority in the villages in our country," it is necessary to restore land to the peasants. To ensure the establishment of " a peasant land-ownership system, or, in other words, private ownership by the peasants of the land " (as stipulated by the current PKI party programme) [48] land must, therefore, be taken from

---

[46] Mao Tse-tung, *Analysis of the Classes in Chinese Society, op. cit.*, pp. 2, 4, 8–9, 13–15. See also Mao Tse-tung, *Selected Works* (London: Lawrence Wishart, 1954), Vol. I, pp. 138 *et seq.*

[47] *DNAPT*, Vol. II, pp. 292–293, 542–543; D. N. Aidit, " Kibarkan Tinggi Pandji-Pandji 'Tanah Untuk Petani' dan Rebut Kemenangan Satu Demi Satu," *Bintang Merah*, Vol. XV (1959), pp. 217–219.

[48] *Material for the Sixth National Congress of the Communist Party of Indonesia, op. cit.*, p. 94. Adoption of the Leninist and Maoist principle of outright individual landownership for the peasant did not come about until 1954. Between 1945 and 1953 the PKI advocated that though land should be redistributed, the land from the landlords should be vested in the village collectivity as a whole, to be re-allocated

the landlords and given to the peasants. But not all landlords are subject to redistribution. For of the two basic enemies confronting Indonesia, imperialism and feudalism, the former is the " most basic," and in practice this means that only " imperialist " landlords, *i.e.*, those who support various subversive rebel movements in Indonesia, should suffer expropriation now. The " patriotic " landlords, *i.e.*, those who join in opposing the rebel movements supported by the imperialists, are not now confronted with a demand for expropriation, but only with a demand that the rent paid by their tenants be reduced from the traditional 50 per cent. to 40 per cent. of the crop. While the " contradiction " between the " imperialist " landlords and the " people " is a " basic " one—that is it can be resolved only by force—the " contradiction " between the " patriotic " landlords and " the people " is not basic, that is it is of the order of a "contradiction among the people," capable of being resolved " by peaceful means, by democratic and mutually persuasive and mutually beneficial negotiations."

In thus broadening the base of his united front, Aidit has not only managed to bring the compradors on the side of " the people " in certain specific anti-imperialist frames of action as we have seen, but also a sizeable segment of the landlords. With respect to the latter tactic there is, of course, a reference point in Mao, though not in Lenin. In 1938, within the context of the new united front resistance to the Japanese invasion, Mao Tse-tung had counselled that " the landlords should reduce rent and interest, but at the same time the peasants should pay rent and interest and unite with the landlords against foreign aggression "; ten years later Mao was to speak of " the enlightened gentry " and of " rich peasants with democratic leanings " both of whom could constructively participate on the side of the revolution.[49] Aidit's distinction between " patriotic " and " imperialist " landlords coincides with Mao's analysis in this respect too.

It should also be noted that in distinguishing between " imperialist " and " patriotic " landlords, Aidit was elaborating on a theme which had been introduced by Muso as early as 1948 in " The New Road " resolution. That resolution also had demanded that " rich " peasants

---

to the peasant's use as the village government decided. (*Cf. Bintang Merah*, November 17, 1945, and *Djalan Baru Untuk Republik Indonesia*, 1953, *op. cit.*, p. 29). This deference to traditional village communalism may have been framed with a view to direct "sovietisation" of the land. In March 1954, Aidit, however, advocated that land be taken from the landlords and be given directly to the peasants " as their own private property " and this principle the party adopted. D. N. Aidit, *The Road to People's Democracy for Indonesia* (General Report on the Political and Organisational Situation, delivered at the Fifth National Congress of the Communist Party of Indonesia, March 1954) (Djakarta: Jajasan Pembaruan, 1955), p. 32.

[49] Mao Tse-tung, *The Question of Independence within the United Front* (Peking: Foreign Languages Press, 1960), p. 1; Mao Tse-tung, *Selected Works*, Vol. IV (Peking: Foreign Languages Press, 1961), p. 209.

who had opposed the Indonesian Revolution should have their land confiscated forthwith, while those " rich " peasants who had supported the revolution would be allowed to keep enough land for their own use. Though on other occasions Aidit has emphasised that the struggle against imperialism and feudalism within the framework of the bourgeois-democratic revolution must be waged simultaneously,[50] it is equally clear that to him the anti-imperialist campaign is primary and that peasant victories on the anti-feudal front can come only " one after the other," as Aidit has said, *i.e.*, more gradually. Hence the apparent solicitude presently shown the " patriotic " landlords in PKI theory and tactics.

The " rich " peasants generally have more than enough land for their own use, but tend to work it themselves. Some, however, also lease out their excess land, lend money and are " by nature semi-feudal." In a sense they stand in between the peasantry and the landlords, but their " productive activities will continue to be utilised for a certain period to come " and that is why they too can participate in the anti-imperialist phase of the revolution and join the national united front. The " middle " peasants are economically independent; they do not lease out land and do not act as moneylenders and like the " poor " peasants often are victims of the grip of the landlords on the rural economy. That is why they not only can join the anti-imperialist phase of the revolution, but " they can also accept Socialism," and they are a reliable ally of the proletariat. Like Mao, Aidit equates the " middle " peasants with the petty bourgeoisie of small traders, intellectuals, lesser officials, and so on. Aidit also emphasises that the " middle " peasantry is particularly important for the revolution, because after the agrarian revolution—that is after the end of feudal relationships—the self-sufficient " middle " peasants with their plots of land will " comprise the majority in the countryside." Before the agrarian revolution, however, the majority of the rural society is composed of " poor " peasants and landless agricultural labourers, unable to make a living from their miniscule holdings or wages, exploited by moneylenders and through the feudal services they must perform for their landlords. Following Mao, Aidit characterises the poor peasantry as the " village semi-proletariat." For Aidit the poor peasants " are the largest force pushing the revolution forward," are " the most reliable of the allies of the proletariat," but they, like the " middle " peasants, can only be liberated under the leadership of the proletariat.[51]

These three divisions of the peasantry are not based on exact definitions of the size of land holdings in each division, although recent PKI land reform proposals suggest that the borderline between " middle "

50 *DNAPT*, Vol. II, pp. 287–288.
51 *Ibid.*, Vol. II, pp. 292–293.

peasants and " rich " peasants is a holding of either about twelve acres of irrigated fields, or eighteen acres of irregularly irrigated fields, or again twenty-four acres of unirrigated fields.[52] Above this lies the category of " rich " peasants and landlords, below it—sometimes far below it—the category of the poor peasantry begins. As part of its intense campaign to win adherents among the peasantry the PKI under Aidit has carried on extensive research in land tenure patterns in Indonesia, which has revealed very high concentrations of land ownership in the hands of a few peasants and landlords in many areas.[53] These PKI data confirm the analyses made by non-Communist investigators, at least in Java. Great stress continues to be placed by the PKI in improving the conditions of the peasantry and the Party's organisational literature abounds with directions and programmes to win peasant support.[54] Of particular interest is the special effort made by the PKI to win a following among fishermen,[55] whose living conditions closely parallel that of the peasantry, and whose support broadens the popular foundation of the united front.

THE ROLE OF THE COMMUNIST PARTY

" The Indonesian Revolution will not succeed unless it is under the leadership of the Indonesia proletariat," Aidit has written,[56] and the united front of " the people " requires the highly politically-conscious proletarian Party as its vanguard. At no time may the popular base of the united front be narrowed; on the contrary, the Party has the obligation always to seek to broaden mass support. As M. H. Lukman, the PKI's first vice-chairman, once put it: " We must always remember the terms for attracting the moderate forces . . . we must also be able to prove our power and our arguments against imperialism and against the reactionary forces in the country with successes which can be experienced also by the moderate forces." [57] The strengthening of the Party involves development of political appeals also to non-proletarian quarters (as Lenin had put it in his *What is to be Done?* (1902): " To bring political knowledge to the *workers* the Social-Democrats must *go among all classes of the population*, must dispatch units of their army *in all directions. . . .*").

52 *Cf.* the remarks of PKI parliamentary deputy Nungtjik in *Review of Indonesia*, September–October 1960, p. 20.
53 Asmu, " Masalah Land Reform," *Bintang Merah*, Vol. XVI (1960), pp. 14–28.
54 " Kesimpulan Mengenai Laporan Tentang Pekerdjaan Partai Dikalangan Kaum Tani," *Bintang Merah*, Vol. XV (1959), pp. 190–194; D. N. Aidit, Asmu, Mau Tje-tung, *Untuk Bekerdja Lebih Baik Dikalangan Kaum Tani* (Djakarta: Jajasan Pembaruan, 1958); *Undang-Undang no. 2, tahun 1960 Tentang Perjandjian Bagi Hasil* (Djakarta: Jajasan Pembaruan, 1960); *Suara Tani*, November 1959, pp. 3–4; January 1960, p. 3; *Kehidupan Partai*, June 1960, pp. 97–100.
55 " Kesimpulan Konferensi Nasional Tani PKI Tentang Masaalah Nelajan di Indonesia," *Bintang Merah*, Vol. XV (1959), pp. 196–200.
56 *DNAPT*, Vol. II, pp. 294–295.
57 *Harian Rakjat*, April 5, 1958.

Though the PKI has foresworn armed resistance to the government for
the moment, it would agree with Mao's directive at the time of the anti-
Japanese war that " the main task confronting the Party of the Chinese
proletariat has been to unite the largest possible number of allies," [58] and
PKI support today (though with some reservations) for Sukarno's new
National Front and for Sukarno's concept of the unity of the major
political currents, including the Communists, in the country (NASAKOM)
mirrors the Party's policy of developing unity and maximum mass appeal
in this anti-imperialist phase.[59]

But as Aidit pointed out as early as 1954, " in the struggle to create
a united national front, both by co-operation with various political parties
or by co-operation with people of various trends and ideologies, the Party
must not become merged with them. The Party must preserve its
political, ideological and organisational independence." [60] This approach
also closely reflects Mao's wartime policy of preserving " independence
within the united front " and of declaring a " national " struggle (*i.e.*,
against the Japanese) to be a form of the class struggle. In opposing
imperialism (which Aidit today never wearies of describing as Indonesia's
" most basic " enemy) the class struggle must be subordinate, Mao had
argued, and hence the relative independence of parties and classes should
be preserved in the first phase of the revolution.[61] With this tactic Aidit
wholly agrees; he has opposed in Indonesia proposals of a complete
merger or dissolution of the political parties at this time, he has urged
freedom of partisan political expression, and in general has favoured the
independence of class interest and partisan movements within the united
front.

The principle of " independence within the united front," as evidenced,
for example, in the July 7, 1937, agreement between Chiang Kai-shek
and the Chinese Communists, reflects, of course, an experience of major
importance to all Asian Communists today, namely the disaster which
befell the Chinese Communists in the mid-nineteen-twenties, when on
Stalin's orders they wholly merged with the Kuomintang and were subsequently all but destroyed by Chiang. From the point of view of class
theory what this merger meant was that the bourgeois-democratic
elements in the first stage of the revolution came to swallow up the
revolutionary proletariat and its vanguard in the Party. This experience
undoubtedly, still plays a role today in the current tactical and doctrinal
tension between Moscow and Peking, in which the latter accuses the

[58] Mao Tse-tung, *Problems of War and Strategy* (Peking: Foreign Languages Press,
    1954), p. 6.
[59] See M. H. Lukman, *Tentang Front Persatuan Nasional* (Djakarta: Jajasan Pembaruan,
    1960) and *Madju Terus Menggempur Imperialisme dan Feodalisme!* (Djakarta: Jaja-
    san Pembaruan, 1961).
[60] *DNAPT*, Vol. I, p. 249.
[61] Mao Tse-tung, *The Question of Independence Within the United Front, op. cit.*, p. 4.

former of seeking to curtail the revolutionary proletarian forces in underdeveloped countries, and of supporting unreliable bourgeois-nationalistic
elements as part of a policy of general peaceful co-existence in which
war is no longer considered necessary for the triumph of world Communism.[62] The lesson to be learnt from the Chinese experience is that the
Party must always retain its identity in the national front and its militant
aggressiveness, for only in that way can it provide the bourgeoisie and
other non-proletarian forces of that front with proper leadership.   The
potential " vacillation " and " treachery " of the bourgeoisie not only
made a victim once of the Chinese Communists (e.g., in 1926–27) but,
as Aidit has argued, also of Indonesian Communists, for example in
the period between 1948 and 1951.   In those years the PKI, demoralised
and weakened by its unsuccessful coup in Madiun, sought to establish
a new base of strength by trying to win indiscriminate favour in bourgeois-nationalist quarters, only to fall victim to the razzias of the
bourgeois Sukiman government in Indonesia in 1951.   From an international point of view, Party independence means that Communist Parties
everywhere must continue to press for an aggressive confrontation with
" imperialism."   A muscular display of Party independence and Party
criticism must never be abandoned just for the sake of " peaceful co-
existence," or of winning adherents in non-proletarian groups.   It is,
therefore, perhaps hardly surprising that in the current ideological and
strategic dispute between Moscow and Peking, Aidit is wholly on the
side of the latter.

   Related to the above questions is the problem of the class origin of
Communist Party members.   Both Mao and Aidit make the peasantry
the basic force, and the agrarian revolution virtually the essence of the
revolution.   In the dark days of 1930, when the Chinese Communists
were in desperate straits, Mao reiterated his belief, expressed even earlier,
that " it is also a mistake for any of our Party members to fear the
development of the power of the peasants lest it become stronger than
that of the workers and hence detrimental to the revolution." [63]   The
revolution in " semi-colonial " China, Mao went on, will never suffer
just because the peasants become stronger than the workers; the revolution will fail only if the workers cease to give leadership to the peasantry.
The same approach is to be found in Aidit.   Though the Indonesian
industrial proletariat is small it can readily lead the peasant masses,
especially the mass of poor peasants and landless agricultural workers,
because of their class identity.   This stress on the identity between the

---

62 See Edward Crankshaw, " Khrushchev and China," The Atlantic Monthly, May 1961,
   pp. 43–47.
63 Mao Tse-tung, A Single Spark Can Start a Prairie Fire (Peking: Foreign Languages
   Press, 1953), pp. 12–13.

industrial and the rural proletariat, and again between the petty bourgeoisie and the " middle " peasantry, is to be found in the class analysis of both Mao and Aidit as we have seen, and suggests a reflection of the Leninist principle that it is less the class origin and more the degree of political consciousness of Communist Party members and their allies which determines the success of the revolution.

In developing this political consciousness proper theoretical training of cadres is the indispensable first step. " A person who is flabby and shaky in questions of theory," Lenin said in *What is to be Done?*, " is not a revolutionary but a wretched amateur," and in his historical description of the PKI Aidit has attributed the failure of Party programmes in the past to the lack of training in Marxist-Leninist fundamentals among cadres.[64] Organisational expertise is not enough, Aidit has argued, for party cadres " cannot possibly understand thoroughly why, for example, the nature of the Indonesian revolution at the present time is not socialist but bourgeois-democratic . . . if they do not understand Marxist-Leninist philosophy." [65]

Since Aidit's advent the internal power structure of the PKI has also undergone a complete revision, and the increasing emphasis on Leninist " democratic centralism," Party discipline and " the principle of self-criticism " has been particularly effective as the Party has steadily grown.[66] As in all Communist Parties this process has had to be steered along the course of approved flexibility and in between the extremes of dogmatic rigidity and heretical subjectivism.

The " uniqueness " of the historical situation in Indonesia has led Aidit to warn explicitly against a slavish adoption of Maoist methods in Indonesia. During the Indonesian Revolution (1945–49), " one of the basic mistakes of the Party in studying from the Chinese revolution at that time was that the Party only tried to find out the similarities between the Chinese revolution and the Indonesian revolution, but did not discover the differences, did not notice the peculiar conditions of Indonesia." [67] For example, according to Aidit the geographical conditions of Indonesia did not lend themselves to the waging of guerrilla warfare as in China. As a result the Party went down to defeat. Today Aidit and the PKI have made fully their own the dictum of Lenin's essay *Struggle for Power and " Struggle " for a Pittance* (1906), that " the mass struggle for freedom has passed through and will always pass through the most diverse and often unexpected stages: it cannot be otherwise, because of the

[64] See, *e.g.*, *DNAPT*, Vol. I, pp. 410–412.
[65] D. N. Aidit, "Pembangunan Organisasi Penting, Tapi Lebih Penting Lagi Pembangunan Ideologi," *Bintang Merah*, Vol. XV (1959), p. 244.
[66] B. O. Hutapea, " Dua Sjarat Utama dari Partai Tipe Lenin: Sentralisme dan Disiplin," *Bintang Merah*, Vol. XVI (1960), pp. 124–130.
[67] *DNAPT*, Vol. I, pp. 421–422

immense difficulty of the struggle, the complexity of its problems and the changeable composition of those who are struggling." [68] The current PKI programme states explicitly that every nation will proceed on its own path to Socialism in accordance with its national peculiarities.[69]

On the other hand the danger of "right" and "left deviations" are equally emphasised in Aidit's address, and warnings against the "disgusting" revisionism of the Yugoslav Communists (and at one time even of Gomulka in Poland) appear frequently in PKI literature. It is particularly noteworthy that the Maoist syllabus of errors, the analysis of, e.g., "extreme democratisation," "individualism," "adventurism" and "right opportunism" are standard topics for continued discussions in PKI meetings.[70] The "method of knowing the situation," the "method of study" and "the importance of synthesising experience at the correct time" are the most effective ways of combating these errors, a PKI directive has it,[71] and at no time in its history has the PKI managed to make its Party organisational structure so thoroughly "Bolshevised" in the Leninist sense as today.

With its widened concept of the proletariat and its allies, based on political consciousness rather than on strict class affiliation or even on the individual's relationship to the production process, and stressing the "independence" of different ideological currents and social groupings within the united front, the Party is in a position effectively to determine its targets during the first, anti-imperialist and anti-feudal, phase of the revolution. It is perhaps this basic approach which, with only few if any modifications, is applicable to the underdeveloped countries of Africa, the Middle East, Asia and Latin-America, and which makes the Chinese or Indonesian experiences, along with their Leninist foundations, into a model for Communist tactics in those parts of the world.

---

[68] *Lenin on the Revolutionary Proletarian Party of a New Type* (Peking: Foreign Languages Press, 1960), pp. 10–11.   See also V. I. Lenin, *The National Liberation Movement in the East, op. cit.*, p. 18: " The international revolutionary movement of the proletariat does not and cannot develop evenly and in 'identical forms in different countries. . . .   Every country makes its own valuable contribution, adding new features to this common stream. . . ."

[69] *Material for the Sixth National Congress of the Communist Party of Indonesia, op. cit.*, p. 97.

[70] See by Mao Tse-tung, *Combat Liberalism* (Peking: Foreign Languages Press, 1954); *On Practice* (Peking: Foreign Languages Press, 1958), pp. 19–22; and *On the Rectification of Incorrect Ideas in the Party* (Peking: Foreign Languages Press, 1953), pp. 6–7, 13–15, 18.

[71] " Beberapa Pengalaman Dalam Melawan Subjektivisme," *Kehidupan Partai*, June 1960, pp. 102–105.

THE MIDDLE EAST: SINO-SOVIET DISCORDS

W. A. C. Adie

THE Sino-Soviet conflict appears to have many levels, only a few of which can be mentioned in a single article. Just below the surface of their misleading ideological polemics, the Soviet and Chinese communists seem to be arguing about economic and military integration and division of labour and the role of mass movements in the revolution [1]; their policies reflect the internal problems facing the regimes, but, for ideological reasons, each must claim universal validity for them. These policies do not merely differ; they compete, literally, on the same ground.

China and Russia are now engaged in a struggle for control of the world communist apparatus, [2] and of the forces it has proved its ability to exploit; primarily, they are trying to divert to their own purposes the movement towards emancipation and modernisation in the vast intermediate areas of Asia, Africa, and Latin America. In the development of this struggle, the countries of the Near and Middle East occupy a special place, and it was over the Lebanon-Iraq crisis (1958) and the Indo-Tibetan border question (1959), that Sino-Soviet policies clashed obviously enough to attract worldwide attention.

In their propaganda since 1960 the Chinese have been coupling complaints about Russian economic aid with hints that Moscow is trying to hold back the revolution in general. China's militant policy, reflected internally in the 'three red banners' (general line, great leap forward, people's communes), finds expression in foreign policy in calls for a sort of world-wide Boxer rising against 'US imperialism'. The thought behind it is that throughout the world the masses, mobilised under Chinese inspiration, have a power greater than the atom bombs wielded by the USA and the USSR. 'Man, not weapons, decides the issue of war'.

China's support for armed struggle throughout the world has been mainly verbal, but she has, in fact, taken concrete action to promote strife, notably in Algeria, tropical Africa, and the Middle East.[3] It may well be that China, in exporting pamphlets on guerrilla warfare in competition with Soviet exports of steel mills and bombers, is not

---

[1] See in particular the articles written by Liu Shao-chi, Teng Hsiao-ping and Lin Piao for the 10th anniversary of the CPR; they defend the Chinese technique of mass movements—the people's revolutionary war in which the country encircles the cities, the communes and so on—and assert that it is of international significance, but reveal the close connection between the internal mass line and the need to modernise national defence, i.e. establish the security of the regime. (English translation by Foreign Languages Press, Peking, 1959).

[2] Cf. Edvard Kardelj, *Socialism and War* (London, 1962), p. 12.

[3] This action has mainly taken the form of providing funds and equipment, and training selected cadres in guerrilla warfare, such as the small Cameroonian group who were apprehended with their notes from the Peking course still on them.

consciously so much interested in war as an end in itself, but in the opportunities for ' united front ' work that a war atmosphere provides.

ON the ideological plane, the conflict between Mao and his opponents appears in the form of complicated arguments about the role of the national bourgeoisie and the right way to exploit ' peace ' and ' national liberation ' movements.[4] To oversimplify, Mao's concept of New Democracy (a bourgeois revolution led by the communist-dominated united front, merging uninterruptedly into a socialist revolution) is set against a modified form of the old Comintern policy (two-stage revolution, led first by the national bourgeoisie and then by the CP), to which the Moscow conference of 1960 gave the label ' *national* democracy '. The Chinese object to the Russians arming national-bourgeois India, Indonesia, etc., to the disadvantage of China; according to them, communists unite with the bourgeoisie in order the better to struggle against its reactionary tendencies. Russian hints at a disarmament deal with the United States on the basis of the status quo (including Formosa?) have also inclined the Chinese to try to divert the ' peace movement ' from pacifism into the path of mass violence. in support of ' national liberation ' struggles in underdeveloped countries.

In order to understand this Chinese attitude, it is necessary to go back to the beginning of the Soviet drive to the East—or at least to its renewal in 1955.[5] Even before Stalin's death there were signs that the USSR was trying to exploit Asian pacifism and neutralism. Representing the reaction to communist aggressions as evidence of Western warmongering and neo-colonialism, Soviet propaganda sought to attach these forces to the bloc economic system, by forming a ' united front ' with them ostensibly against colonialism and war. This united front was eventually embodied in the 'Afro-Asian People's Solidarity Organisation ' with its seat in Cairo. In 1954, China was allotted the role of bell-wether [6]—in fact, operations had already started in 1952 with the Asian and Pacific Peace Conference in Peking—but instead of leading the other nations of Asia into the Soviet fold, within five years she had set up as shepherd herself. The critical moment in this process is hard to pin down, but it seems that one important turning-point was the Middle East crisis of 1958. It came at a time of ferment inside China, but perhaps the fundamental reason why Soviet and Chinese policies clashed in the Middle East (as later over India) is the special connexion existing between the Middle and Near East

---

[4] For the background, see John H. Kautsky, *Moscow and the Communist Party of India* (London, 1956).

[5] The debate over support for the national bourgeoisie goes back to the second congress of the Comintern in July 1920, when the label ' national-revolutionary ' was attached to bourgeois-democratic movements to signify that communists would support them only to the extent that they could infiltrate and exploit them; now we have ' States of National Democracy,' a similar compromise formula.

[6] Moscow broadcasts described China as ' a brilliant sun which had arisen on Asian soil—an example for all peoples of Asia struggling for independence ' (30 October 1954).

and the Soviet and Chinese minority races in Central Asia, to which both regimes call attention in their propaganda.

Facing each other across the Central Asian heartland, they are both moving into it with policies of winning over the local nationalities, and sending technicians and workers to exploit their resources; this colonisation of Central Asia, largely inhabited by Moslems, forms the keystone of the present plans of both China and Russia for building up their industrial strength; parts of the area have been long—and recently—disputed between the two powers; in fact hints of continuing Chinese irredentism still appear from time to time.[7] Both China and Russia have stressed the close connexion between their nationalities policies in Central Asia and their policies towards the underdeveloped and uncommitted countries of Asia, Africa, and Latin America. In fact, there is a tendency in Moscow and Peking to regard the 'third world' in terms of their own experience with Central Asian peoples, as a sort of extension of the traditional Russian 'East' and the Chinese 'Western regions' respectively,[8] and to carry over into it the jujitsu combat between the two Empires which has been going on in Asia for centuries. For obvious reasons nothing much is heard about Sino-Soviet friction in Central Asia itself. But when the world communist movement began its drive into the Afro-Asian world after the 1954 Geneva conference,[9] the divergence of Soviet and Chinese policies was soon revealed, notably at the congresses of the respective parties in 1956.

Post-Geneva Soviet policy, as it emerged at the 20th and later congresses of the CPSU and in countless articles and broadcasts, seems to boil down to the following (though there have been divergent trends): Stalin's bloc was to thaw out into a co-prosperity sphere with blurred edges· united by oil pipelines, linked power grids, and exchange of specialised products. As a *sodruzhestvo* (commonwealth) it was to be integrated through Comecon and rely on the USSR for nuclear defence. Following the example of Afghanistan, the countries of the East would gradually become more and more like Soviet Republics through the strengthening of the state sector of the economy, the presence of Soviet technicians in its key positions and in the armed forces, and so on. At the same time disarmament negotiations, united front work with socialist

---

[7] Apart from Mongolia, potential Chinese claims exist against Tajikistan and the Ussuri Province of the Soviet Far East (including Vladivostok). See K. Mehnert in *International Affairs*, October 1959, H. Bechtoldt, *Aussenpolitik*, January 1951, and Allen S. Whiting, 'Sinkiang and Sino-Soviet Relations,' *China Quarterly*, No. 3, 1960.

[8] The 'East' (*Vostok*) in Leninist writings means roughly any underdeveloped area from Morocco to Kamchatka. The Chinese *Hsiu* or Western Regions included what is now Soviet Central Asia, Afghanistan, etc.

[9] Several writers have pointed out that Geneva made the world safer for local war and the *fait accompli*—this may have been the Chinese view; an article by Ahmed al-Maghrebi in *World Marxist Review* (August 1961) seems to express Soviet appreciation of the fact that the U.N., under conditions of 'nuclear blackmail,' has a tendency to embody the neutralism and irresponsibility of small nations as a sort of new big power, which may be turned against the West by communist-stimulated 'world public opinion,' and defeat it without fighting.

and pacifist elements, and economic competition should hasten the collapse of capitalism under the weight of its internal contradictions, and peacefully bring Western Europe into the economic system of communism.

IN this process, an important part was assigned to the development of Soviet Central Asia in accordance with what Mukhitdinov, at the 21st congress, called an 'international nationalities policy'. Although Khrushchev is on record as explaining that China need not join his economic system because she is big enough to build one of her own, on balance the evidence indicates that the USSR has wanted and needed close co-operation and co-ordination of plans with China.[10] But the Chinese approach is different; Mao thinks not in terms of gradually building the material-technical base for socialist society with Soviet aid, but of rapidly collectivising and mobilising the masses in order to build heavy and defence industry; for him the social change is the pre-condition, not the result, of economic change, and this change has to be revolutionary and violent, both on the local and the world scale. The task of the CCP, wrote Mao, ' is not to go through a long period of legal struggles before launching an insurrection or war, not to seize the cities first and then occupy the countryside· but to take the other way round '.

Mao now applies to foreign affairs the strategy that brought him victory inside China, the strategy of dividing the opposition and winning over sections of it to his united front. Greeting the 8th congress of the CCP in September 1956, the *People's Daily* wrote: ' Our party considers the united front a magic wand, like party-building '; in order to build up China, it said, we should not only mobilise all the positive forces within the country but also ' unite the working class and progressive people in all the countries of the world '. In other words, the world must help to build a strong China, not a strong bloc including China under Soviet tutelage.

The ' international united front ' is the Chinese alternative to the Soviet *sodruzhestvo*. In two important articles in *Red Flag* (Nos. 11 and 12, 1961) Li Wei-han clearly showed that, as the basis of Mao's internal united front was the ' protracted peasant revolutionary war ' under his leadership, so the basis of the ' great unity of the Chinese people and the peoples of the world ' is the ' national liberation struggle ', fought according to Mao's methods of revolutionary war and under Chinese leadership.

---

[10] Pekshev in *Vneshnyaya Torgovlya* (September 1959, 81–83) clearly criticises the Chinese system of making yearly agreements with the USSR; since a quarter of the USSR's trade with the bloc is with China, this makes advance planning difficult. See Klinkmüller in *Osteuropa*, May 1960, and his book written with M. E. Ruban, *Die Wirtschaftliche Zusammenarbeit der Ostblockstaaten* (Berlin 1960), p. 254. China can no doubt sympathise with Albanian complaints that Tito sent ' experts ' to make the Albanian economy dependent on Yugoslavia's, and tried to buy agents in the military leadership to oppose the Party line (Liu Fen-chih in *Shih-chieh Chih-shih*, 10 November 1961). Conversely, the Russians could be thinking of China when they criticise Albania for making inordinate demands for aid and indicating resentment of their aid for Afro-Asia (Konstantinov in *Kommunist*, December 1961).

Li Wei-han also dealt with the extension of the united front among the overseas Chinese, who were intended to act as a link and extend the international united front in the countries where they reside.[11] Burhan Ed-Din Shahidi, the Chinese counterpart to Mukhitdinov, dealt with the extension of the united front to the Islamic world in a separate report. His visit to the Arab world, during which he met President Nasser and other leaders,[12] had led him, he said, to realise more deeply the great influence exerted by the party's nationality policy, united front policy, and religious policy. 'There are 300 million Islamic believers in the world', Burhan went on; 'most Islamic countries are in the Asian and African regions'. Their struggle against imperialism was on the upsurge. He accordingly concluded that the party's internal united front work must be carried on (to provide a suitable basis) and the international united front work must be strengthened, by exchanging visits and missions, mutual economic aid, and so forth. Like Mukhitdinov, he stressed the connexion between internal and external policy towards minor nations— but the Chinese and the Russian policies were different.[13]

Was this Chinese activity co-ordinated with the Soviet drive? In the opinion of President Nasser, one of the drive's targets, at that time it was. It was Chou En-lai who set his mind at rest over the possibility of importing tanks, not ideas, and paved the way for Shepilov's famous arms deal, and it was also he who charmed Nehru over Tibet and the 'Five Principles'.

There is no space here to go into all the internal reasons the Chinese had for disagreeing with overall Soviet policy, whatever may have been co-ordinated between Moscow and Peking in 1954. In 1956–57 both Khrushchev and Mao faced serious difficulties at home; their different reactions to these were reflected in the different policies each recommended to the world communist movement, particularly in the Middle East. In spite of Burhan's call for caution in implementing the united front, the Chinese were soon faced with increasing trouble in Tibet, a revival of separatism in Turkestan (which may, as before, have looked to Russia for support), and such minor incidents as a revolt in Chinghai led by a vice-president of the tame China Islamic Association, Abdulla Ma Wen-chu. This put a new complexion on the possibility of united fronts with bourgeois and religious leaders.

11 Fan Tzu-ying in *Nan-fang Jih-pao*, 9 April 1956.

12 President Nasser told the present writer that Burhan speaks good colloquial Iraqi, apparently acquired during a sojourn in Mosul. During the Mosul riots of 1959 Burhan was reported in Iraq on a goodwill mission.

13 For one thing, the Chinese system of 'regional autonomy' (as in Tibet) is theoretically more centralised than the Russian system of Republics; one aspect of de-Stalinisation in the USSR has been delegation of powers to the Republics. But the 'autonomy' of areas like Sinkiang has remained largely on paper (cf. Saifudin and Ulanfu at the 8th CCP congress). It is interesting that the Ili Kazakh Autonomous *Chou*, scene of the Soviet-sponsored revolt of 1944, produced the largest number of officials purged for 'rightism' and 'nationalism' in 1958. They were accused, *inter alia*, of poisoning Sino-Soviet relations.

Apart from all this, there was the question of oil. The world's largest known deposits of petroleum lie in the Moslem world. And perhaps this is the main reason why, as a recent study points out, 'China is potentially a major Middle Eastern power '.[14] It is obviously intolerable for China to depend for most of her oil supplies on Russia, who could cut off the little she does sell to China at any time. It is estimated that by 1965 the USSR will have an exportable oil surplus of a million barrels a day, and is already able to ' sell oil and influence people ' in such a way that it is not always certain whether trade is being used for political ends or the other way round.

China needs oil for industry, for transport, and for agricultural mechanisation, and her own oil industry is fairly rudimentary. However, there is apparently no question of a friendship pipeline from Russia to China; it could be that for technical reasons the USSR can only supply the oil on conditions unfavourable to China. In any case, the implications of the oil position for Chinese and Russian attitudes to the Middle East are obvious enough.[15]

WHEN the congresses of the two parties met in 1956, Soviet policy had already made its breakthrough in the Middle East; the Soviet drive began with a sudden revival and expansion of Soviet Oriental studies in April 1955 and the revaluation of such leaders as President Nasser.[16] Then followed the famous Egyptian arms deal by Shepilov, then Soviet foreign minister, now in disgrace.

In August 1957, a new era began with the firing of the Soviet ICBMs. There was a marked difference in Soviet and Chinese reactions to this event. A few days before, a promising Syrio-Soviet economic agreement had been signed, and the Syrian Chief of Staff replaced by a reputed communist sympathiser, Colonel Bizri. While communist propaganda worked up a war scare, Khrushchev bombarded Western socialists with letters suggesting they ' unite ' with the USSR to prevent aggression. Khaled Bakhdash, the veteran Kurdish leader of the Syrian Communist party, mobilised his 15,000 odd supporters to spread rumours of invasion, and, from Tirana, Marshal Zhukov gave warning that ' the Soviet Union will not remain with its hands folded. We are all ready to strike ' (24 October). Suddenly the crisis fizzled out, and Zhukov was purged on charges of opposing Party control of the armed forces, and of being inclined to adventurism, both in foreign policy and in running the Defence Ministry.

---

[14] Walter Laqueur in *The Soviet Union and the Middle East* (London 1959), p. 349.
[15] Less obvious, perhaps, is the connection of oil with the Taiwan problems; if it were settled, China could safely rely on seaborne oil supplies instead of being tied to Russia by a trickle across the steppes. On Soviet oil policy see *Problems of Communism*, February 1961. Soviet oil sells at about 50 rubles a metric ton to Western Europe, but 86½ to China.
[16] From the ' madly reactionary terrorist ' of Vatolina's book of 1954 *Imperialisticheskaya Borba za Afriku i Osvoboditelnoe Dvizhenie Narodov* (p. 99 ff), Nasser became the man who contributed to the success of the Bandung conference.

Khrushchev's treatment of the sputniks and of the collapse of the sixth five-year plan (from which they served to divert attention) was aimed at demonstrating his thesis about the power of the communist bloc as the main factor for ensuring peace, and at building up necessary ' business-like relations ' with the outside world. His argument that what was good for Russia was good for the revolution failed to convince the Chinese or other Asian revolutionaries. To them his mood may have appeared as one of complacent and unrevolutionary gradualism.

China was now weaker than ever vis-à-vis Russia, though within a stronger bloc. While Mao has a genius for making a virtue of necessity and finding the good side to a bad thing, he may well have felt that the situation was one which must be changed as soon as possible. A new mood in the CCP found full expression in the swing towards radical ' go-it-alone ' policies, relying on the ' guerrilla style of work '.

If Khrushchev wanted to use the November 1957 meeting of Communist parties to confirm the acceptance of his peaceful competition line by the world communist movement, he found the Chinese hard to deal with; the CPSU delegation by no means got its own way. Liu Shaochi observed later (in May 1958) that the meeting ' marked the beginning of a new stage in the international communist movement '. At the Moscow meeting Khrushchev went a long way to conciliate the Chinese. But in January 1958 an authoritative *Pravda* article dilated on the possibility of alliances between communists and socialists to achieve revolution by parliamentary methods, and hinted that more than one party might be allowed to exist after it, ' as in China '. Hopes still appeared to centre on Egypt and the Afro-Asian Solidarity movement based on Cairo; it was thought that Nasser's apparent alignment with Soviet foreign policy would force him to give them and their ' peace partisans ' the same freedom of action that they enjoyed in India and Indonesia.[17]

In January 1958, just after the Afro-Asian Solidarity conference, Khaled Bakhdash arrived back from Moscow and held a meeting of the Syrian and Lebanese Communist parties at which it was decided (in apparent opposition to the Soviet line) that they must abandon the united front with the Ba'ath socialists. Partly as a result of his adventurist activities, Syria hastily united with Egypt to form the UAR, his party was suppressed, and he had to flee the country without getting any support from the Russians. At this time, *Pravda* (27 February 1958) wrote, ' the front line of the liberation struggle runs through North Africa . . . five Arab countries form an unbroken chain between the imperialist West and oppressed tropical Africa '. But the Russians were not so interested in *armed* struggle as the Chinese. A few days before, Chou En-lai had strongly emphasised to the National People's Congress the importance of the fighting in Algeria, Yemen, Ifni, and Oman, implying that it was at

---

17 Cf. Ponomarev in *Pravda*, 7 January 1958. Bulganin's letter to Nasser of 8 January assumes such an alignment.

least as important as the sputniks in making the imperialists ' sober up '
and accept the Soviet ' peace proposals '.

In April, Nasser visited the USSR and (as he told the present writer),
spoke plainly to Khrushchev about the activities of Bakhdash; he refused
to allow communists freedom to organise in the UAR. This must have
been a considerable disappointment to Khrushchev; he believed that
Nasser's prestige in the Arab world depended on Soviet support—and
also, perhaps, that Nasser could not rely on his mechanised units, to
which Soviet advisers were attached. On a previous occasion Khalid
Mohieddine, the ' Red Major ', had attempted to lead them against
Nasser.[18]

KHRUSHCHEV'S handling of the Middle East crisis widened the Sino-
Soviet split once more. While the Chinese called for arms and
' volunteer armies '[20] to ' oppose aggression ' in Iraq, Khrushchev
seemed to be using the opportunity to wrest concessions from the West
—over Berlin, for example—at a summit conference, which the Chinese
condemned as useless. At a meeting of the World Peace Council in
Stockholm, the Chinese delegates spread alarm by their warlike attitude
and attacks on ' unprincipled pacifism ' and ' hesitation to oppose
aggression ', clearly aimed at the USSR.

After a period of confusion[21], Khrushchev went to Peking and a
communiqué was issued implying he had agreed with Mao about the
need to ' oppose aggression '. However, in the Quemoy crisis, which the
Chinese started immediately after Khrushchev's departure, it became
clear that he did not share the Chinese view that ' US occupation ' of
Formosa was a form of aggression. Soviet support of China was limited
to maintaining the status quo and backing propaganda demands for
China's admission to the United Nations. The mysteries of the Quemoy
crisis deserve an article in themselves; it seems clear enough that questions
of army-party relations, nuclear weapons and ' Mao's military thinking '
were involved.[22] At the Mao-Khrushchev talks, their Ministers of Defence,
Malinovsky and P'eng Te-huai, were present. In August, Deputy Premier
Nieh Jung-chen had written: ' we should and absolutely can master in
not too long a time the newest techniques concerning atomic fission,

---

[18] G. Vaucher, *Gamal Abdel Nasser et son equipe* (Paris 1960), p. 139.
[19] According to the *People's Daily*, the trouble about the Yugoslav programme was that
it appeared at a time when ' the world is at a new historic turning point, with the
East wind prevailing over the West,' and there was (*read*: should be) a ' sharpening
struggle between the communist and non-communist camps ' (5 May 1958).
[20] See *People's Daily*, 21–22 July 1958.
[21] On 2 July, Mr. Macmillan proposed a meeting in the Security Council; the Chinese
condemned it, but on the 23rd Khrushchev approved it, whereupon it became a
' major step for peace.' But on the 28th Khrushchev reverted to his previous idea of
a meeting of heads of Governments, and finally on 5 August he called for a meeting
of the UN General Assembly.
[22] And beyond this, the 3-cornered game of negotiations between the US, the USSR,
and China ; see the chronology in *Europa-Archiv*, 20 January 1959.

thermonuclear reaction . . . rockets'. And Marshal Liu Ya-lou said earlier that when China got her bomb 'another new turning point will probably be reached in the international situation'.[23]

'Since the imperialists are thus insulting and oppressing us', said Mao, 'we need not only a powerful regular army' (dependent on the USSR for heavy weapons) but also 'to step up the building of militia divisions.' The militarisation of labour for the 'great leap' was one way of dealing with the peasant problem, while tightening control over civilian and military experts. And since the 'great leap' was associated with the doctrine of a sharpening struggle with imperialism on the world front, the Chinese not only gave verbal support to such struggles, but actively sought to promote them.

THE Iraq revolt offered opportunities for a reappraisal of communist policy towards the bourgeois-nationalist governments of under-developed countries. Flying to Moscow from Yugoslavia to find out whom Khrushchev was going to support, Nasser was put off with a vague reply; shortly afterwards, the Soviet Ambassador in Iraq reportedly gave Kassem material calculated to set him against Nasser. It was obvious that Iraq, with more resources and fewer trained personnel than Egypt, was suitable for transformation into a 'socialist beacon' in the Arab world, both a model of Soviet aid and a centre for the 'Arab liberation movement', while Nasser's eyes should be diverted towards Africa.

Khalid Bakhdash attacked the policy of support for bourgeois nationalists in the *World Marxist Review* (September 1958) and Academician Yudin, Soviet Ambassador in Peking, even criticised Nehru, the original model of neutralist-bourgeois with whom a united front could be formed.

But the policy of support for such leaders was reaffirmed, in spite of some criticism of Nehru and Nasser, at the 21st congress of the CPSU in February 1959. Khrushchev and Mukhitdinov spelt out the implications of 'peaceful coexistence and economic competition' for the East, as embodied in the seven-year plan and the 'international nationalities policy'. The countries of socialism, said Mr Khrushchev, correctly using the opportunities inherent in the socialist order, will *more or less* simultaneously reach the highest phase of communist society. But this time it was clear the Chinese were not so using their opportunities, as he implied in an attack on premature attempts at communism elsewhere in the report. Instead, he commended Kazakhstan and Central Asia, and Mongolia in particular.

[23] *Liberation Army Daily*, 23 May 1958. His article appeared during a campaign against professionalism in the forces, the real background to which appears to have been the fact that modernisation and centralisation of the forces and their training, though favoured in 1955, tended to weaken the control of Party committees and increase dependence on Soviet equipment and advisers. Hence on 1 August Marshal Ho Lung warned against relying on outside aid instead of on the 'mobilisation of the masses.'

On 1 February 1959, after three months of negotiations, a new Sino-Soviet aid agreement was signed by Khrushchev and Chou En-lai; it seemed that since the Chinese central committee meeting of 28 November —19 December 1958, the CCP had moved back towards the Soviet line on internal economic policy, and were prepared to coordinate their construction plans with the USSR (to a certain extent) for the next nine years, on the understanding that all the socialist countries would reach communism together (previously the USSR was to reach it first, and so today).[24]

But as far as revolutionary policy abroad was concerned, the Chinese still advocated top-speed advance. In practice, they supported the forward policy of Bakhdash who, according to Nasser's information,[25] hoped to create a communist-controlled ' Fertile Crescent ' consisting of Syria, Iraq, Lebanon, and Jordan.

Chinese ideologists registered their dissatisfaction with Russian gradualism in a symposium on the ' Liberation Struggle ' held with their Russian counterparts, an account of which appeared in the Moscow *International Affairs* (March 1959). Their line was that ' it is necessary to rally all the peace forces for relentless struggle '; nothing but good had come of the two World Wars and the Korean War, and to fight the US was to defend peace, because ' US enslavement is a kind of daily warfare without bloodshed.'

At the World Peace Council meeting in Moscow in February, this line found favour. Immediately on his return from Moscow in March, Aziz Sharif, leader of the Iraq peace partisans and a central committee member of the Iraq Communist party, brought several thousand of his men to Mosul and incited disorders, which prematurely set off an anti-communist coup by nationalist officers in touch with Syria, and ended with communal massacres of anti-communists and Moslems by Kurds, Yezidis, and Christians. According to reports sent in by S. Kondrashov, the special correspondent of *Izvestiya,* army units and government offices were purged of ' reactionaries and saboteurs ' after the revolt; the population, he noted, was being organised by such bodies as the Democratic Union of Youth, the Peace Partisans, the Peasant Unions, the Women's League, and particularly the ' People's Resistance Forces ', which had recently been formed to ' watch public order, suspicious elements, reactionaries, and those who had participated in the old regime.'

In spite of such short-term successes, the Mosul revolt was actually a blow to communist influence in the Middle East; Nasser immediately

---

[24] In his remarks against primitive, ascetic ' levelling communism ' at the recent CC Plenum and the 21st Party Congress, Khrushchev gets to the heart of the matter; while he wants more division of labour, the Chinese Utopians really want to *abolish* division of labour and professionalism, and make everyone ' equal.' As Kardelj points out (op. cit.) these are the ' primitive egalitarian aspirations of the rural semi-proletariat.'

[25] In his interview with B. K. Karanjia of *Blitz* (7 March 1959), Nasser said Bakhdash had worked out these plans with his supporters while in Moscow for the 21st congress and at a Pan-Arab communist congress held in Baghdad in February.

denounced the communists as foreign agents, and a holy war (Jehad) was launched against them by his powerful propaganda machine. The *People's Daily* attacked him in an editorial which stressed that the real way to achieve Arab unity was to help in the fighting in Algeria, Oman, etc., while *Red Flag* attacked his slogan ' neither East nor West ' and implied that he was ' reconciled with imperialism '. Tito, too, was bitterly attacked for having ' secret relations ' with the Mosul affair.[26] Khrushchev himself, on the same day that a mass anti-communist rally was held in Cairo, told an Iraqi government delegation in Moscow that he would not support any ' premature ' union of Arab states and reaffirmed his preference for Iraq over the UAR because its internal system was more ' progressive ' (16 March 1959).

After Mosul, communists and opportunists who jumped on their band-wagon pursued an excessively ' progressive ' policy in Iraq; various front organisations spread confusion and disrupted commerce, agriculture, and education. By May, the media of information appeared to be more or less under communist control and men reputed to be pro-communist held key economic posts. More important, the infiltration of the army was such that senior officers were concerned at the threat to security. On 29 and 30 April, the Communist party issued two statements, demanding licensing of political parties and the participation of communists in the Government; they thought that their success in ' organising the masses ' should be reflected in its composition. As the communist organ *Ittihad ash-Sha'ab* put it, in the popular field things were going according to ' evolutionary plans ', but reactionary elements remained in the Government.

At the end of April, Kamel Chaderchi, leader of the left wing of the National Democratic party, left for Moscow for medical treatment, according to the Baghdad announcement, though this was not mentioned in Moscow media. Communist sources hinted that he was regarded as a suitable candidate for the Presidency of Iraq, a figurehead alternative to Kassem. But in his May Day speech Kassem rejected the communist demands and refused to license a return to activity of the political parties.

After manoeuvring by the national democrats, the communists had to withdraw their demands. They compensated this failure by strengthening the front organisations, which were now coordinated by a ' Liaison Committee of Unions and Organisations ' which continually put forward

---

[26] *People's Daily*, 20 March, and *Hung ch'i* (Red Flag) of 18 March. At the Bulgarian Communist Party congress shortly after these events, Bakhdash accused ' emissaries of the revisionist clique of Belgrade ' of working in the Arab countries ' not only to isolate the Arab communist movement from the general communist movement and to disunite it, but also to divert the national liberation movement from its natural line of struggle against imperialism and especially of struggle against American imperialism.' In connection with his tour of Afro-Asian countries, *People's Daily* published an article against Tito entitled ' Beware the trafficker in poison ' on 22 February (the UAR national day); the same phrase was used in Kassem's anti-Nasser propaganda.

communist demands such as the execution of nationalists, further purging of the government and army, and the ' arming of the masses '.

Realising that the party was becoming isolated, and perhaps on Soviet orders, the Iraqi communists took a step back in the second half of June, and began to campaign for the revival of a ' national front '. On 28 June they presented a memorandum to Kassem, proposing a Charter for this front. It carefully avoided all reference to communism, or even socialism, and instead advocated ' guided democracy ' and the establishment of ' democratic parliamentary rule '. Far from reflecting Chinese ideas, it seemed closer to those of Aidit of Indonesia and in accordance with the policy of the 21st congress of the CPSU.

Kassem rejected these demands at a press conference on 5 July. A few days later the politburo of the Iraq Communist party issued a defiant declaration: the militant wing of the party, who favoured a fight rather than support for Kassem's bourgeois regime, seemed to have gained the upper hand. Radio Peking immediately publicised this declaration, while Moscow ignored it, and continued to speak kindly of Kassem. On the anniversary of the revolution (14 July) a rising described by Kassem as ' anarchist ' and involving communist-penetrated Kurdish troops at Kirkuk finally induced him to adopt serious measures against communist infiltration of the forces and administration. He said later that it had been intended to overthrow his regime by risings in Baghdad and three other towns, as well as Kirkuk. Among those inculpated was Siddiq Fallahi, president of the Trade Union Federation. A number of communist trade unions were dissolved and the ' People's Resistance Force ' was suspended. Many people were released from prison, where they had apparently been put without Kassem's knowledge as a result of communist or other intrigues. Reports reaching Beirut and Cairo indicated that the ' anarchists ' in question were would-be communists, particularly Kurds and Christians, supported by the Chinese and certain Stalinists among the East Europeans, but not by the USSR. On 17 August, *Pravda* published the Iraq party's self-criticism, which was not reported in China. In 1960, during the ensuing polemic with China, the Soviet press referred to Iraq as an example of advancing ' premature slogans ' of socialist transformation when conditions for them had not matured.

SINCE their establishment of diplomatic relations with Iraq on 25 August 1958, the Chinese had been attempting what some local press-men called a ' massive penetration ' of the country; apart from its intrinsic importance, it was also a useful link with Algeria. Particular attention was given to the educational system: Abud Zalzala, Inspector-General of Education, was president of the Iraq-China association. Aziz Sharif was also reported to have Chinese support; he was certainly carrying out a policy of ' struggle ' approved by the Chinese and damaging to the official Soviet policy. Another friend of the Chinese was Kassem's own brother-in-law, Colonel Mehdawi; on the morning of the execution of nationalist officers, tried by his television court for their part in the Mosul affair, he left for China to attend the meetings held to celebrate the tenth anniversary of the Chinese People's Republic.

Speeches made at these meetings in Peking by Bakhdash and other Middle Eastern communist leaders showed a bias towards the Chinese militant line; Bakhdash accused Nasser (who was still on good terms with Moscow) of imposing a terroristic dictatorial anarchistic regime on the people of the UAR in the interests of the ' Bank of Egypt clique ' and of a rapprochement with US imperialism. The Iraq delegate said his party would never forget the Chinese stand in support of the 14th of July revolution, which had stopped Anglo-American intervention. (At Bucharest, on 21 June, Khrushchev was to claim that it was the USSR which prevented war spreading in the Middle East in 1956, 1957, and 1958.) By this time Mao and Khrushchev appeared to be completely divided over the question of relations with the USA, and Khrushchev left Peking without signing any joint communiqué. By January of the following year, the Chinese were complaining that the Russians were trying to isolate them in order to make a deal with the United States.

In spite of signs of a recrudescence of Chinese communist influence after the Ba'athist attempt on Kassem's life in October 1959, the situation in Iraq soon became more like that in the UAR, with some, though not all, of the communist lines of advance blocked.

Although Soviet propaganda later complained that Kassem had ' embarked on the path of reaction since July 1959 ', Mikoyan was most affable to Iraq's ' bourgeois nationalist' leaders when he visited the country in April 1960. He was asked by a Chinese journalist in Baghdad how the Soviet position on economic aid to Afro-Asia differed from the Western position. It seemed, from his reply, that Mikoyan took this as a provocation. The Soviet position, he said, was just as favourable to the Afro-Asians as that of the Chinese government. They did not regard these countries as raw material appendages of industrially developed countries, as spheres of influence or of capital investment.[27]

It was, of course, in April 1960 that the Chinese launched their all-out attack on the Soviet policy of gradualism in Afro-Asia and of parleys with capitalism. At the WFTU congress held in Peking during June, Liu Chang-sheng and other Chinese communists upheld the radical line and engaged in ' united front work from below ' with members of other parties. After the third congress of the North Vietnam Laodong party, at which they repeated this performance, Harekrishna Konar, representing the West Bengal CP, returned to tell the Indian CP of Chinese complaints against Russia, which soon leaked to the press and were publicly countered by the Russian complaints against China.[28] Thus the stage was set for the

[27] See on this D. S. Zagoria in *Problems of Communism*, March/April 1961.
[28] According to an article in *Link* (16 October 1960), Konar revealed that the Chinese dismiss the possibility of a peaceful transition to socialism anywhere. A later article (30 October) set forth Russian complaints that the Chinese had been meddling in international communist organisations and urging the ' peace partisans ' to engage in anti-imperialist and anti-capitalist mass actions.

November 1960 meeting of the 80-odd communist parties, at which Khrushchev again tried to obtain general agreement on his policies, and again failed to manage the Chinese. Before the conference opened, a number of authoritative articles (such as Ponomarev on ' Peaceful co-existence, a vital necessity ', and E. Zhukov on ' New National States of Asia and Africa ') indicated that the Soviet government was sticking to its policy of supporting such politicians as Nasser, Kassem, and Nehru, in spite of a certain disillusionment, and the Asian-African communists must just make the best of it.

A great deal has already been written about this meeting; thanks to the recalcitrance of Teng Hsiao-ping and Liu Shao-chi it resulted in a declaration which looks close to the Russian line when read in Russian, and close to the Chinese when read in Chinese. Both sides have subsequently quarried from it those quotations which accord with their own point of view, but the Chinese tend to quote it more often, while the Russians tend to fall back on the theses of their own party congresses.

It appears from the material published since the 22nd congress that Khrushchev was determined to use it to secure agreement with his policies and programme in the world communist movement and at home. In spite of his multi-megaton bomb, he again came up against Chinese opposition and Chou En-lai left Moscow prematurely to discuss with his colleagues what to do about Albania.

THE most recent documents indicate that Khrushchev and his supporters are trying to represent the new CPSU programme as a development of the 1960 meeting of communist parties, with the approval of the whole communist movement. It is stated again and again that ' the Soviet experience is a compass for the other countries ', ' the Russian model reveals to all countries something, and something very essential of their near and inevitable future ', and so on. It is also repeated that any attempts at economic development in isolation (due to narrow-minded nationalism in the guise of rigid dogmatism) ' deprive the given country of the advantages accruing to it as a member of the socialist world system and undermine its technical and economic independence from the capitalist system '.[29]

' Although they have no faith in the principles of peaceful coexistence, the Albanian leaders say they are prepared to apply these principles to

[29] Recent Moscow broadcasts to China have stressed the importance of the CMEA oil pipeline and power grid, and drawn attention to Soviet help to China's power industry. Addressing the foreign experts at a banquet in Peking, Chen Yi remarked that this year the Chinese would achieve greater victories under the guidance of the Three Red Banners and ' relying on our own industrious hands.' According to the CPSU programme, ' the line of socialist construction in isolation, detached from the world community of socialist countries . . . retards the rates of growth of production and makes the country dependent upon the capitalist world. It is reactionary and dangerous politically.' A Moscow broadcast to Indonesia (6 January 1962) also attacked the idea of building socialism separately as ' politically dangerous ', and protested that the USSR was ready to develop cooperation with the CPR ' in the future.'

relations between socialist states. Theoretically this is nonsense and politically it is pernicious'. Their sabotage of the stipulations of the Warsaw treaty and the Charter of the Council for Mutual Economic Aid cut across the proposal for a 'peace zone' in the Balkans; 'this is not vigilance, but passivity'.[30] Such quotations abound, and they obviously have a bearing on China as well as Albania: in particular, the repeated advice to the 'dogmatists' to take account of present-day realities. So far, this barrage has not moved the Chinese; they still argue uncompromisingly that 'investigation and study' show that the contradictions between imperialism and socialism, imperialism and the oppressed peoples, etc., really exist. 'There is only one way to solve these contradictions, that is revolutionary struggle by the people of various countries. There is no alternative'.[31]

The Russian alternative remains much the same as before, though expressed in terms of the formulas 'national democracy' and 'opposing export of counter-revolution', which were adopted at the 1960 Moscow meeting, apparently with the aim of stealing just enough of the Chinese left-wing thunder to satisfy Asian revolutionaries without alarming Western pacifists.[32]

The January 1962 *World Marxist Review* contains an article by the Algerian communist leader Larbi Bouhali with the significant title 'The Building of Communism and the Liberation Struggles of the Arab Peoples'. He points out that the USSR has extended to the UAR credits to the amount of 292,500,000 new rubles, in spite of Nasser's 'reactionary internal policy'. In accordance with agreements concluded in March 1959 and August 1960, Iraq got credits totalling more than 164 million new rubles. The Arabs can receive more aid only if world peace is consolidated—'that is why the programme of the CPSU devotes so much attention to the fight for peace, disarmament, and the conclusion of a peace treaty with the two German states'. Moreover, if the Arab peoples are to benefit from this aid they must influence their governments to cooperate closely with the Soviet Union.

The Algerian FLN is known to have a 'tough' wing which the Chinese have been trying to win over. Will the experience of Iraq have to be repeated in Algeria? There is no evidence that the Chinese have been successful in their approaches to the FLN, and there is no reason to suppose that Afro-Asian and Latin American countries will prove any more vulnerable in the long run to Chinese blandishments than they have been to those of the Russians. After the first flush of novelty, disillusion usually sets in, and experts trickle home, whether they are Soviet oilmen or Chinese rice-growers.

---

[30] *World Marxist Review*, January 1962, pp. 8, 16.
[31] *People's Daily* editorial, 1 January 1962.
[32] In *Neues Deutschland*, 23 December 1960, H. Matern defined 'national democracy' as a 'tactical formulation which can help [communist parties] in the anti-imperialist countries freed from the colonial yoke to carry out the democratic and socialist revolution.'

In sending home the experts, or severely curtailing their activities, Asian and African countries are only following China's example. In 1935, according to the official histories of the CCP, the Chinese revolution freed itself from the almost fatal interference of the Comintern and the effects of Stalin's feud with Trotsky on its affairs; history and geography still imposed on China a special relationship with the USSR in 1950, but the experts went home just the same in the end. The events of recent years indicate that leaders of the revolution in more fortunately situated countries of the East will not allow Khrushchev or Mao to wreck them in the interests of *their* irrelevant feud, or foist on them subversive ' experts '.

Khrushchev and Mao are not really arguing over whether to keep the revolution creeping, or make it ' leap forward ', at the risk of war. Their two regimes, heirs to vast multi-national land empires destined to compete for Central Asia, have inevitably been seeking to orient the communist movement and its front organisations towards the different policies dictated by their own needs and interests. For analogous reasons the other underdeveloped countries will all work out their independent formulas for social and political development in an increasingly polycentric world.

AFRICA: NATIONALISM AND COMMUNISM

Fritz Schatten

AS Africa's rush towards continental independence approaches its goal, and on its maps there is a shrinkage in the last posts of colonialism, a corresponding increase is occurring in research and speculation on the present influence and the future chances of communism on that continent. If the number of journalistic efforts on the theme were to be taken as a criterion, by today the black continent would in fact be covered in a close net of red power posts, if not completely delivered into the hands of communism. But Africa—a fact of which everyone seeking the right approach must sooner or later become aware—is different; here, to an even greater degree than in Asia or Latin America, it is advisable to guard against hasty conclusions and prophecies. There is little in this continent on which one can actually depend, and the Soviet experts on Africa not least of all must realise that. For the persistent revolutionary ferment of Africa in itself discourages the formation of any lasting affiliations—it embraces almost every intellectual and political sphere; everything appears to be in the melting-pot of radical change, and the ideas that have been approved in the rest of the world break down almost completely here.

What is meant by socialism in Africa? Almost every nationalist group south of the Sahara uses this label, and it is an ever-recurring surprise to see the impartiality with which even those politicians who lean to the right pass themselves off as 'socialists of firm principles'. To judge by their own statements, these men—to name only a few to begin with—are socialists: Sekou Touré of Guinea, Kwame Nkrumah of Ghana, Antoine Gizenga of the Congo; and, in contrast perhaps to the philosophising President of Senegal, Léopold Sedar Senghor, they would reject all connection with social-democracy or other forms of playing at socialism in attempts at reform. Are they therefore orthodox communists, or, to use a different formula, has this communism any serious chances in the groups governed or influenced by them? Sekou Touré's reply at least, one would think, provided a clear negative in his forcing the recall of the Soviet ambassador Solod from Conakry. And yet, almost at the same time as Sekou Touré ensured the collapse of a 'communist conspiracy' in Guinea, was not his close adherent Diallou Seydou displaying thoroughly radical pro-communist sympathies at the Stockholm conference of the World Peace Council (16–19 December 1961)? And are there not constantly in Guinea itself, and epecially among the youthful element, more or less tolerated discussions on 'scientific socialism'?

The position in fact—and not only with regard to Guinea—is confusing, and even the Soviet communists have to admit this. In a recent
publication Professor Ivan Potekhin, the leading Soviet authority on
Africa, who himself in many essays has revealed high expectations about
the early triumph of Soviet communism in Africa, expresses himself
thus: ' Which path of evolution is to be chosen, the capitalist or the
socialist? This question is exercising all the countries and peoples of
Africa. Yet great masses of the population in Africa either cannot
imagine at all what socialism is, or have only a vague notion of it. They
do know, however, that socialism is something good, that it is a social
order which takes into account the interests of the workers '. And
Potekhin adds resignedly: ' In Africa socialism is much talked of; the
ideas of socialism are widely diffused, but discussion is mainly concerned
with ideas that are not in accordance with scientific socialism '.[1]

A similar conclusion is reached in the periodical *The African
Communist*, in an article by N. Numadé, an African. He maintains first
of all that the Africans are turning ' more and more to a socialist
solution ', and gives a definition of socialism when he writes: ' We know
that only socialism—i.e. the conquest of the power of the state through
the workers and peasants *under the guidance of the communist party,*
the community ownership of the means of production, which facilitates
bold planning—is capable of developing industry and agriculture within
the shortest term and raising material and cultural living standards. No-
one who makes a serious study of the trends and developments of the
African movement towards freedom can fail to see the direction being
taken by the countries of Africa, the growing influence of socialist ideas '.
Yet the author seems, as it were, to shrink from the force of this assertion,
for he qualifies it by going on to say: ' Naturally one must take care not
to over-estimate the position '. For there were still ' many African
leaders ' who thought nothing of ' making fervent speeches against
colonialism to-day and sitting down to-morrow with the colonial masters
for a private conversation on the " communist threat " '.[2]

The derogatory undertone is, however, entirely misplaced. The
attitude of ' many African leaders ' outlined by Numadé applies only to
a few, and thus is entirely untypical, more especially as regards the
conversations about a ' communist threat ' with the ' colonial masters '.
There is in Africa no perceptible anti-communism in the European or
American sense of the term; it is thoroughly unpopular in that continent,
where it is widely viewed as an attribute of colonialism. What, then, is the
source of the clear conflict between euphoria and disappointment which
finds expression, for example, in Numadé's statements? I believe that it
results primarily from the fact that the communists, and particularly the
Soviet communists, are not capable of grasping the *African mentality* and

[1] Ivan Potekhin, ' Afrika: itogi i perspektivy antiimperialisticheskoy revoliutsii ', in
Aziya i Afrika sevodnya, No. 10, 1961.
[2] *The African Communist* (London), No. 5, 1961.

that they make the same mistake as do many observers in the West : they take the verbal similarity, often extremely close, of statements made by African nationalists and by communists, as proof of a complete identity. In this, moreover, they are encouraged by many African actions which on the other hand encourage the hope that their classical style communism will meet with no difficulties in Africa.

THIS misunderstanding is not new. It could be discerned as long ago as the twenties, when the first contacts occurred between African nationalism (or its earliest manifestations) and communism. At that time in France, England and America, African students with radical leanings were privileged guests at communist gatherings—they served, so to speak, as incarnate alibis for the essential internationalism of the communist parties of these countries. The efforts made by the communist parties of France and Great Britain, entrusted by the second Comintern congress with significant tasks in Africa, were, however, wrecked by the peculiar conflict between communism and French or English nationalism. The attitude of the British and French Communist parties to the question of the colonial struggle for liberation was far from being consistent. With biting sarcasm and derision Manuilsky, at the fifth congress of the Communist International (June 1924), declared:

> About a year ago the Communist International addressed an appeal to the colonial slaves in which it called upon them to rise against their masters. When this appeal reached one of the local branches of the Communist party of France in Algiers, Sidi-Bel-Abbes, that local group passed a resolution condemning this appeal of the Comintern. . . . Further, I venture to ask the French party members where the documents are in which the Communist party of France proclaimed to all the world the liberation of the colonies. . . . Considerable blame for passivity in the field of colonial propaganda has been earned by our English members. . . . In all the documents that came before us on the attitude of the English party to the colonies, we did not find one single declaration in which the English members had clearly and unequivocally demanded the separation of the colonies from the British Empire.[3]

More than twenty years later Maurice Thorez, at the 11th congress of the French CP, expressed himself just as vaguely on the policy of French communists in the colonies. He, like Etienne Fajon, characterised the ' Union Francaise '—and that means the policy of a French assimilation of the colonial peoples—as the ' most propitious framework ' for the aspirations of the overseas territories.[4]

In these circumstances those Africans who were originally in sympathy with communism were naturally discouraged rather than won over for good, an effect which followed more especially in French-speaking Africa on the collapse of the ' Rassemblement Démocratique

---

3 *Protokoll: Fünfter Kongress der K.I.* (Hamburg, n.d. [1924]), pp. 630–632.
4 *L'Humanité*, 26 and 27 June 1947.

Africain' of 1950, although here deeper reasons were also no doubt at work. Taken all in all, the defection of such prominent partisans as Félix Houphouet-Boigny (Ivory Coast) or Gabriel d'Arboussier (Senegal) sprang from a profound mental and spiritual uneasiness: the communists expected from their African adherents unconditional support for the metropolitan communist actions and aims, which were determined for the most part by the international plans of communism drawn up in Moscow. At the same time, however, they refused to take into consideration the special African needs, conditions, wishes, and aspirations. Thus communism was entirely arbitrary in extending its class pattern—to single out only one characteristic point—to the African situation. With absurd consistency it discounted all 'non-proletarian' Africans who opposed colonialism as 'disguised lackeys of colonialism'. *Narody Afriki* (The Peoples of Africa), a book that appeared in Moscow in 1954, for example, described Kwame Nkrumah's Convention People's party and the first government formed by Nkrumah as 'a shield behind which is concealed in reality the dominion of British imperialism'. As recently as 1955 the periodical *Sovetskoe Vostokovedenie* wrote that the 'anti-imperialist and anti-feudalist revolution' in Africa could never triumph in league with the national bourgeoisie, but 'only on the basis of the alliance of workers and peasants and led by the communists'. [5] In other words, communism largely ignored the genuine nationalist movement in Africa, which was taking shape with ever greater speed, and it also failed to notice that those Africans—especially in the 'Rassemblement Démocratique Africain'— who had associated themselves with the communists had some connection with them, but no formal engagement.

A N important reservation of principle—primarily of an ideological and religious nature—was in the past made by many African politicians who became connected in any way with radical socialism. Sekou Touré in an interview summed it up in the words: 'I believe that Marxism supplies important theses on the history of mankind. Dialectical and philosophical materialism make it possible to interpret social and economic facts in a way which leads, for instance, to a denial of the existence of God. Now in the African countries, and especially in Guinea, you will not find any man or woman without belief in God. Even if someone tells you he is a fetishist or has no religion at all—he too is a believer'. [6]

[5] *Sovetskoe vostokovedenie*, Nos. 5–6, 1955. Four years later the British communist Idris Cox admitted: 'In reality, however, political independence was achieved, after the second world war, in India, Indonesia, Ghana and other countries under the leadership of the national bourgeoisie' (*Problems of Peace and Socialism*, No. 8, 1959).
[6] Fernand Gigon, 'Guinée Etat-pilote'. Quoted in Franz Ansprenger, *Politik im Schwarzen Afrika* (Cologne, 1961), p. 292.

A similar view was expressed by the Ghanaian politician Kofi Baako in a lecture on ' Ghana's conception of socialism '. He said: ' I draw your attention to the religious feelings amongst the people. No Ghanaian, no African for that matter, is atheist. Deep down in him are the spiritual stirrings which move him to worship the gods of his ancestors. . . . No matter how much educated, no matter how much sophisticated, his whole being instinctively rejects the projection that life on earth is the end. . . . It stands to reason, therefore, that any political ideology that has no room for these basic facts will not be acceptable and if imposed would only mean strife and social upheaval. You will appreciate, therefore, that the type of society which we are seeking to create in Ghana would last and bring peace *if the existing conditions and traditions are taken into consideration* '.[7]

It is clear that with this the monopolistic claim of communist ideology is punctured at a critical point. Indeed in practice this aspect is very frequently the cause of serious conflict between orthodox communists and African comrades. Several students who have very recently broken off their studies in the Eastern bloc provide a living proof of this. In most cases they were actually Africans who had held important offices in communist groups or front organisations. One of them, who here may stand for several, Mahdi Ismail from Somalia, having spent four years studying in the Eastern bloc and acting as interim representative of a Somalian radical trade union organisation, was actually a member of the British Communist party. As one of several reasons for his break with communism he cited the ' inability of the communist officials in their abstract and cold philosophy ' to satisfy the ' spiritual needs of the African students '. Through their disdain of religious feelings, their cold, purely utilitarian attitude and aims, the communist officials of the Eastern bloc had, in Ismail's view, placed themselves on a level with ' representatives of the capitalist West, who just as soullessly pursue their own profit and, while they do so, worship God without believing in him '.[8] Walter Kolarz draws an apt parallel with many varieties of Asian communism when he writes: ' The Afro-Marxist, like the Buddhist Marxist of Burma, has no use for Marxism as a universal materialist ideology governing all aspects of life, as it has been usually understood in Europe '.[9]

Another, no less significant, factor is the different view of the general political situation held by the African socialist. The surge of the African struggle for liberation has not carried him in spirit at all beyond the boundaries of Africa. It is *Africa* that for him forms the motive, the field and the goal of his struggle, not an abstract world proletariat to which he might feel pledged. With Kwame Nkrumah he substitutes for ' Proletarians of all countries, unite!' the formula ' People of Africa,

---

[7] Lecture given at an International Seminar of Christian Students in Accra, 19 August 1961. Manuscript in possession of the author.

[8] In a conversation with the author, 30 December 1961, in Bonn.

[9] ' Communism in Africa ', in *Problems of Communism*, November–December 1961.

unite!', which is perhaps extended to the peoples of all colonies and very frequently strikes the fundamental chord of race. In the mind of the African the world is divided far less into 'capitalists' and 'proletarians' than into 'rich whites' and 'poor coloured people', and the dream of many is directed, not towards an 'International of the Workers', but towards an 'International of the Coloured'. The Soviet leaders, who have no doubt recognised this phenomenon, are trying to master it by making even greater use in their policy towards Africa of officials and experts from the Soviet Asian republics. In many cases, however, this has the same effect as the more or less abortive attempt of the American State Department to place coloured United States citizens in diplomatic posts in Africa and Asia: the intention behind it is too transparent.

BUT let us return to the division of the world into 'poor' and 'rich' countries or zones. The African who, after he has studied in or paid visits to America or Western Europe, comes into the Eastern bloc often has to make very strenuous efforts to discover those 'fundamental differences' which, according to communist propaganda, are supposed to exist between West and East. He arrives in a relatively ordered, highly industrialised, technically developed world, the impression it makes being enhanced by means of the normal programme for visits in Soviet Russia or Czechoslovakia or East Germany. The African guest is taken into giant steel works and automated machine tool factories, while the technical 'exploits of socialism' are depicted unceasingly—even to the sputniks and luniks and the space ships of Gagarin and Titov. All this may be impressive, but for the average visitor from Africa it is at the same time confusing and depressing. He becomes aware of what appears to be an infinite distance between the social and economic status of his home and the state of the Eastern bloc, the same distance as that yawning between Africa and the highly developed states of the West. To be sure, the African is met with the constant refrain that 'all that' is the result of 'only' forty or forty-five years of 'socialist construction'; but whether these references are able to make up for the impression of distance, which is frequently the dominant one from the outset, must—to judge from the reports of many Africans—be very much open to doubt. Some, like Mamadou Dia, Prime Minister of Senegal, who holds socialist views, will not be able to rid themselves of the feeling that the Soviet Union has 'succeeded in socialist construction, but at the expense of the soul', and agree with Léopold Sedar Senghor: 'The paradoxical element in socialist construction in the communist countries, at least in the USSR, is that it approximates more and more to the capitalist construction of the United States'.[10]

Nevertheless there is a 'fascination of communism', to which, and perhaps even with special intensity, Africans succumb. It is always there

[10] Senghor: Rapport sur la Doctrine et le Programme du PFA, in *Congrès Constitutif du PFA* (Dakar, 1959), p. 51 ff.

when parallels to the African situation can be detected, and that is the case in much greater measure in China and Yugoslavia than perhaps in the USSR and in Moscow's European satellite states. It is quite evident that the African perceives very clear differences between these three 'models', and his approach to communism is marked by the fact that he finds it at a time when the 'Third Rome' has already to a great extent forfeited its character of being the sole centre of communism. He has been born, as it were, into a polycentric communist world, in which it is no longer a question of the one and only, but of several and quite varying paths of socialist development.

The parallels between China and Africa are drawn not only in the propaganda of Peking. A typical statement is that made to the Paris *Figaro* by Barry Diawadou, Minister of Education in Guinea, after a journey to China in 1959: 'Since my return I have been fully convinced of the effectiveness of the Chinese methods. I was profoundly impressed by the similarity between the economic questions that China has been able to solve and the problems that are of common concern today to all the peoples of Africa. I learnt there what can be achieved when the living forces of a nation are summoned in aid. With due regard to the differences of proportion we shall now do the same thing.' [11]

It is the similarity—whether imagined or genuine—of the starting-point that impresses the African friends of China, the fact that the zero point of construction is still visible everywhere in China. Whoever from Africa chooses the much used delegation route Soviet Union—China is confronted everywhere in the USSR with imposing evidence of a highly-developed civilisation and industrialisation; in Mao's country, on the other hand, even when selection of objects for show is most careful, he constantly comes upon evidence of the half-finished. The poverty of the population is just as apparent as the primitive nature of many of the methods of production and the products. And, as the reports of African travellers in China show, those in charge there make no effort at all to conceal this state of affairs. Precisely here, of course, lies the great chance for demonstration of *shared characteristics*. From nothing, the Africans are assured, the Chinese People's Republic within one decade has made a huge 'leap forward' on the economic side. While for the colonialists and their Chinese 'vassals' (Chiang Kai-shek) China's rise to the level of capitalism had been conceivable, the new China had resolved to pass direct from the 'semi-colonial' and 'semi-feudal' stage to socialism, and thus skip the 'agonising stage of capitalism'. For the rest, such successes as the African guests discovered in China were based, so they were told, not on foreign aid and the application of the most modern techniques, but on the new organisation of the masses and of their labour power under the rigorous leadership of the party.

It was just this that inspired a man like Cofie-Crabbe, Chief Executive Secretary of the Ghanaian Convention People's party, and made

11 J. Jacquet-Francillon, 'En Afrique—la Chine arrive', *Le Figaro*, 25 December 1959.

him speak in March 1962 at a CPP gathering of the attractiveness of the
Chinese path, which was 'a model' for Ghana.[12] Even before this the
Guinean Parti Démocratique (PDG) had reacted in a similar way, and
the programme evolved in 1959 of *investissement humain*—unpaid
collective labour for the construction of schools, health centres, roads,
etc.—is quite obviously based on Chinese models. (To a certain extent
the Republic of Mali has in the meantime adopted the same programme.)
On the other hand, however, reports of the development of some pilot
collectives in Guinea on the model of the Chinese communes were probably very much exaggerated. Here, and indeed for the whole of Africa,
it is a question of drawing a sharp distinction between cooperative and
collective experiments. Naturally, in a continent where the soil has
always been cultivated by joint endeavour, there is a strong inclination
towards cooperatives in the modern style. Any attempt, however, at
regimentation in collectives will undoubtedly call forth opposition, as
indeed happened on the occasion of an attempt in Guinea early in 1960.[13]
I have not met a single African who has given unreserved praise to the
Soviet collective farms or the Chinese communes, yet I know many who
were impressed by the Israeli kibbutz and the Yugoslav form of agricultural cooperative.

IF, with the left radical groups of African nationalism, communist China
is frequently given preference over the Soviet Union, this must be
ascribed mainly to its sharper anti-colonialist agitation. Soviet policy is
in many concrete cases extraordinarily opportunist—especially the intensified compliments directed since 1955 towards the national bourgeoisie,
even the team-play with Nasser at the expense of the Egyptian Communist party, the coexistential overtures to the Emperor of Ethiopia
and his feudalistic regime, the relatively swift recognition of Adoula in
the Congo and the dropping of Gizenga—these and similar acts have
repeatedly given rise to serious doubts as to the 'revolutionary disposi-
tion' of the Soviet communists, but have perceptibly benefited the 'revolutionary' Chinese. Even in this respect, however, caution is indicated
over any estimation of African-Chinese cooperation in general. Thus
there is little significance in the fact that, for example, the representatives
of Guinea, before the second Pan-African People's Conference, which
took place in Tunis at the end of January 1960, pleaded in the secretariat
of the Afro-Asian Solidarity movement against the Soviets and with the
Chinese, for a 'harder' address to the conference. In the Guinean view
this was not a question of opening the way for China to the African
battlefield, but of inducing the African parties of like mind to the Guinean
to adopt a sharper line against colonialism. The same interpretation is to

[12] Report in the *Deutsche Zeitung* (Cologne), 9 March 1962, quoting the *Daily Graphic*
(Accra).
[13] *Neue Zürcher Zeitung*, Fernausgabe, 16 March 1960.

be placed on the support of Guinea for the Chinese at the conference of the World Peace Council in December 1961 in Stockholm. There it was a question of what main themes should be treated at the world congress announced for 1962. The Soviets voted, with 166 of their own and outside votes, for a congress on general disarmament. Twenty-four delegates, including the Chinese, in opposition to this, expressed their wish for a congress ' for national independence, peace, and disarmament '. In agreement with the chief Chinese representatives, Liao Cheng-chih and Liu Ning-yi, the Guinean Diallou Seydou made this declaration: ' Some said that the main content of our epoch is disarmament. I say that the main content of our epoch is anti-imperialism, anti-colonialism and anti-racial discrimination. I cannot understand any separation of the questions of peace, freedom and independence. We are under armed enslavement and persecution by imperialism and we want arms '.

These words, in themselves, gave little evidence of communist or pro-communist sentiment. They are rather a reflection of radical anti-colonialist sentiment in the leadership of the Guinean government party, and to be clearly distinguished as ' para-communist ' from the attitude of the traditional communist parties.

Whether this label can be also attached to the illegal terrorist branch of the ' Union des Populations du Cameroun ' (UPC) is certainly open to question. This group, which lost Félix-Roland Moumié, its president of long standing, in November 1960 through poisoning in Switzerland, and today is being led by the no less radical Ernest Ouandié from Conakry, has of all African parties entered into the most intimate relations with Chinese communism. Moumié (with whom I had several detailed discussions) was also one of the few Africans who had absorbed a large measure of universalist communist ideology. Even as a student at the Ecole des Medicines in Dakar, he had made trips to the Eastern bloc, and after a short-lived friendship with Nasser he intensified from 1957 onward his cooperation with the Soviets, who up to the beginning of 1960 were largely responsible for the financial resources and the development of UPC cadres. Soviet policy with regard to Cameroun, however, began to change just before it become independent on 1 January 1960. On 3 January 1960 Moscow's emissary Firyubin had a long conversation with the Cameroun President Ahidjo in Garoua, Northern Cameroun, in which the Soviet diplomat is supposed to have undertaken to enlist the support of the Moumié group. Later the Cameroun Foreign Minister Okala reported to the parliament of Yaoundé that he had discussed the matter in New York with Khrushchev after the opening of the UN session in the autumn of 1960, and the latter had said to him (Okala): ' I have told Monsieur Moumié that a revolution cannot be organised from outside. . . . Go back to Cameroun to suffer with your fellow-countrymen, and gain power in the legal way through elections.' [14] Such a challenge was bound to arouse extreme indignation in a type of

[14] *Neue Zürcher Zeitung*, 13 January 1961.

man so power-conscious, fanatical, and aggressive as Moumié, and in a
long conversation with the author, which took place in Conakry in April
1960, he spoke in terms of absolute contempt of Soviet policy towards
Africa, demonstrating on the other hand fervent veneration of the Chinese
communists. They were, he said, 'true communist revolutionaries and
internationalists'. Finally he produced a copy, dedicated to him by Mao
Tse-tung, of the latter's essay on 'Questions of Strategy in the Partisan
Struggle', and triumphantly emphasised it with the words: 'Here you'll
find out what is going to happen in Cameroun.'

In a similar and equally unrestrained manner Niawue Nicanor, permanent representative of the UPC in Rabat, in an interview in September
1960 with the Hsinhua News Service, sided with Chinese communism.

> The daily growing interest that the Chinese people manifest for our
> struggle in Cameroun is a material proof of their clear adherence
> to the principle of the anti-imperialist fight and of proletarian
> solidarity. From the great Chinese contribution the courage of the
> Cameroun people draws an added inspiration to continue and
> intensify the revolutionary struggle. The rich experience of China
> during its 28-year-long victorious fight . . . offers a valuable example
> for the African peoples, especially as the conditions of life and of
> struggle in Africa do not greatly differ from those of the old China.[15]

That the Soviet-Chinese differences in the Cameroun question still persist
was shown in September 1961. On a Soviet invitation a small diplomatic
delegation from Cameroun went to Moscow to discuss the improvement
of reciprocal relations. At the same time, however, a group of the UPC
led by the Moumié supporter Ouandié was making a stay in Peking.

ALTHOUGH the growing influence of Chinese communism, with its
pronounced trend towards revolutionary rejection of compromise,
can be demonstrated in various small groups of African radicals, the
radical wing of the UPC still forms an exception; but even in this case
some reservations must be registered. The adherents of the UPC in
Cameroun itself are influenced by the ideas of Moumié or even of Mao
Tse-tung only in an ephemeral way. Amongst them there is a mingling
of genuine social rebelliousness against a reactionary upper stratum with
political adventurism and unpolitical gangsterism. The majority would
probably be surprised if they were credited with communist motives in
their fight. Communism in Africa, and this does not apply only to the
UPC, is an affair of the élite, or—to put it more precisely—of a section
of African intellectuals obviously psychologically inclined that way.
Among these are, first of all, those young avantgardists who after the
second world war studied in Western Europe and who were repelled by
capitalism, individualism, the spiritual and moral confusion of the West;
but who also in many cases after returning to their homelands were no

[15] New China News Agency, 11 September 1960.

longer capable of renewing their original social ties with their community. It is precisely this personal dilemma which brings into all the greater prominence the general misery of Africa. Their sociological awareness, schooled in the West, brings into starker relief than ever the low state of the economy, the misery of the masses, the backwardness of certain institutions (such as chieftainship). Since action must be taken swiftly and in a thorough-going way, and the capitalist path is discredited in Africa, it is only natural that in seeking after solutions they come upon the prescriptions of communism, which, moreover, go far towards meeting their own needs. The adoption of forms and methods of the anti-traditionalist one-party rule, of democratic centralism, even of the principle of criticism and self-criticism—as accepted by the government parties of Ghana and Guinea—of economic planning, of state monopoly, etc., is in fact regarded by many political groups in Africa as indispensable, and in some countries—such as Ghana, Guinea, Mali—it is already in full swing. Objectively this development may lead to an approximation to the image of communist states. Subjectively, however, it is still in the first place a matter of attempting to adapt some of the outward forms of communism, or, to put it more precisely, of attempting to amalgamate foreign and specifically African elements. Several African politicians have quite rightly pointed to the fact that, for example, the one-party state with the leader having unrestricted power represents the national projection and modernisation of the traditional rule by chiefs. ' What our constitution has done ', Kofi Baako declared, ' is to identify the government of the country with one person, so that the popular conception of a ruler as a father and the nation as one large community of brothers and sisters would be recognisable to the people '.[16]

Undoubtedly Nkrumah's regime, with its increasingly pronounced features of political and moral perversion—personality cult, elimination of opposition groups, and so on—has already departed a long way from the humanitarian basis of such avowals. Even in Guinea—and with greater limitations in Mali—not infrequently one might suspect that such statements are really designed as camouflage. In tendency and principle, however, we are undoubtedly concerned here with a serious attempt to establish a synthesis. In the process the adaptation of partial elements of orthodox communism is accompanied by the appeal to Africa's own history, by the emphasis on specifically African forms of existence (négritude, personalité africaine), and by nationalistic and pan-African missionary zeal. Afro-communism is the appropriate expression for it.

AFRO-COMMUNISM is certainly not pleasant for the West; it implies a radically anti-Western mood and attitude; an Afro-communism exalted to the position of a binding doctrine encourages the spread of orthodox communist ideas and at the same time facilitates orthodox

---

[16] Kofi Baako, loc. cit.

communist infiltration. Internationally, it leads to new and varied kinds of affiliation, to teamwork perhaps in the front organisations or in UNO. But it is at the same time a demarcation, it draws a boundary line rejecting the monopolistic claim of a communist control-station outside Africa, denying the validity of communist ideology in toto for Africa. Orthodox communism inevitably provokes a conflict at the point where it touches upon the African segment of Afro-communism. That became evident in Guinea in November/December 1961, and what happened there may well be repeated in like manner in Ghana and Mali.

Afro-communism is young and no one can at the moment predict its evolution. To a certain extent its location cannot even be identified; but the fact that at present no communist parties worth mentioning exist in tropical Africa is not to be ascribed only to the tactical considerations of Moscow; it also reflects the incapacity of orthodox communists to adapt ideology and policy to the special conditions of Africa and to do justice in some degree to the natural vehemence of African nationalism. Yet this is not only a present dilemma for orthodox communism, and limited only to Africa. It is permanent and universal, even if in Eastern Europe, for example, it is concealed by Soviet power politics.

The path of Africa is uncertain. The political and ideological contours of this continent, which has been startled out of a long twilight and shaken by an explosive development, are still vague, and undoubtedly they will in the long term experience many profound changes. But the entry of Africa into modern history is taking place in a phase of increasing differentiation in the forms of world politics, and the approach that this continent has already found and in future may find to communism is characterised by the growing differentiation in communism itself. For the socialist-minded African of the year 1962, inspired by Marx, this communism presents itself in a varied, polycentrist form; and the realisation of this may encourage and spur him on to strive after the African stamp of socialism suited to himself and to his country.

LATIN AMERICA:
CASTRO'S COURSE

Boris Goldenberg

THE opposing tendencies towards 'monocentrism' and 'polycentrism' are the natural outcome of changing conditions. Before the war monocentrism was dominant because there was only one communist party in power, in a country which was both great and isolated, both powerful and underdeveloped. So it came about that the world communist movement was transformed into an instrument of that communist party. It had to follow a line which was at each turn 'deduced' from its particular and changing *national* interests, which were in turn identified with those of *world* communism, although in fact these were frequently in conflict with the political necessities of the individual communist parties. So long as other territories fell under the sway of communism mainly or only because of their open or veiled conquest by the Soviet Union, monocentrism remained in force, in spite of the official dissolution of the Communist International. The tendency towards polycentrism could only make headway after communist parties had taken power by their own means, independently of the Russian communists or Soviet state power. This happened first in Yugoslavia and then in China, and from 1948 on polycentrism appeared, leading first to the excommunication of Tito and his comrades, and later to the scarcely veiled dispute with China within the official communist fold.

Now a new centre of communism seems to have arisen in Cuba. Here there was a socialist revolution *sui generis*, without any help from Russia, and the official communists came to power by a new and highly original road of infiltration. Although by itself the island appeared much too small and unimportant to constitute a really new centre of revolution, it has a particular significance as the first communist state established in Latin America. This aspect was underlined by Khrushchev in his report on the communist conference in 1960 of 81 communist parties.

> During the last years a new front of struggle against American imperialism has arisen in Latin America. . . . Its peoples are showing in their struggle that the American continent is by no means a possession of the USA. Latin America reminds one of an active volcano.

The spread of communism to the whole sub-continent would be an overwhelming triumph for the East, and this possibility has been opened by Castro's victory and by its unique features which, indeed, seem to have inaugurated a new kind of communism.

There is much to be said for the thesis that underdeveloped countries which have entered upon the process of industrialisation provide a particularly fertile soil for the reception of Marxism. They suffer under the initial effects of economic modernisation, but they cannot and do not want to go back to the pre-industrial stage; on the contrary, they are bent on rapid industrial progress. Marxism is at one and the same time a protest against the evils of early capitalism *and* a promise of overcoming them through industrial development; it is a protest against the poverty of the masses, their exploitation and oppression, as well as against all feudal, capitalist, and imperialist fetters which hinder rapid development. This appears to be true with respect to Latin America in particular. Most Latin American countries are in an intermediate stage of development, which gives the communist movement better chances than it finds either in more backward countries, in which conditions do not favour revolution, or in the highly developed countries, where a revolutionary socialist movement can be considered neither probable nor necessary.

IN countries like Argentina, Brazil, Chile, Mexico, Uruguay, industrialisation and the objective possibilities for establishing socialism have grown together with sharp contradictions and social discontent. Their average per capita income and their index of urbanisation are much higher than in most countries of Africa and Asia (except Japan); they all have highly modern economic sectors, side by side with pre-capitalist ones; they have a fairly numerous middle class and there is no hostility to modernisation. The whole sub-continent is characterised by a fundamental discrepancy between its potentialities and their realisation. A rational use of the existing productive factors (land, labour, capital, even entrepreneurial talents) would permit much higher living standards than those enjoyed by the majority of the population, which lives at subsistence level. Latin America is the continent with the highest rate of population growth, where the social cleavages are particularly great, where the masses, driven forward by the ' revolution of growing expectations ', are becoming aware of their relative impoverishment and conscious of the need of radical change.

These economic and social conditions are the combined result of underdevelopment and misdevelopment. The first grew out of internal, the second out of external factors. Underdevelopment was the outcome of Latin American history since Spanish times, misdevelopment followed from the impact of foreign capital and the forces of the world market. The socially and politically dominant classes hindered the development of a modern economy, while external forces deflected the course of its evolution, transforming the area into an object of exploitation geared to foreign needs. With the penetration of foreign capital, the Latin American oligarchies were transformed into partners and allies of foreign powers. So it came about that the struggle against these foreign factors— not quite adequately fused under the term ' imperialism '—was to become potentially a struggle agains the ruling classes of Latin America : anti-imperialism contained the seed of anti-capitalism.

Despite these favourable conditons, the communist parties of Latin America remained weak and unimportant. In 1959 it was estimated that the numerical strength of all the communist parties in Latin America did not exceed 240,000—80,000 in Argentina, 40,000 in Brazil, another 40,000 in Venezuela, 30,000 in Chile, 17,000 in Cuba. A recently published Russian handbook gives fairly similar figures, the number for Argentina (1960) being 100,000; Cuba is not mentioned; but membership of the other parties is, according to this handbook, rather lower than in the 1959 estimates—35,000 in Venezuela, 25,000 for Brazil, 20,000 for Chile. According to the same handbook the communist movement in Latin America has grown comparatively slowly since 1939, when it numbered 90,000. It now represents barely 5% of total communist membership in non-communist countries; in 1939 the corresponding figure was 12%. The same weakness is shown in electoral results. In those countries in which the communist party is legal and participates in elections, the percentage is low—the highest was reached recently in Chile, where, in 1961, it got nearly 12 per cent of the total vote.

The main reason for the discrepancy between communist possibilities and communist results is monocentrism. The several communist parties were from the beginning under the predominant influence of the Russian communists, who at this time, when the United States was not yet the 'main enemy', knew and cared little about what happened there, while the strategical and tactical zig-zags they imposed on the Latin American communists ran counter to the interests and sentiments of Latin American radicals.

It is true that communists encountered many difficulties: the Latin American radical intellectuals were mainly and primarily nationalists and individualists, while the labour movement was frequently influenced by anarcho-syndicalist traditions. The communists were anti-nationalist and disciplinarians. The ideology of Latin American radicals was rooted in strong preferences for individual freedom and democracy and was expressed in a peculiar Spanish phraseology. Communists spoke a 'Russian Spanish', regarded individual freedom as petty-bourgeois nonsense, and deprecated democracy. Latin American intellectuals were voluntarists, with a tendency to ultra-radicalism, and were suspicious of any compromises. The communists were revolutionary opportunists who, largely because of the sudden changes imposed on them from Moscow, frequently collaborated with men and parties regarded by the national revolutionaries as reactionary.

Other embarrassments arose out of objective factors: the communists were urban groups, unable to mobilise the agricultural population; in the towns they found a proletariat divided into a minority of organised workers whose outlook was largely trade-unionist, and a majority of badly-paid, unsettled, unorganised workers who could almost be classed as 'lumpenproletariat'. They were also hampered by unsuccessful attempts to interpret the social reality of their countries in Marxist terms which, when not irrelevant, were over-simplified.

They might have overcome those difficulties had they not been fettered by monocentrism, which dictated their *Weltanschauung*, their terminology, and their strategy. As the communists were unable to give expression and leadership to the revolutionary discontent which began to increase after the economic crisis of 1929–1933, it was channelled into other movements which grew out of the Latin American soil: radical-democratic, more or less socialist, and anti-imperialist parties like the Peruvian APRA, the Accion Democratica in Venezuela, the Autenticos in Cuba, the followers of Figueres in Costa Rica, of Arevalo in Guatemala; into bonapartist or semi-fascist movements like Peron's ' Justicialism' in Argentina and, to a certain extent, Vargas' movement in Brazil, as well as in parties which outgrew their original Peronist features and became socialist, like the MNR in Bolivia. From the early thirties onwards the social and political changes occurring in Latin America went far deeper than those which used to be called ' revolutions'. These included the anti-Machado revolution of 1933, the radicalisation of Mexico under Cardenas (1934–1940), the Guatemalan revolution which started in the 1940s, the establishment of Justicialism in Argentina, the democratic revolution of Figueres of 1948, the Bolivian revolution, the fall of the Rojas Pinilla dictatorship in Colombia, and that of the Perez Jimenez dictatorship in Venezuela (1958), where Accion Democratica reconquered power, after its short-lived victory of 1945.

SUBSEQUENT events brought disillusion in their train. The Cuban revolution of 1933 was frustrated (with the active help of the United States) and gave rise to the first Batista regime and later to the victory of the Autenticos, whose rule was characterised as much by wholesale corruption as by rather modest social reforms and anarchic liberty and ended in Batista's coup d'état of 1952. The Mexican revolution seemed merely to have opened the way to capitalist development; Peron was overthrown, to be replaced by an unstable democracy, and Justicialism lost its attraction outside Argentina proper. The Guatemalan revolution, becoming radical and infiltrated by communists, was crushed by a military rising assisted by the United States, and left only the legacy of increased anti-Yanquism throughout Latin America. The fall of Rojas Pinilla in Colombia was followed by the re-establishment of what appeared to be the old oligarchic rule. The Bolivian revolution went from crisis to crisis; the Venezuelan remained a political without becoming a social revolution, radical enough to frighten the capitalists (and so increasing economic difficulties) but not radical enough to satisfy many of those who had been in its favour. The APRA was after thirty years not yet in power, although it had considerably toned down its radicalism and its anti-imperialism. It was in this situation that Castro appeared and it is against this background that the Cuban revolution must be seen.

Here was an authentically Latin American revolution, grown out of the womb of the continent, speaking its language, answering to its desires, overcoming its frustrations. It was led by a romantic, truly revolutionary *caudillo*, whose promise of a third way between capitalism and communism, ' neither bread without liberty nor liberty without bread ', appealed to all Latin American radicals. He did not compromise after coming to power: the old corrupt bureaucracy was destroyed, the army dissolved, the barracks transformed into schools, the masses armed. The rich were made poor and the poor richer, prices were reduced and wages increased; a radical agrarian revolution was begun; the educational monopoly of the propertied classes was broken and culture brought to the people. Foreign enterprises were confiscated, and so were most of those belonging to Cuban capitalists. The ' Yanquis ' were mercilessly attacked by this courageous little David proclaiming the rights of Latin America against the exploiting Goliath of the North. This was the picture as it appeared to most Latin Americans, and it stilled rising doubts.

True, there were no elections in Cuba. But what had elections meant up to then? True, there was no ' rule of law ' and no freedom of the press. But what had the law been except a guarantee of the privileges of a small minority who owned the press as well? Perhaps there was less individual liberty—but the losers seemed to be for the most part the members of the old ruling classes, whereas real liberty, liberty to do something, was greater for the masses. There seemed to be an exaggerated dependence on Russia; but were not the Americans to blame for this, those imperialists of the North who had refused to help the revolution? The official communists were acquiring more power, but Castro remained at the helm and the communists seemed to be only serving and accepting a revolution *sui generis*, and subordinating themselves to its laws.

Illusions are difficult to destroy, for they feed on wishes and have their roots in past frustrations. Even after Castro had publicly buried the idea of the possibility of any ' third road ' between the two blocs, accepted Marxism-Leninism, and subordinated himself to monocentrism, the myth of the new, unique, and independent road to socialism, which he had proclaimed and at first even followed, persisted. Castro's revolution had indeed been unique. The communists had been less radical than the 26th of July movement and rather baffled by what had happened.

According to official communist conceptions, which have allegedly been confirmed by the Cuban experience, Latin American revolutions are primarily anti-imperialist, directed against foreign (North American) domination; bourgeois-democratic, overthrowing the rule of feudalism and of the commercial classes linked to imperialism, the compradores; they arise out of a mass movement leading to civil war; they are based on a broad popular front composed of the national bourgeoisie, the industrial workers, and the peasants. They can succeed only if, inside that popular front, there exists a united front of the lower classes under the hegemony of the workers and their vanguard, i.e., the communist party.

The Cuban revolution contradicted this idea at every point.

The revolution was started, not against imperialism, but against the Batista dictatorship. It was conducted under the banner of representative democracy and of social reforms to be realised inside the framework of the 1940 constitution. If anti-imperialism had a certain importance as the ideology of frustrated intellectuals, it was weaker in Cuba than in almost any other Latin American country, and had steadily diminished since the 1930s. The most progressive representatives of the national bourgeoisie, who formed the first revolutionary government in 1959, were —not without reason—attacked by the communists for being pro-American. The urban workers were not anti-imperialist, if only because so many of them employed in Yanqui enterprises had good positions, while the agricultural workers were interested in the higher prices paid for sugar on the American market. There was no conflict between the comprador and the national bourgeoisie, and no struggle against feudalism, because there was none in Cuba—the Cuban latifundia having been mainly capitalist enterprises.

The fall of Batista did not follow from any mass movement, and there was hardly anything which could be called civil war. The masses—especially those of the middle class—helped the small groups of urban terrorists and mountain fighters, and the pressure of public opinion and passive resistance led to the collapse of a demoralised, corrupt, terroristic, and inefficient machine, whose soldiers refused to fight the guerrillas. There were fewer than one thousand dead on both sides in the military encounters of 1956–1958.

Among those who fought against Batista, the workers were the least active. Blas Roca, the Communist party secretary, wrote in 1959 :

> The main form of struggle was armed struggle in the countryside, while the strikes, boycott of elections and other actions by the working class and the urban masses played only a subsidiary role. The armed struggle was initiated by the petty bourgeoisie. Working class action could not be the decisive factor of the revolution owing to a number of circumstances, such as the split in the ranks of the working people effected by the pro-imperialist bourgeois elements, the bureaucratic control of the trade unions . . . the weight of ' economism ' in the labour movement and the tendency to solve all issues through the official trade-union leadership (*World Marxist Review*, August 1959).

The guerrilla groups could not be regarded as a peasant army, if only because they were so small that the concept ' army ' was inapplicable. According to Castro himself, his total forces numbered no more than 180 in April 1958, after sixteen months of struggle. At the end of December, immediately before the victory, they had risen to 803—although tens of thousands hastened to jump on the band-wagon in the first weeks of

January, only to be dismissed and purged later on. Urban elements, especially intellectuals, formed the majority of the officers. As to the peasants, Guevara wrote:

> The soldiers that made up our first guerrilla army came from the part of this social class which shows its love for the possession of land most aggressively, which expresses most perfectly the spirit catalogued as petty bourgeois; the *campesino* fights because he wants land, for himself, for his children; he wants to manage it, sell it, and make himself rich through his work.[1]

ALTHOUGH the majority of the lower classes were certainly in favour of social reform, they were by no means favourable to a socialist revolution. Castro was right in declaring that, if people had known that the small band of guerrilla fighters were ' Marxists-Leninists ', ' it is possible that we never would have been able to descend to the low-lands ' (speech of 20 December 1961). This lack of revolutionary spirit was not only due to the trade-unionist attitude of the workers and to apathy among the peasants, but also to the social reforms introduced after the 1930s, mentioned in an official pamphlet approved by Castro himself, and published in 1959 in Havana in Spanish and English under the title *Political, Economic and Social Thought of Fidel Castro*.

> Cuban distributive policy since 1933, with its higher salaries, eight-hour day, paid vacations, social security, etc., has produced a more just division of the national income, that is, of the total profits of all the companies, proprietor, partnership, or co-operation, existing in Cuba. Previously this income went into the hands of a few; now it goes to many.

If only because the Cuban revolution contradicted all communist predictions and tenets, it could not have been carried out by them or under their leadership; it remained, therefore, unique, even after Castro's rise to power. The negligible influence of the communists over the workers is shown by the fact that, in the elections for the Trade Union Congress held ten months after Castro's victory, the communists were able

---

[1] *Monthly Review* (New York), July–August 1961. These peasants were the first victims of their illusions and of Castro's promises. Neither they nor the cooperatives got property, but only its usufruct—as Castro now admits: ' The idea of introducing " cooperatives " was put in the Agrarian Reform Law during our flight to the Sierra [to sign the law]. . . . We debated whether the land should be given as property or in usufruct. We said, well—in reality it will be the same thing, but let us put " property " in order that our enemies shall not be able to use this against us. What the cooperatives have is obviously only " usufruct " of the land . . . they are not allowed to sell the land ' (Speech of 20 December 1961, *El Mundo*, Havana, 22 December 1961). The small minority of individual peasants who got ' titles of land ' are prohibited from selling, mortgaging, dividing, or bequeathing it. They are moreover organised in a state-directed institution and controlled by the Institute for Agrarian Reform. Réné Dumont and others have underlined that Cuba is the only case in which the revolution proceeded almost immediately to ' collectivise ' agriculture. Castro was more radical than the official communists.

to muster only about 10 per cent of the votes. A large majority of the delegates were opposed even to the inclusion of communists in the new leadership, and it needed personal pressure from the Castro brothers to overcome their resistance, and a long process of expulsion and pressure to transform the trade unions into state institutions run by official communists.

The social revolution which began after Batista's downfall resulted from the interplay between the charismatic leader's radicalism and the practical outcome of his decisions. The economic result was rapid social-isation; politically it led to the destruction of all representative institutions and, in foreign policy, to a close association with the USSR. All this was achieved in a highly original way which marked the first ' humanist ' phase of the revolution. There was no apparatus, no official leading party, no ideology. Economic policy was characterised not by austerity or productive investment, but by conspicuous consumption and disinvest-ment. The political structure was that of a ' totalitarian democracy ', ruled arbitrarily by a charismatic leader backed by enthusiastic masses, whose adherence was cemented by the benefits they had received, by hopes for the immediate future, and by an artificially enhanced hatred of the Yanquis. Failing to recognise that this dynamic but irrational humanism, with its anarchy, its voluntarism, its disregard for all economic laws, could only be a passing stage and was bound to increase all the difficulties of the country, Latin Americans accepted the new socialist gospel according to Castro, while frustrated radicals, angry young men, and gullible liberals from many countries were only too happy to find a new creed. All kinds of scarcities and economic dislocation appeared from the end of 1960 on, and their growing seriousness was for the first time publicly admitted during the production congress of August 1961 (which showed by the way that the apparently extraordinary achievements of the agrarian reform proclaimed shortly before had been nothing but illusion). Austerity *had* to come, and with it rationality, the inclusion of communists in the government, the establishment of a totalitarian machine, and the ' bolshevisation ' of humanism. Socialism was forced on the masses from above. Sharply criticising the workers, Castro accused them of having sold their revolutionary birthright for a plate of lentils; the only duty of workers under capitalism was the struggle for the conquest of power (*Obra Revolucionaria*, 15 December 1960). Answering the (then legal) Trotskyists who had criticised the government for frustrating the desire of the workers to take over industrial enter-prises and giving them, instead of ' real soviets ', ' technical advisory councils ', Guevara declared:

> The main defect of the technical advisory councils is that they were not created under the pressure of the masses. They are a bureau-cratic creation, introduced from above in order to give the masses an organ they had not demanded—and in this consists the error (*pecado*—literally ' sin ') of the masses (*Obra Revolucionaria*, 15 May 1961).

In November 1961 Castro complained that 'those small peasants who are everywhere giving us so many headaches, are allergic to the cooperatives—they cannot even bear to hear them mentioned' (*Revolucion*, 11 November 1961).

As the reality turned out so different from theory, theory had to be adapted, by a reinterpretation of history, to the new necessities.

IN this reinterpretation the guerrilla bands became a peasant army; the general strike proclaimed at the moment of the victory (to frustrate the utopian plans of a small and powerless minority to establish a provisional non-revolutionary government) was seen as a proof of the leading role of the workers; the five weeks during which Castro was not Prime Minister, having left formal office to persons he himself had nominated and who had no other legitimacy, were presented as a period of 'dual power' in which Cardona was cast in the role of Prince Lvov or Miliukov, while the peasant army (whose very core had soon to be eliminated, because of its counter-revolutionary confusions) was equated with soviets; the conflicts between Castro and Urrutia were given a class meaning, although the first conflict had in fact arisen because Urrutia wanted to close all casinos immediately, whereas Castro was in favour of maintaining them provisionally so as not to increase unemployment. Contradicting his foreign admirers, who had accused the Americans of refusing to give Castro the help he had asked for, Castro declared emphatically (in his speech of 1 December 1961) that he had never envisaged asking the Americans for help or of playing the Russians off against the Americans or vice versa. This he denounced as unworthy. There was no 'third way' of blackmail. The former humanist promises had already been condemned as deviations from the true way, committed by unmentioned persons: 'it is very dangerous for a country about to carry out a serious and profound revolution to fall prey to demagoguery and illusions that the living standards of the people can be immediately bettered' (*Obra Revolucionaria*, 26 March 1961).

Even the thesis that a revolution can only be successful if it is led by communists was now confirmed, since Castro declares that he has been a 'Marxist-Leninist' all along, before he started his struggle. This was now said to have been the reason why an independent 26th of July movement was not set up. Soon after victory, he said in his speech of 1 December 1961, he had said that the only programme of the '26th of July' would have to be a Marxist-Leninist one, and there was no need to have two parties with identical programmes.

Gently chiding those like Sartre and Wright Mills who had believed in the uniqueness of the Cuban revolution, President Dorticos now declared:

> I would like to remind you of some considerations advanced by several well-meaning foreign visitors . . . who came during the first period of our revolutionary process . . . Many of them, in good faith but suffering perhaps from limited vision, told the world that

the Cuban revolution was a revolution which was realised in an
exceptional way, growing out of practical experience, without a
revolutionary theory . . . This became popular even among some of
our people who were good revolutionaries and emotionally bound
to the revolution . . . Today, after three years, these versions have
been refuted (*El Mundo*, 30 December 1961).

Up to now the Cuban revolution has been regarded by international
communism as a model for Latin America. But in fact it is highly
improbable that it could be repeated in other countries of the sub-
continent. It was led by a romantic who fought, officially, under the
banner of the re-establishment of representative democracy, and directed
against a dictatorship which up to 1958 enjoyed United States support
but provoked a growing hatred among all sections of the Cuban people.
Castro was backed by the bourgeoisie—Guevara wrote later that he saw
nothing exceptional ' in the fact that the bourgeoisie, or at least a good
part of it, showed itself favourable to the revolutionary war against
tyranny '—by the entire younger generation, and by the peasants yearn-
ing to own the land. It could count on at least the tacit sympathy of
the middle classes and the workers, and on the less tacit sympathy of the
Church. The dictatorship had been upheld by an inefficient and corrupt
army whose soldiers refused to fight; together with many of their
officers, they could entertain some hopes for their future under Castro.
Castro had indeed proclaimed his goodwill towards all ' honest members ' of the armed forces, even going so far as to appoint, on 1 January
1959, Colonel Rego Rubido as Chief of the Army—only to dismiss him
quite unceremoniously shortly after.

If all classes of the Cuban people were indeed quite unaware of
what was in store for them, so too were the Yanquis. In the article
already quoted Guevara wrote:

> The condition that we could call exceptional is that North American
> imperialism was disoriented and could not measure the true depth
> of the Cuban revolution. . . . When imperialism wanted to react,
> when it realised that the group of inexpert youngsters that marched
> in triumph through the streets of Havana had a clear understanding
> of their political duty and a firm determination to live up to that
> duty, it was already too late (*Monthly Review*, July–August 1961).

Once in power, Castro was free to do as he pleased. There was nothing
to hamper him—the army and police forces were dissolved, the old
pre-Batista parties (with the exception of the communists) were disorganised, the Church was particularly weak, with fewer than 700 priests,
most of them foreigners, for a population of six and a half million. The
many social, economic, and professional organisations shared in the
general confusion and initial enthusiasm and were rapidly purged of
counter-revolutionary elements. The way was open for the adoption of
a new ideology.

As Cuba is so largely dependent on Russia and the Soviet bloc, the Yugoslav and Chinese gospels had no chance. Blas Roca had already condemned the Albanian way in Moscow, and the 'personality cult' was to be abolished even in Cuba. Although the Russians refrained from underwriting the Cuban revolution fully, the 'Year IV', the 'year of the plan', seemed to have opened under the sign of monocentrism and of Cuba's transformation into a Moscow bridgehead.

MARCH 1962 was, however, to bring an extraordinary change—a reversal to Castroist independence, an affirmation of a Cuban or Latin American 'Marxism-Leninism-Castroism'.

The facts, in so far as they are publicly known, are the following: On 16 March Castro attacked certain unnamed persons and the Committees for the Defence of the Revolution for their ultra-radicalism and terrorism, which had driven away people the revolution badly needed and made many Cubans foes of the new regime. At the same time he protested against the unwarranted interference of revolutionary organs in the work of the ministries, which had led to disorganisation. He hinted at the necessity of a purge. Less than a week later the names of those composing the new secretariat of the ORI—the provisional ruling party of the Cuban revolution—were published. The old communists were in a minority, much weaker than on another list of twenty-five leading members of that party which had been published as recently as 9 March. In a sensational speech on 26 March, Castro then attacked Anibal Escalante, one of the three top leaders of the traditional communists, whose name had appeared among the leaders on 9 March and who had been in charge of organising the ORI. Escalante was accused of sectarian deviations from Marxism-Leninism, of having introduced a personality cult of his own, and of having used his position to build up an apparatus composed of his own most trusted followers. In the same speech Castro attacked the pretensions and claims of the old communists, and condemned their intention to push other revolutionaries aside and to monopolise the revolution.

Although it is difficult to give an adequate interpretation of these events, including the fact that the other leading communists seem to be backing Castro's stand against their old comrade, the whole episode looks like a power-struggle between Castro and his closest friends on the one side, and the old communists on the other, and a reaffirmation of Castro's revolutionary independence inside the fold of Marxism-Leninism.

The underlying causes of this rather sudden eruption of a power-struggle must be sought in personal rivalries reinforced by the unexpected profundity of the economic crisis.

Castro is exceedingly vain, and intolerant of systematic criticism. The communists, although never completely trusting this 'ultra-leftist amateur', and privately criticising the errors of 'anarchistic humanism',

had always taken care to flatter the leader whom they needed in order
to entrench themselves in power. Castro, on the other hand, while
suspecting the communists of being less enthusiastic 'Fidelistas' than
they pretended to be, and recognising that some of his policies had
indeed been mistaken, needed the communist cadres both because of
their quality and because of their close relations with Moscow. A
certain tension between the old communists and the Castroists remained
and showed itself in the slowness with which the definitive party of the
Cuban revolution was taking shape. The more the experienced old
communists entrenched themselves in its provisional machine, the more
difficult became the position of old friends of Castro, and the more
problematic his own personal future. The announcement of his own
'Marxism-Leninism' has to be seen partly as an element in this struggle
for power: it gave Castro a new legitimacy inside the communist camp
and could enhance it even in the eyes of Moscow. Till the end of 1961
—and maybe later—Castro still hoped that the growing economic
difficulties could be overcome with the help of Eastern specialists and
goods and in loyal collaboration with the old communist cadres. But
the specialists have criticised the lack of organisation in Cuba, while
Russia was either unable or unwilling to make those extra economic
efforts which alone could have averted the rapid and catastrophic
worsening of the economic situation. Once the crisis had broken out,
and even the sugar prospects appeared much bleaker than the Cuban
government had thought, there was an urgent need to find scapegoats
other than the Yanquis. It is possible that some of the old communists
now felt strong enough to come into the open with their criticisms of
the leader and his mismanagement. At this moment Castro succeeded
in turning the tables on them, exploiting the resentment of many revolutionaries and the perennial unpopularity of the old communists among
the Cuban people. This led to a reaffirmation of his 'independence'
and, maybe, to a split in the ranks of the communists themselves, who
know quite well that their chances in Cuba and Latin America would
be considerably lessened by an open conflict with Castroism.

In 1948 the struggle between Tito and Stalin broke out on the
question of the ultimate control of the Yugoslav 'apparatus'. Although
he was a Marxist-Leninist of an old vintage, Tito wanted to be master
in his own house and resented the attempt of the Soviet NKVD to
recruit members of the Yugoslav security police. His eventual polycentric independence resulted from the fact that Stalin thought otherwise.

Khrushchev's attitude towards Castro is different: however strong
may have been the communist criticisms of the 26 July movement, and
whatever reservations about Castro's leadership the Russians may have
shared with the old Marxists-Leninists of the Escalante 'fraction', once
the conflict broke out, the Russian party came out openly and clearly
for Castro, ignoring for the time being any misgivings the Cuban 'old
communists' may have had. It accepted Castro's condemnation of

Escalante for trying to build up positions of power for himself within the Integrated Revolutionary Organisation and took with good grace Castro's decision to create a six-man secretariat in the new and only party, of whom only one is an old communist. This marks the distance between the era of Stalinist monocentrism and the present polycentric situation.

The Soviet line was given clearly in a long, unsigned (*i.e.*, official) article published in *Pravda* on 11 April 1962. Profusely quoting Castro's 26 March speech, it explicitly approves his condemnation of the 'dogmatism' and 'sectarianism' of Escalante. It underlines the need for the unity of the ORI by urging the 'old and the young party cadres' (*i.e.*, the old communists and the new Marxists-Leninists of Fidelista provenance) to collaborate harmoniously under Castro's leadership. It derides the speculations of the *New York Times* about the possibility of an eventual breach in communist unity in Cuba. And it extols Castro's speech as the Cuban application of Leninist self-criticism, pointedly asserting that the decision to exclude Escalante had been taken unanimously by all the members of the ORI directorate.

But it is also true that the article contains some oblique hints against 'leftist' deviation, a criticism which coincides with the strategic line of the 'old communists' as compared with the 'dynamic' policy of Castro. It declares that party unity

> was forged in the course of the realisation of the agrarian reform, the nationalisation of *imperialist* properties, and other measures preparing the *gradual* transition of Cuba to the stage of a socialist transformation in the towns and villages.

The words in italic show the moderation recommended, which was contrary to what Castro had in fact done; but by now he has probably grasped his 'ultra-leftist' errors, and has been given an official blessing from Moscow. *Pravda* announced that his actions are completely in line with the letter and the spirit of the Moscow declaration of the 81 Communist parties, and solemnly repeated that

> the Cuban Republic, as was clearly stated by the head of the Soviet government, N. S. Khrushchev, can always rely on the help and support of the Soviet people.

To give up Castro would for Moscow be unwise, because of the consequences it might have on revolutionary prospects in Latin America. For the moment this undoubtedly plays into the hands of Fidel and strengthens his hand against all critics, including the communist 'old guard'. His position is thus a reflection of the new dialectical relationship between the 'monocentric' and 'polycentric' tendencies within the international communist movement.

List of Contributors

W. A. C. ADIE formerly worked on Far Eastern affairs at the British Foreign Office and in the area, and is now a Research Fellow at St. Antony's College, Oxford.

P. ALEXANDRE is professor at the Ecole Nationale des Langues Orientales Vivantes in Paris.

EVELYN ANDERSON, journalist, is the author of *Hammer or Anvil: The Story of the German Working Class Movement.*

J. F. BROWN, history graduate of Manchester University and former Research Fellow at the University of Michigan, now lives in Europe and has written a number of studies of East European affairs.

MELVIN CROAN is a member of the Department of Government, Harvard University, where he offers a course on Soviet foreign policy. He recently contributed to a volume on *Revisionism* (New York: Frederick A. Praeger, Inc., 1962).

PIERRE FOUGEYROLLAS, author of *Le Marxisme en Question* (1959), and *La Philosophie en Question* (1960), is on the editorial board of the magazine *Arguments* and teaches at the University of Dakar.

GIORGIO GALLI is the author of *Storia del Partito comunista italiano, La sinistra italiana nel dopoguerra, La sinistra democristiana,* and other books on Italian politics.

BORIS GOLDENBERG studied sociology in Heidelberg. From 1937 to 1960 he lived in Cuba. He is a specialist in Latin American affairs.

WILLIAM E. GRIFFITH is a Research Associate at M.I.T.'s Center for International Studies. He has completed a book on Albania which will be published shortly.

ERNST HALPERIN, Swiss journalist, served as a correspondent of the *Neue Zürcher Zeitung* in Belgrade, 1949-53, and in Vienna, 1953-56. From 1957 to 1961 he was correspondent for several West German newspapers in Warsaw. He is the author of a book on Tito, *The Triumphant Heretic,* and a frequent contributor to Swiss and German papers.

GEOFFREY HUDSON is head of the Far Eastern Department of St. Antony's College, Oxford, and the author of *The Far East in World Politics, Questions of East and West,* etc., etc.

K. A. JELENSKI, essayist and art critic, lives in Paris. He is on the editorial board of *Preuves.*

JUSTUS M. VAN DER KROEF is Associate Professor of Political Science at the University of Bridgeport, Conn. His books include *Indonesia in the Modern World, Indonesian Social Evolution: Some Psychological Considerations* and *The West New Guinea Dispute.*

BORIS LEVITSKI, author of *Vom roten Terror zur sozialistischen Gesetzlichkeit,* is scientific contributor to the Friedrich Ebert-Stiftung in Bonn.

PROFESSOR EMANUEL SARKISYANZ specialized in Burmese studies at the University of Chicago and is now at the University of Freiburg, Switzerland.

ROBERT A. SCALAPINO, author of *Democracy and the Party Movement in Prewar Japan,* and co-author of *Parties and Politics in Contemporary Japan,* is Chairman of the Department of Political Science at the University of California, Berkeley.

FRITZ SCHATTEN, journalist, is the author of *Afrika—Schwarz oder rot?,* a study of nationalism and communism in tropical Africa, which will appear later this year in English.

GEORGE URBAN is the author of *The Nineteen Days,* an account of the 1956 revolution in Hungary, and of *Kinesis and Stasis* (British Studies in Germanic Languages and Literatures), 1962.